IR35 Defence Strategies

IR35 Defence Strategies

Fourth Edition

David Smith LLB CTA

Tottel Publishing Ltd, Maxwelton House, 41–43 Boltro Road, Haywards Heath, West Sussex, RH16 1BJ

© Tottel Publishing Ltd 2009

All rights reserved. No part of this publication may be reproduced in any material form (including photocopying or storing it in any medium by electronic means and whether or not transiently or incidentally to some other use of this publication) without the written permission of the copyright owner except in accordance with the provisions of the Copyright, Designs and Patents Act 1988 or under the terms of a licence issued by the Copyright Licensing Agency Ltd, Saffron House, 6–10 Kirby Street, London EC1N 8TS. Applications for the copyright owner's written permission to reproduce any part of this publication should be addressed to the publisher.

Warning: The doing of an unauthorised act in relation to a copyright work may result in both a civil claim for damages and criminal prosecution.

Crown copyright material is reproduced with the permission of the Controller of HMSO and the Queen's Printer for Scotland. Any European material in this work which has been reproduced from EUR-lex, the official European Communities legislation website, is European Communities copyright.

A CIP Catalogue record for this book is available from the British Library.

ISBN: 978 1 84766 291 0

Typeset by Phoenix Photosetting, Chatham, Kent
Printed and bound in Great Britain by Athenæum Press, Gateshead, Tyne and Wear

Author's foreword

Much has changed since the last edition of this book in 2004, not least of all a change of title! The reference in the old title to the Commissioners is no longer appropriate, following the introduction of the Lower-tier and Upper Tax Tribunals from 1 April 2009. The new appeals regime is described in the latter chapters of 'IR35 Defence Strategies', and the Tax Tribunal rules are included for ease of reference.

In practice, the Tax Tribunals should not be too dissimilar to the General and Special Commissioners in terms of the conduct and relative informality of appeals. This book therefore draws upon practical experience of numerous appeals before the Commissioners, in the form of various 'case studies'.

Many more cases have been heard and everything from *Ansell v Richardson* in 2004 to the recent Dragonfly High Court decision is commented on. A number of very important non IR35 cases (but still concerned with tax status) have been heard both by the Special Commissioners and in the High Court. These too are explained.

As mentioned, I have also added a number of real life 'case studies' mainly towards the latter chapters of the book. They offer a practical and sometimes amusing (some would say disturbing) insight into dealing with HMRC in the real world.

HMRC have extended the use of regional appeals units and although not the main focus of this book IR35 has been affected by the managed service company legislation.

The final chapter of the book deals with something of a general update on IR35 with further food for thought. For many thousands of small businesses IR35 and how 1 to argue it remains a major factor in their tax affairs. As always my message is 'get the facts, apply the correct legal principles to the facts and have the courage to argue with HMRC where it is justified'.

David Smith
Milton Keynes
April 2009

The views expressed in this publication do not necessarily represent the views of Tottel Publishing. No responsibility can be accepted by the Publisher or the Author for action taken as a result of information contained in this publication. It is essential that individual legal and, where appropriate, taxation advice be taken.

Preface

'What's it all about? Does being caught by IR35 really make that much difference?'

An IT contractor passed away and at the Gates of Heaven was asked if he wanted to spend eternity in Hell or Heaven. Somewhat puzzled he asked for a week's trial in each. Down he went to Hell where, to his surprise, he came across a beautiful Caribbean beach, an enchanting sunset, all his old pals and limitless food, drink and partying. For a whole week he had a wonderful time.

The next week he spent in Heaven playing a harp on a cloud. It was fine, but a bit dull after his week in Hell.

At the end of his week in Heaven he was asked to make his decision, 'where would he prefer to spend eternity?' All things considered he decided Hell was by far the better option and he couldn't wait to get back to the partying.

Down he went to Hell but this time instead of the Caribbean beach party he was greeted by flickering flames, torment and desolation.

Calling out to the Devil he said, 'I don't understand. I was down here last week and it was great. Non-stop partying, beautiful Caribbean sunsets, all my old pals—the lot. This time it's all gone. All there is now is flames, torment and desolation.'

In desperation he shouted at the Devil, 'What's changed?'

'Ah', said the Devil, 'it's really quite simple. You see last week you were *contracting*—but now you're *permanent!*'

(Author's note—while being a very old joke, the sentiment remains!)

About the author

David Smith graduated in Law in 1981 and later had legal research published. Following a career in commerce he joined the Inland Revenue (as was) as a direct entrant Inspector of Taxes via the Civil Service Commission. He has been in the private sector since 1989 both as the tax partner in two accountancy practices and as a founding director of Accountax in 1996.

For many years David has specialised in status disputes, particularly in the construction industry, though many other self-employed workers have been defended, including supermarket trolley collectors, chicken catchers and even nuns. More recently workers who have been subject to IR35 challenges have been successfully defended. He can be contacted at Accountax on 08450 660035 or mail@accountax-ltd.com

Acknowledgements

I would like to thank Sarah and Sarah at Tottel for their professional, enthusiastic and courteous support. I would also like to thank the whole team at Accountax for once again proving that yes, tax can be fun! Happy days and thanks for the journey! Daniel Cobelli needs a special mention as he has made a substantial contribution to this edition. Finally my thanks to Mark McLaughlin for updating the latter chapters in relation to the new tax tribunal system.

Contents

Author's Foreword	v
Preface	vi
About the Author	vii
Acknowledgements	viii
Table of Cases	xvii
Table of Statutes	xxiii
Table of Statutory Instruments	xxvii

1 Introduction to IR35: its consequences and common misunderstandings — 1
- The background — 1
- IR35 in brief — 1
- The history of IR35 — 2
- Major consequences of IR35 applying — 8
- Dispelling the misunderstandings of IR35 — 10
  - IR35 misunderstanding 1—there is a new status test — 10
  - IR35 misunderstanding 2—liability rests with the agency/end user — 11
  - IR35 misunderstanding 3—HMRC published guidance accurately summarises the law — 12
  - IR35 misunderstanding 4—having less than 5% of the shares in the intermediary company means that IR35 will not apply — 12
  - IR35 misunderstanding 5—standard agency contracts fail IR35 — 13
  - IR35 misunderstanding 6—completion of time sheets indicates direct employee status — 13
  - IR35 misunderstanding 7—the mere existence of a limited company ensures that the worker is not a disguised employee of the client — 14
- Summary — 14

2 Planning to beat IR35: the four basic principles in outline — 15
- 1. A critical analysis of the IR35 legislation — 15
- 2. Agreeing and implementing contractual terms which fall outside IR35 — 15
- 3. Understanding HMRC's IR35 compliance process — 16
- 4. Taking an IR35 appeal to the Tribunal — 16
- Applying the four principles — 16
- Summary — 17

3 Analysing the IR35 legislation for possible escape routes — 18
- ITEPA 2003, Pt 2, Ch 8 — 18
  - ITEPA 2003, s 49(1)(a) — 19

Contents

	ITEPA 2003, s 49(1)(b)	19
	ITEPA 2003, s 49(1)(c)	22
	The National Insurance legislation	23
	Summary	24
4	**Why understanding case law is important**	**25**
	The hierarchy of the tribunals and the courts	26
	Understanding law and fact	28
	Summary	29
5	**The major case law decisions and status criteria**	**30**
	Introduction	30
	Substitution	32
	External and internal rights of substitution and sub-contracting	32
	HMRC's view of substitution	39
	Hiring helpers	43
	Contracts which are silent on substitution	43
	Summary	44
	Mutuality of obligations	44
	Why is mutuality of obligations so important?	44
	Understanding what mutuality of obligations means	45
	The case law	50
	HMRC's view of mutuality of obligations	54
	Summary	56
	Control	56
	Can control be implied?	62
	Delegated control	63
	Summary	64
	Other factors case law recognises as important	65
	Important factors	65
	In business on own account	65
	An alternative approach: are engagements an incident of a continuing 'profession'?	67
	Intention of the parties	69
	Financial risk and chance of profit	72
	Freedom to offer services	73
	Previous HMRC determinations	74
	Minor factors	75
	Provision of equipment	75
	Employee style benefits	76
	Basis of payment	76
	Recognised custom and practice	77
	Summary	77
6	**Crucial question 1: who is the client?**	**78**
	Where does the contractual relationship lie?	78
	Where is the financial relationship?	78
	The agency is not acting as a mere introducer	79
	Commercial contracts with many parties	79

	ITEPA 2003, Pt 2, Ch 8	80
	HMRC's view	80
	Summary	81
7	**Crucial question 2: what contractual arrangements are needed to defeat IR35?**	**82**
	Mindsets and modus operandi	83
	The bigger picture	83
	The way forward and looking beyond the contract	83
	Important contract terms and conditions	85
	Personal service, mutuality and control	85
	Other important contract terms and conditions	89
	Factors of secondary importance	94
	Lack of employee benefits	94
	Provision of equipment	95
	Basis of payment	95
	General considerations	95
	Summary	96
8	**Crucial question 3: is the agency/end-user contract relevant?**	**97**
	Why the agency/end-user contract may not be relevant	98
	ITEPA 2003, Pt 2, Ch 8	99
	The doctrine of privity of contract	102
	Common sense and equity	103
	Existing case law	105
	Summary	106
9	**Crucial question 4: is the personal service business an agency within ITEPA 2003, Pt 2, Ch 7?**	**108**
	The agency trap	108
	How can the agency trap be avoided?	109
	Demonstrate that the strict terms of ITEPA 2003, Pt 2, Ch 7 have not been met	109
	Demonstrate that 'services' and not 'personnel' are being supplied	111
	Summary	112
10	**Crucial question 5: do composite companies defeat IR35?**	**113**
	Background	113
	The managed service company (MSC) rules	113
	'Umbrella' companies	114
	Summary	114
11	**Analysing IR35 case law**	**115**
	IR35—the cases	115
	Battersby v Campbell	115
	F S Consulting v McCaul (Inspector of Taxes)	116
	G S Ltd v Gregory	117
	Synaptek Ltd v Young (Inspector of Taxes)	118
	Misplaced reliance on *F S Consulting Ltd v McCaul*	120

Lime-IT Ltd v Justin (Officer of the Board of Inland Revenue)	122
Tilbury Consulting Ltd v Gittins	124
Future Online v S K Faulds (Inspector of Taxes)	129
Ansell Computer Services Ltd v Richardson (HM Inspector of Taxes)	131
Usetech Ltd v Young (Inspector of Taxes)	133
Future On-Line Limited v S K Foulds (HM Inspector of Taxes)	135
Netherlane Limited v York	137
Island Consultants Limited v HMRC	140
First Word Software Limited v HMRC	143
Datagate Services Limited v Revenue and Customs Commissioners	144
MKM Computing Limited v HMRC	146
Larkstar Data Ltd v HMRC	148
Alternative Book Company Limited v HMRC	150
Dragonfly Consulting Limited v HMRC	152
Appeals units	157
Summary	157

12 Should an HMRC contract review be requested? 158
Summary 162

13 Appraising a case, interest penalties and directors' personal liability and can IR35 be reversed? 163
Interest charges 163
Penalties 163
    The 'new' regime 164
    The 'old' regime 164
Personal liability 165
Can IR35 be 'reversed'? 166
Summary 166

14 How HMRC will target IR35 cases 167
1. Ticking the 'service company' box on Form P35   167
2. Examination of the taxpayer's self-assessment return   168
3. Routine compliance visits   168
    Information and inspection powers   169
4. Submission of a contract review to HMRC   169
5. Powers under TMA 1970, s 16   169
6. Informants   170
7. Random enquiries   170
8. Research teams   170
9. Schemes advertised as 'Avoiding IR35'   170
Summary   170

15 HMRC interviews and IR35 strategies 172
The start of the inspection 172
Factsheets and Codes of Practice 176
    Issue of Factsheet EC/FS 4 176
Contracts 177
Employment and special status inspectors 178

Factors the inspector will consider	180
What is the client's business?	180
Are other workers doing the same job?	181
How did the worker get the job?	182
Is the worker in business on his own account?	182
Control	182
Personal service	183
Provision of equipment	184
Financial risk	185
Opportunity to profit	186
Mutuality of obligation	186
Entitlement to holiday pay, sick pay etc	187
Termination	187
Exclusivity	188
Intention of the parties	189
Notes of interview	189
Developments in tactics	190
Information notices	190
End-user evidence	191
Customer service or compliance enquiry	191
A new approach to substitution	191
Conclusion	192
Summary	192

16 Appeal formalities and strategies in an unresolved IR35 dispute — 193

Making an appeal	193
The Tax Tribunals	195
Internal reviews	196
Getting the appeal listed for hearing	197
The 'lost art' of advocacy	197
How a hearing is arranged	198
A note on calling HMRC's bluff	201
Doing the pre-hearing homework	201
Summary	202

17 Preparing for an appeal hearing — 203

Introduction	203
Before the hearing	204
Agreed statement of facts	204
Who should prepare the statement of facts?	206
The question for determination	207
Administrative procedures	208
What needs to be done	211
Opinions count for nothing	211
Documentation	212
Bundle A	212
Bundle B	213
The practitioner's own documents	215
Clarifying what determination is being sought	215

Witnesses	215
Witness summons	218
Summary	220

18 Presenting an appeal — 221
Location	221
Representation	222
The First-tier Tax Tribunal	222
The Tax Tribunal judge	224
The inspector	224
The layout of the meeting room	225
The proceedings	225
1. Addressing the Tribunal and introducing the client	227
2. Presenting a brief summary	228
3. Calling and examining witnesses	230
4. Cross-examination of the taxpayer and the appellant's witnesses	232
5. Re-examination of the taxpayer and his witnesses	233
6. Questions asked by the Tribunal	234
7. Legal submissions by the practitioner (probably given later after all evidence has been heard)	234
8. Summarising the taxpayer's case	235
9. The inspector responds	236
10. Cross-examining the inspector's witnesses	236
11. Re-examination by HMRC	239
12. Questions by the Tribunal	239
13. HMRC make their legal submissions (possibly immediately after the appellant's legal submissions)	239
14. HMRC summarise their case	240
15. The taxpayer's final summary	240
16. The decision	240
Notes on presentation style	241
A mistake to avoid	242
Summary	242
A blueprint for an IR35 defence and appeal	243

19 What happens after the appeal hearing — 244
If the taxpayer has won	244
If the taxpayer has lost	246
What lessons can be learnt	247
Summary	247

20 The advice clients need now — 248
1. Agree and implement a sound written contract	248
2. Maintain due diligence records to show the contract is implemented	248
3. Educate the client	250

21 Closing reminders and latest developments — 251
The nuclear option revisited?	252
What exactly is the issue for determination?	253

Another contract to be considered?	254
The future of IR35	255
Appendix 1: ITEPA 2003 Pt 2 Ch 8	257
Appendix 2: SSCBA 1992 s 4A	267
Appendix 3: SI 2000/727	270
Appendix 4: Tax Bulletin 45 extract	281
Appendix 5: The Tribunal Procedure (First-tier Tribunal) (Tax Chamber) Rules 2009 SI 2009/273	292
Appendix 6: The Tribunal Procedure (Upper Tribunal) Rules 2008 SI 2008/2698	311
Index	339

Table of Cases

[References are to paragraph numbers and appendices]

A

Abbey Life Assurance Co Ltd v Tansell. *See* MHC Consulting Services Ltd v Tansell
Action Contracts (East Midlands) Ltd v Ablitt; Action Contracts (East Midlands) Ltd v Asfordby Storage & Haulage Ltd, UKEAT/0568/07/ZT, EAT, [2008] All ER (D) 456 (Jul) 5.77
Addison v London Philharmonic Orchestra [1981] ICR 261, EAT 5.134, 5.148
Airfix Footwear Ltd v Cope [1978] ICR 1210, [1978] IRLR 396, (1978) 13 ITR 513, EAT 5.77, 5.78, 5.82, 5.93
Alpine (Double Glazing) Co Ltd v Secretary of State for Social Services 1982 (unreported) 5.184
Alternative Book Co Ltd v Revenue and Customs Commissioners [2008] STC (SCD) 830, Sp Comm 11.247–11.262
Ansell Computer Services Ltd v Richardson (Inspector of Taxes) [2004] STC (SCD) 472, [2004] STI 1995, Sp Comm 11.112–11.120, 11.208, 11.290, 15.80, 19.17
Arctic Systems. *See* Jones v Garnett (Inspector of Taxes)
Australia Mutual Provident Society v Chaplin (1978) 18 ALR 385 .... 4.11, 5.17, 5.23, 5.24, 5.26, 5.28, 5.37, 5.46, 5.62, App 4

B

BSM (1257) Ltd v Secretary of State for Social Services [1978] ICR 894, QBD .. 5.162, 5.180
Barnett v Brabyn (Inspector of Taxes) [1996] STC 716, 69 TC 133, Ch D .. 5.175, 5.176, 11.116
Battersby v Campbell (Inspector of Taxes) [2001] STC (SCD) 189, [2001] STI 1498, Sp Comm 11.2–11.7, 11.40, 11.290
Baylis (Inspector of Taxes) v Gregory [1987] STC 297, [1986] 1 WLR 624, [1986] 1 All ER 289, [1986] STC 22, (1986) 83 LSG 200, (1986) 130 SJ 16, Ch D ... 11.17
Bhadra v Ellam (Inspector of Taxes) [1988] STC 239, 60 TC 466, (1988) 85(2) LSG 37, Ch D.. 5.135, 5.136
Brady (Inspector of Taxes) v Hart (t/a Jaclyn Model Agency) [1985] STC 498, 58 TC 518, Ch D 6.8

C

Cable & Wireless Plc v Muscat; sub nom Muscat v Cable & Wireless Plc [2006] EWCA Civ 220, [2006] ICR 975, [2006] IRLR 354, (2006) 103(12) LSG 30, (2006) 150 SJLB 362, CA 1.22, 21.12, 21.13, 21.14
Calder v H Kitson Vickers (Engineers) [1988] ICR 232, CA 5.160
Carmichael v National Power Plc [1999] 1 WLR 2042, [1999] 4 All ER 897, [1999] ICR 1226, [2000] IRLR 43, (1999) 96(46) LSG 38, (1999) 143 SJLB 281, HL 4.7, 4.13, 4.18, 5.68, 5.72, 5.77, 5.85, 5.90, 5.93, 11.151, 11.183, 18.62

Table of Cases

Castle Construction (Chesterfield) Ltd v Revenue and Customs Commissioners
 [2008] SpC 723, [2009] STI 91, Sp Comm 5.137
Catamaran Cruisers Ltd v Williams [1994] IRLR 386, EAT 1.70
Chilcott v Inland Revenue Commissioners [1982] STC 1, 55 TC 446, [1981] TR 357,
 DC 3.24
Clark v Oxfordshire HA [1998] IRLR 125, (1998) 41 BMLR 18, CA 5.77, 5.84
Cornwall CC v Prater; sub nom Prater v Cornwall CC [2006] EWCA Civ 102, [2006]
 2 All ER 1013, [2006] ICR 731, [2006] IRLR 362, [2006] BLGR 479, (2006)
 156 NLJ 372, CA 5.76, 11.183
Costain Building & Civil Engineering Ltd v Smith [2000] ICR 215, EAT ... 8.46, 8.47

D

DPP v Schildkamp [1971] AC 1, [1970] 2 WLR 279, [1969] 3 All ER 1640, (1970)
 54 Cr App R 90, (1969) 119 NLJ 1116, (1970) 114 SJ 54, HL 3.24
Datagate Services Ltd v Revenue and Customs Commissioners [2008] STC (SCD)
 453, [2008] STI 146, Sp Comm 11.202–11.215, 11.290
Davies (Inspector of Taxes) v Braithwaite; sub nom Davies (H.M Inspector of Taxes)
 v Braithwaite [1931] 2 KB 628, 18 TC 198, KBD 5.152, 5.153, 5.154,
  11.23, 11.25
Dragonfly Consulting Ltd v Revenue and Customs Commissioners; sub nom
 Dragonfly Consultancy Ltd v Revenue and Customs Commissioners
 [2008] EWHC 2113 (Ch), [2008] STC 3030, [2008] BTC 639, [2008] STI
 2032, (2008) 105(35) LSG 22, Ch D 3.28, 5.164, 7.46, 11.263–
  11.290, 21.4, 21.19, 21.21

E

Electronic Data Systems Ltd v Hanbury, EAT/128/00, EAT, [2001] All ER D 369
 (Mar) 5.92
Express & Echo Publications Ltd v Tanton [1999] ICR 693, [1999] IRLR 367,
 (1999) 96(14) LSG 31, CA 4.15, 5.17, 5.30, 5.31, 5.32,
  5.34, 5.35, 5.36, 5.38, 5.37,
  5.42, 5.45, 5.46, 5.47, 5.48,
  5.58, 5.59, 5.73, 5.117, 5.159,
  5.184, 7.11, 7.46, 11.31, 11.50,
  11.278, 15.68, 15.82, 17.27,
  18.62, App 4

F

FS Consulting Ltd v McCaul (Inspector of Taxes) [2002] STC (SCD) 138, [2002]
 STI 209, Sp Comm 8.20, 8.52, 11.8–11.15,
  11.23, 11.33, 11.34, 11.35,
  11.36, 11.290
Fall (Inspector of Taxes) v Hitchen [1973] 1 WLR 286, [1973] 1 All ER 368, [1973]
 STC 66, 49 TC 433, [1972] TR 285, (1972) 117 SJ 73, Ch D .... 5.153, 5.154, App 4
First Word Software Ltd v Revenue and Customs Commissioners [2008] STC (SCD)
 389, Sp Comm 11.188–11.201, 11.290
Future Online Ltd v Foulds (Inspector of Taxes); sub nom Future Online Ltd
 v Faulds (Inspector of Taxes) [2004] EWHC 2597 (Ch), [2005] STC 198,
 76 TC 590, [2005] BTC 226, [2005] STI 190, (2004) 148 SJLB 1283,
 Ch D 6.14, 11.93–11.110,
  11.132, 11.133, 15.38

G

G S Ltd v Gregory (2002) Special Commissioner Mr Sadler SpC 11.15, 11.17

Table of Cases

Global Plant Ltd v Secretary of State for Health and Social Security; sub nom Global Plant Ltd v Secretary of State for Social Services [1972] 1 QB 139, [1971] 3 WLR 269, [1971] 3 All ER 385, (1971) 11 KIR 284; (1971) 115 SJ 506, QBD 5.17, 5.22, 5.24, 5.137, 5.172

H

HMRC v Wright. *See* Revenue and Customs Commissioners v Wright
Hall (Inspector of Taxes) v Lorimer [1994] 1 WLR 209, [1994] 1 All ER 250, [1994] STC 23, [1994] ICR 218, [1994] IRLR 171, 66 TC 349, [1993] STI 1382, (1993) 90(45) LSG 45, (1993) 137 SJLB 256, CA (Civ Div); affirming [1992] 1 WLR 939, [1992] STC 599, [1992] ICR 739, (1992) 136 SJLB 175, Ch D .... 4.7, 4.14, 5.14, 5.17, 5.27, 5.29, 5.34, 5.141, 5.149, 5.153, 5.167, 5.173, 5.179, 11.139–11.143, 11.186, 15.49, 15.55, App 4
Hellyer Brothers Ltd v McLeod; Boston Deep Sea Fisheries v Wilson [1987] 1 WLR 728, [1987] ICR 526, [1987] IRLR 232, (1987) 84 LSG 1056,(1987) 131 SJ 805, CA 5.77, 5.83
Hewlett Packard Ltd v O'Murphy; sub nom O'Murphy v Hewlett Packard Ltd [2002] IRLR 4, [2002] Emp LR 54, EAT 1.70, 5.69, 5.77, 6.9, 8.45, 8.49

I

Interlink Express Parcels Ltd v Night Trunkers Ltd [2001] EWCA Civ 360, [2001] RTR 23, (2001) 98(20) LSG 43, CA 5.131
Island Consultants Ltd v Revenue and Customs Commissioners [2007] STC (SCD) 700, [2007] STI 1871, Sp Comm 11.165

J

JL Window & Door Services and Molloy v Revenue and Customs Commissioners [2009] SpC 733 .... 5.137
Jobsin Co UK Plc (t/a Internet Recruitment Solutions) v Department of Health; sub nom Jobsin.co.uk Plc v Department of Health [2001] EWCA Civ 1241, [2002] 1 CMLR 44, [2001] Eu LR 685, (2001) 98(33) LSG 29, CA 9.22
Jones v Garnett (Inspector of Taxes) [2007] UKHL 35, [2007] 1 WLR 2030, [2008] Bus LR 425, [2007] 4 All ER 857, [2007] STC 1536, [2007] ICR 1259, [2007] 3 FCR 487, 78 TC 597, [2007] BTC 476, [2007] WTLR 1229, [2007] STI 1899, (2007) 157 NLJ 1118, (2007) 151 SJLB 1024, HL 18.13, 21.26

L

Lane v Shire Roofing Co (Oxford) Ltd [1995] IRLR 493, [1995] PIQR P417, CA .. 5.174
Larkstar Ltd. *See* Revenue and Customs Commissioners v Larkstar Data Ltd
Lee Ting Sang v Chung Chi-Keung [1990] 2 AC 374, [1990] 2 WLR 1173, [1990] ICR 409, [1990] IRLR 236, (1990) 87(13) LSG 43, (1990) 134 SJ 909, PC (HK) 5.174, 7.45
L'Estrange v F Graucob Ltd [1934] 2 KB 394, KBD 7.58
Lewis (t/a MAL Scaffolding) v Revenue and Customs Commissioners [2006] STC (SCD) 253, [2006] STI 1272, Sp Comm 5.137, 16.1
Lime-IT Ltd v Justin (Inland Revenue Officer); sub nom Lime-IT Ltd v Justin (Officer of the Board of Inland Revenue) [2003] STC (SCD) 15, [2002] STI 1653, Sp Comm 5.38, 5.149, 11.41, 11.53, 11.55, 11.68, 11.290, 15.53, 15.80, 16.1
Lynch v Thorne [1956] 1 WLR 303, [1956] 1 All ER 744, CA 7.11

Table of Cases

M

MHC Consulting Services Ltd v Tansell; sub nom Abbey Life Assurance Co Ltd v Tansell [2000] ICR 789, [2000] IRLR 387, (2000) 97(19) LSG 43, (2000) 150 NLJ 651, (2000) 144 SJLB 205, CA 8.43

MKM Computing Ltd v Revenue and Customs Commissioners [2008] STC (SCD) 403, [2008] STI 139, Sp Comm 11.216–11.228

MacFarlane v Glasgow City Council [2001] IRLR 7, EAT 5.17, 5.38, 5.49, 11.32

McLeod v Hellyer. *See* Hellyer Brothers Ltd v McLeod

McManus v Griffiths (Inspector of Taxes) [1997] STC 1089, 70 TC 218, [1997] BTC 412, (1997) 94(33) LSG 27, Ch D 5.121, 5.183, 18.15

McMeechan v Secretary of State for Employment [1997] ICR 549, [1997] IRLR 353, CA 5.77, 5.85, 5.88, 5.98, 15.57

McMenamin (Inspector of Taxes) v Diggles [1991] 1 WLR 1249, [1991] 4 All ER 370, [1991] STC 419, [1991] ICR 641, Ch D 5.17, 5.23, 5.25, 5.29, 5.60, 15.47

Malik v Bank of Credit and Commerce International SA (In Liquidation); sub nom BCCI SA, Re; Mahmud v Bank of Credit and Commerce International SA (In Liquidation) [1998] AC 20, [1997] 3 WLR 95, [1997] 3 All ER 1, [1997] ICR 606, [1997] IRLR 462, (1997) 94(25) LSG 33, (1997) 147 NLJ 917, HL 5.73

Market Investigations Ltd v Minister of Social Security [1969] 2 QB 173, [1969] 2 WLR 1, [1968] 3 All ER 732, (1968) 112 SJ 905, QBD .. 5.121, 5.143, 5.144, 5.145, 5.146, 5.153, 11.120, App 4

Massey v Crown Life Insurance Co [1978] 1 WLR 676, [1978] 2 All ER 576, [1978] ICR 590, [1978] IRLR 31, (1978) 13 ITR 5, (1978) 122 SJ 791, CA ... 5.132, 5.159, 5.161, App 4

Maurice v Betterware UK Ltd [2001] ICR 14, EAT 7.50

Midland Sinfonia Concert Society v Secretary of State for Social Services [1981] ICR 454, QBD 5.168, 5.181

Montgomery v Johnson Underwood Ltd; sub nom Johnson Underwood Ltd v Montgomery [2001] EWCA Civ 318, [2001] ICR 819, [2001] IRLR 269, [2001] Emp LR 405, (2001) 98(20) LSG 40, CA 5.1, 5.68, 5.69, 5.77, 5.82, 5.88, 5.89, 5.90, 5.91, 5.93, 5.111, 5.117, 5.123, 5.128, 5.138, 8.48, 11.82, 11.115, 15.57, 15.58, 18.63

Morren v Swinton and Pendlebury BC [1965] 1 WLR 576, [1965] 2 All ER 349, 63 LGR 288, DC 5.122, 5.123, 5.139, 11.182

Motorola Ltd v Davidson [2001] IRLR 4, EAT 8.46, 8.47, 8.49

N

Narich Pty v Commissioner of Payroll Tax [1984] ICR 286, EAT 5.112, 7.11, 20.6, 20.7

Nethermere (St Neots) Ltd v Gardiner; sub nom Nethermere (St Neots) Ltd v Taverna [1984] ICR 612, [1984] IRLR 240, (1984) 81 LSG 2147, (1984) 134 NLJ 544, CA .... 5.77, 5.82, 5.93, 11.109, 11.144–11.164, App 4

North West Ceilings Ltd v Reid. *See* Reid v North West Ceilings Ltd (t/a Shopspec)

O

O'Kelly v Trusthouse Forte Plc [1984] QB 90, [1983] 3 WLR 605, [1983] 3 All ER 456, [1983] ICR 728, [1983] IRLR 369, CA 5.72, 5.76, 5.77, 5.78, 5.79, 5.80, 5.81, 5.98, 5.148, 5.169, 5.187, 5.189

O'Murphy v Hewlett Packard Ltd. *See* Hewlett Packard Ltd v O'Murphy

Table of Cases

P

Parade Park Hotel v Revenue and Customs Commissioners [2007] STC (SCD) 430, [2007] STI 1183, Sp Comm 5.141, 15.70, 16.1
Propertycare Ltd v Gower, UKEAT/0547/03/ZT, EAT, [2004] All ER (D) 16 (Jan) 5.69, 5.77, 5.92

R

R (on the application of Professional Contractors Group Ltd) v Inland Revenue Commissioners; sub nom Professional Contractors Group Ltd v Inland Revenue Commissioners; R v Inland Revenue Commissioners, ex p Professional Contractors Group Ltd [2001] EWCA Civ 1945, [2002] STC 165, [2002] 1 CMLR 46, [2002] Eu LR 329, 74 TC 393, [2002] BTC 17, 4 ITL Rep 483, [2002] STI 40, (2002) 99(9) LSG 31, (2002) 146 SJLB 21, CA (Civ Div); affirming [2001] EWHC Admin 236, [2001] STC 629, [2001] Eu LR 514, [2001] HRLR 42, 3 ITL Rep 556, [2001] STI 669, (2001) 98(20) LSG 44, (2001) 151 NLJ 535, QBD (Admin) 1.3, 1.65, 5.39, 5.77, 5.93, 5.171, 6.6, 7.3, 8.19, 8.27, 11.20, 12.8, 13.10, 15.58
R (on the application of the PCG) v IRC. *See* R (on the application of Professional Contractors Group Ltd) v Inland Revenue Commissioners
Ready Mixed Concrete (South East) Ltd v Minister of Pensions and National Insurance; Minister for Social Security v Greenham Ready Mixed Concrete Ltd; Minister for Social Security v Ready Mixed Concrete (South East) Ltd [1968] 2 QB 497, [1968] 2 WLR 775, [1968] 1 All ER 433, 4 KIR 132, (1967) 112 SJ 14, QBD .... 5.1, 5.10, 5.17, 5.18, 5.20, 5.24, 5.26, 5.29, 5.33, 5.34, 5.37, 5.39, 5.46, 5.69, 5.82, 5.89, 5.90, 5.111, 5.115, 5.116, 5.117, 5.122, 5.123, 5.125, 5.137, 5.138, 5.141, 5.190, 7.25, 7.28, 11.82, 11.84, 11.219, 11.270, App 4
Reid v North West Ceilings Ltd (t/a Shopspec) [2001] Emp LR 551, EAT .. 5.127, 5.132, 5.133
Revenue and Customs Commissioners v Larkstar Data Ltd [2008] EWHC 3284, Ch D 1.60, 11.229–11.246, 11.290, 21.3
Revenue and Customs Commissioners v Wright [2007] EWHC 526 (Ch), [2007] STC 1684, [2007] BTC 596, [2007] STI 337, Ch D 4.3, 5.137, 21.21
Robb v Green [1895] 2 QB 315, CA 5.73

S

Serco Ltd v Blair, EAT/345/98, EAT 8.46, 8.47
Shell (UK) Ltd v Lostock Garage Ltd [1976] 1 WLR 1187, [1977] 1 All ER 481, (1976) 120 SJ 523, CA 7.11
Sidey v Phillips (Inspector of Taxes) [1987] STC 87, 59 TC 458, (1987) 84 LSG 342, (1987) 131 SJ 76, Ch D 5.191
Smith (National Minimum Wage Compliance Officer for the Inland Revenue) v Hewitson (t/a Executive Coach Catering Services) (2001) unreported, EAT/489/01, EAT 7.11
Stapels v Secretary of State for Social Services (15 March 1985, unreported): 5.121, 5.122, 5.123, 15.44
Stevedoring & Haulage Services Ltd v Fuller [2001] EWCA Civ 651, [2001] IRLR 627, [2001] Emp LR 690, CA 5.77, 5.93, 7.11
Stoddart v Cawder Golf Club, EAT/87300, EAT 5.158

Table of Cases

Stuncroft Ltd v Havelock, EAT/1017/00, EAT, [2002] All ER D 292 (Jan) .   5.77, 5.92, 5.93, 15.58
Swan (WF & RK) (Hellenic) Ltd v Secretary of State for Social Services (18 January 1983, unreported) 5.118
Synaptek Ltd v Young (Inspector of Taxes) [2003] EWHC 645 (Ch), [2003] STC 543, [2003] ICR 1149, 75 TC 51, [2003] BTC 8044, [2003] STI 529, (2003) 100(22) LSG.31, Ch D 5.59, 5.76, 5.77, 5.83, 5.93, 6.10, 7.24, 8.4, 11.18, 11.19, 11.22, 11.23, 11.28, 11.29, 11.30, 11.31, 11.34, 11.36, 11.78, 11.114, 11.290

T

Tilbury Consulting Ltd v Gittins (Inspector of Taxes) (No 2); sub nom Tilbury Consulting Ltd v Gittens (Inspector of Taxes) [2004] STC (SCD) 72, [2003] STI 2278, Sp Comm 6.10, 11.56–11.67, 11.69, 11.76, 11.88, 11.92, 11.290, 15.80, 16.1, 17.55, 18.94

U

Usetech Ltd v Young (Inspector of Taxes) [2004] EWHC 2248 (Ch), [2004] STC 1671, 76 TC 811, [2005] BTC 48, [2004] STI 2220, (2004) 101(40) LSG 29, Ch D 8.20, 8.52, 11.13, 11.121, 11.123, 11.125, 11.126, 11.127,11.290, 13.18

W

WHPT Housing Association v Secretary of State for Social Services [1981] ICR 737, QBD....................................... 1.69, 4.5, 5.19, 5.158, 5.188
Walls v Sinnett (Inspector of Taxes) [1987] STC 236, 60 TC 150, DC 4.16
Warner Holidays v Secretary of State for Social Services [1983] ICR 440, QBD .. 5.191
Wickens v Champion Employment [1984] ICR 365, (1984) 134 NLJ 544, EAT ... 5.73
Williams v Evans (Inspector of Taxes); Jones v Evans; Roberts v Evans [1982] 1 WLR 972, [1982] STC 498, 59 TC 509, (1982) 126 SJ 346, Ch D 3.12
Winter v Westward Television (1978) unreported 1.71, 8.43, 8.51

Y

Yewens v Noakes (1880–81) LR 6 QBD 530, CA 4.8, 5.108, 5.121
Young & Woods v West [1980] IRLR 201, CA 5.162

Table of Statutes

[References are to paragraph numbers and appendices]

C

Commissioners for Revenue and Customs Act 2005
  Sch 4
    para 102(1) .... App 1
        103(1)(a) .... App 1
        105 .... App 1
Companies Act 1948
  s 332 .... 3.24
Contracts (Rights of Third Parties) Act 1998 .... 8.31

D

Disability discrimination Act 1995:   8.44

E

Employment Rights Act 1996
  s 230(1), (2) 4.1
Employers' and Workmen Act of 1875 .... 5.109

F

Finance Act 2000
  s 144 .... 13.16
  Sch 12 .... 1.34, 11.70
    para 1(1) 11.136
        22 .... 1.34
Finance Act 2003
  s 136 .... 1.11
    (2) .... App 1
    (3)(b)(i) .... App 1
  Sch 36 .... App 1
  Sch 42
    para 1 .... App 1
  Sch 43 .... 13.5
    para 1 .... App 1
Finance Act 2004
  s 61 .... App 1
  Sch 12
    para 17(2) 13.5
  Sch 35
    para 56 .... 13.5

Finance Act 2007 .... 13.6, 13.9
  s 97 .... 13.5
  Sch 3 .... 13.5
    para 3 .... App 1
  Sch 24 .... 13.5
Finance Act 2008 .... 15.4, 15.10, 15.18, 15.79
  Sch 36 .... 14.12, 15.8
Finance (No 2) Act 1975
  s 38 .... 1.12
Freedom of Information Act 2000:   15.20

G

Goods Vehicles (Licensing of Operators) Act 1995 .... 5.131

H

Human Rights Act 1998 .... 15.22

I

Income Tax Act 2007
  s 1030(1) .... App 1, App 2
  Sch 1
    para 289 .... App 2
        429 .... App 1
  Sch 2 .... App 1, App 2
Income Tax (Earnings and Pensions) Act 2003 .... 6.15, 10.4
  s 19 .... App 1
    32 .... App 1
  Pt 2, Ch 7 (ss 44–47) 1.11, 3.10, 3.26, 8.16, 9.1, 9.5, 9.10, 9.12, 9.25, 9.26
  s 44 .... 1.12, 1.53, 9.1, 9.2, 9.12
    (1)(a) 9.13, 9.14, 9.15, 9.21
       (c) 9.18
    45 .... 1.12, 1.53, 9.1
    46 .... 1.12, 1.53, 9.1
    47 .... 1.12, 1.53, 9.1

Table of Statutes

Income Tax (Earnings and Pensions)
Act 2003—*contd*
- s 47(3) 9.3, 9.10, 9.25
- Pt 2, Ch 8 (ss 48–61) ... 1.34, 2.3, 3.1, 3.4, 6.11, 8.5, 8.6, 8.26, 11.70, 17.16, 17.33, App 1
- s 48 .... 1.12, App 1
  - (2)(aa) 10.7
- 49 .... 1.12, 3.4, App 1
  - (1) 11.70
    - (a) 1.7, 3.4, 3.5, 3.6, 3.7, 3.9, 3.26, 3.31, 6.11
    - (b) 3.4, 3.10, 8.8, 8.11, 8.16, 8.25, 8.28, 8.31, 11.70
    - (c) 3.4, 3.6, 3.9, 3.20, 3.27, 5.3, 5.155, 6.13, 6.14, 8.1, 8.6, 8.8, 8.14, 8.17, 8.21, 8.22, 8.28, 11.70
  - (3) 3.12, 3.23, 3.28
  - (4) 3.21, 3.27, 6.13, 8.1, 8.7, 8.8, 8.14, 8.25, 8.28
- 50 .... 1.12, App 1
- 51 .... 1.12, 1.62, 3.14, App 1
  - (1) 3.14
    - (b) 1.12, 1.62, 1.63
  - (2) 3.14
  - (3) 3.15
  - (4) 3.15
- 52 .... 1.12, App 1
- 53 .... 1.12, 3.17, App 1
- 54 .... 1.12, 1.42, 1.46, App 1
- 55 .... 1.12, App 1
- 56 .... 1.12, App 1
  - (3) 3.19
- 57 .... 1.12, App 1
- 58 .... 1.12, App 1
- 59 .... 1.12, App 1
  - (3) 3.18
- 60 .... 1.12, 1.62, 3.15, App 1
- 61 .... 1.12, App 1
- 62–77 .... 1.12
- 229 .... App 1
- 233 .... App 1
- 337–342 .... App 1
- 398(2) .... App 1

Income Tax (Earnings and Pensions)
Act 2003—*contd*
- s 688A 10.4, 10.8
- Sch 2
  - para 12(3) 8.16
- Sch 5
  - para 58 .... 8.16

Income Tax (Trading and Other Income) Act 2005
- Sch 1
  - para 586 .... App 1

M

Master and Servant Act 1889 ..... 5.109
Master and Servant Act 1902 ..... 5.109

N

National Minimum Wage Act 1998
- s 54 .... 4.1

S

Social Security Administration Act 1992 .... 11.4
- s 114 .... 13.16
- 115 .... 13.16
- 121C 13.14
- 121D(4) 13.15

Social Security Contributions and Benefits Act 1992
- s 4A .... 1.33, 2.3, 3.1, 3.22, 3.23, 3.31, App 2
  - (2) 3.28

Social Security Contributions and Benefits (Northern Ireland) Act 1992
- s 4A 3.1, 3.22

Social Security Contributions (Transfer of Functions etc) Act 1999
- s 8 .... 16.2, 16.3, 16.4, 16.8, 16.26, 17.31, 17.33, 17.36, 18.36
- 9A 15.9

T

Taxation and Chargeable Gains Act 1992
- s 155 .... 3.12

Taxes Management Act 1970
- s 16 .... 14.16
- 20 .... 15.71, 15.73, 15.74, 15.77, 15.78, 15.79

Taxes Management Act 1970—*contd*
  s 20(1) 15.79
      (3) 15.79
      33 .... 13.20, 13.23
      49 .... 16.5
      (2)(b) 16.5
      49A 16.14
      49C 16.14
      49E 16.14
      54 .... 16.19
      98A(4) 13.9
      114 .... 11.17

Tribunals, Courts and Enforcement
   Act 2007 .... 4.10, 18.21
   s 11 .... 19.4

W

Welfare Reform and Pensions Act
   1999 .... 5.120
   s 75 .... 1.33, 3.1, 3.22, App 2
   76 .... 3.1, 3.22
Workmen's Compensation Act
   1897–1943 .... 5.109

Table of Statutory Instruments

[References are to paragraph numbers and appendices]

F

First-tier Tribunal and Upper Tribunal (Composition of Tribunal) Order 2008, SI 2008/2835 .... 18.11

I

Income Tax (Pay As You Earn)) Regulations 2003, SI 2003/2682
- reg 69 .... 1.42
- 72 .... 13.17
- 73 .... 1.42
- 80 .... 1.17, 5.137, 16.1, 16.2, 16.3, 16.4, 16.8
- 82 .... 1.42
- (2) 13.4
- 97 .... 15.8, 15.9

S

Social Security (Categorisation of Earners) Regulations 1978, SI 1978/1689 .... 9.1

Social Security Contributions and Benefits Act 1992 (Modification of Section 4A) Order 2003, SI 2003/1874
- art 3, 4 .... App 2

Social Security Contributions and Benefits Act 1992 (Modification of Section 4A) Order 2007, SI 2007/2071
- art 2(2) .... App 2
- (3)(a)–(c) .... App 2
- (4)(a), (b) .... App 2
- (5) .... App 2

Social Security Contributions (Intermediaries) (Northern Ireland) Regulations 2000, SI 2000/728 .... 1.33, 3.1, 3.22

Social Security Contributions (Intermediaries) Regulations 2000, SI 2000/727 .... 1.33, 3.1, 3.22, 17.33
- reg 1–4 .... App 3
- 5 .... 3.28, App 3
- 6 .... 11.9, App 3
- (1)(a) 6.11
- 7–12 .... App 3

Social Security (Contributions) Regulations 2001, SI 2001/1004
- Sch 4
- para 26 .... 15.8

Special Commissioners (Jurisdiction and Procedure) Regulations 1994, SI 1994/1811
- reg 18 .... 11.39

T

Tax and Civil Partnership Regulations 2005/3229
- reg 13 .... App 1
- 139 .... App 1

Tribunal Procedure (First-tier Tribunal (Tax Chamber) Rules 2009, SI 2009/273 .... 18.5, 18.6, 18.21, 18.39, 18.40, 18.79, 19.14, 19.15, App 5
- r 16 .... 17.54
- 39 .... 19.4
- 40, 41 .... 19.6

Tribunal Procedure (Upper Tribunal) Rules 2008, SI 2008/2698 .... App 6

W

Working Time Regulations 1998, SI 1998/1833 .... 11.285, 21.16

Chapter 1
Introduction to IR35: its consequences and common misunderstandings

The background

1.1 Other than the poll tax, no piece of tax legislation has received such orchestrated criticism and lobbying as IR35. Sources close to the Treasury suggest that, if they had the chance again, the government would choose a less contentious approach to this legislation, which had some good arguments going for it. The legislation is poorly worded, creates massive uncertainty and, on reflection, changing the law to make national insurance payable on close company dividends might have been an easier and more successful approach.

IR35 in brief

1.2 In essence, IR35 simply says that if a worker who renders personal service is a disguised employee of his client then he should be subjected to the same tax and national insurance deductions as other regular employees. In principle no reasonable person would have a problem with this. Bogus self-employment should no more work than complex artificial offshore trust schemes.

1.3 However, in recent years, the government has developed policies in several areas of tax, seemingly based on straightforward financial expediency often dressed up as something else. It has been suggested that IR35 is not really an issue about fairness or equity, but is an exercise in improving financial yield for the Treasury. It carries with it the spin of modern politics and was expressed in such emotional language that it was heavily criticised by Mr Justice Burton in the Professional Contractors Group's (PCG's) judicial review application in the Spring of 2001. He said:

> 'It appears to me to be wholly regrettable and unnecessary that such colourful language was used in the first press release' (*R (on the application of Professional Contractors Groups Ltd and others) v IRC* [2001] EWHC Admin 236, [2001] STC 629 at 640).

The approach is not restricted to the so-called Friday to Monday disguised employees who might be subject to a legitimate IR35 challenge. All manner of skilled consultants who have been running their own businesses for many years are potentially caught.

1.3 *Introduction to IR35: its consequences and common misunderstandings*

If HMRC wanted to stamp out national insurance avoidance by the use of dividends taken by close company shareholders (a legal planning strategy), why was it necessary to extend IR35 to partnerships and unincorporated workers who are not able to take dividends?

1.4 Some commentators believe that there was political pressure to 'trickle down' the liability away from the agencies and end users to the personal service businesses at the bottom of the chain. This avoids traditional status disputes where the putative employer risks the liabilities, interest and penalties.

The history of IR35

1.5 There is limited value in going over the whole history of IR35 in detail. The fact is, it is on the statute book and it has survived quite unscathed. The initial judicial review challenge failed and although the right to appeal was eventually given to the PCG in June 2001, the Court of Appeal in late 2001 felt unable to strike out the IR35 legislation.

1.6 The initial press release in the Budget of March 1999 was entitled 'IR35' and gave the basic thrust of what was behind the initiative. It was concerned with 'Avoidance of Tax in the Provision of Personal Services'. Yet most personal service businesses are primarily concerned with obtaining work, not avoiding tax or national insurance. In order to obtain work, agencies often have to be used and agencies require contractors and freelancers to incorporate so they, the agencies, can avoid having to operate payroll deductions. Once incorporated, a business may pay less tax and NICs, but that is often a by-product of incorporation, not a reason for it at the outset.

1.7 Arguably this was misleading, because the main area of 'avoidance' with so-called personal service businesses is national insurance avoidance by the taking of dividends. Although the Contributions Agency and HMRC merged in 1999 it would be going too far to assume that tax avoidance means the same thing as national insurance avoidance. It should also be recognised from the outset that IR35 has always been concerned with 'personal' service. Not only is this word used extensively in the various press releases on the subject, it is also used throughout the legislation itself. As will be seen later, one of the principles of defending oneself against IR35 is to show that there is a genuine business-to-business relationship where 'personal' service is not required. This represents one of the major opportunities in avoiding IR35 and the practitioner should not lose sight of the fact that IR35 has always been aimed at *personal* service for the purpose of a business carried on by a client (ITEPA 2003, s 49(1)(*a*)).

1.8 HMRC have long accepted, and this has been confirmed in their internal manuals, that where a limited company which in law is a separate third party genuinely enters into a contract, then this will be a contract between that limited company and its client. In other words, it is not a contract between the personal service business's controlling shareholder and the clients.

1.9 Many successful individuals, ranging from sportsmen to pop stars, form limited companies in order to exploit their commercial attributes. Putting a limited company between the worker and the client is a perfectly legitimate form of business and HMRC have been quite happy to accept this so long as the substance matches the form.

1.10 It should be noted that the mere insertion of a company will not divorce the worker from the client where the company is inserted only as an administrative convenience or a sham, and case law both recent and old, shows that in such circumstances the insertion of the company can effectively be ignored. This is discussed in more detail later in this chapter.

1.11 The essential thrust of IR35 is aimed at the so-called 'one-man band' limited company commonly used in the IT, engineering and oil and gas industries. The legislation was extended by FA 2003, s 136 to domestic workers, such as nurses, nannies, chauffeurs and butlers, engaged by service companies. This was achieved by removing the requirement that services must be provided to a business. Ironically, one of the main reasons why there are so many personal service limited companies is because of the introduction of ITEPA 2003, Pt 2, Ch 7, dealing with agency workers.

1.12 The so-called 'agency rules' found in ITEPA 2003, ss 44–47 (and their national insurance equivalent regulations) were introduced originally in F(No 2)A 1975, s 38. In essence, the legislation states that, where a worker contracts with an agency, then the agency will have to make deductions of PAYE and national insurance as if the worker were an employee of the agency even though in law he is not.

1.13 The agency rules do not apply where the worker incorporates into a limited company. This means that, where the worker operates as a limited company, the agency is not obliged to make the PAYE and national insurance deductions that would otherwise have to be made if the worker operated as an individual or as a partner in a firm.

1.14 It is not known for sure why limited companies were excluded from the original agency regulations, but the fact is they were. It is for this reason that the overwhelming majority of workers who contract with agencies (with the exception of unskilled or semi-skilled workers, such as warehouse pickers) are effectively forced into incorporating, so that the administrative burdens of operating PAYE and national insurance are lifted from the shoulders of the agency. Indeed, several agencies and accountancy practices specialise in forming limited companies for such workers and then deal with their accounting requirements.

1.15 Had the legislation not given an exception to limited companies there would not now be the need for legislation in respect of the widespread use of them. But use of limited companies within the law is not the same as abuse. It is regrettable that the tone of the IR35 debate has given the impression that contractors who have incorporated, for a variety of commercial reasons other than fiscal, are 'tax cheats'.

1.16 *Introduction to IR35: its consequences and common misunderstandings*

1.16 Some commentators have questioned whether IR35 is needed at all. For many years HMRC have been concerned with establishing correct tax status and the Contributions Agency has been concerned with establishing the correct national insurance status. For example, in previous years there was a massive targeting of the construction industry.

1.17 It could be argued that if a worker is a disguised employee of his client there is already a mechanism for challenging his tax status, through the use of determinations under reg 80 of the Income Tax (Pay As You Earn)) Regulations 2003, SI 2003/2682. However, there is a fundamental difference with the reg 80 route. If HMRC were to challenge a worker's tax status under a reg 80 determination and succeed, the liability for paying over the appropriate deductions would rest with the employer *not* with the worker's own personal service company.

1.18 Practitioners will understand that under IR35 any liability to hand over extra tax or national insurance in respect of the disguised employee is a liability of the personal service business itself and not the fictional deemed employer.

1.19 As the IR35 issue became increasingly controversial throughout 1999, it was soon made clear by the end users that they would not want to carry any liability under IR35. At one stage it was considered that the liability to make the appropriate deductions would rest with the agencies used commonly by IR35 at-risk businesses. But again, pressure of one kind or another resulted in the liability falling on the personal service business itself.

1.20 The personal service business worker can find himself in a particularly difficult position. On the one hand his company may be liable (and in certain circumstances he himself may be personally liable—see Chapter 13) to make significant extra tax and national insurance deductions as if the worker were in receipt of a traditional salary. Yet at the same time the worker will not get the benefit of any employee rights from the fictional employer, rights which would be afforded to other regular employees.

This raises the question 'what is the difference between a deemed employee and an actual employee?' and the only way it can be answered is to remember that IR35 creates a fictional salary only for the purposes of extracting PAYE and national insurance.

1.21 Various pressure groups have suggested a so-called 'nuclear option', whereby any worker who is deemed to be caught by IR35 should make his case for employee rights with the client. Indeed, in the judicial review case Mr Justice Burton said that, under the circumstances, the worker's solicitor would be able to send a 'pretty strong letter' claiming employee rights with the client.

1.22 There have already been several court cases where a worker, despite contracting via a limited company, has successfully claimed employment law rights either from the end user or the agency through whom he contracted. Equally, there are cases where workers have failed in similar circumstances. Having successfully washed their hands of any strict legal liability in respect of IR35 deductions both agencies and end users should be aware that it is almost certain that claims against them will increase. This trend is evidenced in the Hewlett Packard tribunal case of 2001. Whilst outside the scope of this book, the employment law case *Cable & Wireless plc v Muscat* [2006] All ER (D) 319, CA is worthy of note. In that case, an individual worked for Cable & Wireless through an agency, which contracted with his personal service company. The Court of Appeal held that the individual was in fact an employee of Cable & Wireless under an implied contract of service. The notional employment contract was effectively a real contract, which gave the individual real employment rights.

1.23 A further irony is that many of the IR35 at-risk workers were previously employees made redundant in the early 1990s and who have shown the courage and initiative to form their own businesses. The government regularly trumpets its policy of assisting small businesses, but in many ways IR35 is a major hindrance for the entrepreneur.

1.24 As stated at the beginning of this chapter, no reasonable person would have serious difficulty in accepting the proposition that a worker who is really a disguised employee should be taxed in the same manner as other genuine employees. During a House of Commons debate the Paymaster General commented that people who were 'the same as an employee' should, as a matter of fairness, pay the same amount of tax as regular employees. It was explicitly stated that IR35 is aimed at relationships which have the 'essential characteristics' of direct employment. The prerequisites of a contract of employment are more fully explained in Chapter 5 where it will be seen that according to the strict letter of the law specific tests have to be met before a worker can be classified as an 'employee'.

1.25 In one sense, this phrase hints at an IR35 defence strategy. To avoid IR35, any worker needs to show, in light of the above statement, that he is not the same as other employees and that his relationship does not have the essential characteristics of employment. This comes down to an examination of his working relationship and his contractual terms and conditions and is considered in Chapters 4, 5 and 7.

1.26 Where a worker is presently acting as a disguised employee he should take advice to change the method by which he operates and the contractual terms and conditions he works to, so that in future he falls outside of IR35.

1.27 The original IR35 press release did not go into extensive detail. Passing reference was made to the so-called Friday to Monday scenario, where a worker who is a direct employee under PAYE on the Friday and comes back on the Monday as a self-employed worker despite the fact that to all intents and purposes he is working for the same people at the same premises doing the same job. But the key here is 'to all intents and purposes'. Tax status is determined by the terms and conditions of the working relationship between the two parties and there are many examples of workers who have changed their tax status 'overnight', but have genuinely done so by entering into different terms and conditions from those that went before.

The courts have made it clear that parties can renegotiate the terms and conditions whenever they wish and the tax and national insurance consequences will then flow from those terms and conditions, so long as the new terms are not a sham.

1.28 *Introduction to IR35: its consequences and common misunderstandings*

1.28 The approach of the government to IR35 seems to have been more akin to 'once an employee always an employee', but this simply doesn't stand up in law. Furthermore, HMRC tend not to argue that a person who is self-employed cannot become an employee!

1.29 The original press release indicated that a process of consultation with various representative bodies would proceed, but it has been widely reported that very little change came about as a result of this consultation process. One month after the press release a further paper was produced in April 2001. However, the emphasis on the consultation process changed somewhat and it was made clear that, although the April document was up for discussion, it was not in fact a 'consultation document'.

1.30 The April paper advanced some principles whereby IR35 would apply. Emphasis was placed on whether the worker was controlled, but a let-out clause allowed the client the freedom not to make deductions under PAYE if it knew that 'substantially' all of the monies referable to the work done had in fact been paid to the worker as a salary. This is because salaries are already subject to PAYE and national insurance. This was seen by many, especially the clients, as unworkable. The April document was roundly criticised from many quarters.

1.31 In September 1999, a further press release advanced matters considerably and formed the basis of the final legislation. It was accepted that the onus to make the appropriate PAYE and national insurance deductions should fall on the shoulders of the personal service business, confusingly called the 'intermediary' in the legislation.

1.32 Just as significantly, the control test described in the April document was dropped in favour of the traditional common-law tests that determine the borderline between employed and self-employed income. The so-called control test, which many years ago had been the single most important criterion in determining status, had been played down over the preceding 25 years or so. All commentators agree that a more comprehensive test, looking at a far wider range of individual factors beyond mere control, must give a more informed and balanced approach to this difficult issue.

1.33 IR35 subsequently resulted in further legislation. The first deals with the national insurance aspects of IR35 and is contained in the Social Security Contributions and Benefits Act 1992, s 4A (as inserted by the Welfare Reform and Pensions Act 1999, s 75). That legislation enabled statutory regulations to be introduced at a later date (namely, the Social Security Contributions (Intermediaries) Regulations 2000, SI 2000/727, and Northern Ireland equivalent regulations in SI 2000/728). The primary legislation, the subject of a very well informed and closely argued debate in the House of Lords, was eventually enacted, although not before the Lords initially rejected it and remitted back to the House of Commons, much to the government's chagrin.

1.34 The tax legislation was initially published in early 2000 and was included in FA 2000, Sch 12 and thereafter superseded by ITEPA 2003, Pt 2 Ch 8 ('Application of provisions to workers under arrangements made by intermediaries'). At the

Introduction to IR35: its consequences and common misunderstandings **1.39**

time many practitioners noted that Royal Assent would not be granted until the midsummer of 2000, yet the legislation would be retroactive and apply to services performed from 6 April 2000. Payments received after that date, for services performed before 6 April 2000, were not included within the IR35 provisions. Conversely, any sums received before 6 April 2000 in respect of services performed from 6 April were within the IR35 provisions (FA 2000, Sch 12 para 22, now repealed). This ensured that it was not possible to forestall the legislation by arranging for pre-payments to be made for services to be carried out after the introduction of the IR35 rules.

1.35 The lack of genuine consultation, and the lack of attention to workable detail, in the early forms of IR35 led to fierce criticism of HMRC. As a public service, and one to be strongly welcomed, HMRC have now devoted substantial publicity to the whole issue of IR35, including reproducing the press releases, *Tax Bulletin* articles and a series of frequently asked questions on their website (http://www.hmrc.gov.uk/ir35/index.htm).

1.36 HMRC have claimed that IR35 is not as complicated as some people have made out. The author has noted, however, that HMRC had themselves posted a total of 105 frequently asked questions concerning IR35 on their website! This figure was correct at the time the first edition of this book was published. The latest figure has risen to 120, so one can only assume IR35 has become even more complicated.

1.37 Despite this more helpful and informative approach to IR35, many practitioners will not be aware that on occasion HMRC have had had to change their own answers to their own FAQs; worryingly without seeming to notify anyone in the profession, the PCG or the public that they had changed their response, despite the fact that the question asked in one case the author was made aware of was an extremely fundamental one.

1.38 The introduction of IR35 has been controversial and many feel that HMRC have not listened to reasoned and reasonable arguments. In many ways, a lack of proper consideration of the views of genuinely interested parties gave rise to the judicial review challenge of the PCG. When the matter was aired in court under the scrutiny of an independent and highly perspicacious High Court judge, the arguments against and the concerns with IR35 were given a fair hearing.

1.39 HMRC have published many articles on IR35, not all of which are perceived as giving an accurate or up-to-date analysis of the case law. *Tax Bulletins* 41, 45, 47 and 51 all contain HMRC's view of the new legislation. *Tax Bulletin* 45 is perhaps of most use as it shows, in the celebrated examples of Gordon, Henry and Charlotte, how extraneous business factors and a commercial history and modus operandi can enable a personal service business to escape IR35. Unfortunately, some inspectors do not apply the Charlotte 'standing back approach' when they should and this is discussed in more depth in Chapter 11. *Tax Bulletin* 41 contains useful information on the appeals process and is worth studying. Unfortunately it is not entirely reliable and this is touched on in Chapter 12.

1.40 *Introduction to IR35: its consequences and common misunderstandings*

Major consequences of IR35 applying

1.40 This section is not designed to be a detailed analysis of all the consequences, fiscal or otherwise, of being caught by IR35. It is a timely reminder of the principal disadvantages of IR35 and, as such, encouragement to take steps and advance arguments to show IR35 does not apply. Many websites (such as www.contractoruk.co.uk) exist with 'calculator' facilities to show the exact difference in take home pay, where different rates of pay can be entered. HMRC's website also contains many frequently asked questions in calculating the deductions due under IR35 (http://www.hmrc.gov.uk/ir35/faq.htm).

1.41 The main fiscal disadvantage of IR35 is that income referable to what is called a 'relevant engagement' will be treated as if it is traditional salary and this deemed salary will therefore be subjected to PAYE and national insurance deductions.

1.42 Typically, contractors take a high proportion of their 'drawings' as dividends, which carry no national insurance and can also be tax advantageous, particularly for those who need only draw around £35,000 per annum to live.

The IR35 rules do not prevent the contractor from continuing to take dividends, but he will, at the end of the tax year, have to make a deemed salary calculation in accordance with the rules in ITEPA 2003, s 54 (see Appendix 1) and hand over the deductions by19 April (by virtue of Income Tax (Pay As You Earn) Regulations 2003, SI 2003/2682, reg 69). This clearly gives very little time, and deductions paid late will usually attract interest (under SI 2003/2682, reg 82). Furthermore, form P35 will have to be completed by 19 May (in accordance with SI 2003/2682, reg 73); this is also not a very generous time limit. Here the contractor will have to decide what to answer in box 6 which asks 'have you operated the Intermediaries Legislation (sometimes know as IR35) or the Managed Service Companies Legislation?'

As such there is the potential downside of having to pay substantially extra national insurance and, potentially, extra tax, along with there being a tight administrative deadline for completing the forms and making the necessary declarations.

1.43 It is not all bad news. First, the income which is deemed to be in respect of relevant engagements and which must be subject to the IR35 deductions can first be reduced by a flat 5% expense together with a claim for certain other specified extra expenses.

The 5% covers administrative help, marketing costs, certain insurances, professional fees and, among other things, training. The 5% need not be actually expended—it is given automatically.

1.44 Secondly, for those contractors who have only part of their income caught under the IR35 rules (because not all of their work amounts to relevant engagements) they may escape IR35 deductions completely. This is because many contractors already take a traditional salary, either as a tax planning strategy in using up lower rate earned income bands or to 'frank' pension contributions. In fact, out and out so-called 'abuse' of dividends is unusual.

This means that a contractor could escape all IR35 deductions. For example, a

Introduction to IR35: its consequences and common misunderstandings **1.49**

contractor may have £75,000 of work during a year and one-third of it might be caught as a 'relevant engagement'. However, if a salary of £20,000 is already being taken then this, together with the 5% deduction of £1,250 (being 5% of the income from the relevant engagement), has to be deducted. This means that potentially £25,000 less £1,250, ie £23,750, is caught under the IR35 rules but £20,000 is already being taken as a salary. Furthermore, specific extra expenses can also be deducted, including certain professional subscriptions, capital allowances, some forms of pension contributions and employer's national insurance contributions paid for the year in question.

It will be readily appreciated that the IR35 'bill' may well be nil.

1.45 The beauty of the 'deemed salary' is that it can be covered and cancelled by any salary taken, even if the salary taken related to an engagement which was outside of IR35. This is the case even if the salary was paid earlier in the year than when the relevant engagement occurred. For example, a salary drawn in the early part of the tax year, during a period when the income generated by the personal service business was *not* from a relevant engagement, can be offset as salary in respect of a relevant engagement *later* in the tax year.

1.46 The legislation in respect of the calculation of the deemed salary is contained in nine steps in ITEPA 2003, s 54 (see Appendix 1).

It should be noted that the deemed salary calculation is not the same as a corporation tax computation. The latter still has to be completed on normal taxation principles.

1.47 In the corporation tax computation, deductions will be available for salaries paid, employer's national insurance contributions, the deemed salary calculation and the national insurance arising on it and other expenses, including travel, professional indemnity insurance cover, capital allowances and other normal miscellaneous expenses.

The company's actual profit and loss account will be very different to the CT computation. It will show deductions for salaries paid, the employer's national insurance thereon, the employer's national insurance on the deemed salary, the PAYE on the deemed salary, the employee's national insurance on the deemed salary plus capital allowances, travel, professional indemnity insurance cover and any normal miscellaneous expenses.

1.48 It is possible to have a situation where the allowable employment income expenses are exceeded by the actual expenses of the company. Where this is the case there may be insufficient funds to pay out a high enough salary to cover the deemed salary. Yet the shortfall would be caught by the rules and tax and national insurance would become payable.

1.49 The exact extent of any greater tax and national insurance take will of course depend on many different factors unique to each personal service business and contractor. The main point is that contractors who have traditionally taken large dividends and low salaries will be hit hard.

There have been suggestions that the extra duties arising on the typical personal service business and contractor is in the region of £7,000 per annum. As there are

1.49 *Introduction to IR35: its consequences and common misunderstandings*

thought to be in excess of 100,000 small businesses potentially affected by IR35, it is clear why HMRC are keen to implement it.

1.50 A further consequence of IR35 is that a contractor who wishes to retain substantial funds in his company and shelter them at the lower corporation tax rates will not be able to do so. This is because income from relevant engagements will be treated as a deemed salary (subject to the 5% deduction) and will be deemed to have been paid whether or not this has actually happened.

A note on double taxation and a warning.

1.51 Despite HMRC's assurances to the contrary, it *is* possible to have double taxation under IR35. This arises where a deemed salary is calculated but not drawn. The tax and NIC is paid over and then in the new financial year an *actual* salary is taken in respect of the 'deemed' salary from the previous year. Where an actual salary is taken, the previously paid deemed salary deductions cannot be set off, hence full deductions of PAYE and national insurance have to be made again in respect of the actual salary. Dividends can avoid this.

A warning should also be sounded at this stage. Some practitioners who are not sure whether IR35 applies to their client, advise the contractor to take an actual salary and play safe, and in so doing there cannot be any come-back under IR35. The problem with this is if the contractor later decides the advice he was given was wrong, and he wishes to review whether he really was within IR35, he will have a major problem. This is because if an *actual* salary has been taken this cannot be reversed, even if it is accepted by HMRC that IR35 did not apply for the period in question.

It would be far better to pay the liabilities on the 'deemed' salary. If the situation was then revisited and IR35 was found not to apply, a supplementary P35 could be submitted and tax/NIC reclaimed.

Dispelling the misunderstandings of IR35

IR35 misunderstanding 1—there is a new status test

1.52 This misunderstanding is an easy one to deal with yet remains misunderstood by many potentially affected by IR35.

Initially there was to be a new statutory 'control' test to determine whether or not a worker was a disguised employee and hence caught by IR35. This was dropped in favour of the existing common law tests developed over the years through the courts.

1.53 The reasons for this volte face are not entirely clear, but it is suggested that practical difficulties with a statutory control test had already been encountered in relation to ITEPA 2003, ss 44–47 (the agency rules) and the national insurance equivalent regulations.

1.54 Furthermore, it is clear that many specialist contractors are simply *not* controlled, particularly in respect of 'how' they do their work. This is, after all, because they are specialists. Old case law going back to the mid 1960s acknowledged that 'control' can only be an issue where there is scope for it. It might seem a non-starter for HMRC to devise a 'control' test when, almost by definition, there is very limited scope for it in the case of the typical personal service business expert.

1.55 A new statutory 'control test' could have been extended to 'rights of' rather than de facto control, but this would have been difficult to put into legislative form in any meaningful way. The background to this is that sometimes HMRC argue that even if there is no actual control the control test might still be satisfied if the client retains a theoretical 'right' to control the worker. It is of course very difficult to prove or disprove a theoretical right of control. Where HMRC realise there is no actual control, they will still sometimes argue that there was a 'right'. If the proposed control test had been extended to a 'right of', as well as actual, control it would have been a formidable line of attack for HMRC.

For whatever reason, the existing case law precedents were found to be preferable.

Case law also gives the opportunity for the law to develop in an organic way by reflecting the ever-changing workplace environment.

1.56 The first misunderstanding of IR35 is quite simply clarified by appreciating that no new status test has been brought in. It is no harder now, post-IR35 to escape the status of 'disguised employee' than it was pre-IR35. Self-employment has not become a special or rare category.

Those practitioners who dealt with the Contributions Agency's and HMRC's attacks on self-employment in the construction industry in the late 1990s will remember the impression given by many tax officers to the effect that the 'law on status' had changed. Of course it had not changed, but many companies went along with it. IR35 is the same. The law on determining self-employment has not changed.

IR35 misunderstanding 2—liability rests with the agency/end user

1.57 This misunderstanding is still one that many agencies and end users consider to be fact. This relates to the issue of liability under IR35 and once again shows how fear, uncertainty and doubt have come about from the early draft versions of IR35.

Quite simply, the liability for deducting and paying over the appropriate tax and national insurance rests with the personal service business, the so-called 'intermediary' and not with the agency or end user.

Perhaps the use of the word 'intermediary' was never wise as this, in itself, has caused much confusion. But to this day agencies and end users still believe that they are somehow liable if they change contractual terms and conditions which allow the worker to escape IR35. They will not be liable and have nothing to fear. More recent experiences suggest that agencies and end users are getting to grips with IR35 and may have become more flexible when it comes to amending contract terms in order to assist avoiding IR35.

1.58 It should be noted that, in certain limited circumstances, the director of the personal service company may be personally liable for IR35 deductions. This is discussed in greater depth in Chapter 13. It should also be noted that where a company

1.58 *Introduction to IR35: its consequences and common misunderstandings*

falls within the Managed Service Company legislation (introduced in 2007) liability under the MSC rules can personally fall on the worker and certain other individuals or corporate entities. The new MSC rules are beyond the scope of this book, but the MSC rules are looked at in broad terms later.

IR35 misunderstanding 3—HMRC published guidance accurately summarises the law

1.59 The third misunderstanding of IR35 is that HMRC's published guidance is an accurate summary of the legal criteria to be applied in determining whether a worker is a disguised employee—it is not. However in fairness IR35 has now developed through case law to the extent that little reliance is placed on such guidance and practitioners seem to have wised up to the fact that such publications are not law and are prepared to remind the inspector and Tribunal of this fact.

1.60 HMRC and other non-statutory booklets can be used to good effect as the decision in *Larkstar Ltd* shows (see Chapter 11). This is a 2008 General Commissioners' decision that was appealed to the High Court ([2008] EWHC 3284 Ch), but was subsequently remitted back to the decision is still awaited at General Commissioners for re-hearing by a differently constituted panel, on the grounds that the Commissioners had misdirected themselves in relation to two of their considerations and one finding of fact. That case is commented on in Chapter 11.

IR35 misunderstanding 4—having less than 5% of the shares in the intermediary company means that IR35 will not apply

1.61 There is the common misunderstanding that, by having less than 5% of the shares in the intermediary company, the worker cannot be caught by IR35. This is quite wrong and many schemes set up along these lines fail.

1.62 This is because the legislation (ITEPA 2003, s 51, see Appendix 1) employs a much wider test in determining whether the IR35 rules apply in cases where the intermediary is a company. It states that IR35 may apply if the worker has a 'material interest' in the intermediary. Material interest is not determined only by a straight 5% shareholding in the intermediary company. Instead, material interest is, broadly, beneficial ownership or the ability to directly or indirectly control more than 5% of the company's ordinary share capital, possession of or the right to acquire more than 5% of the company's distributions or entitlement to receive more than 5% of the assets available for distribution among participators in a close company. Furthermore, a material interest can be the worker's alone, or the worker's with one or more associates, or an associate's alone, or an associate's with other associates. It should also be noted that an associate is widely defined by ITEPA 2003, s 60 (see Appendix 1).

1.63 However, even where there is no material interest, the worker can still be caught by IR35 if either he or an associate receives (or is entitled to receive) payment or another benefit not chargeable under employment income directly from the intermediary company, which can 'reasonably be taken to represent remuneration for services provided by the worker to the client' (ITEPA 2003, s 51(1)(*b*)).

IR35 misunderstanding 5—standard agency contracts fail IR35

1.64 HMRC have said that standard agency contracts are caught by IR35 (see *Tax Bulletin* 45, dated February 2000). This is too general. It is probably fair to say that the majority of existing standard agency contracts are more likely than not to be caught by IR35, but this is because of their poor drafting in terms of IR35 and the conditions they contain. It is not the fact that they are 'standard' or 'agency contracts' which makes them fail. In fact, a standard contract may fall outside the scope of IR35 if it contains appropriate clauses, which, when agreed and implemented, ensure the worker is not a disguised employee. In the early days of IR35 many agencies were reluctant to alter their standard contracts which had of course been drawn up many years previously and when IR35 was not an issue. Some of the more proactive agencies saw flexibility over terms and conditions as a positive marketing strategy and they were only too pleased to agree more 'IR35 friendly' terms if it meant getting a particular worker placed with a client. In recent times and as the UK economy heads from downturn to recession it is clear that work is scarce and once again workers have less influence over amending contract terms.

1.65 There is nothing wrong or artificial in both parties agreeing to use a standard form contract. Not only is this practice widespread in other aspects of commercial and domestic life, but it was actively encouraged by Mr Justice Burton in the PCG Judicial Review in the High Court (*R (on the application of Professional Contractors Group Ltd) v IRC* [2002] STC 165). The judge anticipated that the various parties would get together and agree standard terms which would take the relationship out of IR35.

1.66 In fairness to HMRC, their statement effectively said that standard agency contracts, even if caught by IR35, would tend to be ignored if they were for less than a month in duration. Unfortunately, this has often been misconstrued as meaning that any standard agency contract which lasts for longer than one month is automatically caught. This of course is not the case. It *may* be caught, but detailed reference has to be made to the terms and conditions it contains.

IR35 misunderstanding 6—completion of time sheets indicates direct employee status

1.67 Despite HMRC guidance to the contrary (ESM 0518), the widely promoted HMRC view is that the use of time sheets is a strong indicator of direct employment by the client. This is misleading for two reasons.

1.68 First, the reality is that the overwhelming majority of regular employees do *not* complete time sheets! If completion of a timesheet is so indicative of direct employment status, why is it that most employees do not fill them in?

1.69 *Introduction to IR35: its consequences and common misunderstandings*

1.69 Secondly, even though some regular employees do complete time sheets, there is no specific reference to 'time sheets' as a relevant factor to be taken into account in any tax status decision made by the courts. In a little-known national insurance case *WHPT Housing Association Ltd v Secretary of State* [1981] ICR 737 (discussed at **5.158**) completion of time sheets was not held against the taxpayer who was found to be self-employed. This case is not in the HMRC manuals. There may be an argument that, at most, time sheets are one minor factor in assessing whether the worker is a direct employee of the client, but only in industries where it is the norm for direct employees to complete time sheets. However, there may be other much stronger factors suggesting the worker is not a disguised employee for which there is express judicial authority.

IR35 misunderstanding 7—the mere existence of a limited company ensures that the worker is not a disguised employee of the client

1.70 Case law heard prior to IR35 in the context of determining status for employment law purposes has made it clear that the mere insertion of a limited company as an administrative convenience will not establish self-employed status. If the real contract is between the worker and the client, then the company can be ignored. It has to be emphasised that the inserted company tends to be ignored when the *worker himself* wants to ignore it. This was demonstrated in the 2001 case of *O'Murphy v Hewlett Packard* [2002] IRLR 4 and the earlier case of *Catamaran Cruisers Ltd v Williams* [1994] IRLR 386.

1.71 Not all workers who seek to deny the existence of their own company succeed. One notable failure was in the 1978 case of *Winter v Westward Television* (1978), unreported, heard by the Employment Appeals Tribunal. Mr Winter was represented by a Mr Tony Blair, a former employment lawyer, latterly involved in politics.

Summary

1.72 There are many myths and misunderstandings regarding IR35 and practitioners and their clients should be aware of them. The correct position is as follows:

1 There is no new 'status' test. The existing case law precedents are what matters.
2 The liability under IR35 rests with the personal service business and not the agency or the end user.
3 HMRC-published guidance does not accurately summarise the law.
4 Having less than 5% of the shares in the personal service business will not automatically provide an IR35 defence.
5 Standard agency contracts of whatever length do not automatically fail IR35 and many agencies are becoming more flexible.
6 The completion of time sheets is not in itself an indication of direct employment by the client.
7 The mere existence of a limited company does not in itself prevent a worker from being a disguised employee of the client.

Chapter 2

Planning to beat IR35: the four basic principles in outline

2.1 IR35 can be resisted effectively. This brief chapter outlines the main IR35 defence strategies in principle.

Taking a wider view of the IR35 landscape, there are four main strategies to be considered, all of which can be used either in isolation or as part of a co-ordinated approach to show IR35 may not apply in any particular given circumstance.

1. A critical analysis of the IR35 legislation

2.2 The purpose of this approach is to examine the legislation in fine detail, with the aim of establishing, or at least questioning, whether the legislation applies in principle at all. It has been too readily assumed that the wording of the legislation automatically catches all personal service businesses. However, if it can be shown that this is not the case then IR35 will simply not apply.

2.3 Chapter 3 analyses the primary legislation, ITEPA 2003, Pt 2, Ch 8 together with the Social Security Contributions and Benefits Act 1992, s 4A. It examines the conditions that must be satisfied before IR35 applies, and it suggests some arguments based on the rules of statutory interpretation to defeat the presumed application of IR35.

2. Agreeing and implementing contractual terms which fall outside IR35

2.4 A person's tax status is determined by the terms and conditions of his working relationship. There has been a great deal of commentary about the so-called 'hypothetical' contract IR35 requires to be constructed. The legislation contains no such phrase as 'hypothetical contracts'. It simply asks whether the circumstances are such that, had the contract been entered into directly between the worker and the client, those terms and conditions would amount to disguised employment.

2.5 A detailed understanding of the case law on employment status (explained in Chapter 5) is essential if the practitioner is to demonstrate that a worker is not a disguised employee of the client. Chapter 7 takes this a stage further by considering

2.5 *Planning to beat IR35: the four basic principles in outline*

in detail what terms need to be agreed in the contract in order to help ensure that the contract itself does not fall foul of IR35.

2.6 Tax inspectors, and indeed the Tribunal, will always prefer to see hard physical evidence and proof of contentions being made. It is, therefore, strongly recommended that many small matters, which in themselves will not necessarily win the argument, should be subject to a 'paper trail' or due diligence process. This is also something the PCG advocates.

2.7 If one is attempting to show that contract terms fall outside IR35 and reference is made to, say, professional indemnity insurance or website advertising, then copies of the appropriate certificates and website print-out should be retained. Even very well paid contractors may not raise a formal invoice on company stationery, but this is exactly the kind of evidence which would indicate a genuine business with a proper business organisation. Accordingly, contractors should always be encouraged to document their business activities thoroughly.

3. Understanding HMRC's IR35 compliance process

2.8 The third principle of defeating IR35 is to have a clear understanding of what will happen when HMRC wish to challenge under IR35. This is dealt with in Chapter 15.

4. Taking an IR35 appeal to the Tribunal

2.9 If a dispute cannot be resolved by argument with the inspector, the only alternative to backing down is taking the case to the tax tribunal. Most practitioners have little experience of conducting contentious appeals, particularly where large sums of money could be involved. Chapters 16 to 18 give a clear step-by-step guide through the process.

Applying the four principles

2.10 The four principles of defeating IR35 clearly require a comprehensive knowledge and understanding of the legislation, case law, HMRC interview techniques and what is required to mount an effective appeal at the tax tribunal.

2.11 The overwhelming majority of tax practitioners and clients have not been involved in a contentious appeal hearing, with all that that involves, including adducing evidence, cross-examining witnesses and making legal submissions. Chapters 16 to 18 contain highly detailed practical guidance on how to take a case to the Tribunal.

2.12 This chapter is deliberately called 'planning' to beat IR35, because a successful defence strategy will not come about by coincidence or apathy. Personal service businesses and their advisers need to take proactive steps *now* to help ensure that the IR35 rules do not apply. The purpose of this chapter is to help the practitioner focus on the main strategies of beating IR35 and to underline the important message that homework and planning are needed now in order to deal with the challenge, should it come.

2.13 It is suggested that HMRC are more likely to target easy cases, which tend to be the businesses who have neglected to deal with the essential detail which shows that they fall outside the scope of IR35. The tax courts are littered with the bones of unsuccessful taxpayers who never quite got around to doing what they had to in order to protect themselves. Those who argue that had they organised their tax affairs in a slightly different way they would have received a less harsh tax treatment will receive no sympathy from the inspector, the Tribunal or the courts.

Summary

2.14 Planning a defence against IR35 is all about having an attitude of challenge and a questioning approach. Remaining independent and avoiding the label of 'disguised employee' does not require the worker to fit into some unique category or privileged special case. It should never be forgotten that beating IR35 is not about proving the worker is self-employed; instead, it is about proving the worker is not an employee of the client. The two are not the same.

However, planning to beat IR35 and applying the four basic principles do need careful consideration and forethought. There is a big prize at stake after all. The following chapters will give the open-minded and proactive practitioner a wealth of arguments, advice and guidance on how the four principles can be used in practice.

Chapter 3

Analysing the IR35 legislation for possible escape routes

3.1 It is often assumed, in the author's view far too readily, that the IR35 legislation—to be found in ITEPA 2003, Pt 2, Ch 8, the Social Security Contributions and Benefits Act 1992, s 4A (as inserted by the Welfare Reform and Pensions Act 1999, s 75) or its Northern Ireland equivalent the Social Security Contributions and Benefits (Northern Ireland) Act 1992, s 4A (as inserted by s 76) and the Social Security Contributions (Intermediaries) Regulations 2000, SI 2000/727 (or, for Northern Ireland, SI 2000/728)—will somehow automatically apply to all personal service businesses.

3.2 It is suggested that a more questioning and critical approach to analysing the legislation will reveal opportunities for demonstrating that IR35 does not apply. In other words, IR35 may be a complete non-starter for certain personal service businesses. In the author's view, the legislation is not well worded; it offers some very arguable points; and the tax legislation is worded differently from the national insurance legislation. Yet many advisers and contractors take a fatalistic view of IR35. They see the only argument as one of attempting to show that the terms of their contract take them outside IR35.

3.3 Certainly, IR35 does not apply if it can be shown that the personal service business worker is not a 'disguised employee' of the client; hence the heavy emphasis on contractual terms and conditions and the working relationship. But it would be preferable to avoid the 'disguised employee' argument by showing that the IR35 legislation simply does not apply at all. If it can be shown that, in principle, the intermediaries' legislation does not apply, there will be no need to examine contracts, working relationships or anything else. In a situation where the practitioner is working within the tight financial restraints of limited fee budgets a 'knock out' blow will be preferable to a long and drawn out fight, one which may only result in a narrow win on points and which can be a harrowing process. Quite simply, IR35 may well be a club the personal service business does not have to join.

ITEPA 2003, Pt 2, Ch 8

3.4 The key paragraph in the chapter that defines the engagements to which the IR35 rules apply is ITEPA 2003, s 49. This section sets out three requirements (listed in s 49(1)(*a*), (*b*) and (*c*)), and *all* of these have to be satisfied before the worker can fall within the scope of the rules. Broadly, para 1 requires that there must be three parties: the worker, the intermediary and the client. The worker must personally perform, or be under an obligation to perform, services for the purposes of a business carried on by the client (s 49(1)(*a*)). Those services are performed not under a contract between the worker and the client but under 'arrangements' involving the intermediary (s 49(1)(*b*)). Finally, the circumstances of the arrangements are such that, were there a direct contract between the client and the worker, the worker would for tax purposes be regarded as an employee of the client (s 49(1)(*c*)).

Each of the separate three requirements in para 1 is examined below in turn.

ITEPA 2003, s 49(1)(a)

3.5 The first condition for IR35 to apply is covered in ITEPA 2003, s 49(1)(*a*). This requires that:

> 'an individual ("the worker") personally performs, or is under an obligation personally to perform, services for another person ("the client")'.

There are two main points here. First, there is a twin test of 'performs' or 'obligation to perform'. Second, the services have to be performed *for a client*.

3.6 The test of 'performs' or 'obligation to perform' is carefully worded. The word 'performs' ensures that the test looks at what actually happens, as opposed to whether there is an unused right of substitution. In other words even if there is a right of substitution but in fact the worker carries out the duties personally then he is still within the scope of s 49(1)(*a*). He may of course escape IR35 on the 'right of substitution' under s 49(1)(*c*).

3.7 It should be noted that the test in s 49(1)(*a*) requires that it is the worker (and not the personal service business) who must perform or be obliged to perform the services. Therefore, s 49(1)(*a*) would not seem to be met if it can be shown that it is the personal service business (as opposed to the worker) which is under the obligation to perform services. This anomaly could have been avoided if the legislation stated that the Schedule applies when either the worker *or* his intermediary personal service company performs, or is under an obligation to perform, the services. However, s 49(1)(*a*) did not use this wording, and this is potentially to the taxpayer's benefit.

3.8 This raises the question as to what happens in the situation where a substitute is in fact sent to provide the services. The mere fact that a substitute may be sent suggests that the worker is not under an obligation to give personal service (and, indeed, he does not actually perform the services on any occasion when the substitute is sent). It would seem reasonable to interpret this as meaning that the greater the possibility of providing substitutes, the more likely it is that IR35 does not apply.

3.9 Suppose Fred Bloggs, a director/shareholder of Fred Bloggs Computer Services Ltd, sends a substitute for, say, two weeks out of a six-month contract. In this situation, it is suggested that there are two possible interpretations of s 49(1)(*a*).

3.9 *Analysing the IR35 legislation for possible escape routes*

The first is that the IR35 rules will still potentially apply to the times when the substitute is not sent. The second possible interpretation is that IR35 will not apply at all to that particular contract because personal service has not always been given. In the author's experience, HMRC are increasingly willing to exclude from IR35 the income arising under the whole contract when either a substitute is actually sent or where there is a not unreasonably fettered right to send a substitute, although they will often seek third-party confirmation of the right.

It should also be noted that the right to send a substitute may also preclude a worker from being viewed as a disguised employee of the client, and thereby not satisfying the test in s 49(1)(*c*), discussed below.

ITEPA 2003, s 49(1)(b)

3.10 Section 49(1)(*b*) provides the second condition that must be met if the legislation is to apply. It requires that:

> 'the services are provided not under a contract directly between the client and the worker but under arrangements involving a third party ("the intermediary")'.

In other words, the services must not be provided directly by the worker to the client, but via an intermediary. IR35 will not apply if there is not at least one intermediary. Obviously, if the worker does not use an intermediary, but simply provides services to the client directly, the worker falls outside the scope of Pt 2, Ch 8. This is possibly the easiest method of escaping IR35, but before the worker gets too excited it must be remembered that he would, in the absence of an intermediary, then be subject to the normal case law in determining whether he is an employee of the client or is self-employed, and would almost certainly be caught by the agency rules (Pt 2, Ch 7) if he contracted with an agency.

It is an interesting moot point to ask what the position would be if the worker entered into a contract personally but on terms which stated he would provide the services via his own limited company. Could it not then be argued that IR35 cannot apply as s 49(1)(*b*) has not been met because the contract *is* directly between the worker and the client? If not why not?

3.11 In the early days of IR35 there was much confusion surrounding the term 'intermediary'. Indeed, it is odd that the legislation does not include a comprehensive definition of that term, when there are definitions for so many other words and phrases for which the meaning is more immediately obvious (such as 'tax year'). What is clear is that the word 'intermediary' does not mean the agency in the classic personal service business/agency/end-user chain. The intermediary is the business that provides the services. Typically, the intermediary is a one-man limited company or a partnership.

3.12 The statutory provision which comes closest to defining the meaning of intermediary is ITEPA 2003, s 49(3). This states that the term 'third party' includes 'a partnership or unincorporated body of which the worker is a member'. Arguably, this phrase is unclear. Do the words 'of which the worker is a member' apply to both partnerships and unincorporated bodies? In other words, does s 49(3) mean that an intermediary includes any partnership, or only those partnerships of which the worker is a member? In many ways, this is similar to the debate concerning the interpretation of the phrase 'fixed plant or machinery' in relation to assets qualifying for rollover relief under TCGA 1992, s 155. (In that instance, it was held in *Williams v Evans* [1982] STC 498 that the word 'fixed' qualifies for both plant and machinery.) Again, this is arguably another ambiguity in the legislation, and it illustrates the types of issues that can be raised with HMRC.

3.13 Even disregarding this point, not all intermediaries are within the scope of IR35. Specific requirements must be met if Ch 8 is to apply, and these requirements depend on the type of intermediary in question.

3.14 ITEPA 2003, s 51 sets out the requirements where the intermediary is a company. This section is clear evidence, if any were needed, that the legislation is intended to apply to situations where the work is provided by an intermediary company. It provides that an intermediary company will only be within IR35 if the intermediary is not an associated company of the client by reason of them both being under the control of the worker (or the worker and another person) (ITEPA 2003 s 51(1), (2)). Furthermore, the worker must either have a material interest in the intermediary or receive payments or benefits from the intermediary which can reasonably be taken to represent remuneration for services provided by the worker to the client.

3.15 A material interest is, in this context, widely defined as 5% by reference to ordinary share capital, dividend rights, or, in the case of a close company, entitlement to assets (ITEPA 2003, s 51(4)). The interests of associates (defined by ITEPA 2003, s 60; see Appendix 1) can be taken into account for the purpose of the material interest test (ITEPA 2003, s 51(3)).

3.16 Where the intermediary is a partnership, the requirements depend on whether or not the payments or benefits are received (or receivable) by a worker as a member of the partnership. If they are, there are three alternative tests. The first is that the worker and his relatives (ie, spouse, parent or remoter forebear, child or remoter issue, brother or sister) are entitled to at least 60% of the profits of the partnership. This requirement would not therefore be met if at least 60% of the profits went to more remote family members, such as uncles and aunts.

The second requirement is that most of the profits of the partnership are derived from services within IR35 provided to a single client (or a single client and his associates). There is no statutory definition of the term 'most' in this context, so it should probably be given its usual meaning of the majority of or over half.

The third requirement is that the partnership profit sharing arrangement for any of the partners is based on the amount of income generated by that partner from IR35 services. This requirement is clearly intended to catch partnerships that would not otherwise fall within IR35 which are used as a means of passing income resulting from IR35-type engagements to that worker. If the payments etc are received (or receivable) by a worker who is not a member of the partnership, then the tests are the same as those where the intermediary is an individual (ITEPA 2003, s 52).

3.17 *Analysing the IR35 legislation for possible escape routes*

3.17 Where the intermediary is an individual, there is a single test: the worker must receive (or be entitled to receive) payment or benefit from the intermediary which can reasonably be said to represent remuneration for services provided by the worker to the client (ITEPA 2003, s 53). The language of that provision (ie 'a payment or benefit ... received or receivable ... which can reasonably be taken to represent remuneration for services') is deliberately wide, so that it catches any income other than that which is truly unrelated to the services provided to the client.

3.18 Of course, there may be more than one intermediary. The most common example of this is in the worker/personal service business/agency/client scenario. In such a case, the above rules apply separately to each of the intermediaries in determining whether they are within the scope of IR35 (ITEPA 2003, s 59(3), see Appendix 1).

3.19 IR35 cannot be escaped merely by using a foreign intermediary. However, IR35 does not apply in circumstances where no employment income liability would arise if the services were provided directly by the worker to the client (ITEPA 2003, s 56(3)). This could be by reason of a combination of the residence status of the worker, the residence of the client, or the place in which the service was provided. An example of this is where a non-resident worker performs duties outside the UK. He would not be charged to UK tax under general principles Therefore, IR35 cannot bring those earnings into the charge to UK tax merely because they are provided via an intermediary.

ITEPA 2003, s 49(1)(c)

3.20 Section 49(1)(c) is often thought of as the key test. It states that the Schedule applies where:

> 'the circumstances are such that, if the services were provided under a contract directly between the client and the worker, the worker would be regarded for income tax purposes as an employee of the client'.

It requires the circumstances to be considered with a view to seeing if the worker is a disguised employee of the client. As there is no separate test for employment status under IR35, all of the tests for employment in the existing case law are relevant. For a discussion of relevant case law, see Chapter 5, and Chapters 6–8 in the context of who is the client, recommended contract terms and the relevance of the agency/end-user contract.

3.21 The legislation specifically provides that the 'circumstances', in this context, include 'the terms on which the services are provided, having regard to the terms of the contracts forming part of the arrangements under which the services are provided' (ITEPA 2003, s 49(4)). This means that it is necessary to examine the contractual terms under which the services are provided. This is discussed further in Chapter 7.

The National Insurance legislation

3.22 The relevant primary legislation is the Social Security Contributions and Benefits Act 1992, s 4A (as inserted by the Welfare Reform and Pensions Act 1999, s 75). The equivalent Northern Ireland legislation is the Social Security Contributions and Benefits (Northern Ireland) Act 1992, s 4A (as inserted by s 76). The detailed regulations are contained in the Social Security Contributions (Intermediaries) Regulations 2000, SI 2000/727; the equivalent Northern Ireland provisions are contained in the Social Security Contributions (Intermediaries) (Northern Ireland) Regulations 2000, SI 2000/728.

3.23 There is a similar point to be raised in relation to the sidenote to SSCBA 1992, s 4A. The sidenote reads: 'Earnings of workers supplied by service companies etc'. It is notable that the sidenote of s 4A specifically includes a reference to personal service companies (unlike the tax legislation in ITEPA 2003, s 49(3)). But in terms of demonstrating that IR35 may not apply, the words 'workers supplied' in the sidenote are potentially very helpful. The extent to which sidenotes are relevant in interpreting the legislation is a reasonably complex issue, and readers are referred to *Bennion: Statutory Interpretation* (Butterworths, 5th edn, 2008). In general, the sidenote is part of the Act which was passed by Parliament, and may therefore be used in interpreting the legislation. As with headings, sidenotes are necessarily brief and therefore potentially of limited use.

3.24 But there is case law which supports the assertion that modern judges consider it proper to take account of sidenotes, and gather what guidance they can from them. In *Chilcott v IRC* [1982] STC 1, Vinelott J said (at 23) that the sidenote was 'a permissible ... [and] useful guide throwing further light on the mischief aimed at'. An example of a case which shows the usefulness of sidenotes is *DPP v Schildkamp* [1971] AC 1, in which the scope of the Companies Act 1948, s 332 was restricted by its sidenote.

3.25 There is, therefore, judicial authority for using the sidenote in interpreting the section. If the national insurance legislation is aimed at 'workers supplied', as the sidenote states, does this not mean that where a worker is not supplied but instead a 'service' is given, then by definition the regulations cannot apply? This would seem to be a very arguable proposition. The national insurance legislation was introduced prior to the tax legislation and it is to be noted that the tax legislation does not have a similar rubric about 'earnings of workers supplied'. One wonders whether the government spotted this, and wanted to avoid it for the purposes of the tax legislation.

3.26 One of the main strategies in defeating IR35 is to show that there exists a genuine business-to-business relationship to supply services. Not only does this show there is no personal service as required by ITEPA 2003, s 49(1)(*a*) but it also avoids a potential agency problem under ITEPA 2003, Pt 2, Ch 7. Likewise, it is arguable that the national insurance consequences of IR35 can be avoided where it can be shown that the workers are not being supplied, but instead services are being undertaken.

3.27 *Analysing the IR35 legislation for possible escape routes*

3.27 Otherwise, the national insurance legislation is reasonably similar to the tax legislation in relation to determining the scope of IR35. It should be noted, however, that there are one or two discrepancies. First, the tax legislation defines the word 'arrangements' as being those entered into by the intermediary (s 49(4)), whereas the national insurance legislation fails to provide such a definition. Secondly, the hypothetical contract under the national insurance legislation is not defined as a 'direct' contract between the worker and the client, whereas it is so defined in the tax legislation (s 49(1)(*c*)). These differences may prove important when arguing a case as the IR35 'assessments' may be tax, or national insurance, or both.

3.28 Somewhat confusingly, SSCBA, s 4A(2) provides a definition of the term 'intermediary', which is also defined in SI 2000/727, reg 5, and which is referred to in reg 6(1)(*b*), whereas the tax legislation defines 'third party' instead (at ITEPA 2003, s 49(3)). It is suggested that this shows, if nothing else, that the legislation is poorly worded. The differences between the two sets of legislation have been commented on in several cases, most recently in the *Dragonfly* litigation heard both by the Special Commissioners and on appeal in the High Court. Following some highly detailed dissections of the provisions the view seems to be that while there are differences they were not intentional; nor do they create a practical problem of major significance.

3.29 Other arguments based on statutory interpretation are available to the practitioner, but in the real world it seems likely that IR35 cases will be won or lost on an examination of the circumstances and arrangements of the hypothetical contract.

Summary

3.30 All too often it is assumed that the IR35 rules automatically apply because it is thought that the situation in question would seem to be one for which the IR35 rules were intended. No assumptions should be made without first looking at the detailed rules. Is the intermediary a relevant one within IR35? If the worker does not actually provide the service, is he (and not the personal service business) the person who is obliged to perform the services? Is the IR35 challenge under the tax or national insurance legislation? The rules are not the same.

3.31 Furthermore, the legislation itself contains a number of ambiguities, particularly, it is suggested, as regards ITEPA 2003, s 49(1)(*a*) and the use of the words 'workers supplied' in the sidenote to SSCBA 1992, s 4A. There are some arguments to be raised on the basis of statutory interpretation—and it is legitimate to raise them. Statutory interpretation is not mere word play or sophistry, and to dismiss it as such is failing to take advantage of the full range of defence strategies available to the practitioner. Indeed, many a court case has turned on the interpretation of seemingly straightforward legislation, let alone these rules, which contain a number of ambiguities.

Chapter 4
Why understanding case law is important

4.1 There is no useful definition in the legislation of a contract of service (direct employment), or a contract for services (self-employment).
The Employment Rights Act 1996, s 230(1) says:

> 'an employee means an individual who has entered into or works under (or worked under) a contract of employment'.

And s 230(2) goes on to add:

> 'a contract of employment means a contract of service or apprenticeship whether express or implied and if express oral or in writing'.

The same definition appears in the National Minimum Wage Act 1998, s 54.

4.2 In the absence of a detailed statutory definition of employment and self-employment it is necessary to turn to the court decisions over the years where the status of a person has had to be decided. This is why case law is so important. There is nothing else to go on. Despite this, in an exchange of correspondence with Accountax, a tax inspector declared that case law 'is not relevant to IR35'. Such a lack of understanding is breathtaking. HMRC will often go on a detailed 'fact finding' initiative, only to discover that the facts they are seeking are not recognised by case law as being relevant. Accountax has witnessed many examples of inspectors who refuse to address case law. By ignoring case law until the last minute they fail to apply the correct tests that, ultimately, the courts will apply.

4.3 It should be noted that many of the court decisions are not directly concerned with income tax or national insurance; some are concerned with employment law rights, such as unfair dismissal or the entitlement to holiday pay or sick pay, and others with industrial accidents. In any event, the court has had to decide whether or not the person concerned was employed or self-employed and a huge body of case law has built up. HMRC are quite happy to refer to employment law rather than pure tax or national insurance cases where appropriate, as the ESM demonstrates in many places. Without doubt HMRC have made strenuous efforts to update their internal guidance manuals, but as Anne Redston has correctly pointed out on the lecture circuit there are still too many shortcomings.

The relevance of employment law decisions was considered in two recent cases. In *HMRC v Wright* [2007] EWHC 526 (see Chapter 5) the High Court made it clear

4.3 *Why understanding case law is important*

that employment law cases are relevant even if it is 'tax status' that is in issue. In some respects the phrase 'tax status' is misleading because what is actually being ascertained in 'employment' status. Once that has been done the tax and national consequences simply flow from that status.

4.4 When arguing that a client falls outside of IR35, it is too easy to rely on personal opinion or on a sense of what is fair and equitable. When corresponding with HMRC or representing clients at the Tribunal, the mere opinion of the advocate counts for nothing. While it may be possible to put forward a very reasonable view based on common sense this will carry limited weight.

4.5 On the other hand, quotations from case law decisions give arguments authority and will be convincing. Not only does case law enable points to be made but it will also enable the inspector's arguments to be rebutted. A good example of this might be where the inspector claims that the completion of a time sheet is an indicator of direct employment. Yet a search of all tax cases, going back to the nineteenth century, reveals that the phrase 'time sheets' has never been mentioned once. In an attempt to refute the inspector's arguments this would be pointed out. Indeed there is a national insurance case, *WHPT Housing* [1981] ICR 737, discussed at **5.158**, where it was accepted that completion of time sheets indicated *self-employment*.

4.6 It is important to be able to quote the words the judges have actually used. There are many useful publications which give summaries of the case law judgments. Whilst such publications are extremely useful, they rarely quote the actual words the judges have used, and it is that wording which will carry the greatest weight.

The hierarchy of the tribunals and the courts

4.7 Practitioners should be aware of the pecking order of the tribunals and courts. Quotations from the more senior courts, particularly recent decisions, will carry most weight. One should also be aware of the inspector quoting from a particular case when it was heard in the lower courts despite the fact that the higher courts overturned the decision on appeal. A good example of this is HMRC's habit of quoting only the High Court judgment in *Hall v Lorimer* [1992] STC 599. What HMRC seem to forget is that the case went on to be heard by the Court of Appeal, and it is the judgment of the senior court which is more important and carries more weight. As it is, the Court of Appeal in this case supported the decision of the High Court, but Lord Justice Nolan in the Court of Appeal made some extremely important judicial comments that HMRC often fail to recognise, because in error they concentrate their efforts only on the High Court judgment. They do this because it suits them.

Likewise with *Carmichael v National Power Plc* [1999] 1 WLR 2042. MRC have been known to quote the Court of Appeal decision despite the fact that it was overturned by the House of Lords.

4.8 Although old law is by no means bad law—in fact often the reverse—the employment scene is shifting, and quoting up-to-date law will be far more impressive than quoting decisions from half a century ago.

Why understanding case law is important **4.13**

An example of this is the 1880 case of *Yewens v Noakes* (1880–81) LR 6 QBD 530, CA which introduced the idea of the 'control' test, but spoke in terms of the 'master/servant' relationship. This style of language goes back to a time when 'master/servant' had a specific meaning in the social hierarchy and this phrase should not be taken as being synonymous with 'employer/employee'. The phrase 'master/servant' carries a peculiarly Victorian flavour and, bearing in mind the case quoted was heard in 1880, this is hardly surprising. Indeed, the word 'servant' had a technical meaning that would hardly be applicable in the twenty-first century. So old cases must be seen in their historical and social context.

4.9 It is important to quote, wherever possible, up-to-date case law judgments that have taken into account the modern world and which can be applied easily to present-day circumstances. If the up-to-date case law quoted is from a senior court, then all the better. It should cause no great surprise that the inspector may be unaware of very recent case law. Despite the ready availability of case law judgments on the internet, the Head Office of HMRC are not always prompt in disseminating new cases to the districts. Various tax inspectors have confirmed this to the author.

4.10 The hierarchy for a tax appeal depends on whether it is subject to the 'old' or 'new' appeal system.

Under the appeal system before 1 April 2009, the case was first heard by the General Commissioners or Special Commissioners. The Commissioners were the tribunal of first instance, and from the Commissioners an appeal could be made to the High Court on a point of law or on the basis that no reasonable tribunal could have reached the decision it came to. This is dealt with in greater detail in Chapter 19. From the High Court it is possible to appeal to the Court of Appeal and, ultimately, to the House of Lords, in certain circumstances.

Following the Tribunals, Courts and Enforcement Act 2007, as from 1 April 2009 a new tribunal system applies, whereby the General and Special Commissioners and High Court will no longer have a role to play in tax appeals. Instead a two-tier tribunal with a 'leap-frogging' to the Court of Appeal will replace the Commissioners. The two-tier tribunal system is discussed in Chapter 16 and following Chapters.

4.11 The House of Lords also hears certain appeals from Commonwealth countries in the Privy Council. An example of this is the *Australian Mutual v Chaplin* (1978) 18 ALR 3854 case of 1978 which is important in the context of substitution clauses and which is mentioned in HMRC's internal guidance manuals (see ESM 0531).

4.12 Prior to the merger of the Contributions Agency with HMRC, a Contributions Agency appeal would be by way of asking the Secretary of State to lay down a question for determination at a Secretary of State's Tribunal, usually presided over by an independent barrister. This appeal process ended in April 1999, when the two departments merged.

4.13 As far as employment law is concerned, the case is initially heard by the Employment Tribunal (formerly called the Industrial Tribunal). This is usually a three-person tribunal with a qualified Chairman and two lay members. On appeal,

4.13 *Why understanding case law is important*

the case is referred to the Employment Appeals Tribunal who may hear appeals on a point of law or on the basis that the Employment Tribunal could not have reasonably reached the conclusion it did on the facts. The Employment Tribunal normally consists of three members, including one professional judge and two laymen. On appeal from the Employment Appeals Tribunal the matter is referred to the Court of Appeal and thereafter to the House of Lords.

A good example of this is the *Carmichael v National Power* case of 1999 which started in the Employment Tribunal and finished in the House of Lords. This case is also a good example of why it is important to read the leading judgment of the senior court, as in this case the House of Lords, in a fairly readable ten-page judgment, overturned a 28-page judgment in the Court of Appeal.

Understanding law and fact

4.14 Both practitioners and tax officers may become confused between the facts of the case and the legal precedents they set. It must be understood that the facts will vary from one case to another in 99% of cases. There will be similarities, but also differences. It is a mistake to say that *Hall v Lorimer* [1994] 1 WLR 209 does not apply to a particular case because that case involved a vision mixer and the present case involves a computer programmer. Yet this mistake is often made.

4.15 The plain truth is that the overwhelming majority of cases can be distinguished on the facts—and this will always be the case. HMRC also recognise that the courts have consistently stressed that every case must be decided on its own particular facts (see ESM 7009). What is of concern are the legal precedents laid down by the courts and tribunals in the judgments which become the binding precedent for future cases. For example, the important 1999 Court of Appeal case of *Express and Echo* [1999] ICR 693 lays down, among other things, that where a substitute can be sent then, as a matter of law, the worker cannot be an employee. It is not relevant that the worker, in that case, was a newspaper delivery man.

4.16 It is important not to compare and contrast facts from one case with those of another as a means of establishing legal precedent. In *Walls v Sinnett* [1987} STC 236 an experienced judge stated that simply comparing facts offers no possibility of assistance. What may be compelling in one case may be less important in another, and this of course is quite correct. What need to be identified are the universal legal principles which can be applied to the facts as established.

4.17 The courts lay down principles through the process of *stare decisis* (ie abiding by legal precedents set by other, usually superior, courts). Although case law develops over the years and different glosses are placed on earlier decisions, it is this emerged trail of legal authority which forms the basis of understanding what the current state of law is.

4.18 A great deal has been written as to whether the process of determining status is one of fact, law or both. Esoteric arguments can be found throughout case law judgments, a prime example being *Carmichael v National Power* where many pages in the Court of Appeal's judgment were devoted to this question.

4.19 The main reason it is so important is that a superior court or tribunal can only interfere when there is an appeal on a point of law, or where the conclusion reached by the lower tribunal was so perverse that no reasonable tribunal properly conducting itself could possibly have come to that conclusion. Superior courts will not interfere in findings of fact if the finding was within the band of possible conclusions.

4.20 The distinction between law and fact can be seen in the following example. If the tax tribunal establishes as a fact that there is an unfettered right to send a substitute but then decides the worker is an employee, this would be appeallable as a point of law. However, if the tribunal concludes that a substitute could not be sent, that would be a finding of fact and not appeallable (unless totally perverse considering the evidence available).

4.21 So is status fact or law? The answer is probably a bit of both, or, as the courts describe it, a mixed question of fact and law. It is generally accepted that, where a relationship is entirely reflected in a written agreement, then it is a question of law as to what the relationship is. On the other hand, the whole matrix of facts often needs to be considered and this will be the case with IR35, as there is a case for bringing in the broader modus operandi of the contractor and the way he runs, and has run, his business.

4.22 One learned commentator suggests that fine distinctions between fact and law can be substituted with a more common-sense approach: was the decision right or wrong? Although one sympathises, the distinction remains important in terms of the prospects of an appeal succeeding in the higher courts, as higher courts do not see their role as one of re-hearing and re-evaluating simple fact.

Summary

4.23 Court decisions remain the single most important source of guidance in demonstrating that a worker is not a disguised employee of the client. Facts will vary from one case to another but binding precedents are principles that remain, and they must be fully understood and quoted when the need arises.

Chapter 5

The major case law decisions and status criteria

Introduction

5.1 There are hundreds of cases in the various tribunals and courts that have been concerned with 'status'. The 1968 High Court decision in *Ready Mixed Concrete v Ministry of Pensions and National Insurance* [1968] 2 QB 497 is seen by all commentators as the seminal authority for the modern law of status. In an often reaffirmed judgment Mr Justice McKenna said:

> 'I must now consider what is meant by a contract of service. A contract of service exists if the following three conditions are fulfilled: (i) the servant agrees that in consideration of a wage or other remuneration he will provide his own work and skill in the performance of some service for his master. (ii) He agrees, expressly or impliedly, that in the performance of that service he will be subject to the other's control in a sufficient degree to make that other master. (iii) The other provisions of the contract are consistent with its being a contract of service.'

Point (i) covers substitution and mutuality and point (ii) covers control.

It is tempting to concentrate only on the more recent and more senior case law decisions, as such decisions will necessarily carry more weight than old cases which may now be out of favour. It is essential, however, to be aware that the case law regarding tax status is an ever-developing and ever-changing body of law, which often revisits some of the earlier case law decisions. For example, in the Court of Appeal decision in *Montgomery v Johnson Underwood Ltd* [2001] EWCA Civ 318 in March 2001, several references were made to case law going back to the 1960s and, very clearly, the court was strongly influenced by some of those earlier decisions.

5.2 Employment law cases (eg concerning unfair dismissal or entitlement to holiday or sick pay) may also be relevant in determining status for IR35 purposes. There is a difference in emphasis between cases involving tax and national insurance law and those concerning employment law; the latter are generally brought where the individual is seeking to obtain employee rights, and this may colour the interpretation of them when considered in relation to tax cases. However, employment law cases are still relevant. Indeed, HMRC themselves, where appropriate, refer to employment law cases in the ESM as well as pure tax or national insurance cases. Many employment law cases are important because the tribunal usually has to consider the preliminary issue of the worker's status before the substantive employment law issue (eg unfair dismissal) can be determined.

5.3 It should also be noted that the existing case law largely concerns the distinction between employment and self-employment. In practice, the IR35 debate is usually expressed in similar terms. But, strictly, IR35 is about establishing that the worker is *not* in effect an employee of the client, rather than showing he is self-employed (ITEPA 2003, s 49(1)(*c*)). Indeed, the most common IR35 situation is where a worker is an employee of his own company, and is not, therefore, self-employed. However, the existing case law is essential in showing that the worker is not a disguised employee of the client, as there is no separate test for employment status under IR35.

5.4 Some of the cases mentioned are 'unreported'. This does not mean they are not binding legal precedent. What it does mean is that, for a variety of reasons, the case did not appear in the regular law reports. Firms of court transcribers nonetheless have the judgment typed and these are available and can certainly be used in argument. The professional accountancy bodies should be able to assist practitioners in obtaining transcripts.

5.5 It is therefore necessary to appreciate that although the law changes it is more often than not a question of new glosses or approaches being placed on existing case law, with perhaps more modern attitudes towards the employment scene being taken into account.

5.6 On the other hand, it would be a mistake, in the author's view, simply to take a chronological analysis of all case law in an attempt to see what the current legal approach to tax status might be. There is a mass of case law pulling in decisions from different areas such as employment law, tax and national insurance status, industrial accidents and others, and a study of all relevant decisions going back over the last 100 or so years would be overwhelming.

5.7 The better approach to be taken is to analyse the more important strands or criteria relating to tax status, such as substitution, control, mutuality of obligations, financial risk and intention. It can then be seen, for example, how these significant areas have developed over the years. A similar approach can then be taken with the other criteria, such as mutuality of obligations.

5.8 An analysis of the law using this method will not only lead to a better appreciation of what is important in the early twenty-first century when considering tax status, but will give a clear sense of historical development of the more important criteria.

A handful of IR35 appeals were heard before the General and Special Commissioners. These are not legally binding precedent but are of interest. They are considered in Chapter 11.

5.9 *The major case law decisions and status criteria*

Substitution

5.9 The reason substitution is so important is that when an individual person is directly employed, he is expected to give his personal service. A direct employee works under a contract of service. On the other hand, a self-employed person or a commercial business, be it a limited company or partnership, undertakes to supply services. It is thus said to operate by way of a contract *for* services as opposed to a contract *of* service.

5.10 Substitution is, therefore, crucially important. If a person does not have to give personal service, but can instead send a substitute or delegate in his place, then that person cannot be an employee, as the vital prerequisite of personal service is missing. This need for personal service is one of the prerequisites of a contract of employment and is discussed in the context of the *Ready Mixed Concrete* case of 1968 at **5.18** below.

External and internal rights of substitution and sub-contracting

5.11 There is, in the author's opinion, a distinction between internal substitution, external substitution and sub-contracting of a contract. In order to defeat IR35 specifically, or a tax status challenge generally, it is important to demonstrate that there is a genuine business-to-business relationship as opposed to a 'disguised employment' relationship.

5.12 Therefore it follows that, if a one-man limited company computer contractor wants to demonstrate that it is a genuine business, it should be able to show that it has the right to send a substitute on its own behalf to carry out the contract works. This defeats all challenges that personal service is required. It should be remembered that a limited company is a separate legal entity and if the company has the right to send a substitute in its place then that is what can be described as an 'external' right of substitution.

However, where the business has the right to reallocate or substitute its own internal personnel to carry out the contract works, that is to say it may substitute one of its existing employees for another, then this can be described as an 'internal' right of substitution.

5.13 It is considered that a genuine right to send an external substitute would carry slightly more weight than the right merely to send a different existing employee, that is an internal substitute.

5.14 This view is held for two reasons. The first is that important case law such as *Hall v Lorimer* [1994] 1 WLR 209 talks about substitution in the context of 'hiring in' a substitute. Similar phrases have been mentioned in other case law decisions and this type of language leads to the conclusion that the courts anticipate a substitute being called in from outside the business not merely reallocated from the existing internal resources of the business. Why else would the phrase 'hiring in' be used?

Secondly, the issue of substitution often raises arguments about the 'reality' of the right. The fact is that the overwhelming majority of personal service limited companies potentially affected by IR35 are one-man band businesses with one director/employee who is the sole fee earner. As such the reality is that an internal substitution clause is quite meaningless because there simply are no other employees who could be sent or reallocated by way of substitution. HMRC would quite rightly be suspicious of such a clause.

5.15 Sub-contracting a contract is different from substitution. Substitution is concerned with appointing a third party to stand in the place of the personal service business whereas sub-contracting, or authorised delegation, is concerned with arranging for the obligations to be carried out by a third party. These two approaches are not quite the same, but in all cases the responsibilities under the contract cannot be passed to a third party. As a matter of general contract law it is generally thought that it is not possible to assign contractual liabilities (for a detailed discussion, see Cheshire, Fifoot and Furmston *Law of Contract* (Butterworths, 15th edn, 2006). Novation is, therefore, the only method by which the contractual responsibilities can be transferred to another party. Under this method, all the parties (say, A, B and C) must make a new contract, which effectively replaces the previous one, in which A releases B from his obligation to provide the services, and C agrees to assume those responsibilities.

5.16 The right to sub-contract the contract works to a third party without the need to seek the client's permission and without other unreasonable constraints is an overwhelmingly strong indicator of self-employment. The court cases have tended to concentrate on the right of substitution, rather than sub-contracting, but the two concepts are closely related. There can be no question that the unqualified right to sub-contract the work would also be an overwhelming indication of a genuine business relationship as opposed to disguised employment. This is simply because in either case personal service is not required.

5.17 As stated above, the law has recognised the need for personal service as a prerequisite for direct employment status for many years. Although the concept is mentioned in many case law decisions the most important are, in chronological order:

- *Ready Mixed Concrete (South East) Limited v Minister of Pensions and National Insurance* (High Court) [1968] 2QB 497;
- *Global Plant Limited v Secretary of State for Health and Social Security* (High Court) [1972] 1QB 139;
- *Australian Mutual Provident Society v Chaplin* (Privy Council) (1978) 18 ALR 3854;
- *McMenamin v Diggles* (High Court) [1991] 1 WLR 1249;
- *Hall v Lorimer* (Court of Appeal) [1994] 1 WLR 209;
- *Express and Echo Publications Limited v Tanton* (Court of Appeal) [1999] ICR 693; and
- *Macfarlane and Skivington v Glasgow City Council* (Employment Appeals Tribunal) [2001] IRLR 7.

It is interesting to note that the majority of the above seven cases were not concerned with tax status, which is a good example of how relevant case law needs to

5.17 *The major case law decisions and status criteria*

be drawn from other areas of the law including employment law rights and national insurance matters.

5.18 In the 1968 *Ready Mixed Concrete* case it was stated by McKenna J ([1968] 1 All ER 433 at 440B) that:

> 'freedom to do a job either by one's own hands or another's is inconsistent with a contract of service, though a limited or occasional power of delegation may not be'.

It should be noted that this phrase has been reaffirmed many times in more recent case law, but the final few words relating to a limited or occasional power of delegation have not been approved—a fact often missed by HMRC.

5.19 The judge also commented that, in order for there to be a contract of service, that is a relationship of direct employment, the worker must provide 'his own work and skill'. The concept of personal service being a prerequisite to a relationship of direct employment was thus clearly spelt out. Many cases have subsequently reaffirmed this. In a decision which receives little publicity, in *WHPT Housing* case [1981] ICR 737, the High Court said 'the principal obligation undertaken by the employee is to provide *himself* to serve' (author's emphasis).

5.20 However, as can be seen from these words, the High Court in *Ready Mixed Concrete* took the view that where the right to send a substitute is 'limited' or where the substitute can only be sent in restricted occasional circumstances, then such a qualified right may not be inconsistent with a direct employment relationship. As stated above, this aspect of McKenna J's quotation has been played down, but it has nonetheless given HMRC the opportunity to resist the right of substitution where such right is fettered, and this has for many years been HMRC's counter argument to a claimed right of substitution.

5.21 The words of McKenna J deserve closer analysis. He did not say that a limited right to send a substitute would be an indicator of direct employment. He said a limited right *may* not be inconsistent with direct employment. This is a subtle difference and for many years HMRC's view that a limited right of substitution is ineffective has not been subject to the challenge it deserves. It was noted by Mr Justice Burton in the PCG judicial review challenge in 2001 that this restrictive interpretation of substitution by HMRC may be difficult to justify.

5.22 The practical difficulties over an unworkable internal right of substitution were stated above and a salutary lesson should be learnt from the 1971 case of *Global Plant*. In this case there was a qualified right to send a substitute, but the High Court had little hesitation in reaching the conclusion that the clause was a sham. Shams do not work, whether in the context of substitution or anything else, and it must be stressed that for a substitution clause to carry any weight it must be genuinely entered into and not simply part of a paper-signing exercise.

5.23 Before looking at the important 1991 case of *McMenamin v Diggles*, the *Australian Mutual v Chaplin* case from 1978 is worth mentioning. This was a case referred to the UK Privy Council from the Australian courts. Lord Fraser referred to substitution by using a different phrase:

> 'the power of unlimited delegation is almost conclusive against the contract being a contract of service'.

Interestingly the same court said that where: 'there is nothing in the written contract to prevent (the worker) from delegating the whole performance of the task' this would give an implied right of substitution. This important quotation is generally not known by many tax inspectors and it should be brought to their attention.

5.24 By the late 1970s there was, therefore, a trail of case law starting with *Ready Mixed Concrete* and running through to the *Australian Mutual v Chaplin* case, wherein the courts were increasingly accepting that the right to send a substitute or delegate was so inconsistent with a contract of employment that any worker with such a right would not be deemed to be a direct employee. The important qualification from the *Global Plant* case is that the substitution clause and the right of substitution must be genuine and not a sham and if it is to be relied upon it should not be qualified.

5.25 The 1991 case of *McMenemin v Diggles* developed the concept of substitution somewhat further. This was a High Court case concerned with the income tax status of the worker who operated as a barristers' clerk. He was formerly an employee of many years' standing who renegotiated his terms and conditions and claimed thereafter to be self-employed. His tax status was challenged by the Revenue. The main argument run by the Revenue was that the position of barristers' clerk was an 'office' and in accordance with the Taxes Act should automatically trigger PAYE deductions under Employment Income. The court, however, stated that the phrase 'barristers' clerk' was nothing more than a description.

According to his contract the taxpayer had the implied right to send a substitute to fulfil the clerking services he was to provide. This was because he was obliged to provide other less senior clerks and support staff and, by definition, this meant that he was not obliged personally to perform all the services himself. He had the further right to undertake the senior clerking services himself or to provide an alternative head clerk so long as the alternative head clerk had at least ten years' experience. It is understood that the taxpayer conceded that he could not readily supply an alternative head clerk with ten years' experience yet this clause was not held to be a sham. He had the clear contractual right to provide a substitute head clerk and the court accepted that the right was genuine.

5.26 In retrospect it might have been more fruitful for the Revenue to have argued that placing the ten years' experience 'qualification' on the alternative head clerk amounted to such a fettering that it was rendered ineffective under the dictum of McKenna J in the *Ready Mixed Concrete* case. It will be remembered he said that a 'limited' right of substitution may not carry with it the same importance as an unlimited right to send a substitute. Again, perhaps the Revenue could have referred back to the *Australian Mutual v Chaplin* case, where the court referred to the 'power of unlimited delegation'. It seems quite clear that the taxpayer did not have the 'power of unlimited delegation' as the alternative head clerk had to have at least ten

5.26 *The major case law decisions and status criteria*

years' experience. The Revenue seemed not to have picked up on this point, but instead concentrated their arguments on the taxpayer having an 'office'. The Revenue lost and did not take the case any further. There were many other factors in this case which were on the taxpayer's side and in some ways it is surprising that the Revenue wanted to take the case as far as the High Court where, having lost, a binding precedent, together with the attendant publicity, was brought to the attention of practitioners.

5.27 In 1993, the Court of Appeal reached an important decision in *Hall v Lorimer*. In that case, the Revenue challenged the tax status of Mr Lorimer but lost the argument at the Special Commissioners. The Revenue appealed, but again lost in the High Court. The Revenue appealed once more to the Court of Appeal and lost unanimously. In the context of substitution *Hall v Lorimer* is not, in the author's view a leading case. The case is more important in terms of the general approach to be taken in considering tax status and, in particular, the importance of having multiple clients and the unimportance of the provision of equipment and premises, especially where the taxpayer is merely supplying personal skills and services.

5.28 However, the case did mention the issue of substitution. The taxpayer undertook almost 600 separate engagements and in around six of these sent a substitute. The court took the view that in the context of six occasions out of 600 this would not necessarily have an impact on the remaining engagements where a substitute was not sent. In other words, simply because a substitute was sent for approximately 1% of the total engagements this did not necessarily imply that there was a right of substitution for all the other engagements. Compare this to the *Chaplin* case quotation at **5.23** above in respect of written contracts which are silent on the issue of substitution.

5.29 In the *Lorimer* case substitution was considered more in the context of the actual physical sending of a substitute, whereas the *McMenanin v Diggles* case and later case law tends to concentrate on the right to send a substitute as opposed to the actual sending of one. It should be noted and heavily underlined that the taxpayer in *Hall v Lorimer* did not have a written right of substitution and it is believed that it was for this reason that the court was unwilling to imply that a general right of substitution existed. The lesson here is simple: do not leave these things to chance. If the parties have genuinely agreed a right of substitution this should be clearly spelt out and committed to writing. *Hall v Lorimer*, being a relatively recent Court of Appeal authority, contains many useful hints on how to determine status. Unfortunately, it is also a case that can be seen to move away from the fundamental approach of *Ready Mixed Concrete* to a more vague multi-factional approach, whereby a picture is painted from the accumulation of detail. While this offers flexibility, it also produces uncertainty. Case law in the last five years has reverted to a more fundamental approach on substitution as well as other factors.

5.30 The very important case of *Express and Echo Publications Group v Tanton*, heard by the Court of Appeal in 1999 dealt with the issue of substitution in an extremely clear-cut and robust manner.

Practitioners are encouraged to read this fairly brief Court of Appeal judgment given by Lord Justice Peter Gibson. The case concerned a newspaper delivery driver who had previously been treated as a direct employee. He was subsequently re-engaged, doing essentially the same work but in a self-employed capacity. The worker was given a self-employed contract which he never signed. He then questioned his employment status.

5.31 In fact he sought advice from the Revenue, who were so convinced that he was an employee, that the law report stated the Revenue would 'countenance no other view whatever'. This was a very clear pronouncement by the Revenue which was unanimously rejected by the Court of Appeal.

5.32 Interestingly, however, the Revenue did not challenge the putative employer on the grounds that they were employing Mr Tanton, and instead Mr Tanton took Express and Echo Group through the employment tribunals and the case ended up in the Court of Appeal. Despite many indications of direct employment, the court held Mr Tanton was in fact *not* an employee.

5.33 Lord Justice Peter Gibson said that, in establishing employment status, the first question to be asked is whether or not there are any terms of the engagement which are inherently inconsistent with a contract of service. If there are, the question of status is concluded at that point and there is no need to consider the whole range of other factors usually taken into account in status decisions. This simple and fundamental approach is to be welcomed, and reaffirmed the *Ready Mixed Concrete* approach.

5.34 This is, in the view of the author, an important shift in the approach to determining status. In previous cases throughout the 1980s, culminating in *Hall v Lorimer* in 1993, the common approach was to gather all the relevant facts, with no one fact being conclusive on its own, with a view to painting a picture and coming to a balanced conclusion. However, *Express and Echo* reverts to a more fundamental approach. Put simply, any terms which are inherently inconsistent with a direct employment relationship will rule out any possibility that the contract as a whole is one of direct employment.

The author's interpretation of this return to a more fundamental approach is also recognised by Deakin and Morris, professors of law, in their respected text *Labour Law* (Butterworths, 4th edn, 2005).

On analysis this approach must be correct. If there are any terms which are so at odds with a direct employment relationship it stands to reason that direct employment cannot be appropriate. This approach continues the much more clear-cut line of reasoning from the *Ready Mixed Concrete* case, which took a fundamental view of status criteria.

5.35 In the *Express and Echo* case what was inherently inconsistent with a contract of service was that Mr Tanton had the right to send a 'suitable' substitute. In the words of Lord Justice Peter Gibson ([1999] IRLR 367 at 370):

> '... it is in my judgment, established on the authorities that where, as here, a person who works for another is not required to perform his services personally, then as a matter of law the relationship between the worker and the person for whom he works is not that of employee and employer'.

5.35 *The major case law decisions and status criteria*

This is a classic example of a succinct and helpful quotation with real legal authority. Note how clear this quotation is. It does not say that a right to send a suitable substitute is an important factor—it is a determinative factor.

5.36 Two further points emerge from the *Express and Echo* case. First, Mr Tanton did in fact send a substitute on a couple of occasions, although the court referred to the importance of the *right* not the actuality of sending a substitute. Secondly, and quite rightly, the judge said that if a clause is a sham it should be exposed as such and discredited.

5.37 What is interesting is that the right to send a substitute was fettered in the *Express and Echo* case to the extent that the substitute had to be 'suitable'. One might argue that any right to substitute, delegate, or sub-contract carries with it an implied term that the substitute is competent or 'suitable' to do the work. But by putting the word 'suitable' into the equation is this not a fettering of the 'unlimited power of delegation' referred to in the *Australian Mutual v Chaplin* case? Perhaps it is, but it is a fettering which the court clearly found to be *reasonable*. In other words, the restriction to being able to send only a suitable substitute did not weaken the right of substitution. It should be remembered that in the *Ready Mixed Concrete* case of 1968 the judge said that a limited power of delegation *may*, and only may, weaken the personal service argument.

5.38 The question as to how far a substitution clause has to be fettered before it loses its value is amply demonstrated in the *MacFarlane and Skivington* case of 2000. Here some gym instructors had a substitution right which Glasgow City Council claimed prevented them being employees on the authority of *Express and Echo*. However, once the substitution clause was analysed carefully it was clear that it was so fettered and qualified that in truth it did not amount to a right of substitution at all. The clause in question restricted the right to send a substitute to those occasions when the worker was 'unable' (not merely unwilling) to work; any substitute to be sent had to come from a pre-approved list maintained by the Council; when a substitute was required the Council themselves would organise this; and the Council (not the original worker) would pay the substitute. On examination this was not a sufficiently open-ended substitution clause and the Council could not rely on it to defeat the workers' claim that they were direct employees.

In a witty observation the tribunal pointed out that the best that could be said about the substitution clause in this case was that if the worker did send a substitute she probably would not have been in breach of contract but that was as good as it got!

An unfettered right of substitution will defeat IR35, as will a right of substitution which is fettered only to the extent that the substitute must be reasonably suitable. So much is clear.

Substitution clauses which merely allow the personal service business to 'offer' a substitute are not reliable. No doubt it is open for any worker to approach his client and suggest or 'offer' a substitute, but such a stance would be totally speculative. The client, clearly, could refuse the offer. So the right to 'offer' a substitute is of little value. What is needed is a right to send one.

It is not uncommon to see substitution clauses where the original worker must work alongside the substitute during the handover period. One would naturally

The major case law decisions and status criteria **5.42**

expect the original worker to liaise with his substitute as a matter of practicality, but to impose a handover period might appear to be too restrictive a fettering. However, the 2002 Special Commissioners judgment in *Lime-IT Ltd v Justin* [2003] STC (SCD) 15 dealt with this specific issue. Dr Avery Jones placed great emphasis on the substitution clause, which contained a handover period, and the clause was one of the major factors that helped defeat IR35 in that case.

5.39 A further case law gloss on substitution came in the March 2001 judicial review challenge to IR35 initiated by the Professional Contractors Group (in *R (on the application of Professional Contractors Group Ltd) v IRC* [2001] EWCA Civ 1945). Mr Justice Burton, delivering the High Court judgment, criticised the Revenue's largely strict and narrow interpretation of substitution. The Revenue's view that a restricted right, or the need first to obtain the client's permission would necessarily prove fatal to a substitution clause was not accepted by the judge. He felt too narrow an approach was unwise.

However, it should be remembered that his remarks, while very interesting were arguably obiter dicta. This means they were remarks said in passing only and as they were not directly connected to the European Law he was considering such remarks do not amount to binding legal precedent. It is likely that HMRC will see it this way and early IR35 appeals have shown this—see Chapter 11.

HMRC's view of substitution

5.40 The reader should perhaps concentrate on the law rather than being overly concerned with HMRC's views, but when dealing with an IR35 challenge substitution is one of the most significant aspects and, whether HMRC's approach is right or wrong, their view of this issue will have to be dealt with. Furthermore, knowing in advance how HMRC view substitution will give the practitioner forewarning of what he is dealing with.

5.41 In late 2000, HMRC significantly modified their view of substitution by taking a less narrow view of the issue, and made some major changes to their Manual. However the revised 2008 version of HMRC's Employment Status Manual contains some very notable changes in the way HMRC are now approaching the issue of substitution. It is apparent that HMRC are now reverting back to a stricter approach. For example, HMRC are alert to contracts containing clauses that appear to give a right of substitution, but which are not genuine (see ESM 3355 'Considering the evidence: ineffective or sham substitution clauses').

5.42 HMRC have acknowledged the important case of *Express and Echo Publications Group v Tanton*, heard in the Court of Appeal in 1999. They have publicly stated that, according to the *Express* case, where a substitute can be sent this would 'probably' indicate that the worker was not an employee. The specific words of Lord Justice Peter Gibson should be remembered, as he said something quite different. In his judgment the right to send a substitute would 'as a matter of law' preclude the worker from being an employee. Practitioners will note the difference between 'probably' and 'as a matter of law' and may conclude that HMRC were

5.42 *The major case law decisions and status criteria*

loath to embrace the full impact of the *Express* decision on the important subject of substitution.

5.43 Being generous to HMRC they perhaps made their comments in the context that not all substitution clauses necessarily preclude direct employment, as the substitution clause may be significantly fettered or qualified. If this is what they meant to say, however, then they should have said it unequivocally. HMRC's view that a right of substitution would 'probably' preclude direct employment is clearly not a fair precis of what the judge said.

5.44 This important observation once again underlines the importance of reading what the judges say rather than taking at face value an interpretation devised by a third party with its own interests to protect.

5.45 HMRC have gone into much greater detail in addressing substitution in their internal manuals. HMRC accept (at ESM 0530) that: 'an essential element of an employment is that the worker provides personal service'.
Unfortunately, it then goes on to say that if the worker is free to utilise a third party to do the work or to help him then it is 'unlikely' that the worker is an employee. The words of the judgment in the *Express* case must be borne in mind because HMRC have played down the significance of personal service and substitution in this extract.

5.46 In the more detailed guidance in ESM 0530 onwards, HMRC make reference to the *Ready Mixed Concrete* case, *Australian Mutual v Chaplin* and the *Express and Echo* case and at last this important topic is given the technical analysis it deserves. HMRC now accept (at ESM 0531) that it is 'most unlikely' that any worker who has the right to send a substitute will be an employee.

5.47 Despite the above statement in ESM 0531, the author has noticed HMRC are taking a now somewhat regressive approach to substitution. HMRC previously stated in ESM 1052 (now obsolete) that:

> 'where a worker does not have to perform the work personally and can hire a substitute to carry out the work, that is inconsistent with employment and the worker will be self-employed regardless of other factors such as control etc'.

The phrase of note being 'will be self-employed regardless of other factors'. However, HMRC's revised 2008 Manual at ESM 0533 now states:

> 'Where a substitution provision is not as strong as that in the Tanton case, it will probably lead to the conclusion that there is a requirement for personal service.'

It goes on to say:

> 'a right to send a substitute is only an indicator of self-employment and not determinative by itself. However, where a worker has a wholly unqualified right to provide a substitute, the courts may well consider that to be a strong indicator of self-employment or determinative by itself.'

5.48 This new approach is a far cry from HMRC's previous position. In the author's opinion, HMRC have faltered in their approach by suggesting that if a substitution provision is not akin to that in the *Tanton* case, it will probably lead to the conclusion that there is a requirement for personal service. Lord Justice Peter Gibson's judgment did not reflect this opinion and HMRC should be reminded that little is gained from comparing the facts of one case to another.

5.49 HMRC point out that in its view the right to provide a substitute must be genuine, the engager (by which it means the client of the personal service business) must not have an unreasonable right of veto over the substitute and that the worker must himself engage and pay the substitute. The author considers this approach to be both reasonable and in line with the *MacFarlane and Skivington* case heard in 2000.

5.50 HMRC devote some detailed analysis in asking whether the right of substitution is genuine and whether the right to reject a substitute effectively renders the right worthless. It is quite correct to do so. Helpfully, HMRC guidance (at ESM 0530) advises that:

> 'The fact that an engager can limit the choice of substitute to a suitable person does not necessarily mean that there is no real right.'

This is an extremely clear and unequivocal statement by HMRC, and in the author's experience many inspectors and compliance officers are unaware of it. It should be quoted to HMRC without hesitation.

5.51 In other words, HMRC accept that where there is a right to send a substitute but that substitute can be rejected if he is not suitable, the right to send a substitute in these circumstances will still be treated as effectively unfettered.

HMRC previously stated in their old guidance that, where the client can reject the substitute in one of three circumstances, the right of substitution will *not* be treated as being fettered and will still safeguard self-employment. The three special circumstances given were:

1 Rejection of the substitute because of his inability to do the work effectively or within a reasonable timescale.
2 Rejection of the substitute if he is a known troublemaker.
3 Rejection of the substitute because other workers refuse to work with the person in question.

5.52 Readers should be aware that these concessions have now been removed from HMRC's ESM; however there is no harm in quoting these circumstances to HMRC as part of a persuasive argument. Nonetheless, there is a major risk in relying too heavily on these circumstances since case law itself does not recognise troublemakers or bad team players as acceptable fetters. Further the fact that these concessions have been removed from HMRC's ESM means there is a real danger that HMRC will adopt a stricter approach and personal service businesses that have deliberately used an HMRC previously 'approved' watered down substitution clause may well find themselves in trouble. It may be embarrassing for HMRC to

5.52 *The major case law decisions and status criteria*

backtrack but it is quite capable of doing this. The internal instructions are, after all, only HMRC's guidance. They are not law.

As such, it is strongly recommended that an unfettered right is agreed, or one which is restricted only to the extent that the substitute has to be suitably qualified or experienced.

5.53 Although HMRC are alert to the possibility of sham substitution clauses being put into contracts, they also accept that unless there is good reason to doubt the bona fides of the substitution clause it should be accepted at face value.

5.54 ESM 0537 acknowledges that:

> 'disproving a claim to rights of substitution can be difficult. Unless there is reason to doubt a claimed right of substitution it may normally be accepted at face value'.

That said, HMRC's ESM 0530 now instructs tax officers to make a number of checks and obtain evidence to support whether or not a right of substitution is genuine. These include checking if the right is included in a written contract, obtaining evidence to support any verbal agreements and where it is alleged that a right is an implied term of the contract, evidence to support this view. Further ESM 0530 instructs tax officers to check whether or not a substitute has actually been sent. In the author's experience this had led to a number of tax officers refusing to accept a right of substitution where a substitute has not been sent, despite ESM 0530 stating:

> 'Remember that the fact that a right is not exercised does not mean that it does not exist.'

5.55 ESM 0537 makes it clear that unless there is reason to doubt the claimed right of substitution it 'may normally be accepted at face value'. In practice, HMRC will not accept a substitution right at face value without speaking to the client. HMRC should be challenged when they fail to follow ESM 0537 without good reason. A further practical difficulty is that the person at the end user who is approached for confirmation of the substitution right might be (and indeed is likely to be) completely unaware of what the actual contractual position is between the end user and agency on the one hand and the agency and personal service business on the other. If the end user via the human resources department or department manager merely offers their personal opinion, perhaps in a brief telephone conversation, what use is that in terms of reliable legal evidence? It is submitted very little.

5.56 Unfortunately, despite the clear guidance at ESM 0537 and 0530, too many tax officers are far too reluctant to acknowledge that genuine substitution rights exist, and attempt to put the contractor to some trouble by making him prove the right. This is in spite of the clear guidance at ESM 0538 which places the onus on HMRC to show the substitution right is a sham, and not on the contractor to show it is not.

5.57 ESM 0538 advises the tax officer that if he wishes to ignore a claimed right of substitution he must find the evidence to show that the claimed right does not exist. In such cases the tax officer is advised that he should 'always speak to the engager and the worker', yet HMRC have no legal authority to require either party to attend a personal interview—a point not understood by many practitioners.

5.58 It is a pity that the manuals go on to give the tax officer proactive advice to justify ignoring a claimed right of substitution while at the same time advising that a right of substitution should normally be accepted at face value. It all seems to be rather inconsistent and HMRC should be challenged.

In the author's view this is a straightforward matter of tactics on HMRC's part. It knows in law that the right to send a substitute (so long as it is not unreasonably fettered) will preclude direct employment as per the *Express and Echo* judgment. HMRC must, therefore, go out of their way (contrary to the official guidance, whereby a right of substitution should normally be accepted at face value) to try to disprove the right, because, should an IR35 or tax status appeal turn on the issue of substitution, HMRC know that the law is against them.

5.59 Sometimes HMRC will argue that a worker is necessarily employed because he has no *obligation* to send a substitute. But this is to twist the case law into something at odds with the leading cases. A reasonable substitution clause is a silver bullet, but the lack of one is not a fatal flaw.

More recently HMRC's approach to the substitution issue has once again hardened. Following *Synaptek Ltd v Young (Inspector of Taxes)* [2003] EWHC 645 (Ch) High Court appeal (see Chapter 11), HMRC now argue that a fettered substitution clause must be put into practice before it can be seen as effective. This is not quite what *Synaptek* said and it is submitted that *Express Echo* remains a more accurate statement of the law and as a Court of Appeal authority takes precedence.

Hiring helpers

5.60 It almost goes without saying that the right to hire helpers is an overwhelming indicator of self-employment, as the need for personal service would no longer be present. The 1991 case of *McMenamin v Diggles* is a good example of this.

5.61 Furthermore, if a worker (or in the strict context of IR35 the personal service business) has the right to hire and/or actually hires other workers as employees or self-employed consultants then this would also indicate a business modus operandi, with the attendant risks and costs. Any genuine and not unreasonably fettered right to send a substitute or hire help, by definition breaks the personal service obligation and defeats IR35.

Contracts which are silent on substitution

5.62 Where there is no written right to send a substitute, the personal service business is faced with the difficult task of proving, on the balance of probabilities, that the right to send a substitute exists, despite the useful extract from *Chaplin*'s case noted at **5.23** above.

5.62 *The major case law decisions and status criteria*

Without question it is possible to have an oral right to send a substitute, but a clear written term provides much better evidence and is open to less cross-examination. For the purposes of clarity all important terms should be recorded in a signed, dated contract.

5.63 It should be remembered that where there is no right to send a substitute at all, or where the right is significantly fettered, this does not mean of itself that the worker is a disguised employee. A properly worded genuine right to send a substitute precludes direct employee status, but a lack of such a right does not in itself mean that the worker is a disguised employee of the client. Where there is no right other factors have to be considered and in particular mutuality of obligations, control and financial risk.

The simple fact that a substitute cannot be sent does not mean IR35 bites, it merely means that IR35 has not been automatically defeated ab initio.

Summary

5.64 The case law shows, and HMRC (perhaps reluctantly) accept, that where there is a genuine right to send a substitute, so long as the right is not unreasonably fettered, then as a matter of law the worker will not be an employee of the engager. As such, the right of substitution is a very effective factor in demonstrating that the worker is not a disguised employee of the client. However, attempts by HMRC to seek third-party confirmation when there is no good reason to doubt the substitution right should be pointed out as being contrary to ESM 05375. Don't hold your breath.

Mutuality of obligations

5.65 To many practitioners and tax officers alike, no other aspect of employment status causes as much difficulty and confusion as mutuality of obligations. This is further evidenced by the many academic articles written on this subject.

The author has researched mutuality of obligations extensively, including interviewing leading academics. Where relevant the results of this research will be brought out in the following paragraphs.

Why is mutuality of obligations so important?

5.66 Mutuality is such an important fundamental that without it there cannot be a contract of employment. Current case law looks to see if the 'irreducible minimum' to create a contract of employment is present. If it is not there the contract cannot be a relationship of direct employment. The irreducible minimum includes mutuality of obligation. The case law discussion below looks at this in more depth.

5.67 Like the issue of substitution, mutuality of obligations has developed through various court cases over the years. At times mutuality of obligations has been very much the single most important factor in determining status, not least during the early and mid-1980s. Yet at other times, particularly in the mid-1990s, the concept was given less importance.

5.68 Current legal precedents, and in particular *Carmichael v National Power Plc* [1999] 1 WLR 2042 House of Lords case in 1999 and *Montgomery v Johnson Underwood Ltd* [2001] EWCA Civ 318 Court of Appeal case in 2001, again indicate that mutuality of obligations is an extremely important factor in status disputes generally and potentially IR35 in particular.

Understanding what mutuality of obligations means

5.69 There seems to be ongoing confusion when similar sounding terminology is used. This can usefully be cleared up:

Mutuality of obligations—this relates to the ongoing relationship between the parties and involves a high level of commitment to each other. This is fully explained below at **5.70** et seq below.

Mutual intention—this is what relationship the parties to a contract wish and intend to create and this could be either a relationship of direct employment or self-employment. It is quite different from mutuality of obligations. The parties' intention is important, see **5.155** et seq below.

The essentials to create any contract—this is the three attributes that all arrangements need before they can harden into a formal contract and are discussed below.

The irreducible minimum to create a contract of service—this is the whole basis of creating a contract of employment as originally developed by McKenna J in the 1968 *Ready Mixed Concrete* case and centres on the trinity of personal service, control and, more recently, mutuality of obligations. This is discussed at **5.90** below, having been reaffirmed in the *Montgomery v Johnson Underwood* case of 2001. Thus it can be seen that these terms are both important and different.

For a binding contract to exist both parties must have the intention of entering into legal relations with each other, there must be an offer and an acceptance and valuable consideration must pass between the parties. However, the mere offer and acceptance of a specific piece of work does not amount to mutuality of obligations in the context of employment status.

This important point has been underlined in the obiter comments made by Burton J in the PCG judicial review hearing at the High Court (see **5.100** below) and also in the 2001 *Hewlett Packard* Employment Appeal Tribunal decision.

Mr Justice Burton said that the obligation of the client 'to pay the money' is not enough to establish mutuality of obligations, and this was confirmed in *O'Murphy v Hewlett Packard* [2002] IRLR 4.

More recently, in *Propertycare Ltd v Gower* (EAT 547/03, [2004] All ER (D) 16 (Jan)), His Honour Judge Peter Clark said:

'the cases, starting with *Ready Mixed Concrete* show that mutuality of obligations means more than a simple obligation on the employer to pay for work done; there must generally be an obligation on the employer to provide work and the employee to do the work. That is how we understand the first of McKenna J's tests in *Ready Mixed Concrete*.'

5.70 *The major case law decisions and status criteria*

5.70 In the sense of establishing employment status, mutuality of obligations is concerned with a deeper degree of commitment, trust and confidence between the parties, such that they have a higher plane of obligations beyond the mere offer and acceptance of work.

5.71 Mutuality is not a concept liked by HMRC and wherever possible it plays down the importance of this factor. Tax officers may point out that employment status is not necessarily the same thing as tax status, although practitioners will note that HMRC will quote employment law cases when it suits them. When arguing IR35 cases practitioners will constantly come across inspectors who insist that mutuality of obligations is necessarily established by the simple giving and doing of work. While HMRC head office specialists concede the position is more complex than this, the message seems not to have filtered down to district level.

5.72 As pointed out in *Labour Law* (Deakin and Morris, Butterworths, 4th Edition, 2005), mutuality of obligations in the context of employment contracts has a specific meaning 'which refers to the presence of mutual commitments to maintain the *employment relationship* in being over a period of time' (author's emphasis). Some commentators believe that this ongoing commitment must extend to a situation where there is no work available and the 1999 *Carmichael* case suggested this. If work runs out but the worker nonetheless receives a retainer payment then it could be argued that the higher plane of obligations has been at least partially met and mutuality of obligations established. This would perhaps also be the case where the worker is obliged to give up work elsewhere and be 'on call' and give his time to a particular paymaster when required to do so, or where the 'employer' is under an ongoing duty to find work for the worker.

As Deakin and Morris point out, every type of contract contains binding promises but a contract of employment requires the 'second tier of obligation consisting of mutual promises of future performance'. They neatly précis the whole concept of mutuality of obligations by saying that 'at the first level there is an exchange of work for remuneration. At the second level there is an exchange of mutual promises of future performance. The second level—the promise to employ and to be employed—provides the arrangement with its stability and with its continuity as a contract'.

This two-tier approach to mutuality develops an earlier theory of Professor Mark Freedland of Oxford in his 1976 *The Contract of Employment*. This book has recently gone into its second edition and is re-titled *The Personal Employment Contract* (Oxford Monographs on Labour Law).

The author has exchanged e-mails with Dr Deakin of Cambridge who concedes that the 'two-tier' test is one of 'impression' rather than strict case law. The author has also interviewed Dr Brodie of Edinburgh University who reviewed Freedland's book in the *Industrial Law Journal* (March 2004). Dr Brodie believes that mutuality is either in the nature of simple payment in return for work, or it requires a higher plane of obligations! As he recognises, case law has described mutuality in many different ways and there is no absolutely clear definition. Arguably Freedland's 'two-tier' approach of mutuality was ahead of its time, as the *O'Kelly v Trusthouse Forte Plc* ([1984] QB 90) case some seven years later referred to mutuality in the context of an obligation to maintain the employment relationship in the future—see **5.79** below.

5.73 The case of *Wickens v Champion Employment* described the employment relationship as requiring care and continuity ([1984] ICR 365 at 371E). The *Express and Echo* decision in 1999 referred to 'trust and confidence' ([1999] IRLR 367 at 370), both being inherently required in a contract of service as established by the House of Lords in *Malik v BCCI* [1980] AC 20, and this idea of a higher plane of obligations can be readily recognised. Indeed, in the old case of *Robb v Green* [1895] 2 QB 315 the court recognised that a master/servant, relationship required the worker to 'serve with faith and fidelity'. Quaint language perhaps, but the point is made.

For mutuality of obligations to be present the bilateral element of the obligations should not be overlooked. If a work provider is obliged to offer work but the work doer is not obliged to do it, or if the work provider is not obliged to offer work but the work doer is obliged to accept it when offered, then there will be no mutuality of obligations, just unilateral obligations, and this is fundamentally not the same thing.

5.74 If either the work provider is not obliged to offer work or the work doer is not obliged to undertake work offered there is no mutuality of obligations even though there may be unilateral obligations.

This does *not* mean to say that the worker is necessarily self-employed and certain workers fall into a no man's land where the courts have held that they have a contract *sui generis* (of its own kind). In other words it is neither a contract of employment nor a contract for services (self-employment).

5.75 Some tax officers consider that mutuality of obligations is the same thing as a mutual intention to create self-employment. It is not and this is a basic error. HMRC have long held the view that the intention of the parties as to what type of relationship they have created is not a factor to be taken into account unless the overall position is ambiguous and finely balanced. However, the intention of the parties as to whether they have created employment or self-employment is not the same thing as mutuality of obligations. The parties' intention is important—see below.

5.76 It must be remembered that defeating IR35 is not about proving self-employment. It is simply a question of showing that the worker is not an employee. There are four further areas of mutuality of obligations worth commenting on.

The first is often overlooked but could prove useful. If the personal service business is entitled to no notice (or very little notice) of termination of its contract then it can be argued that the higher plane of care and continuity inherent in mutuality of obligations is by definition missing and many contracts do have zero termination periods. On the other hand if a long period of notice has to be given to the personal service business then it could be argued that this indicates some element of 'care and continuity'. Often the personal service business itself has to give quite a long period of notice, but this is normally for the protection of the agency's interests. Chapter 11 notes the comments of Mr Justice Hart in this respect in *Synaptek Ltd v Young (HMIT)*. In essence the point was made that if there is no mutuality in the sense that this means an obligation to offer work, then why would a period of notice be needed? Turning this around, does the existence of a period of notice imply mutuality. In pure legal theory the answer is probably 'yes', but notice periods are

5.76 *The major case law decisions and status criteria*

often inserted for practical and commercial reasons and not as oblique evidence of a lack of mutuality.

Secondly, some commentators have suggested that mutuality of obligations can exist *during* an individual contract and as such the presence of mutuality of obligations will be established within the relationship. As such, they argue, the IR35 defence of 'lack of mutuality' is not available. It is submitted that this is incorrect and such an approach fails to appreciate the true meaning of mutuality, that is to say the *ongoing commitments to maintain* the employment relationship. A huge difficulty is that if mutuality amounts to an obligation to offer/do work at what point in time is the 'obligation' to be identified? Before a contract is offered there is no obligation to offer it. This suggests no mutuality. Once the contract is offered and accepted then clearly there is an obligation to complete the contract. Is mutuality established at this point? What if once the contract is offered and accepted either party can unilaterally withdraw within the contract? These questions can only be answered once a definition of mutuality can be devised.

There are four possible definitions of mutuality.

1 Mutuality as mere consideration, ie payment in respect of work.
2 An obligation to offer/accept work throughout a contract.
3 An obligation to offer/accept future work.
4 The higher plane test of trust and confidence.

Case law suggests that 1 and 3 are at the extremes and 4 is less reliable. Perhaps 2 is the correct middle ground. Indeed in the *Cornwall County Council v Prater* [2006] EWCA Civ 102 decision (see **11.183**) it was specifically accepted that while there may be no ongoing obligations to offer further work after a given contract has ended there may still be mutuality of obligations within a particular stint of work. The author thinks that must be correct if (and it is a big 'if') the wording of the contract justifies such a conclusion. If a contract states 'if you accept this piece of work you must complete it and cannot terminate the contract and we, the work provider, must honour the contract and cannot terminate it' then clearly mutuality of obligations apply during that limited period.

If all mutuality of obligations means is the bundle of contractual rights and promises (as opposed to the higher plane of commitments identified earlier) then the whole concept of mutuality becomes meaningless as every contract, be it of service, for services or just getting on a bus, will have 'mutuality' and the doctrine of mutuality of obligations and its special meaning in status would be rendered nugatory. As will be seen below the Court of Appeal and House of Lords have identified mutuality in the context of status as being an area of prime importance and to suggest that there is mutuality of obligations during the subsistence of every contract where work is undertaken is plainly wrong. The mistake made is one of confusing mutuality of obligations (in the proper sense) with mere contractual rights and obligations which all contracts have.

The third area concerns the impact on mutuality of obligations of the length of the contract, where the contract is for a *fixed* period. Is it correct to assume that a contract fixed for a period of say one week has any less mutuality than a contract fixed for say three years? One's gut instinct might say 'yes' but it is submitted that this again misunderstands what mutuality, in the context of employment status, is all about. As stated above, it is not concerned with the contractual rights and promises that subsist during a specific contract, because all contracts of every kind contain rights and promises, or obligations. Mutuality of obligations in its proper employment status context means a high degree of commitment to maintain an ongoing relationship of employment. However, there is a real argument to say that only once a contract of employment is established does mutuality become an issue. In other words, mutuality in the context of the higher plane of trust and commitment is the result of a contract of service, not a determinant of such a contract.

So back to the two fixed-term contracts: one for a week, one for three years. If these contracts were entered into as fixed-term contracts it is suggested that the length of the engagement *itself* does not impact on mutuality of obligations.

It might be that the three-year contract carries with it other terms which may more readily imply mutuality, for example a long period of notice, the right to enjoy other aspects of 'care and continuity' afforded to regular employees, but these issues are separate from the length of the contract per se. Indeed, HMRC now accept that the length of an individual contract is a neutral factor.

It is also suggested that if the one-week contract was automatically renewed or extended week in, week out for a period of three years then this would be more likely to create or imply mutuality than a one-off fixed three-year contract. This concept of mutuality of obligations being capable of slowly crystallising over a period of time is discussed at **5.78** et seq below.

Whenever possible, new negotiated distinct and project-leased contracts should be entered into rather than extensions or rolling renewals of existing contracts. This will make it harder for HMRC to establish mutuality.

Fourthly, if mutuality of obligations, as properly defined, is a prerequisite for a contract of employment, does this mean that a supermarket checkout operator doing a temporary job over Christmas will not be an employee? And if not why not? Again one's gut instinct might be to say it is obvious the checkout operator is an employee. Such a worker surely has all the hallmarks of a regular employee. There is control, no financial risk, no rights of substitution, the intention to be an employee, provision of a uniform, etc, but is there mutuality of obligation? Arguably not, if mutuality, correctly defined, falls within 3 or 4 as described above. This is a one-off temporary assignment for a few weeks' work with absolutely no ongoing mutual commitments. And before the idea of a non-employed checkout operator is dismissed the true nature of mutuality of obligations should be considered carefully and the landmark *O'Kelly* case, discussed at **5.79** below, explored, where the court came to what is to many an unusual decision.

5.77 The leading cases on mutuality are, in chronological order:

- *Airfix Footwear Ltd v Cope* (1978) decided by the Employment Appeals Tribunal [1978] ICR 1210;
- *O'Kelly v Trust House Forte* (1983) Court of Appeal [1984] QB 90;
- *Nethermere (St Neots) Ltd v Gardiner* (1984) Court of Appeal [1984] ICR 612;
- *McLeod v Hellyer Bros* (1987) Court of Appeal [1987] 1 WLR 728;
- *Clark v Oxfordshire Health Authority* (1997) Court of Appeal [1998] IRLR 125;
- *McMeechan v Secretary of State for Employment* (1997) Court of Appeal [1997] ICR 549;
- *Carmichael v National Power* (1999) House of Lords [1999] 1 WLR 2042;

5.77 *The major case law decisions and status criteria*

- *Montgomery v Johnson Underwood Ltd* (2001) Court of Appeal [2001] EWCA Civ 318;
- *R (on the application of Professional Contractors Group and others v IRC* (2001) High Court [2001] EWCA Civ 1945;
- *O'Murphy v Hewlett Packard* (2001) decided by the Employment Appeals Tribunal [2002] IRLR 4;
- *Property Care Ltd v Gower* (2003) decided by the Employment Appeals Tribunal[2004] All ER (D) 16 (Jan);
- *Stuncroft v Havelock* (2001) decided by the Employment Appeals Tribunal [2002] All ER (D) 292 (Jan);
- *Stevedoring and Haulage Services Ltd v Fuller* (2001) [2001] EWCA Civ 651;
- *Synaptek Ltd v Young* (HMIT) (2003) [2003] EWHC 645.

There are other mutuality cases. For example, in the Employment Appeal Tribunal case *Action Contracts (East Midlands) Ltd v Ablitt and another* [2008] All ER (D) 456 (Jul), the appellant successfully appealed on the basis that the Employment Tribunal's finding as to mutuality of obligations between the parties to the case had been arrived at in error. However, the above are the leading authorities and will now be examined.

The case law

5.78 In the 1978 case of *Airfix Footwear v Cope*, it was established that despite there being no formal legal obligation to offer and accept work, such obligations may crystallise over the passage of a long period of time.

In this case the worker carried out work, usually for five days per week for over seven years. Despite this long period of almost constant work the decision was not clear-cut and the tribunal was split. Indeed, there were many factors pointing to self-employment.

It is arguable that mutuality of obligations was misapplied in this case in that its presence was held to indicate direct employment status whereas it is submitted that the correct approach is that a lack of mutuality of obligations precludes direct employment. This is certainly the line later cases took. The *Airfix* case did not go beyond the employment tribunals unlike many of the mutuality cases of later years, which went to the Court of Appeal or indeed the House of Lords.

The work undertaken was essentially unskilled, and part of the reasoning for the decision was that the worker had no technical skill to exploit in the marketplace. This can be readily contrasted with the typical personal service business worker, who may well be an expert or specialist.

Needless to say, HMRC are quite keen to quote the *Airfix* case but it should be seen in the context of an unskilled worker. The *O'Kelly* case, heard in the Court of Appeal five years later took a different and much more extreme view.

5.79 *O'Kelly* was something of a landmark decision and is still considered to be a leading precedent on mutuality despite being over 25 years old. That case concerned unskilled and semi-skilled workers who attended large hotel functions and acted as wine waiters etc on a 'regular casual' basis. Despite their many hallmarks of direct employment status the workers were held to be self-employed. This was because there was no *legal* obligation on the hotel to offer them work nor on them to accept it. The fact that work was regularly accepted, sometimes in excess of 50 hours per week did not alter the position. There was no *obligation*.

The court described the regular offering and accepting of work as nothing more than 'market forces', which should not be confused with legal obligations.

The original employment tribunal found, and the Court of Appeal agreed, that 'it was a purely commercial transaction for the supply and purchase of services for specific events because there was no obligation for the company to provide work and no obligation for the applicants to offer their "*further*" services' (author's italics—[1983] ICR 728 at 744).

5.80 The *O'Kelly* case is also notable in that it established that the mere supply of semi-skilled labour, with few if any of the trappings of being in business, was nonetheless a perfectly legitimate form of self-employment. The court noted that, although there was no great financial risk on the workers, this did not preclude them from being independent contractors.

It also rejected the idea that there was an umbrella or global contract which subsisted throughout the arrangements.

5.81 The case has been criticised by those who seek to establish employment law rights for unskilled or semi-skilled workers, but the precedent is very clear and HMRC do not like it. The author has interviewed several academics who hold the view that *O'Kelly* was mutuality's 'low point', in that it made a lack of mutuality easy to establish and hence employment rights difficult to establish. Many also feel the waiters were badly advised and that an astute lawyer should have given them some sound advice 'over the soup'.

5.82 The case of *Nethermere (St Neots) Ltd v Gardiner* should also be considered. In that case, the tribunal found, albeit by only a majority decision, that an apparent lack of mutuality can crystallise into true mutuality, as in the *Airfix* case. The tribunal identified such obligations as coming into force perhaps after one year of the giving and taking of work. However, in the Court of Appeal Lord Justice Kerr ([1984] ICR 612 at 630E) could *not* accept that:

> 'even a lengthy course of dealing can somehow convert itself into a contractually binding obligation.'

The decision in *Nethermere* was a narrow one and the appeal tribunal felt unable to interfere in the findings of the lower tribunal. The period of one year of work giving rise to employment was rejected in the *Montgomery v Johnson Underwood* case (see **5.88–5.92** below) where the worker was in situ for two and a half years and was held not to be an employee. It was *Nethermere* that first developed the concept of the 'irreducible minimum' needed to create a contract of service. The phrase was developed from the earlier dicta of McKenna J in *Ready Mixed Concrete*. The irreducible minimum contains mutuality and the worker 'must be obliged to provide his own work and skill'. If the emphasis is placed on the word 'must' it can be seen that mutuality amounts to an absolute obligation to do the work. On the other hand, if the emphasis is placed on the words 'his own' then it seems that the issue of personal service and substitution is being addressed, not mutuality as such.

5.82 *The major case law decisions and status criteria*

The author's view is that mutuality, personal service and control are effectively all part of the irreducible minimum needed to create a master/servant relationship, or a contract of employment. In some ways mutuality encapsulates personal service just as it might be argued that control encapsulates personal service. If a worker is obliged to work is this another possible aspect of control?

In any event the 'irreducible minimum' was born in *Nethermere* and it included mutuality of obligations, although no definition was given as such.

5.83 In the important Court of Appeal case of *McLeod v Hellyer Bros* in 1987, Hull-based trawlermen had worked for many years for the same party. Their claim for employee rights was rejected, as mutual obligations did not subsist over the entire duration of the period. This again highlights the essential characteristic of mutuality of obligations: an ongoing commitment of continuity. See Chapter 11 for how the High Court in *Synaptek v Young* developed this in the context of IR35.

5.84 The next notable mutuality decision (*Clark v Oxfordshire Health Authority*) was heard in 1997 by the Court of Appeal and concerned a nurse who was part of a nursing bank. Her terms and conditions were highly consistent with a contract of employment and although she did not work continually for the same 'employer' the question was raised as to whether she had a global contract.

5.85 This important case found there was no global contract and underlined that the concept of mutuality of obligations was very important but not crucial to the issue of status. *Clark's* case perhaps reduced the impact of mutuality, and this is an interpretation which can be placed on the decision in *McMeechan v Secretary of State for Employment* also heard in 1997. However, mutuality became a more prominent factor as a result of the decision of the House of Lords in the 1999 case of *Carmichael v National Power*, which reversed the Court of Appeal ruling. Indeed, in that case Lord Irvine stated ([1999] 4 All ER 897 at 902a) that the workers' claim to be employees 'foundered on the rock of absence of mutuality'.

Rarely is such an unequivocal statement made. This very important recent and senior case once again reaffirmed the importance of the 'irreducible minimum' required to establish a contract of service. Mutuality of obligations was seen as very much part of that minimum.

5.86 It was noted by the court that the workers were not necessarily self-employed. Again practitioners should remember that defeating IR35 is not about proving self-employment—it is about proving the worker is not an employee of the client, which may be somewhat easier.

5.87 HMRC are unhappy that mutuality is being given such importance, but even more recent case law again underlines the relevance of this concept.

5.88 In the 2001 case of *Montgomery v Johnson Underwood Ltd*, the Court of Appeal again referred to the 'irreducible minimum' necessary to create a contract of employment and referred in depth to the importance of mutuality as part of the equation. Earlier cases such as *McMeechan*, which appeared to play down mutuality, were distinguished and the *Montgomery* case provides many strong quotations.

5.89 This case concerned a receptionist who contracted with an agency and carried out her duties at the end user's premises. She worked at the same place for over two and a half years. She was found *not* to be either an employee of the agency or an employee of the end user.

This was because she was not sufficiently controlled to be a servant and there was a lack of mutuality. The *Ready Mixed Concrete* case of 1968 was quoted with approval. This laid down the principle that, as well as having to give personal service (not in issue in the *Montgomery* case itself) and being under the control of the 'master', it was important to establish that the other terms were not inconsistent with a contract of service. A lack of mutuality is such an inconsistent term.

5.90 Lord Justice Brooke ([2001] IRLR 269 at 274) said:

'the concept of an irreducible minimum of obligations was expressly applied by Lord Irvine ... in *Carmichael v National Power*, and there is a consistent line of authority contained in decisions of this court, binding both on this court and inferior tribunals, to the effect that the three elements of a contract of service identified by McKenna J in *Ready Mixed Concrete*, must be present before a contract of service can be identified, *whatever other elements there may be which point one way or another*' (author's emphasis).

5.91 Brooke LJ also pointed out ([2001] IRLR 269 at 275) that this trinity of personal service, control and mutuality had first to be considered before the other general factors. It is only necessary to go to the 'second stage' of considering all the other status criteria if personal service, control and mutuality are first established. If they are not, the status will not be one of employee and the argument need go no further.

5.92 Because part of the 'irreducible minimum' of a contract of service was missing Buckley J said 'whatever contractual arrangements were enjoyed ... she cannot have been an employee'.

This important precedent has been cited in more recent cases heard by the Employment Appeals Tribunal. The case of *Electronic Data Systems v Hanbury and Brook Street Bureau* ([2001] All ER (D) 369 (Mar), EAT 128/00) involved an agency worker claiming, inter alia, unfair dismissal. The Employment Tribunal decided at a preliminary hearing that there was no contract of service, and the EAT had no hesitation in endorsing that conclusion, stating (at para 10) that it was 'plainly permissible' as there was 'no mutuality of obligation ... regardless of the contractual position' between the parties.

The case of *Stuncroft Ltd v Havelock* (EAT 1017/00, [2002] All ER (D) 292 (Jan)) involved a claim for redundancy pay. The EAT overturned the Employment Tribunal's decision, explaining at para 8, that 'want of mutual obligation was a knock out blow'. Strong words indeed.

The EAT allowed the appeal of *Propertycare Ltd v Gower* (EAT 547/03, [2004] All ER (D) 16 (Jan)), an unfair dismissal case.

5.93 The judicial review case brought by the PCG (*R (on the application of Professional Contractors Group v IRC*) contains some helpful, if obiter, remarks by

5.93 *The major case law decisions and status criteria*

Mr Justice Burton on the issue of mutuality that were made at the same time the Court of Appeal was deciding the *Montgomery* case. He criticised HMRC's policy of ignoring mutuality wherever they can and said ([2001] STC 629 at 651):

> 'It cannot be right for the Revenue simply to conclude that mutuality of obligation is not a relevant issue ... it has now recently been emphasised by the House of Lords in *Carmichael v National Power*.'

The Carmichael decision has also been followed in the little publicised Court of Appeal judgment in *Stevedoring & Haulage Services Ltd v AM Fuller and others* [2001] EWCA Civ 651. This case confirmed that where there is a contractual clause negativing mutuality this cannot be overridden by what happens in practice, even if work is offered and accepted on an ongoing basis. The court said at paragraph 11 of the judgment:

> 'the implied terms flatly contradict the express terms contained in the documents: a positive implied obligation to offer and accept a reasonable amount of work (whatever that means) cannot be reconciled with express terms that neither party is obliged to offer or accept any work)

None of the conventional routes for the implication of contractual terms will work. Neither business efficacy nor necessity require the implication of implied terms which are entirely inconsistent with a supposed contract's express terms. This tells us that the lack of mutuality should be committed to writing and not left to chance. In the cases where mutuality crystallised over a period of time (*Airfix; Nethermere*) there was no clause negativing mutuality of obligations as there was no written contract at all.

Mutuality of obligations, affectionately known as 'MOO', is a powerful IR35 defence strategy simply because most agencies, end users and contractors are happy to contract away any such obligations. Practitioners should be arguing it until the cows come home. In *Stuncroft Ltd v Havelock* His Honour Judge Wilkie QC said, at para 8, that a lack of mutuality is a 'knock out blow'. Not merely a persuasive factor but a determinative issue, as it is part of the irreducible minimum. This judgment endorsed the arguments of Clive Sheldon, barrister, who appeared on behalf of HMRC in the *Synaptek* appeal!

Synaptek v Young is analysed in Chapter 11 as it is an IR35 case. However, it can be usefully underlined that that case established that in an IR35 context for there to be sufficient mutuality of obligation, the obligations must endure for the entire period of the notional contract, not merely in isolation.

HMRC's view of mutuality of obligations

5.94 Whereas in the past HMRC have sometimes been suspicious of claimed rights of substitution and have tended to play down the importance of such rights, it has been out and out dismissive of the importance and relevance of mutuality. However, the law is simply not on their side, and it should not be forgotten just how critical of HMRC's view of mutuality Mr Justice Burton was in the judicial review case (see above **5.93**).

5.95 If the fundamental importance of mutuality is acknowledged, that is to say it is a prerequisite of a contract of employment, being as it is part of the 'irreducible minimum' to create a contract of service, then direct employment status can be defeated by ensuring that, in practice and in terms of contractual conditions, mutuality is not implied or created. In general, work providers are quite happy to contract with the work doer on the basis that there is no obligation to provide work to the work doer and equally the work doer is happy to contract with the work provider that he will not make himself available for work in the future.

5.96 In the real world, work cannot be guaranteed and in the context of project based contracts in particular it would be quite unwise for the work provider, in particular, to guarantee ongoing work.

5.97 One of the main reasons that IT and engineering agencies have thrived over the last ten years is simply because there is a requirement for workers to be engaged and released as work flow dictates. Putting to one side the technical legal arguments regarding mutuality of obligations, HMRC could make a greater effort to understand the relevance of ongoing mutual commitments and their general undesirability in the real commercial world. HMRC's approach to mutuality was also criticised by Mr Justice Burton in the PCG case, see para **5.93**. Quite confusingly HMRC do accept in ESM 0543 that mutuality of obligations *is* a consideration to be taken into account. This is all very inconsistent.

5.98 The truth is mutuality is a very important topic and, despite dismissing it as essentially irrelevant to tax status, HMRC go into some considerable detail in their manuals, analysing all the case law and attempting to draw fine distinctions between the various decisions and individual judgments. Needless to say they cannot have it both ways. It is suggested that the importance of mutuality is clearly established in numerous senior court cases, and it is more for reasons of policy than as a result of objective legal analysis that HMRC seek to play it down. The author acknowledges the sterling efforts of Anne Redston who has successfully convinced HMRC to change various paragraphs of the ESM on mutuality and certain other key areas. To this day, HMRC try to play down *O'Kelly* and play up *McMeechan*. They even argued at the Special Commissioners that *Montgomery* was wrongly decided, but it has got them nowhere.

5.99 A twist on mutuality comes out from the judicial review case brought by the PCG. During an exchange before the judgment was delivered HMRC's counsel confirmed that mutuality of obligations was indeed a necessary prerequisite for a contract of service.

5.100 When considering the so-called 'hypothetical' contract between the worker and the client, HMRC's counsel seemed to accept, during discussion in open court, that there could be no mutuality of obligations in an entirely hypothetical contract. Indeed, how can there be? HMRC will now have to argue that there can be mutual obligations in an imaginary contract. Are they going to have to show that there is hypothetical mutuality within a hypothetical contract? If so, it would seem that HMRC have a significant burden in demonstrating that this exists. As Mr Justice Burton pointed out, how can one arrive at the required 'irreducible minimum

5.100 *The major case law decisions and status criteria*

of obligation from someone who doesn't employ you ... when there isn't any obligation at all? What is the obligation of the employer? ... *the obligation [of the client] to pay the money is not enough*' (author's emphasis).

5.101 In the April 1997 *Tax Bulletin*, HMRC acknowledged (in the context of a builder) that regularly accepting work from the same client might simply be a function of the worker managing his business well and he could hardly be criticised for regularly accepting well-paid contracts. Even in the context of IR35 HMRC should be reminded of these comments.

5.102 As ESM 0543 says, 'There must be an irreducible minimum of mutual obligation for there to be a contract of service'. HMRC confirm that even in the context of a notional contract 'you must be able to point to an irreducible minimum which would have existed'. This would seem to present HMRC with a massive challenge where contracts are properly worded.

Summary

5.103 Mutuality is so important in establishing a contract of employment. It requires more than a mere offer and acceptance of work. Arguably, a higher plane of legal obligations is required including continuity and care, trust and confidence as well as the desire to maintain the relationship even during periods when there is no work. At the very least there must be an obligation to offer and accept work for the entire period of the notional IR35 contract. Often this will not exist.

Mutuality of obligations is very much part of the 'irreducible minimum' required to establish direct employment. Quite simply, without it a contract of service cannot exist.

HMRC's view and interpretation of mutuality is at odds with current case law, and their approach has been criticised by the High Court itself.

Control

5.104 Whereas mutuality of obligations has been afforded varying levels of importance over recent years, the issue of control has, if anything, experienced more fluctuating credence over an even longer period. HMRC are very fond of the so-called control test and it still appears as the lead item in many HMRC pamphlets, which purport to explain the criteria to be taken into account in determining status.

5.105 Traditionally, and certainly in the author's experience, HMRC have taken a fairly simplistic approach to the control test. It has often expressed the view that if A can tell B what to do then A is the master of B who is a servant and is, therefore, the employee of A.

5.106 In the construction industry, where the skill level of some workers is at a lower level than, say, IT contractors and engineers, HMRC have been able to push for direct employee status, on the basis that if someone is told what to do or reports to a foreman he is 'controlled'. The control test alone has become a fertile ground for HMRC status challenges, yet this approach, in the author's opinion, seriously misunderstands the law. It is submitted that control is a prerequisite for a contract of employment but its existence per se does *not* automatically create direct employment status.

5.107 The reason control is important stems from the Victorian concept that a master would control his servant. It should be noted that the word 'servant' had a specific meaning in Victorian legislation and was not synonymous with the word 'worker'. A servant would always be a worker, but a worker would not necessarily be a servant. The idea was that a servant was subject to his master's control and therefore by definition if a person controlled another he would be his employer in the context of status, as he would be his master. The very words master and servant carry with them an old fashioned feel, which is not surprising in the context of the origin of the phrase. Indeed, in eighteenth and nineteenth century Britain (and going back to Roman times) a person's 'status' in society would automatically put him under the command of another superior person.

5.108 Throughout the mid-twentieth century the courts tended to concentrate on the issue of control as the single most important factor in determining status. Indeed, there are precedents going back as far as the nineteenth century which stressed this single issue, such as *Yewens v Noakes* (1880–81 LR 6 QBD 539, CA) where Lord Justice Bramwell gave the leading judgment. It has, however, been said that the dictum of Bramwell LJ on control has been misapplied almost from the moment of its emergence.

5.109 This is because the word 'servant' designated a specific category of employees who were subject to the Master and Servant Acts and the Employers' and Workmen Act of 1875. Furthermore, under the Workers' Compensation Acts different categories of workers enjoyed specific entitlements. This was the context in which 'servants' had to be identified—*not* in the context of tax status generally.

5.110 The so-called 'control test' was used extensively until it was considered that the test had severe limitations. For example, a ship's captain who would be an employee would nonetheless be quite uncontrolled when he was captaining a ship on the high seas. To put this into a more modern context a brain surgeon within the National Health Service who is regarded as an employee is nonetheless not controlled by the hospital, certainly not as to the manner in which he performs his operations. HMRC are very keen to compare typical IR35 at risk workers with ships' captains and brain surgeons. This is flawed. The true IR35 test is to compare IT contractors with IT employees, oil engineers with oil engineers and not with unrelated professions.

5.111 It was eventually realised that the control test was not a single criterion which could accurately predict or establish status. Although the concept was still regarded as important up to the late 1960s, its importance appeared to diminish in the 1980s and 1990s. Only in recent case law, such as the *Montgomery* Court of Appeal case in 2001, has the control factor again become a much more significant indicator as to status. It should be remembered that control is important as a prerequisite of a contract of service. It is *not* a factor which on its own establishes a

5.111 *The major case law decisions and status criteria*

contract of service and in this sense the law has certainly moved on. It is only one part of the irreducible minimum required. As MacKenna J said in the *Ready Mixed Concrete* case ([1968] 1 All ER 433 at 441A):

> 'An obligation to do work subject to the other party's control is a necessary ... condition of a contract of service.'

5.112 Case law indicates that control can have relevance in respect of the what, how, where and when work is executed but for there to be sufficient control to indicate a master/servant relationship, there has to be a significant degree of interference in the manner in which the work is carried out. The *Narich Pty v Commissioner of Payroll Tax* [1984] ICR 286 case in 1984 found the worker to be an employee because, in fact, she was 'tied hand and foot' in the way she did her work. It would be unwise to turn this round and say that control only exists where a worker is tied hand and foot, but use of this kind of language implies that control is not satisfied in the context of master/servant relationships at a superficial or low level.

5.113 This latter point should be clearly understood. Control is not synonymous with mere supervision or direction. These latter two are weakened, less intrusive versions of control. The ability of a client to require a worker to report to him or sign in and out of a building may amount to nothing more than a proper regard for health and safety considerations, which is not the same thing as true control.

5.114 Perhaps in recognition of the changing realities of the modern working arena, or for other reasons not fully understood, the courts moved away from the strict control test. It was seen as unworkable and unreliable as a simple foolproof test.

5.115 As an alternative to the discredited control test, the so-called 'part and parcel' or 'integration' test was popularised in the 1950s and 1960s. This concentrated on establishing whether the worker had become part and parcel of the putative employer's business. This test, to some extent developed by the maverick judge Lord Denning, itself became discredited when it was realised that many genuinely self-employed workers were part and parcel of the 'employer's' business, while workers who were clearly direct employees were not part and parcel of the 'employer's' business. MacKenna J in *Ready Mixed Concrete (South East) Ltd v Minister of Pensions and National Insurance* ([1968] 1 All ER 433 at 445F) commented that the test raised more questions than he knew how to answer.

5.116 Hence, two single and fairly strict tests (control and integration) were discredited and subsequently the courts tended to take a more holistic approach by looking at the whole balance of factors, with a view to seeing whether the worker was in 'business on his own account'. This also became known as the 'economic reality' test. This approach was popular throughout the 1970s, 1980s and early 1990s, and moved away from the more fundamental approach to status developed by McKenna J in *Ready Mixed Concrete*. Subsequently, the 'in business on own account' test has been downgraded to 'useful' rather than 'fundamental', and more recent case law has reverted to the stricter *Ready Mixed Concrete* approach.

5.117 At the present time it is suggested that the correct approach to status is as laid down in the *Express and Echo* case heard in the Court of Appeal 1999 and is to ask whether there are any terms of the contract which are inherently inconsistent with direct employment. This builds precisely upon McKenna J's 'trinity' in *Ready Mixed Concrete*. If there are, the status debate is concluded and the worker will not be an employee of the client. If there are no such inherently inconsistent terms, then all other factors have to be put in the melting pot and a balanced picture painted from the accumulation of detail available. When considering the whole melting pot of factors control will always be a consideration and, following *Montgomery*, a very important one.

5.118 To show just how far the control test per se was played down in the 1980s one need only consider the judgment of Mr Justice McCullogh in *Swan (WF & RK) (Hellenic) v Secretary of State for Social Services* (18 January 1983, unreported). He said (at page 34H of the judgment):

> 'it is now also well recognised that men who are subject to a very considerable degree of control may nevertheless be independent contractors'.

He went on to say that the best example of this would be a labour only subcontractor in the building industry—a comment to be remembered when dealing with construction industry status challenges.

5.119 It is submitted that, although the issue of control is a wide topic, the most important aspect of control is the 'how'. Often HMRC will say that having to perform the task at a particular place or at a particular time are equally important aspects of control indicating a master/servant relationship. In the author's view this is faulty reasoning. If an IT contractor is engaged to attend a bank's premises to service computers in the Directors' Suite on the 10th floor it is quite clear that he will have to carry out the work on the 10th floor where the computers are situated, and may have to carry out the work outside of normal office hours when the computers can be more readily accessed. The reason he works within these 'constraints' is because of the practical realities and requirements of the job specification, not because he is an 'employee'.

5.120 This point was taken in the House of Lords when the Welfare Reform and Pensions Act 1999 was debated at length. One of their Lordships suggested that if a householder instructs a plumber where to fit a new radiator and the plumber complies with this he is doing so not because he is the employee of the householder but because the radiator needs putting in a particular place. It is essential not to allow HMRC to confuse a job specification with actual detailed control as to how the job is completed. HMRC's guidance at ESM 0522 acknowledges that where the nature of the work dictates where the services are to be provided this is not a determining factor. As such, the argument that a contractor is controlled because he has to work at a client's premises can be readily refuted where he has to work there because, for example, that is where the mainframe computer is located.

5.121 Again, the important 'how' aspect of control can be seen in the unreported *Staples* case of 1983 when the Department of Health and Social Security

5.121 *The major case law decisions and status criteria*

challenged the status of a relief chef who worked via an agency in a restaurant. It was accepted as a fact that the chef was controlled, in as much as the hotel dictated particular menus for which the chef had to cook the appropriate food. However, the control the hotel had over the chef went one stage further: not only could they tell him the broad theme of the food but it could dictate the precise dishes the chef had to cook. In these circumstances the DHSS argued that the chef was 'controlled'. The High Court rejected this argument on the basis that the chef could not be told 'how' to cook the food. The importance of the 'how' aspect of control was also highlighted in *Market Investigations Ltd v Minister of Social security* [1969] 2 QB 173 and *MacManus v Griffiths* [1997] STC 1089, and indeed goes all the way back to *Yewens v Noakes* in the nineteenth century.

5.122 An earlier case, *Morren v Swinton and Pendlebury BC* [1965] 1 WLR 576, however, acknowledged that, where a person of some specific professional or technical skill is involved, in that case an engineer, then the possibility of control would be restricted, as by definition there would be little scope for it. In such circumstances the court said that other factors beyond control would have to be taken into account. A consideration of both of these cases suggests a very attractive anti-IR35 argument. The *Staples* case says unless a worker can be told 'how' to do his work he is not controlled, and *Morren* tells us that there is no scope to control an expert. This raises the interesting possibility that an expert is much less likely to be an employee because there is no scope for the prerequisite of control. Interestingly, HMRC accept the full force of this logic and is happy to relegate control to a very insignificant factor in respect of specialists (see ESM 0528). This might sound like 'heads I win, tails you lose'. HMRC emphasise the importance and impact of the control test when it suits them, yet dismiss the concept when it can be shown the worker is very much left to his own devices, but *Ready Mixed Concrete* should not be ignored so readily.

5.123 If the two cases of *Staples* and *Morren* are considered together it can be seen that a specialist cannot be controlled and is, therefore, less likely to be an employee. It is then tempting to move on from control and consider other factors—an approach advocated by HMRC. But they are forgetting that control sufficient to render a worker the servant of his master is a *prerequisite* in establishing a contract of service according not only to the *Ready Mixed Concrete* case in 1968 but the more recent and authoritative decision in *Montgomery v Johnson Underwood Ltd* decided by the Court of Appeal 2001. That case underlined the 'irreducible minimum' for direct employment, part of which is control. This really should cause HMRC major difficulties in the context of highly skilled workers and needs to be explored. *Morren* is not bad law, but it has been superseded by *Ready Mixed Concrete* and *Montgomery*.

5.124 To this day many tax officers at area level maintain that if a worker can be told what to do then he will be a servant of his master and an employee for tax purposes. The importance of the 'how' is overlooked as is the requirement that the control must be so strict that it must amount to a significant interference with the worker. A job spec should not be confused with true 'control', whereby a master/servant relationship is created.

5.125 Control was stated to be a prerequisite of direct employment in the *Ready Mixed Concrete* case of 1968. What the High Court did *not* say was that a person who is controlled is necessarily an employee. To suggest otherwise is to twist the words of McKenna J into something quite different. This tactic is sometimes used by HMRC and should be resisted.

5.126 Practitioners should remember that, before a worker can be an employee, the trinity of a high degree of control, the requirement to give personal service and the other terms not being inconsistent with a direct employment relationship (such as the lack of mutuality of obligations), must *all* be present.

5.127 Despite a general fall from grace, the control factor has remained an issue to consider, but one which carries less influence than it did 30 years ago. However, in *North West Ceilings* [2001] Emp LR 551 (see **5.132** below) discussed below, a different emphasis was placed on the relevance of control; control was to some extent seen as an indicator of employment, rather than a lack of it as a contra-indicator of employment. This approach seems to be more common in employment law cases where the tribunals tend to lean in favour of the worker.

5.128 The *Montgomery* case was not concerned with substitution and personal service; these were simply not issues on the facts. Instead the court referred in detail to the 'irreducible minimum' required to establish a contract of employment as being mutuality of obligations and sufficient control to render the worker a servant of the master. Despite the worker (an agency supplied receptionist) being under the supervision of an end user for a period of well over two years the court found that there was no mutuality, actual or implied, nor was there sufficient control over the worker to make her an employee of either the end user or the agency.

5.129 A lack of mutuality or lack of control are fundamental factors either of which preclude direct employment status on the clear legal precedents laid down by the courts.

5.130 In the past, HMRC have argued that, even if there is no actual control, there may well be a right of control, but it seems that the tribunals and courts are increasingly concerned with actual interference and an actual exercising of control rather than the remote theoretical possibility of it. Practitioners should never lose sight of the fact that in the context of status there must be, in the author's opinion, a significant degree of control, whereby one person is subjugated to the position of being a servant of his master, and without this there can be no contract of service.

5.131 The Court of Appeal was influenced by the control factor in March 2001 in the *Interlink Express v Night Trunkers Ltd* case [2001] EWCA Civ 360, although in the context of IR35 and status generally the case carries little weight. This is because that case was peculiar to the provisions of the road haulage industry (in particular the operation of the Goods Vehicles (Operators Licences) Act 1995), and was concerned with whether a contract can be declared void on the grounds of illegality.

5.132 In the case of *North West Ceilings Ltd v Reid* April 2001, the Employment Appeal Tribunal found the worker to be an employee, despite the fact that

5.132 *The major case law decisions and status criteria*

previously he had been content to be treated as a self-employed subcontractor. HMRC had issued a 714 Certificate and he had also had income subjected to SC60 deductions. Mr Reid had been on a self-employed basis for around four years before he went on the payroll in March 1998.

This was an unfair dismissal case where the worker himself wanted to establish direct employee status (for his own financial gain), and it does not sit well with Lord Denning's comment in *Massey v Crown Life Assurance* [1978] 2 All ER 576 at 581d that a person who makes his self-employed bed should have to 'lie in it'. It is further evidence that tribunals often lean in favour of the claimant worker.

5.133 The Employment Appeal Tribunal in the *North West Ceilings* case felt that Mr Reid was an employee throughout his entire period with North West Ceilings, and it had no hesitation in reaching such a conclusion. The court was influenced by the control that was exercised over Mr Reid and the fact that he was a 'supervisor'. The evidence also showed that there were other employees doing the same kind of work as Mr Reid and they had always been treated as PAYE employees.

Arguably this case shows that control is an influential factor and not just a contra-indicator of self-employment, but the tax treatment of similar workers and Mr Reid's own stance in this case were also very strong factors and even HMRC tend not to cite this case as a mainstream authority.

Can control be implied?

5.134 In *Addison v London Philharmonic Orchestra* [1981] ICR 261, it was argued that as the musicians had to follow the directions and co-ordination of the conductor this implied control. This was rejected by the court and it was noted that the deceased composer himself could be said to have control over the performance as he had written the music in the first place! This equally was not considered sufficient to create control in the sense of a master and servant relationship.

5.135 Sometimes the courts arrive at surprising conclusions. In the case of *Bhadra v Ellam*,[1988] STC 239 concerning an agency-supplied doctor, the question arose as to whether the doctor was controlled within the terms of the agency legislation. It was common ground that the doctor was professionally qualified and it was argued by him that he was not controlled. It should be noted that in the High Court the doctor represented himself and was up against experienced HMRC counsel.

The court decided as a fact that the doctor was 'accountable' up the chain of hospital command and as such there must have been a right of 'control' coming down the chain and, therefore, the control factor was satisfied. If the control factor is present it is almost impossible to escape the agency regulations on any other arguments.

5.136 Although *Bhadra v Ellam* is not a case that is often relied upon, it illustrates that the courts may be willing to imply a right of control. It should be specifically noted that HMRC's own counsel accepted that merely telling a worker what task to do next would *not* amount to control.

Delegated control

5.137 In the case of *HMRC v Philip John Wright* [2007] STC 1684 the question of whether or not control could be delegated was raised. Mr Wright's business was to provide labour to main contractors. Mr Wright would usually give initial instruction to the worker himself, but after that the precise on-site instructions lay with the on-site foreman. HMRC argued that the element of control exercised over the workers by the site foreman must be regarded as delegation by Mr Wright to a third party to exercise the control over the workers which he himself was entitled to exert. In support of their submission HMRC relied on the decision of Lord Widgery Chief Justice in *Global Plant Limited v Secretary of State for Health and Social Security* .

Mr Justice Lewison held that the decision in *Global* did not lay down any principle of law. He found that it was a decision on its own facts and one which would depend on finding that the site foreman was in effect the agent of the employer. This was not the usual way in which building contracts are structured and Mr Justice Lewison stated 'The usual position is that the site foreman is nominated by the main contractor. I would not regard the mere fact that workers were told what to do by a site foreman as amounting to control by Mr Wright. Moreover, the law has, in my judgement moved on since Global Plant.'

A similar approach was taken in the earlier case of *Lewis t/a MAL Scaffolding & Others v HMRC* [2006] SSCD 253 (SpC 527) brought before the Special Commissioners by Accountax. Dr David Williams stated:

> 'I do not accept the argument that the site agents could be regarded as carrying out the control function over the workers for MAL Scaffolding, the site agents have independent statutory safety obligations that apply to employee and employed worker alike.'

In the case of *MAL Scaffolding*, Dr David Williams criticised HMRC's objectivity. The Revenue approached their investigation on the basis that there must be an employment relationship between MAL scaffolding and the workers if one looks hard enough. Officers then went looking on that basis and persuaded themselves they had found what they were looking for. They totally failed to persuade the Special Commissioner. This is a warning to HMRC to take an unbiased objective approach when investigating status and IR35 cases.

In a similar vein it was once noted by Park J during a hearing in the High Court that HMRC would have the whole world on PAYE if it could get away with it!

The decision in *MAL Scaffolding* was relied upon in part by the Special Commissioner in *Castle Construction (Chesterfield) Limited v Revenue & Customs Commissioners* [2008] SpC 723, in deciding that 12 scaffolders as well as a number of other sub-contractors were self-employed. In that case, the Special Commissioner held that the appellant company had correctly classified a total of 314 out of 321 individual workers as self-employed.

The Commissioner did not regard the contracts between the company and workers in this case as very helpful. For example, he commented in relation to a substitution clause included in the contracts that it was 'broadly nonsense' and '... a fiction ... to enhance the "non-employee" case...'. However, the Commissioner considered the facts and case law authority in deciding that 217 bricklayers, 75

5.137 *The major case law decisions and status criteria*

labourers, the twelve scaffolders, six foremen, two supervisors and two slinger signalmen were self-employed.

The remaining seven workers (ie six fork-lift truck drivers and one lorry driver) were considered to be employees. Interestingly, the Commissioner held that it was 'fair and appropriate' that their employment status should only apply in the future, and not for past periods. The effect was that the company would not be liable to pay tax and National Insurance contributions for five earlier tax years assessed by HMRC. It should be noted that *Castle Construction* is not a test case. It was decided on its own particular facts. The Commissioner referred to established lines of authority (or 'material pointers') in reaching his decision, including the familiar tests set out in *Ready Mixed Concrete (South East) Ltd v Minister of Pensions and National Insurance* [1968] 1 All ER 433, ie broadly mutuality of obligations and personal service, control, and whether the other contract terms are consistent with an employment contract.

Another employment status case followed shortly after Castle Construction, which the taxpayers also won. In *JL Window & Door Services and Molloy v Revenue and Customs Commissioners* [2009] SpC 733, the appellant partnership engaged workers on a self-employed basis. Following a review, HMRC concluded that the status of the workers was that of employees under contracts of service, and issued formal income tax determinations (under SI 2003/2683, reg 80) and Notices of Decision for National Insurance purposes on that basis. The partnership appealed. In addition, Mr Molloy was a worker who appealed against the Notice of Decision that he was an employee. The Special Commissioner once again applied established case law to the particular facts of the case, and dismissed HMRC's appeal. In applying the various indicators of status established in previous cases, the Commissioner held that although there was mutuality of obligations in the workers' contracts, the partnership did not exercise a sufficient degree of control over the workers to make itself 'master'. This was sufficient for the Commissioner to decide that the workers were not employees. However, he also stated that he did not find the other provisions of the contracts consistent with their being contracts of service, and that the workers were in business on their own account, albeit in a modest way.

Summary

5.138 The control test used to be considered foolproof as a determinant of employee status, but its significance was played down in the 1980s and its whole historical background has been misunderstood. However, the 2001 *Montgomery* case puts it back in vogue and reaffirms the *Ready Mixed Concrete* approach that control is a prerequisite of employee status but not proof of employee status. It now rejoins personal service and mutuality of obligations in the trinity of essential prerequisites to create a direct contract of employment. And even where it does exist this does not prove of itself that the worker is an employee.

5.139 A significant degree of control is required before a worker can be an employee yet many personal service business workers are beyond control, particularly in respect of how they do their work, as evidenced by their often unique and specialist skills. As such the re-emergence of the control test prerequisite can only be a fillip to IR35 defence strategies and arguments. No doubt HMRC will try to dismiss control in the context of highly skilled workers, but such an approach should be resisted. The *Morren* case has been superseded.

Other factors case law recognises as important

5.140 The essential trinity of personal service (no rights of substitution), control and mutuality of obligations have now been considered in depth and according to the case law if there is a not unreasonably fettered and genuine right to send a substitute; *or* insufficient control to make the worker a servant of his master; *or* a lack of mutuality of obligations, then there cannot be a contract of service, or direct employment.

5.141 This is not to say that the worker will be necessarily self-employed. Often the case law, especially employment law decisions, merely say the worker is not an employee or he falls into the category of having a contract *sui generis*. But this is good enough to defeat IR35, which merely requires the worker to demonstrate that he is not a disguised employee.

HMRC take the view that employment status should be decided on an overall view of a number of work-related factors. This process is known as 'painting the picture'. Their stance is that a status decision has to be made by 'standing back and looking at the picture as a whole', without giving undue weight to particular factors. However, in the 2006 case of *Parade Park Hotel v HMRC* [2007] STC (SCD) 430 the Special Commissioner played down the 'painting the picture' approach endorsed by Nolan LJ in *Hall v Lorimer* indicating that the 'irreducible minimum' must first be considered before looking at the rest of the conditions of the engagement. John Clark stated 'If the conditions listed by McKenna J in *Ready Mixed Concrete* are crucial on the basis that they represent the "irreducible minimum" they must logically take precedence over this "painting a picture" approach'. *Parade Park* is a case that succinctly illustrates the more important aspects of status and is a decision HMRC do not particularly like!

5.142 Of course, the best way to show that the worker is not a disguised employee of the client is to demonstrate that the personal service business is operating independently in a business-to-business relationship. The trinity of substitution, control and mutuality are without doubt the most essential points to consider but there are others. These other points fall into what can be described as important factors and minor factors.

Important factors

In business on own account

5.143 This is not so much a single factor as a general test. It was first alluded to in the *Market Investigations* case of 1969 and came from earlier US precedents. It was put forward as a fundamental test and asked whether the worker could be regarded as being in business on his own account? This has become known as the 'economic reality' test.

5.144 *The major case law decisions and status criteria*

5.144 Mr Justice Cooke said ([1968] 3 All ER 732 at 737I):

> 'Is the person who has engaged himself to perform these services performing them as a person in business on his own account? If the answer to that question is "yes" then the contract is a contract for services. If the answer is "no" then the contract is a contract of service.'

This 'in business on own account' test or approach has been revisited and alluded to many times in the last 30 years but it has been recognised that it has its limitations, as HMRC themselves seem to accept in their internal manuals.

Indeed, the test is a little curious in that in one sense it simply says that if a person is 'in business' that is, self-employed, then he is self-employed!

5.145 As explained in the *Market Investigations* case, the test asked questions relating to the supply of equipment, the method of pay and the level of financial risk. It was also acknowledged that where work was undertaken as part of an existing business then that would help to establish self-employment. Mr Justice Cooke said ([1968] 3 All ER 732 at 738B):

> 'The application of the general test may be easier in a case where the person who engages himself to perform the services does so in the course of an already established business of his own.'

This could be particularly useful for IR35 at-risk businesses which have traded for many years.

5.146 Cooke J added ([1968] 3 All ER 732 at 738C) that an existing business is not *necessary* to establish self-employment:

> '... and a person who engages himself to perform services for another may well be an independent contractor even though he has not entered into the contract in the course of an existing business carried on by him'.

This latter extract should give some comfort to personal service businesses entering into their first contract.

5.147 However, as soon as an approach to status is developed its weaknesses are exposed. What if a person does not have the traditional trappings of being in business, ie he has no stock, premises, staff, etc. Can he still be self-employed? The answer is a resounding 'yes'. There are many examples of self-employed persons who show few if any of the traditional self-employment badges identified in the late 1960s and 1970s. An actor, management consultant, or swimming coach may well have no stock or staff and little apparent financial risk yet they can be self-employed.

5.148 The 'in business on own account test' has been played down in cases such as *O'Kelly v Trust House Forte*, heard by the Court of Appeal in 1983. Here the court took the view that the supply of the 'commodity' of semi-skilled labour was a legitimate form of self-employment.

A similar approach was taken in the case of *Addison v London Philharmonic Ltd*. Mr Justice Waterhouse asked ([1981] ICR 261 at 273A):

> 'were the applicants performing their services at the relevant time as persons in business on their own account? We have no hesitation in answering "yes".'

This was despite the fact the workers concerned were part-time orchestra musicians with *very little* to substantiate that they were running a 'business'. The court commented ([1981] ICR 261 at 273C) that the musicians: 'contributed their own skills and interpretative powers to the orchestra's performances as independent contractors', and the 'in business' approach was played down.

5.149 In the author's view, the business on own account test is, however, still important because it represents not so much a strict test as more of an attitude or mindset. It raises legitimate questions of whether the worker has a business organisation which could include in the early twenty-first century having an office at home, a website presence or a marketing strategy and business plan. These 'personal factors' which may demonstrate a commercial modus operandi were accepted as being important in the 1993 Court of Appeal decision in *Hall v Lorimer*. HMRC have also accepted in the 'Charlotte' example that personal and business factors might take the taxpayer out of IR35 (see Tax Bulletin 45 at Appendix 4). Personal business factors helped the taxpayer in the IR35 case of *Lime-IT Ltd v Justin* (see Chapter 11).

5.150 It is not unreasonable that a person who claims to be running an independent business can demonstrate that he is doing so, by providing examples of his actions which are consistent with his claims, such as being VAT-registered, raising invoices on business stationery, holding insurances and appointing an accountant to draw up accounts in relation to that business. These actions may not, in themselves, prove that he is not a disguised employee of the client, but they do show an approach wholly inconsistent with one who is a regular employee. These differences are important when an appeal is being presented, or arguments are being put to the inspector.

5.151 It will be appreciated that the relevant considerations often start to overlap. Being an independent businessman might equate to a lack of control; having assumed financial risk might be said to be akin with independence and a general 'in business' attitude.

The 'in business' approach remains an important consideration but it is not to be too slavishly followed. It is more of an indicator of attitude rather than a strict test.

An alternative approach: are engagements an incident of a continuing 'profession'?

5.152 The general approach to beating IR35 is one of understanding the law, agreeing terms and conditions which are outside IR35 and demonstrating a general commercial business approach. Some lobby groups and commentators have, however, suggested that there might be a case law shortcut based on an old decision.

5.152 *The major case law decisions and status criteria*

The 1931 case of *Davies v Braithwaite* [1931] KB 628 heard in the High Court by Rowlatt J concerned the correct schedule of charge for an actress. She had enjoyed at least ten different contracts for the three-year period in question, including theatre work, making films and radio appearances.

Some of her earnings were from America. The taxpayer argued that she should be taxed as an *employee* as this would mean her American income escaped UK tax under the then present rules. On the other hand HMRC argued that she should be taxed as a *self-employed* person under what was then Schedule D and that her American income should be taxed in the UK.

HMRC's justification was that she was not controlled sufficiently to be in a master/servant relationship and hence was self-employed. This is another case where principles were sacrificed for expediency.

Rowlatt J held all her income was proper to Schedule D, overturning the Commissioners' decision on the basis that:

> 'where one finds a method of earning a livelihood which does not consist of the obtaining of a post and staying in it but consists of a series of engagements and moving from one to the other ... then each of those engagements cannot be considered an employment, but is a mere engagement in the course of exercising a profession ...' (p 635).

5.153 The parallels with the IT contractor, a professional person moving from one engagement to another seem invitingly easy to make. The author's view is, however, much less optimistic. First, this case was heard when there was a general reclassification of what was to be included in employment income, with the historical emphasis being on 'offices' and 'posts' which had a degree of permanency about them. Secondly, the decision is now over 70 years old and its relevance to the modern world can be questioned. Thirdly, and perhaps most importantly, the case has been distinguished (ie not applied in subsequent case law decisions). There is also perhaps a question mark over whether IT contractors really do move from 'engagement to engagement' with the frequency envisaged in *Davies v Braithwaite*.

In the *Davies v Braithwaite* case itself Rowlatt J said: 'It seems to me quite clear that a man can have both an employment and a profession at the same time, in different categories' (page 635). This then was picked up in a much more recent High Court case, *Fall v Hitchen* [1973] 1 All ER 368 which concerned a professional dancer/actor who argued, on the authority of *Davies v Braithwaite* that he was self-employed. He lost. The *Fall v Hitchen* case approached the status test more from a 'business on own account approach (this new 'test' had been recently developed in the *Market Investigations* case of a few years earlier) instead of the 'in a profession on own account' approach. The court said, quite simply and logically, that if a professional person undertakes a contract that is in fact a contract of employment, it will remain a contract of employment 'notwithstanding that he is at the same time carrying on his profession' (p 376e).

The judge in *Fall v Hitchen*, Pennycuick V-C, quotes extensively from *Davies v Braithwaite*. It seems he was concerned that people were getting the wrong end of the stick with *Davies v Braithwaite*. He said:

> 'I have read those passages partly because they contain an accurate exposition of what Rowlatt J really did decide ... and partly because they show that a

person carrying on a profession may perfectly well hold an office and also, plainly, an employment in the same sphere as that in which he carries on his profession' (p 378d).

Other cases have confirmed this approach, including the Court of Appeal in *Hall v Lorimer* (1993). It seems that having a professional existence proves nothing per se. The terms of the actual contracts entered into need analysing before a status decision can be reached. Those who rely on a pure *Davies v Braithwaite* 'in a profession on own account' approach are skating on very thin ice.

5.154 More recent unpublished Special Commissioners' decisions concerning actors in the early 1990s have shown that standard equity contracts are not caught under employment income. It has been rightly suggested that if the word 'actor' in the standard equity contract was replaced with 'contractor' and the contract then submitted to HMRC for an IR35 review HMRC would almost certainly fail it. This anomaly has been pointed out by Anne Redston (to whom thanks), but in the author's view this is nothing more than an anomaly. Only HMRC know why they did not appeal to the High Court—and they are not telling. As the Special Commissioners' judgment is unreported and unpublished it will not significantly influence HMRC or Commissioners in an IR35 dispute. In the ESM, HMRC mention these cases but play up the factor that the actors engaged in many different professional activities (unlike the dancer in *Fall v Hitchen*). HMRC say all cases have to be dealt with on their own facts. Although there is nothing to be lost in arguing for the 'in a profession on own account' approach à la *Braithwaite*, it would seem far more likely that an argument based on substitution, lack of control and lack of mutuality of obligations, backed by modern case law, will succeed. Accountax has seen the *McGowan and West* judgment and on the facts it was reasonable that the taxpayers won. It is submitted there is nothing ground breaking in the decision.

Intention of the parties

5.155 In relation to IR35, this factor refers to whether or not the parties to the contract (ie the client and the personal service business) intend that the worker is to be a direct employee of the client. Identifying what the parties' wished to create is sometimes called their 'mutual intention'.

It is worth noting that the established case law concerns whether the parties intended that the worker is employed or self-employed. Clearly, the most common situation in an IR35 context is where the worker is an employee of his own company, so the distinction here is not strictly between employment and self-employment. However, the case law remains relevant because, as with case law concerning other factors, it goes towards determining whether the worker is a disguised employee of the client (and therefore potentially within IR35 in accordance with ITEPA 2003, s 49(1)(*c*)) or whether he is running a genuine independent business.

5.156 The intention of the parties is often underplayed by HMRC, but the correct legal position is that it must always be taken into account. That is not to say the

5.156 *The major case law decisions and status criteria*

parties' intention is always a highly influential factor, but it does have to be taken into account from the outset in all cases.

5.157 HMRC now seem to accept this view. In their internal guidance on intention, they start off by saying that (at ESM 0554):

> 'What the parties call their relationship, or what they consider it to be, is not conclusive. It is the reality of the relationship that matters. *Nevertheless the intention of the parties has to be taken into account.* The intention can be decisive where the relationship is ambiguous and where the other factors are neutral.' (Author's emphasis.)

However, it goes on to state that (ESM 0554):

> 'When you have gathered all the facts, you should stand back and look at the bigger picture. *If you consider that the case is borderline, you should then, and only then, look at the intention of the parties.* Where there is mutual intention for a contract of employment or for a contract for services, that will determine the status of the worker.' (Author's emphasis.)

This would seem to be somewhat contradictory. If the intention of the parties has to be taken into account, surely it should be considered in all cases, not merely borderline ones. In the author's experience, HMRC's approach in practice is to try to play down or even ignore completely the parties' intention. This approach should be resisted.

5.158 The relevance of intention is demonstrated by two different approaches. First, and this is an area often not considered by HMRC when disputing status issues, in order for there to be a valid contract there must be an offer and acceptance, consideration and an intention to enter into a legally binding relationship.

Clearly if one party offers work on a self-employed basis and the work is accepted on that basis, and this is coupled with the fact that the intention of the parties was to enter into a legal relationship based on this, then it can be appreciated just how fundamental the whole issue of intention is. This is not just in the context of tax status but in the whole area of contract law generally. This was noted by Webster J in *WHPT Housing Association Ltd v Secretary of State* [1981] ICR 737 He said:

> 'There also seems to me to be considerable force in [the] argument that the original offer and acceptance was to provide services, not service, and that there is no evidence that the nature of the contract changed after its inception.'

The only way HMRC can play down intention is effectively to say the parties' desires to offer and accept work on a business-to-business basis and enter into a legally binding agreement on that basis can be completely ignored. This is not only absurd but no panel of Commissioners would want to ride roughshod over the parties' intentions. This was underlined very recently by Lord Johnston in the case of *Stoddart v Cawder Golf Club* (EAT 873/00, 19 February 2001), heard in the EAT. Although the Tribunal found many factors pointing to employment and the workers

The major case law decisions and status criteria 5.160

had been engaged by the golf club for almost 20 years, this did not allow them to override the stated intention of the parties, which was to have a self-employment relationship. Lord Johnston said (at para 8):

> 'Where persons intend to create a self-employed situation and the ingredients of such can be found, such as method of payment, potential exposure to VAT and a lack of consent to be an employee, it is very difficult for any Tribunal to conclude that the contrary to what the parties intended to achieve had resulted.'

The concept of freedom of contract cannot be ignored so easily.

5.159 Secondly, the established case law recognises that the intention of the parties has to be taken into account in all status disputes, not merely in finely balanced cases as HMRC often claim. Most commentators would perhaps say that it is another relevant and important factor but no more than that. It is less important than, say, substitution or mutuality of obligations but more important than, say, sick pay and holiday pay. Until the *Express and Echo* case of 1999 this would probably be a reasonable approach, but since that decision it is suggested that the intention of the parties must now be given more weight. Indeed, in that case Lord Justice Gibson said ([1999] IRLR 367 at 370) that in a status dispute 'one starts with the common intention of the parties'.

In ambiguous cases the intention will be the deciding factor. An important case on this point is *Massey v Crown Life Assurance*, decided by the Court of Appeal in 1977. Lord Denning said ([1978] 2 All ER 576 at 580a):

> 'It seems to me on the authorities, that, when it is a situation which is in doubt, it is open to the parties by agreement to stipulate what the legal situation between them shall be.'

He also said ([1978] 2 All ER 576 at 580a):

> '... if their relationship is ambiguous and is capable of being one or the other, then the parties can remove that ambiguity, by the very agreement itself which they make with one another'.

He went on to say ([1978] 2 All ER 576 at 581c) that if the parties deliberately arrange to be self-employed even to obtain tax benefits, that is strong evidence that that is the real relationship. This was also approved in the High Court *Swan Hellenic* case of 1983. At page 40, Mr Justice McCullough described the intention of the parties in what was a borderline case, as a 'factor of major significance'.

This is why it is important to have a clear intention clause in any contract that is used to demonstrate that IR35 does not apply (as discussed in Chapter 7).

5.160 An example of another case in which the parties' intention was a key factor in determining status is *Calder v Kitson Vickers and Sons Ltd*. In that case it was held that when parties deliberately agree for the worker to be self-employed, it might afford strong evidence that that was their real relationship. Furthermore, Lord Justice Gibson stated that ([1988] ICR 232 at 250E):

5.160 *The major case law decisions and status criteria*

> 'A man is without question free under the law to contract to carry out certain work for another without entering into a contract of service.'

5.161 There are limitations to the relevance of the intention of the parties. Status cannot be determined merely by applying an artificial label to a relationship. A person who on the terms of his relationship is clearly an employee cannot suddenly become self-employed merely because he is described as such. Nor can a sham relationship of self-employment be legitimised by the use of a label.

Again the *Massey* case illustrates this where Lord Denning said ([1978] 2 All ER 576 at 579i):

> 'The law, as I see it is this: if the true relationship of the parties is master and servant under a contract of service, the parties cannot alter the truth of that relationship by putting a different label on it.'

5.162 The following year a High Court case (*BSM 1257 Ltd v Secretary of State for Social Services* [1978] ICR 894) also clarified that the contract could be ignored if 'in practice the relationship is other than that stated in the contract'.
This was supported in a Court of Appeal case (*Young and Woods Ltd v West*)[1980] IRLR 201).

5.163 It is therefore clear that false labels and sham contracts do not work and must be avoided. But perhaps HMRC should be more concerned with bogus contracts and labels of self-employment which have been 'forced' onto the worker rather than trying to undermine the *genuine* intentions of parties who are very clear as to what kind of relationship they wish to enter into.

5.164 Bogus labelling of a relationship does not change it, nor should it. However, it is suggested that the intention of the parties is considerably more important than HMRC like to acknowledge, and in finely balanced cases it will become the determining factor. In the context of the IR35 notional or hypothetical contract it is no silver bullet defence to say that just because there was no intention to have a contract of service then by definition there cannot be one. However, when inferring the terms and conditions of the hypothetical contract the original intentions of the parties must be a factor to be taken into account. This approach was supported by Henderson J in the case of *Dragonfly Consulting v HMRC* [2008] STC 3030 ChD. Henderson J pointed out that the intention of the parties cannot prevail over the true legal effect of the agreement between the parties, but recognised that in a borderline case a statement of the parties' intention may be taken into account and may tip the balance one way or another.

Financial risk and chance of profit

5.165 This is not an easy area to pin down because financial risk can incorporate so many different factors.

5.166 From the author's experience, HMRC's view seems to be that financial risk is nothing beyond giving a fixed price for a job. Clearly, if an IT contractor gives a

The major case law decisions and status criteria **5.173**

fixed price for writing some software the job might take much longer than anticipated thus resulting in a poorer overall financial return even though an actual 'loss' would still not have been made. It is very difficult for a person supplying his skill to make a 'loss' as such.

But risk comes in many different guises, including the obligation to correct defective work, no guarantee of work or no compensation for work cancelled at short notice, a limited or non-existent period of notice etc.

5.167 Lord Justice Nolan in the 1993 Court of Appeal case of *Hall v Lorimer* specifically noted ([1994] IRLR 171 at 174) that self-employment is characterised by running the risk of bad debts and a lack of work. Dr Avery Jones said in the *Lime-IT* case that the mere fact of invoicing indicates self-employment. This seems to have been overlooked by HMRC.

5.168 In *Midland Sinfonia Concert Society v Secretary of State for Social Services* [1981] ICR 454, the court stated that the question of risk of profit or loss had to be seen in the context of the nature of the work being undertaken. Here the court held that in the context of musicians who merely turned up and performed (like so many IR35 at-risk personal service businesses) the question of profit and loss was 'not particularly appropriate'.

5.169 In the *O'Kelly* case, the court accepted that ([1983] 3 All ER 456 at 465b) in the context of the provision of semi-skilled labour: 'it is not to be expected that there would be a financial investment or participation in the profits or losses of the business'.

So far as provision of equipment is relevant to 'financial risk' see **5.180** below.

Freedom to offer services

5.170 A person running a business should have the freedom to undertake work and exploit his available skills in the marketplace as he sees fit. He should be able to make business decisions and benefit from the sound management of his business.

5.171 One aspect of this is the freedom to contract elsewhere or undertake other work, perhaps in the evenings and the weekends. Mr Justice Burton went so far as to suggest, in the PCG judicial review case (*R (on the application of the Professional Contractors Group and others) v IRC*, that where this happens the contractor would be 'home and dry'. This seems a little optimistic but the point is still made. Having a number of different income streams, particularly where they are running coterminously can clearly help the general 'business on own account' approach to be demonstrated.

5.172 In the *Global Plant* case one of the reasons the worker was found to be an employee was that there was a contractual condition which specifically *prohibited* the worker from carrying out work for other parties without the consent of Global Plant.

5.173 In *Hall v Lorimer* the Court of Appeal determined that ([1994] IRLR 171 at 174) the taxpayer was self-employed because he exploited 'his abilities in the

5.173 *The major case law decisions and status criteria*

market place ... [and] the more efficient he is at running the business of providing his services, the greater is his prospect of profit'.

5.174 However, if a worker is at the beck and call of a client and has to work for that client when work is available then such a restriction of freedom will be a strong pointer towards a relationship of direct employment. It will also demonstrate at least one half of the ingredients of mutuality of obligations, that is the worker's obligation to accept offered work. It will also indicate an aspect of control.

This was demonstrated in the Hong Kong case of Lee Ting Sang v Chung Chi-Keung [1990] 2 WLR 1173 where the client (employer) had 'first call' on the worker's time. This case came to the UK Privy Council as the ultimate court of appeal for Hong Kong cases. Both the Lee Ting Sang decision and the 1995 Court of Appeal decision *in Lane v Shire Roofing Co (Oxford) Ltd* [1995] IRLR 493were concerned with compensation claims for personal injuries which could only be awarded to employees, not the self-employed. It seems clear from the judgments and the comments subsequently made by legal academics that an element of 'public policy' was very much to the fore when the decisions were handed down and the workers were found to be employees. The facts of the Lane decision certainly suggest the worker was a genuine self-employed sub-contractor.

It should be noted that in both cases the workers *wanted* to be treated as employees so they could obtain financial compensation for personal injuries. It is assumed that in IR35 cases the worker will be denying he is an employee.

Previous HMRC determinations

5.175 In *Barnett v Brabyn (Inspector of Taxes)*[1996] STC 716, HMRC argued the worker was *self-employed* when he worked for his father's partnership. The worker disagreed and claimed he was an employee. The case ended in the High Court and HMRC advanced three main reasons why the worker was self-employed. These were that he had input as to the hours he worked, he had expressed an intention to be self-employed and that HMRC had determined his previous years' tax liabilities on the basis that he was self-employed. This was despite the fact that there was a whole raft of direct employment indicators. These are powerful arguments to put to HMRC in any status dispute, including IR35.

The court accepted the worker was self-employed despite him having many hallmarks of direct employment. The court accepted as 'cogent evidence' the previous determinations on a self-employed basis.

5.176 For over four years this case was not included in HMRC's Schedule E manual. To this day many tax officers are unaware of it. HMRC have tried to play this case down on the basis that they had 'special facts' and that there was an unusual family relationship between the worker and the putative employer (father/son). This may have been the case, but they cannot take away the very forceful arguments in favour of self-employment that HMRC persuaded the court to accept. Such arguments can be used in an IR35 context to help demonstrate that the worker is not a disguised employee of the client. The law report ([1996] STC 716 at page 139) confirms that *HMRC* argued:

'It is quite possible for a person to be in business on his own account when all he supplied was his own services without providing any equipment or having any risk of loss of prospective profit.'

This is a devastating passage to quote back to HMRC or the Commissioners. It rather seems that HMRC can be very keen to embrace many of the themes of case law, but only when it suits them.

Of course, *Barnett v Brabyn* came before IR35 legislation. Just because HMRC have previously accepted the personal service business as an independent contractor does not mean that new legislation (ie IR35), will not move the goal posts, but this decision remains highly relevant in looking at how HMRC tried to prove self-employment and it can certainly be used to good effect in argument.

Minor factors

Provision of equipment

5.177 Practitioners may be surprised to see this listed as only a minor factor but in the context of labour only specialists the 'equipment' criterion is something of a red herring. An IT contractor who writes software is not engaged to provide materials. That is simply not the nature of his work. Just as a bricklayer lays bricks and does not necessarily supply them. A window cleaner cleans windows, he does not supply the windows.

5.178 For many years HMRC have insisted in placing the provision of equipment at or near the top of the list of status determinants. It is suggested that the correct question to be asked is 'what is the worker there to do?' If this is to supply his specialist skills, that is only his labour, then it is not an issue of fundamental importance to ask if he also happens to supply equipment. He is not there to do that.

5.179 This was amply illustrated in the 1993 Court of Appeal decision in *Hall v Lorimer*. Lord Justice Nolan ([1994] IRLR 171 at 174) noted that the taxpayer provided no premises, tools, equipment or workshop. He then went on to deliver a masterpiece of common sense. He said, 'No; he does not. But that is not his business.' HMRC conveniently tend to quote only from the High Court in the *Lorimer* case as has been pointed out many times by Accountax and other commentators such as Anne Redston.

5.180 If expensive equipment *is* provided then that will show a greater financial risk because of the capital outlay, but this cannot be turned around by saying that where equipment is not provided the worker is automatically an employee.

The court will take into account the reasons why the client/employer provided the equipment. In the *BSM* case of 1978 driving instructors who had been treated as employees but who converted to self-employed status still had the vehicle provided to them. Despite a High Court challenge by the DSS, the decision was that the drivers were self-employed and the court held the provision of the vehicles did not indicate employee status as they had been provided for 'good practical reasons'.

5.181 *The major case law decisions and status criteria*

5.181 In the *Midland Sinfonia* case the musicians were accepted as self-employed despite the fact that they were merely 'hiring out their skills as occasion arose'. In that case the musicians did provide their own instruments, but the point is they were not providing consumable materials or large pieces of equipment. One violin would last perhaps a lifetime. The parallel is that the IT contractors do not usually provide large computer systems, just their labour. As an attractive alternative it might be pointed out that the contractor provides his brain—perhaps the most crucial piece of 'equipment' a specialist can provide.

5.182 The provision of equipment is, therefore, something of a red herring where skills are being provided and it seems that there is a hint that HMRC might be finally accepting the force of this argument—see ESM 0540.

5.183 In the later case of *McManus v Griffiths* in 1997 HMRC themselves contended that the worker was self-employed. The worker argued that as she had not supplied the premises or equipment to do the job she was an employee. HMRC refuted this and the court agreed that the worker was self-employed. Mr Justice Lightman ([1997] STC 1089 at 1099) said, 'This position is not affected by the fact that the club provided the premises, equipment and services.' See also **5.175** above.

Employee style benefits

5.184 Cause and effect should not be confused. An employee is entitled to certain benefits because he is an employee in law; a person does not become self-employed simply because he does not receive such benefits.

However, where the parties agree that benefits such as sick pay, holiday pay, partaking in a grievance procedure etc will not apply, such factors will be taken into account as status indicators, albeit minor ones.

This is apparent from the case of *Alpine (Double Glazing) Co Ltd v Secretary of State for Social Services* 1982 (unreported)—a case quoted at ESM 0544. More significantly, similar comments were made by Gibson LJ in *Express and Echo Publications Group v Tanton* decided by the Court of Appeal in 1999 ([1999] IRLR 367 at 370).

Perhaps the very contracting away of such benefits also indicates that the parties do not want to have a relationship of direct employment.

Basis of payment

5.185 Traditionally, HMRC have argued that an hourly or daily rate indicates a relationship of direct employment but this approach is not backed up by the case law or commercial reality.

Many self-employed persons charge by the hour. Why should a computer consultant not do the same? On the other hand, many workers get paid by the 'piece' but are regarded as employees.

5.186 In the ESM (at paragraph 0542) HMRC do accept that the basis of payment may not be conclusive, but this is an approach not often taken by tax officers in the field.

5.187   In the 1983 Court of Appeal case of *O'Kelly v Trust House Forte*, it was clearly stated that the method by which remuneration is calculated is not one of the crucial indicators of status.

5.188   In the slightly earlier 1981 case of *WHPT Housing Association Ltd v Secretary of State for Social Services* it was held that being paid by the hour indicated self-employed status as regular employees were paid a salary irrespective of the actual hours they worked. The taxpayer architect however was only paid for the actual hours he worked.

The *WHPT* case is not mentioned in the ESM.

Recognised custom and practice

5.189   In *O'Kelly v Trust House Forte* one of the factors taken into account was that traditionally similar workers had been treated as self-employed. Indeed, the Court of Appeal ([1983] 3 All ER 456 at 465) acknowledged that disregarding the accepted custom and practice of the industry could have 'widespread damaging repercussions throughout the whole industry'.

This extract could be useful in the context of highly skilled consultants, many of whom have been regarded as self-employed for years (and of course in the context of the construction industry also).

Summary

5.190   The factors discussed above carry some weight but the thrust of any case law-based IR35 or general status argument has to be centred on the *Ready Mixed Concrete* and the trinity 'irreducible minimum' without which a contract of service cannot be established. These are personal service, control and mutuality of obligations.

5.191   The overwhelming majority of workers who wish to preserve self-employment have been successful in the courts. HMRC have not won a traditional tax status case in the courts since 1987 (*Sidey v Phillips (Inspector of Taxes)* [1987] STC 87) and the Contributions Agency since 1983 (*Warner Holidays Ltd v Secretary of State for Social Services* [1983] ICR 440). The case law is on the side of those seeking to establish or preserve self-employment, and this should not be forgotten in an IR35 context, where the worker is hoping to demonstrate that he is not a disguised employee of the client.

Chapter 6
Crucial question 1: who is the client?

6.1 This may seem something of an odd question, but it is one of the most important questions to ask. In a situation where the personal service business contracts directly with a typical end user plc (eg a bank or an oil company), the client of the personal service business will clearly be that plc.

In determining whether there is a disguised employment it is necessary to examine the terms and conditions of the contract signed between the personal service business and the end user.

6.2 But what if there is an agency? In the author's experience most IT and engineering contractors provide their services to an agency rather than directly to an end user. There are many sound commercial reasons for doing so.

6.3 Does the existence of an agency make any difference? In the view of the author, it is the agency itself which may be the client of the personal service business. This is for the following reasons.

Where does the contractual relationship lie?

6.4 Although it is possible to find tripartite contractual arrangements which are entered into by the personal service business, agency and end user, these are very rare. The reality is that in 99% of cases involving an agency, the personal service business enters into only one written contract—and that is with the agency.

6.5 It is possible in law to have a situation where two third parties, A and B, can enter into an agreement whereby C benefits despite not being a party to the A/B agreement (eg certain trusts), but such agreements are rare in normal commercial contracts. As such it is felt that the client of the personal service business is the party with whom it has entered into contractual arrangements (ie the agency).

6.6 Regrettably, this was not explored fully in the judicial review brought by the PCG (*R (on the application of the Professional Contractors Group) v IRC* [2001] EWCA Civ 1945).

Where is the financial relationship?

6.7 Where an agency is involved it is the agency which pays fees to the personal service business. The end user does not pay fees to the personal service business. In normal commercial terms a business is paid by the customer or client to whom it has provided services. The personal service business provides services to the agency and in return receives consideration under its contract with the agency. Normal business and commercial practice would therefore regard the agency as the client of the personal service business.

The agency is not acting as a mere introducer

6.8 Some agencies exist only to make an initial introduction, as between the worker, or his business, and the end user. In these circumstances it is possible, and indeed likely, for the agency to 'fall out' of the commercial chain, as following the initial introduction it has no ongoing role to play. An example of this argument (which failed on the facts) can be seen in the 1985 tax case of *Brady v Hart* [1985] STC 498.

6.9 However, in the typical IR35 at-risk scenario, there is a personal service business, agency and end user and once the initial introduction is made the agency does *not* disappear from the scene. It has an ongoing relationship. It continues to charge fees to the end user for the provision of supplied workers/businesses, it takes its margin and then pays out a fee for services provided by the personal service business. In the 2001 EAT decision in *O'Murphy v Hewlett Packard* [2002] IRLR 4, the tribunal accepted that the agency was acting as principal on its own behalf. HMRC's FAQ also admits of the possibility of this, at Agency FAQ 5 (http://www.hmrc.gov.uk/ir35/agency.htm).

For these reasons it is felt that commercial common sense and the reality of the situation is that, where the personal service business contracts with an agency, it is the agency which may be the client of the personal service business and the end user, one removed up the 'chain' is not the client.

The end user will be the client of the agency, but that is another matter and not one relevant to the personal service business.

Commercial contracts with many parties

6.10 To suggest that the agency's client is in fact also the personal service business' client leads to potentially ridiculous situations. It is not unknown for a small agency to contract with a larger agency which in turn may contract with a company which contracts with a subsidiary of a plc group. Are HMRC now suggesting that the personal service business' client is a remote party, five times removed up the commercial chain?

In the author's opinion the Tax Tribunal would find such a proposition preposterous and far removed from the reality of the situation.

In the High Court case of *Synaptek Ltd v Young* [2003] EWHC 645, Synaptek Ltd, Mr Stutchbury's personal service business, contracted with an agency, the agency in turn contracted with EDS and EDS contracted to the Benefits Agency, the 'end user'. Both before the Commissioners appeal and during it HMRC asked whether Mr Stutchbury was a disguised employee of EDS, not the Benefits Agency. Why is not at all clear.

If HMRC maintain the 'end user' is the client why did they not treat the Benefits

6.10 *Crucial question 1: who is the client?*

Agency as the client? There are two likely alternatives. The first is that HMRC were concerned that if the Benefits Agency became the 'deemed' employer this might encourage contractors to take out employment law claims against it. Politically this could be damaging. Second, HMRC have suggested that they will stop going up the chain of parties once it becomes clear that a person is no longer being supplied, but where anonymised services are being supplied. As the EDS/Benefits Agency did not mention Mr Stutchbury, HMRC 'stopped' at EDS as he had been named in the agency/EDS contract. A more worrying interpretation is that HMRC pick the 'client' on the basis of no real logic at all.

In *Tilbury Consulting Ltd v Gittins (HMIT)* [2004] SSCD 72 (SpC 390), an IR35 appeal heard at the Special Commissioners in 2003, the agency Compuware was deemed to be acting as principal, not agent. HMRC had identified Ford, who appeared to be the end user, as the deemed employer, but as Ford had outsourced much of its requirements to Compuware they could never have been the deemed employer. That HMRC could make such a basic error after a two-year enquiry is somewhat worrying. The taxpayer won the appeal. A detailed article on this case, 'Tom, Dick or Roger' by Theresa Naylor of Accountax, appeared in *Taxation* (Vol 152, Issue 3935, 27 November 2003).

Unfortunately, all IR35 cases to have been heard so far have assumed that the 'client' is the end user. However, both *Synaptek* and *Tilbury* show that this is not always the case.

ITEPA 2003, Pt 2, Ch 8

6.11 ITEPA 2003, s 49(1)(*a*) (and SI 2000/727 reg 6(1)(*a*)) makes it clear that, for IR35 to apply, services have to be provided 'for another person (the client)'. Obviously 'another person' has a wide definition and would include a body corporate, partnership or unincorporated body. It seems quite clear that the agency is 'another person'.

6.12 Could it be argued, playing devil's advocate, that the personal service business could be supplying services to two clients, that is the agency *and* the end user, at the same time? This is simply not possible. There is either a contract with the agency or there is a contract with the end user.

There cannot be both at the same time in respect of the same work. In any event how can a worker have two so-called hypothetical contracts in respect of one piece of work?

6.13 The legislation requires the existing contractual terms to be recognised (ITEPA 2003, s 49(1)(*c*) and (4)) so the only hypothetical feature is that the worker is deemed to stand in the shoes of the personal service business.

HMRC's view

6.14 In HMRC's currently published view (ESM 3050), it is necessary to establish the nature of the worker's services and the identity of the person for whom those services are provided, before applying the test in ITEPA 2003, s 49(1)(*c*). HMRC's guidance cites the case *Future Online Ltd v Foulds* [2005] STC 198, an IR35 case, as authority for this approach. In that case the appellant, an IT specialist, argued that the client was an agency, rather than the end user. The court dismissed the taxpayer's appeal, and held the end user required the services of the IT specialist for the purpose of its business (ie supplying computer systems), not the agency. Whilst ESM 3050 does not go as far as to state that HMRC will consider the client to be the end user in every case, it does suggest that HMRC will do so if there is sufficient nexus between the worker's services and the activities of the end user.

Summary

6.15 Where the contractual and financial relationship is with an agency, it is submitted that the agency may be the client of the personal service business. ITEPA 2003 allows this, and commercial and common sense require it. If HMRC have any legislative, case law, commercial or logical authority to assert that the agency is not the client of the personal service business in all cases, perhaps it should publish it. Although the author acknowledges there are other opinions on this specific issue, it would seem beneficial to have them argued comprehensively in court where HMRC's somewhat assumptive view of the end user (however far removed) as client can be challenged. HMRC's lack of consistency on treating the non end user as client in a four-party chain should also be explored.

Chapter 7

Crucial question 2: what contractual arrangements are needed to defeat IR35?

7.1 Ensuring that IR35 does not apply is not a mere paper-signing exercise. It cannot be emphasised strongly enough that entering into a sham contract for services will never defeat IR35. It may lead to accusations of dishonesty and will be exposed in any robust cross-examination from a tax inspector should the case go to the Tax Tribunal on appeal.

7.2 Once the law is properly understood it is then a matter of entering into a genuine commercial business-to-business arrangement, whereby the contractual terms and conditions take into account the case law precedents, with a view to ensuring one is not a disguised employee.

7.3 In some ways this might be considered by some to be a cynical exercise. But so might the IR35 legislation itself. Practitioners should be aware that in the judicial review brought by the Professional Contractors Group (*R (on the application of the Professional Contractors Group) v IRC*) in the High Court, Mr Justice Burton himself suggested ([2001] STC 629 at 651) that it would be wise for the parties to get together and agree terms and conditions which would take them outside IR35. However, any clauses drafted should be genuine, workable and reasonable. Extreme clauses may give the impression that the contract is an exercise in presentation rather than the true terms of the agreement.

7.4 Parties to a contract are free to enter into whatever terms and conditions they wish and it is not open to HMRC or any other government department to dictate what these terms and conditions should be. If the contractual terms and conditions entered into represent the true agreement between the parties then the motivation behind the agreement is not relevant.

If, however, the agreement is a sham and nothing more than a paper-signing exercise then it will be exposed, and will deserve to be exposed, and as such be rendered ineffective.

HMRC's guidance on contracts indicates that they will take into account all contracts in any chain between the worker and client (ESM 3325), and that account must be taken of all the terms on which the services are provided, whether forming part of the written contract or not (ESM 3330). However, the next chapter considers the validity of this approach.

Crucial question 2: what contractual arrangements are needed to defeat IR35? **7.9**

Mindsets and modus operandi

7.5 Many IR35 personal service businesses genuinely agreeing and entering into terms and conditions which help ensure that IR35 does not apply may require a significant change in both the mindset and modus operandi of the contractor. Despite the massive publicity surrounding IR35 and the disastrous fiscal consequences it brings to the contractor, some personal service businesses tend to operate not so much as disguised employees, but actual out-and-out employees.

7.6 In simple terms, in order to ensure that IR35 does not apply, the personal service business and its directors have to stop acting and thinking and contracting as an IR35-caught business and start acting, thinking and contracting as an IR35-exempt business. If this requires a change of attitude and a change of contractual terms and conditions then so be it.

7.7 An example of contractor apathy is the personal service business director who cannot be bothered to raise an invoice on his business stationery because he has already completed a time sheet and believes a formal invoice is unnecessary. He may have a point, but so long as the tax tribunals and courts take into account whether or not the worker has a proper business organisation he would be unwise to ignore such formalities. In brief, contractors must help themselves.

The bigger picture

7.8 Factors outside the signed contract can have a significant influence in determining whether a worker is caught under IR35. An individual contract may not be particularly well worded in respect of IR35, but it might be clear from the 'big picture' that the personal service business is indeed a genuine business and not subject to the intermediaries' legislation. Case law recognises that where there is an existing business it will usually be easier to establish ongoing self-employment as part of that business (see **5.145**). In the example of 'Charlotte' (http://www.hmrc.gov.uk/manuals/esmmanual/ESM3313.htm), HMRC also recognise that other factors beyond the terms of the contract in isolation, can have a significant impact on an IR35 appraisal.

This might be demonstrated by the fact that the personal service business concerned might employ several fee-earning individuals, operate from established business premises with a multitude of different clients, have made substantial investment in equipment and training and perhaps have a website advertising its services. Few if any of these factors will be apparent from examining a contract in isolation.

It should be understood that an absence of these factors will not mean that the personal service business is caught by IR35, but their presence will undoubtedly help establish IR35 exempt status.

The way forward and looking beyond the contract

7.9 Ensuring that IR35 does not apply should, therefore, be seen as a combination strategy. The contractual terms of the genuine working relationship should

7.9 *Crucial question 2: what contractual arrangements are needed to defeat IR35?*

wherever possible reflect criteria which the courts have accepted as giving rise to self-employment and the contractor should operate in a true business-to-business manner, with a demonstrable commercial approach. HMRC have previously given the example of Charlotte whose overall circumstances take her outside of IR35 (see Appendix 4) and while this is only general guidance it helps establish the principle that HMRC will consider outside factors beyond the strict terms of the contract. Arguably, this is all part of the 'business on own account' approach.

7.10 However, HMRC may wish to be satisfied that the written terms and conditions of the contract truly reflect the reality of the working relationship between the parties. The extent to which they are entitled to do this is somewhat limited.

7.11 In *Narich Pty v Commissioner of Payroll Tax* [1984] ICR 286, the court made it quite clear ([1984] ICR 286 at 291A) that, with one exception (described below), it is not possible to look beyond the strict terms of the contract as to the manner in which the parties subsequently acted:

> 'The first principle, is that, subject to one exception, where there is a written contract between the parties whose relationship is in issue, a court is confined, in determining the nature of that relationship, to a consideration of the terms, express or implied, of that contract in the light of the circumstances surrounding the making of it; and it is not entitled to consider also the manner in which the parties subsequently acted in pursuance of such contract.'

> 'The one exception to that rule is that, where the subsequent conduct of the parties can be shown to have amounted to an agreed addition to, or modification of the original written contract, such conduct may be considered and taken into account by the court'.

This begs a rather difficult question. How can HMRC satisfy their curiosity as to whether the parties have subsequently varied the original contract if they are precluded from examining the reality beyond the strict contract terms? If the parties to the contract state categorically that the terms remain as per the written contract how can HMRC force them to discuss the issue? This question is not easily answered, but the courts have made their position quite clear and even HMRC accept that contract terms should be taken at face value, unless there are already good reasons to suggest that they do not represent the reality of the situation. In practice, HMRC are increasingly treating the personal service business/agency contract merely as the starting point in an IR35 investigation. They will be happy to decide IR35 applies on the basis of the lower contract, but if challenged will seek to interview the end user.

Even if a contract term is not enforced this may be because the parties have agreed temporarily to waive that clause. This might seem thin, but this is precisely what Peter Gibson LJ suggested in the *Express Echo* case ([1999] ICR 693). In *Stevedoring and Haulage Services v Fuller* [2001] EWCA Civ 651, it was stated that a specific contractual clause cannot be negatived by what happens in practice. It seems that, in non-IR35 cases at least, the contract is king so long as it is genuine. More should be made of this when arguing IR35.

It has been noted by the author, when defending non-IR35 status, that HMRC are keen to accept at face value, and quote back to the contractor, clauses in a contract

Crucial question 2: what contractual arrangements are needed to defeat IR35? **7.14**

which suggest the worker is caught. In these circumstances they tend not to look beyond the words.

In *Smith (IR) v Hewitson* ((2001), EAT/489/01), a national minimum wage case heard in the EAT in late 2001, it was held that the issue to focus on was the contractual obligations between the parties and not what actually occurred or how the company treated other workers. It is of course HMRC who police the national minimum wage laws.

The contracting market weakened noticeably in 2001/02 and as such the contractor held a poorer negotiating position. Despite the current economic climate, the highly publicised IR35 decisions, the recent legislation against composite companies and the notable decline in the requirement for permanent staff have together placed contractors in a much stronger position to negotiate contractual terms, and agencies are more flexible in what terms and conditions they will agree.

It should be noted that the courts are reluctant to imply further terms into a contract if such implied terms directly contradict express terms that already exist. This is discussed in *Cheshire, Fifoot and Furmston's Law of Contract* (15 edn, 2006) Butterworths.

HMRC may try to imply terms that are contrary to the actual written agreement, but the courts could well reject this approach 'where the parties have entered into a carefully drafted written contract containing detailed terms agreed between them' (*Shell UK Ltd v Lostock Garages Ltd* [1976] 1 WLR 1187 at 1200).

Also, in *Lynch v Thorne* [1956] 1 WLR 303, the Court of Appeal said it could not imply a term which would 'create an inconsistency with the express language of the bargain'. As such any HMRC attempt to ignore an express written term in favour of an HMRC-instigated implied term should be resisted.

Important contract terms and conditions

7.12 Chapter 5 detailed the more important case law precedents. Bearing these in mind it then becomes necessary to incorporate as many business-to-business clauses into the contract as possible and to ensure that they are implemented in practice.

7.13 This section concentrates on the trinity of personal service, lack of mutuality of obligations and lack of control. Suggested clauses are given and it is a matter of negotiation between the parties as to whether they are agreed in practice. However, it must be emphasised that such clauses should reflect the reality of the relationship in order to be effective.

Personal service, mutuality and control

Services not personnel

7.14 As a fundamental strategy, to help ensure that IR35 does not apply, the following cannot be stressed enough. IR35 is aimed at personal service not the provision of services. Wherever possible the contract should be written in terms which show that a person is *not* being supplied (whether named or not), but that a service is being provided.

7.14 *Crucial question 2: what contractual arrangements are needed to defeat IR35?*

This should be clearly spelt out in the contract, any schedules and other correspondence relating to the contract. A genuine business-to-business relationship to supply services will also have the effect of defeating an 'agency' challenge by HMRC (see Chapter 9).

Personal service and substitution

7.15 A recommended substitution clause would read as follows:

> 'The company may use a suitably qualified and experienced substitute or delegate to perform the contract works. The company will notify the client where it intends to substitute or delegate all or part of the contract works. Where a substitute or delegate is used by the company, the client shall have no contractual, financial or legal relationship with the substitute or delegate. The company is solely responsible for arranging payments to the substitute or delegate and the substitute or delegate is answerable only to the company.'

7.16 A generally acceptable but perhaps less robust substitution clause might read:

> 'The company may send a substitute but such substitute may be rejected by the client if the client is reasonably satisfied that the substitute does not possess the necessary skills and experience required.'

7.17 These two clauses are both external substitution clauses and a further internal clause is recommended as follows:

> 'The company may use suitably qualified directors, employees or self-employed persons in order to perform the contract works at its own discretion and may also utilise the services of employees or self-employed persons in an administration capacity. Such persons will be answerable solely to the company and the client shall have no contractual, financial or legal relationship with the hired assistance. Payments to the above persons will be the sole responsibility of the company.'

7.18 A recommended sub-contract clause would read as follows:

> 'The whole or part of this contract for services may be assigned or sub-contracted to any third party provided that the sub-contractor is suitably experienced and qualified. The company will notify the client if any part of the contract works is sub-contracted or assigned. If this occurs the third party will be bound by terms identical to those in this contract.'

7.19 References to the company are of course references to the personal service business.

7.20 Finally, it is important to show that the contract represents a business-to-business relationship to undertake services and not provide workers. Simply

Crucial question 2: what contractual arrangements are needed to defeat IR35? **7.24**

providing workers plays into the first leg of the intermediaries' legislation in that there is a requirement for personal service and it triggers a potential agency problem (see Chapter 9). Contracts should, therefore, avoid the naming of consultants to be provided and concentrate instead on the nature of the services to be provided. It is just arguable that, if the consultants are not named, there is no need for a specific substitution clause on the basis that substitution is somehow implied. However, a clear written right should always be spelt out to avoid any confusion, and to provide good contractual evidence which may usefully be adduced at an appeal.

7.21 A business-to-business relationship for the provision of services should clearly be headed 'Contract for Services' and headings such as 'Contract for the Supply of Consultants' are unhelpful. Indeed, the author has seen contracts which have been held out as being 'IR35 proof' headed 'Contract of Employment for the Supply of Temporary Workers'. Although a reasonable tax tribunal or court may be reluctant to read too much into the headings in a contract such phraseology does not help get the IR35 defence off to a good start! Phrases in a genuine contract for services which are worth avoiding include 'authorised personnel' and 'named consultant'. It is not fatal, however, to name an individual in the personal service business who is to be treated as a point of contact.

Mutuality of obligations

7.22 A suitable clause showing there is a lack of mutual obligations would read as follows:

> 'The client is not obliged to offer work or contracts to the company nor is the company obliged to accept such contracts if offered. The company is not obliged to make its services available at any time. Specifically both parties declare that they do not wish to create or imply any mutuality of obligations whatsoever either during the course of this contract for services or during any period when contract works are not available.'

Generally, the two parties to a commercial contract have no difficulty in confirming in writing that ongoing work does not need to be offered nor that the personal service business needs to make its services available. Unfortunately, many contracts are at risk from IR35 because they remain silent on fundamental issues, such as a lack of mutuality. This is a great pity because, in practice, agreeing such a clause seldom causes a problem.

7.23 When such fundamental issues are not addressed in writing the possibility of awkward cross-examination with inconsistent answers before the Tax Tribunal is a real possibility. As such, contractors should help themselves by ensuring a clear lack of mutuality clause is in the contract terms and conditions.

7.24 Clauses which imply that there is mutuality of obligations are very unhelpful and are not that uncommon. Contracts which have no designated end date and are said to 'continue until either party gives notice to terminate' imply actual mutual obligations and if the contract rolls on from one year to the next there may come a

7.24 *Crucial question 2: what contractual arrangements are needed to defeat IR35?*

time when a tribunal or court may say that the course of dealings between the parties has hardened into mutual obligations. Clauses which say 'work will be allocated' to the contractor also imply mutuality, as in *Synaptek Ltd v Young (HMIT)* [2003] EWHC 645 (see Chapter 11). This does not of itself mean the personal service business falls foul of IR35, but a golden opportunity to demonstrate that IR35 does not apply has been lost.

Control

7.25 Which party has the right of control is determined by the express terms of the contract, and if the contract terms 'deal fully with the matter one may look no further' (MacKenna J in *Ready Mixed Concrete (South East) Ltd v Minister of Pensions and National Insurance* [1968] 1 All ER 433 at 440E). This passage can usefully be quoted to HMRC when they try to ignore a contract. It is therefore important to ensure the 'control' aspect is committed to writing. The most important aspect of control is the 'how' and the following clause is suggested:

'The client shall not control, or have any right of control as to how the company is to perform the contract works.'

7.26 Less fundamental aspects of control are dealt with in the following clauses:

'How the company fulfils its contractual obligations is a matter for the company.'

'The company will use its own initiative in how the contract works are to be completed and will have flexibility as to the hours worked on location but will nonetheless assist the client by making all reasonable attempts to work within an overall agreed deadline, will observe health and safety regulations and will comply with all reasonable operational requirements relating to working hours and security.'

'Start and finish times are at the discretion of the company within an overall programme of contract works which will be verbally agreed from time to time and the company, its directors, employees or consultants are not obliged to seek permission from the client to leave a location at any time.'

7.27 Quite understandably, clients will want to ensure that the services provided meet the required and expected standards. The addition of a clause which makes it expressly clear that 'the company agrees to undertake services in a professional manner at all times and undertakes the services in the capacity of a specialist' may add some comfort for the client.
Such a clause may be strengthened by the additional words:

'The company undertakes that it will devote such time attention skills and ability as the contract works require.'

Crucial question 2: what contractual arrangements are needed to defeat IR35? **7.32**

Assurances as to correcting defective work might make a lack of control clause more acceptable to the client.

The single most important aspect is to show that there is a clause which clearly gives the contractor freedom to undertake services in the manner which he feels is appropriate, so as to show that he is not controlled by the client as to 'how' the contract works are executed.

Summary

7.28 In light of the *Ready Mixed Concrete* case (see Chapter 5) in 1968 and subsequent senior court decisions, the three issues of personal service and substitution, a lack of mutuality of obligations and a lack of control, must be regarded as the essential trinity and prerequisites of a contract of employment. These are the three issues that must be addressed when drafting contracts with IR35 in mind.

7.29 It must be remembered at all times that if the contract does not deal with substitution, mutuality and control this does not mean that the worker is a disguised employee. What it means is that the worker has not automatically escaped IR35 from the outset and that he will have to rely on other factors to establish a genuine business-to-business relationship, which may prove difficult.

Other important contract terms and conditions

7.30 Having considered the trinity of personal service, mutuality and control the remaining important contractual factors need to be considered.

Not all will carry the same weight in every case, but there are clear legal precedents to suggest that they indicate a self-employed relationship. As such they should be spelt out clearly in a written contract for services, and of course implemented.

They fall into two categories: terms which are of primary importance in establishing self-employment and those of secondary importance:

1 Primary importance: financial risk, business organisation, freedom and flexibility and intention.
2 Secondary importance: lack of employee benefits, provision of equipment and basis of payment.

Financial risk

7.31 Traditionally, HMRC take a very narrow view of financial risk and, in the author's opinion, this does not reflect the reality of the commercial world. HMRC see financial risk as giving a fixed price for a job. Clearly, if a contract gives a fixed price for a job and there is the chance that the worker overruns, then he is potentially suffering risk, but the concept goes considerably further than this.

7.32 The following suggested clauses are all indicative of financial risk to a greater or lesser extent.

7.33 *Crucial question 2: what contractual arrangements are needed to defeat IR35?*

7.33 'The company will negotiate the price for the contract works and is obliged to honour any such agreed price.'

In other words, once a price has been agreed, be it for the whole project or a daily or hourly rate, then that price remains fixed.

Of course, the price is often contained in the contract itself (usually in a Schedule), but here we are making it clear that once a price is agreed, the personal service business cannot go back and ask for more. This merely serves to underline that a commercial business decision is being made by the PSB which has to be honoured and which carries an element of risk.

7.34

'Defective work by the company its directors employees consultants substitutes or hired assistants will be corrected by the company at its own cost or in its own time.'

In certain areas this can represent significant financial risk.

HMRC often (erroneously) argue that the risk of correcting defective work is equally indicative of employed status, but this is simply not supported by law. If an employee carries out defective work it is corrected within the normal working day without any form of deduction being made. Tax officers often forget that the doctrine of vicarious liability means that the employer is generally accountable and responsible for any acts of negligence of his employee—including defective work.

The author has seen defective work clauses imposing massive potential financial risk on the contractor and this important factor should not be underplayed.

7.35

'The company will not be entitled to receive payment for cancelled contract works.'

Many IT and engineering contractors who work for an agency have to sign a clause stating that if the agency loses the contract with the end user then the agency will have no financial liability for cancelling the contract with the personal service business. Quite clearly this represents risk.

However, if a bona fide employer fails to win a contract with a client it will still be obliged to offer continuing work or wages to its employees, subject to the normal redundancy rules. Self-employed contractors working via the personal service business do not enjoy such safeguards.

7.36

'The company accepts it has legal risk in respect of public liability and professional indemnity and will therefore pay the costs of such insurance premiums and maintain adequate cover at all times. During the term of this contract for services and for the following six years the company will maintain adequate insurance cover in respect of professional indemnity with cover up to at least £1 million.'

Crucial question 2: what contractual arrangements are needed to defeat IR35? **7.42**

Employees do not maintain such insurance because they are not liable. Self-employed people do because they are so liable.

7.37 Other suggested clauses are:

'The client reserves the right to offset any losses sustained as a result of the company's actions, breach or unsatisfactory performance, from the company's fees.'

'The company acknowledges the volatility of the (IT/engineering sector) and accepts that there is the financial risk of bad debts when operating as an independent business on its own account.'

'This contract for services can be immediately terminated by the client for any reason whatever and no notice is required to be given'.

7.38 Contractors will of course want to weigh the benefits of implementing IR35 proof clauses on the one hand with commercial considerations on the other. The final suggested clause is an extreme example of financial risk with which the personal service business may not feel comfortable. It has also been suggested that if a contract can be terminated without notice, that this represents an element of control over the worker. It is suggested that this is not really the case, as control in an employment sense is concerned with interference in how the work is executed not whether a contract can be terminated.

7.39 It is not unknown for personal service businesses to be extremely reluctant to commit to some of the above terms and conditions because they fear it leaves them exposed. It does. But this is part and parcel of being in business, taking risks and demonstrating significant potential financial liabilities.

7.40 It will therefore be a matter of negotiation as to how far the personal service business wants to take on financial risk, but the narrow HMRC view, that financial risk amounts to giving a fixed price for a job, does not come anywhere near a true evaluation of the concept.

7.41 A further element of financial risk, which generally cannot be gleaned from the wording of a contract alone, concerns what might be a very extensive investment on the part of the personal service business into training and equipment. HMRC have acknowledged that a significant capital investment in training and equipment incurs an element of financial risk and will be taken into account when reviewing tax status—see ESM 0540.

Business organisation

7.42 Personal service businesses wanting to ensure that IR35 does not apply should already be acting in a commercial business-to-business manner, but several clauses can be agreed which will help underline this. Arguably, these clauses are not particularly significant when taken individually, but when considered together they

7.42 *Crucial question 2: what contractual arrangements are needed to defeat IR35?*

show a mindset indicative of an independent contractor as opposed to an employee of a client.

7.43   The following clauses are suggested:

'The company will prepare VAT invoices for contract works undertaken.'

'The company being in business on its own account will have its own business stationery and business cards and will if requested by the client supply a specimen for the client's records.'

'The company will at all times represent itself as an independent business and will in no circumstances represent itself or hold itself out as a representative, servant or employee of the client. The company hereby acknowledges it is in business on its own account and is not part and parcel of the client's business, or any other business.'

'The company will maintain at its own cost appropriate independent office accommodation, telephone system, mobile telephone, fax facility and e-mail facility.'

This final clause may refer to nothing more sophisticated than using a spare bedroom or a study as an office but it is all additional *evidence* that the personal service business is operating as an independent contractor as opposed to a mere employee.

7.44

'The company may advertise its services and may use a business trading name.'

Again, this is a further indication of a general business modus operandi.

Freedom and flexibility

7.45   The following clauses are suggested.

'The company is free to undertake other contracts for services for other parties at any time, either before, after, or concurrently with this contract for services, providing that the provision of services does not create a conflict of interest or prevent the company from providing services to the client.'

'The client acknowledges and agrees that it does not have first call on the services of the company and cannot require the company to give the client any priority over another client.'

It may be remembered from Chapter 5 that a significant factor indicating direct employment status in the case of *Lee Ting Sang v Chung Chi-Keung* [1990] 2 AC

Crucial question 2: what contractual arrangements are needed to defeat IR35? **7.50**

374 was that the employer had the right to insist that the worker gave him first priority when he had work available for him.

Intention

7.46 Some practitioners may be surprised to see 'intention' in the list of the more important factors in establishing self-employment.

However, as is explained in Chapter 5, the intention of the parties is always something to be taken into account, despite HMRC's best efforts over the years. Indeed, in the 1999 Court of Appeal *Express and Echo* case Lord Justice Peter Gibson ([1999] IRLR 367 at 370) went so far as to say that when determining status one 'starts with the common intention of the parties'.

Intention as a factor to be taken into account has always been downplayed by HMRC, but their approach was held to be incorrect by the High Court in the recent case of *Dragonfly Consulting Ltd v Revenue and Customs Commissioners* [2008] EWHC 2113.

As such, although many personal service businesses and the clients may feel it does not need to be said, it is the Accountax view that a clear intention clause must be helpful in establishing genuine independence. The following clause is recommended:

> 'Both parties agree and intend that this legal relationship is one of giving and accepting independent specialist services and specifically is not a relationship of master and servant or employer and employee.'

Summary

7.47 Before looking at factors of secondary importance it is worth reminding practitioners that many contracts potentially fall foul of IR35, not because they are badly written but because they are silent on the fundamental aspects of establishing self-employment (and, therefore, failing to demonstrate that the worker is not a disguised employee of the client). Silent contracts do not amount to good evidence.

7.48 It will not always be possible for the two parties to a contract to agree to all of the above clauses but every effort should be made to agree to as many as possible.

In committing to the suggested clauses, again strictly on the basis that they represent the true agreement between the parties, this will make the personal service business extremely difficult to attack.

7.49 IR35 is no different from any other aspect of HMRC compliance work. There has to be a realistic yield for the money and man hours spent in collecting it and HMRC without question pick on the weaker cases as part of this process.

Contractors should, therefore, make themselves difficult to attack by ensuring that the contractual terms and conditions agreed reflect a genuine business-to-business relationship.

7.50 If, however, the contract as written does not reflect the true arrangements between the parties then one of the parties to the 'agreement' may ask the tribunal

7.50 *Crucial question 2: what contractual arrangements are needed to defeat IR35?*

to establish the true relationship. This was seen in *Maurice v Betterware UK Ltd* ([2001] ICR 14) in the Employment Appeals Tribunal in 2000. Here the workers sought to overturn a signed self-employed contract on the basis that it did not reflect the true arrangements. Mr Justice Keene accepted the argument, and the case was remitted to the Employment Tribunal, so the full and correct position could be established. It should be noted that in this case the workers themselves wanted to establish a relationship of direct employment which, one assumes, the personal service business will not want to do.

Factors of secondary importance

Lack of employee benefits

7.51 HMRC have traditionally taken the view that a lack of employee benefits is not a factor to be taken into account in determining status. They hold the view that employee benefits flow from employment status, not the reverse.

There is certainly a logic to this, but the line of reasoning is not entirely supported by the courts and it is understood that HMRC will now take into account a lack of employee-style benefits as being indicative of a genuine business-to-business self-employed relationship.

7.52 Chapter 5 analyses the relevant case law on employee benefits and bearing this analysis in mind the following clauses are suggested.

> 'The company, its directors, employees and consultants will not be entitled to receive holiday pay or bank holiday pay or special absence paid in any circumstances.'

> 'The company, its directors, employees and consultants will not be entitled to receive sick pay in any circumstances from the client. The company will bear the cost of any health insurance which it may arrange at its own discretion.'

> 'The company, its directors, employees and consultants are not entitled to partake in any grievance procedure offered to employees of the client and as an independent business are not entitled to any employment law rights.'

> 'The company, its directors, employees and consultants are not entitled to receive any company benefits or partake in any pension scheme run by the client. Pension provision may be made by the company at its own discretion for its directors or employees.'

The four clauses above prohibit the company itself from receiving various benefits. Clearly a company cannot receive sick pay etc, but it is worth making this expressly clear in the contract as it can only help strengthen the case that IR35 does not apply. While not being factors of major significance, it is generally easy to agree such terms and conditions and for the sake of clarity they should be committed to writing.

Provision of equipment

7.53 The reality of most personal service business contracts is that the majority of equipment will be supplied by the end user. Contractors tend not to carry mainframes around in their rucksacks! On the basis that the personal service company is contracted to provide skills rather than equipment, as more fully explained in Chapter 5, it is not considered that provision of equipment is particularly relevant. As stated above, if a personal service business does make a significant investment in equipment then that can only help to indicate a financial outlay, which in turn indicates a potential financial risk, but it is certainly not essential to defeating IR35.

7.54 In terms of contractual conditions, it is suggested that where the personal service business does supply computer equipment it warrants that it is technically capable of fulfilling its function and is virus free.

Basis of payment

7.55 It is suggested that attached to the contract for services there is a Schedule which clarifies the basis of payment and invoicing frequency. This is mentioned here only for the purposes of administrative clarity. As explained in Chapter 5, the basis of payment itself is not one of the more important factors in determining status and this is a fact accepted by HMRC.

General considerations

7.56 Practitioners are urged to note that the suggested clauses are not meant to be an all encompassing blueprint contract for services. They represent example clauses relating to the more important aspects of a genuine contract for services.

7.57 The final version of a contract for services will contain many other clauses relating to the commencement and termination date, the actual services to be provided, aspects of intellectual property rights and confidentiality and specific technical legal clauses relating to the construction of the contract.

Practitioners should, therefore, seek further professional assistance in drawing up self-employed contracts, either from a suitably experienced lawyer or specialist tax advisers.

7.58 If a contract is signed but not understood, or not even read, there is good contract law precedent in the 1934 case of *L'Estrange v F Graucob Ltd* ([1934] 2 KB 394) to say that the contract still stands. However, it would be better all round if contracts are carefully considered before they are entered into.

7.59 It is recommended that fresh contracts are entered into as often as is practicably possible. This is not the same as merely adding a further Schedule to an old contract. Such 'rolling' contracts are generally to be avoided as they imply ongoing commitments. It is recommended that quarterly or six-monthly contracts would show that the parties are re-committing themselves to the terms the contract

7.59 *Crucial question 2: what contractual arrangements are needed to defeat IR35?*

contains, and if some of the terms are re-negotiated from one contract to the next, then so much the better.

Summary

7.60 The contractual terms and conditions of the working relationship between the two parties are the single most important piece of evidence to be adduced in an IR35 defence.

Care should be taken in ensuring that not only are the contract terms understood but that they represent the reality of the relationship. Shams do not work.

The suggested clauses detailed above do not purport to take into account other highly important considerations in commercial contracts. The clauses have been designed as a strategy to ensure that the worker is not a disguised employee of the client. As such, personal service businesses may want to take advice on other contractual matters, which in themselves have no real relevance to the IR35 position.

7.61 Non-contractual matters which support a genuine business approach, such as advertising, maintaining an office or website, etc, should all be documented and evidence retained. This 'paper trail' is quite rightly advocated by the PCG as one of those things a contractor can do to help himself.

7.62 Hopelessly unworkable and totally impractical clauses of an extreme nature should be avoided. They add nothing and weaken otherwise credible and realistic contracts.

Chapter 8
Crucial question 3: is the agency/end-user contract relevant?

8.1 In the majority of contracting relationships the personal service business does not contract with an end user but with an agency. Where this is the case, HMRC have, from day one, taken the view that in the common commercial chain of personal service business/agency/end-user the contract, as between the agency and end user, is as relevant as the contract between the personal service business and the agency. They state (at Frequently asked Questions, Contract 2, on their website at http://www.hmrc.gov.uk/ir35/faq_qanda/contract_q2.htm) that:

> 'HMRC will take account of all relevant contracts in order to discover whether the relationship between a worker and a client would have been one of employment, if there had been no intermediary. This would include any contracts between the client and an agency, and between the agency and the worker's intermediary.'

But is this approach valid? Some commentators suggest that it is, but in the author's view it is questionable, and it might be resisted. The reasons are fully explored below but, as a preliminary discussion, it is worth bearing in mind the following recent and real-life application of HMRC's official line on taking into account the agency/end-user contract.

Case study
Accountax represented an IR35 at-risk contractor who was subject to an IR35 challenge from a nominated status inspector. Her personal service business contracted with an agency and a bank was the end user. HMRC requested sight of the agency/bank contract as this was in its view relevant to the 'circumstances' of the 'arrangements' as per ITEPA 2003, s 49(1)(*c*) and (4).

HMRC were not given access to this contract, not least because the personal service business did not itself have access to it. In similar situations HMRC have been known to decline to give an IR35 opinion leaving the personal service business in no-man's land.

However, in a telephone conversation with the author, the status inspector accepted that while she would ideally *like* to see the agency/end-user contract she was in fact able to offer an IR35 opinion without it. For the technical and logical reasons explored below this makes sense, but what is important is that HMRC confirmed this approach in writing.

8.1 *Crucial question 3: is the agency/end-user contract relevant?*

A letter is on file from the status inspector saying that an IR35 opinion can be given on the basis of the personal service business/agency contract alone. There is nothing to suggest this was a rogue decision as the inspector had taken head office advice. This decision arguably demonstrates that HMRC really know that the personal service business/agency contract is the most important one.

Practitioners should note that the letter was not written with caveats about taking into account the agency/end-user contract should it ever be produced. A clear opinion was given by the nominated status inspector. Quite simply the agency/end-user contract was not needed. Unfortunately, in recent times HMRC have universally needed to see the so-called upper contract as well as the contract between the intermediary and agency.

8.2 It is accepted that the approach of this status inspector may be uncommon but, with head office eyes watching how IR35 disputes are unfolding at area level very carefully, it perhaps indicates that HMRC do not always follow their own official line.

8.3 This was a case which the personal service business was prepared to defend on appeal at the Commissioners (as was)—perhaps HMRC preferred to settle the matter to avoid a possible early defeat and the publicity which would ensue. The lesson to be learnt is not to give in at the first hurdle when HMRC ask for the agency/end-user contract.

8.4 HMRC are also on record as saying that, where it seems from the personal service business/agency contract that the worker is caught by IR35, it is not necessary for them to examine the agency/end-user contract. But where it appears that the worker escapes IR35 based on the personal service business/agency contract then it will be necessary to examine the agency/end-user contract. This apparent 'heads HMRC wins, tails the contractor loses' approach should be seen for what it is—an exercise in double standards. HMRC should have a consistent approach; they should maintain that either both contracts are relevant or that only the lower contract is.

In the 2003 High Court case of *Synaptek Ltd v Young* ([2003] EWHC 645 Ch),the chain of parties was: personal service business/agency/EDS/Benefits Agency.

In that case, HMRC did *not* rely on or even adduce the EDS/BA contract. If they maintain all contracts are relevant then surely they should have done so as the BA was the end user. Again, an example of, at best, inconsistency.

Secondly, why did HMRC not argue that the director of Synaptek Ltd was not a disguised employee of the BA?

Why the agency/end-user contract may not be relevant

8.5 It is suggested that there are four main reasons:

- ITEPA 2003, Pt 2, Ch 8;
- the doctrine of privity of contract;
- common sense and equity;
- existing case law.

ITEPA 2003, Pt 2, Ch 8

8.6 The legislation does not seem specifically to deal with the common situation where there is an agency. Despite much commentary on the so-called 'hypothetical' contract alluded to in ITEPA 2003, s 49(1)(c)—incidentally the phrase 'hypothetical contract' does not appear in the legislation and should, therefore, be used with extreme caution—there is a very convincing argument in favour of not taking into account the agency/end-user contract at all when considering whether IR35 applies. HMRC efforts to imply extra terms that have the effect of overriding existing express terms should be resisted (see **8.13**).

8.7 The reasoning is as follows: ITEPA 2003, s 49(4) states that:

> 'the circumstances referred to in (1)(c) include the terms on which the services are provided, having regard to the terms of the contracts forming part of the arrangements under which the services are provided'.

8.8 This needs analysing carefully. It is clear from the wording of ITEPA 2003, s 49(4) that 'the circumstances' in s 49(1)(c) refer to contracts forming part of the 'arrangements'. Crucially, and this is often overlooked, the word 'arrangements' is detailed at s 49(1)(b) as being 'arrangements *involving* a third party (the intermediary)' (author's emphasis). In the author's view, this can only mean the contractual arrangements entered into by the personal service business (the intermediary) and in the personal service business/agency/end-user commercial chain the only contract entered into by the personal service business is the one with the *agency*. The contract between the agency and the end user is not an arrangement involving the personal service business itself, and the worker's day-to-day method of operating at a client's premises, that is, the practical and mundane aspects of the relationship, are equally not arrangements involving the intermediary. They are merely practical day-to-day considerations. The two are quite separate and distinct so it should not be forgotten that s 49(1)(b) refers only to arrangements involving the personal service business.

8.9 If there was a tripartite agreement (which is rare but not impossible), then it might seem reasonable to assume that such an arrangement would have to be considered, as clearly it would be an arrangement involving a third party.

8.10 It could just be conceivable that, where an agency contracts with an end user to supply a specifically named person, it might be considered that this also is an arrangement involving a third party, particularly if the named worker also signs the contract qua worker, not merely qua director of the business. But even this concession to HMRC's approach is unjustified. This is because the arrangement in this scenario would involve the *worker* not the intermediary personal service business and IR35 is aimed, as the Act says, at intermediaries.

8.11 Indeed, s 49(1)(b) specifically points out that the rules are *not* aimed at contracts the worker has directly with a client but only where contracts are entered into under arrangements via a personal service business. In these circumstances HMRC cannot argue that a contract is relevant to the arrangements if it names the

8.11   *Crucial question 3: is the agency/end-user contract relevant?*

individual, when at the same time HMRC acknowledge that the contract is not entered into by the personal service business, and hence is not relevant.

8.12   It is the personal service business' contract with the agency which forms the 'arrangements' included in the 'circumstances'.

8.13   The legislation is not easy to read and it is unhelpful that it is necessary to go back and forth to gain the true meaning of the word 'circumstances'. But, taken a step at a time, it is suggested that the correct conclusion is that it is the contract entered into by the personal service business which is relevant.

8.14   Furthermore, s 49(4) does not mention hypothetical contracts or imaginary contracts. On the contrary, the wording is very much concerned with *the provision of the actual services*. The phrase 'the terms on which the services are provided' seems, if anything, to imply that a set of hypothetical terms is not in issue. It is the terms of the contract under which the services are provided that are relevant and it is submitted that the only hypothetical aspect is that the worker stands in the shoes of the personal service business. It is this substitution of the worker for the personal service business which is the hypothesis (s 49(1)(*c*) refers) and this is discussed below in greater detail.

8.15   In simple terms, unless the personal service business is party to the contract either in its own right or within a tripartite agreement, then any other contracts are not relevant, as they are not arrangements involving the personal service business.

8.16   It is often suggested that the word 'arrangements' has a broader meaning than strict contractual agreements. In determining whether or not matters are 'arrangements' and should, therefore, be taken into account, it is interesting to note that the IR35 rules in Pt 2, Ch 8 do *not* employ a wide definition of that term (whereby arrangements 'include any scheme, agreement, undertaking or understanding, whether or not legally enforceable') that is used in two separate occasions elsewhere in that Act (at ITEPA 2003, Sch 2, para 12(3) (in relation to employee share ownership plans), and Sch 5 para 58 (enterprise management incentives). As such there is no need to give the word 'arrangements' an extended meaning to that laid down in s 49(1)(*b*).

The hypothetical contract—the myth

8.17   As stated earlier, there is no reference in the Act to a hypothetical contract as such. ITEPA 2003, s 49(1)(*c*) asks whether:

> 'the circumstances are such that, *if* the services were provided under a contract directly between the client and the worker, the worker *would be* regarded for income tax purposes as an employee of the client' (author's emphasis).

8.18   It is submitted that on its true construction there is no need to construct a hypothetical contract at all. There is, however, a need to construct a fiction as to *who* the parties to the contract are. In other words, the hypothetical aspect relates to the supposed parties to the contract not the hypothetical terms they are meant to have agreed.

8.19 The fiction created by IR35 is to stand the worker in the shoes of his business to see whether the agreed terms would render him an employee of the client. It is not necessary to construct a new set of terms and conditions.

Regrettably this point was not highlighted in the PCG case (*R (on the application of the Professional Contractors Group) v IRC*) ([2001] EWCA Civ 1945), as that case was concerned with European law, not a detailed interpretation of the Chapter itself.

8.20 It has been readily assumed that an imaginary contract has to be devised. This is not the case. All that is required, by hypothesis, is to ask what the legal relationship would have been if the worker had made the contract himself. There is some logic to this argument, because IR35 is aimed at the artificial insertion of an intermediary (usually a limited company), hence it makes sense to ask what the position would be if the intermediary is simply removed. Clearly this does not require the invention of any new terms and conditions—the worker merely assumes those which his personal business has entered into. However, the comments of the Special Commissioner in the *F S Consulting Ltd v McCaul (Inspector of Taxes)* ([2002] STC (SCD) 138) appeal and *Usetech Ltd v Young (Inspector of Taxes)* ([2004] EWHC 2248 Ch) discussed in Chapter 11 need to be borne in mind.

8.21 This approach of putting the worker in the shoes of his business vis-a-vis the contract with the client will therefore have the benefit of taking into account the actual terms of a real commercial contract as required by s 49(1)(*c*).

8.22 ITEPA 2003, s 49(1)(*c*) refers to the actual circumstances, not hypothetical circumstances, of the services provided. It can be seen from the full text of s 49(1)(*c*) that the so-called hypothetical aspect is the reference '... if the services were provided ... under a contract ... (between) the worker and the client ...'. The Act is envisaging the contract terms remaining constant in respect of the services. It is only the parties to it who are changing. This is the IR35 hypothesis.

8.23 Not only does the Act of itself, on a careful analysis, support this approach, but it has the advantage of avoiding the absurd situation where the contractor, his representative, the inspector, the Tax Tribunal and the courts all have to try to guess the detailed terms and conditions of a non-existent contract not entered into by anyone.

8.24 A further and important justification for putting the worker in the shoes of his personal service business as opposed to inventing hypothetical contract terms can be found in HMRC's own standard contract review letter. This clearly states what the employment relationship would be *if the contract was made directly by the worker*. It does not refer to hypothetical contract terms at all.

The use of 'contracts' (plural) in ITEPA 2003, s 49(4)

8.25 Some commentators and HMRC have suggested that the use of plural 'contracts' in s 49(4) requires a consideration of both the personal service busi-

8.25 *Crucial question 3: is the agency/end-user contract relevant?*

ness/agency contract and the agency/end-user contract. Why else, they argue, is the word used in its plural if the only contract to be considered is the one between the personal service business and the agency? As a preliminary issue those who suggest all the contracts in the chain need to be considered should first address the s 49(1)(*b*) issue at **8.8** above.

8.26 It is submitted that there are two reasons why the use of the plural does not mean that the two different contracts referred to above have both to be considered. First, the whole language of Pt 2, Ch 8 is written in the plural. It refers to 'engagements', 'services', 'arrangements', and 'circumstances' and therefore the use of 'contracts' (plural) merely continues the same style.

Secondly, in deciding whether IR35 applies and to see if the worker is a disguised employee, all the contracts entered into by the personal service business need to be considered. That is, if a personal service business enters into four quarterly contracts during a given year then all four must be considered to see whether IR35 applies to any of them or to the total bigger picture. HMRC have accepted, in the illustration of Charlotte (see Appendix 4), that it is possible to stand back and look at a contractor's whole business history and not just the terms of an individual contract. As such it is quite reasonable, even essential, to look at all contracts entered into by the business to come to the right conclusion. If the schedule merely referred to the 'contract' (singular) this would cause potential difficulties over exactly which contract was being referred to.

8.27 The use of 'contracts' (plural) is quite deliberate and this enables all contracts entered into by the personal service business to be taken into account, both in respect of the deemed salary calculation for the year in question and in order to look at the bigger picture. As further support for this argument, the legislation has been interpreted by Mr Justice Burton as requiring consideration on an individual engagement by engagement basis (*R (on the application of PCG Ltd) v IRC*), which may well mean consideration of several contracts (plural).

8.28 In any event, it should never be forgotten that s 49(1)(*c*), read in conjunction with s 49(1)(*b*) and (4), limits the contracts to be considered strictly to those that the personal service business is a party to.

The doctrine of privity of contract

8.29 The second justification to show that the agency/end-user contract is not relevant is the doctrine of privity. This says that A and B cannot make a contract whereby C is obliged to do something or refrain from doing something. A and B cannot enforce obligations on C by agreeing something between themselves.

8.30 An example of this might be where A agrees with B that C has to buy some goods. Such an agreement has no force because C is not a party or privy to the A/B contract. The idea here is that the end user and agency are represented by A and B and the contractor, C, is not a party to their agreement, and his tax and national insurance obligations should not be influenced by it. It has to be remembered that seldom will the contractor ever get to see the agency/end-user contract and nor will he have any influence over its terms.

8.31 It is fair to say that the doctrine of privity has many exceptions and whole chapters of detailed contract law textbooks are devoted to the topic. But in principle it is straightforward. A person cannot be bound by a contract to which he is not a party.

Not only is the agency/end-user contract not within the scope of s 49(1)(*b*), it is not a contract the personal service business has signed.

In this context the doctrine of privity is not eroded by the Contracts (Rights of Third Parties) Act 1998.

Common sense and equity

8.32 Many of the points raised earlier in this chapter show why the agency/end-user contract, if it is brought into the IR35 equation, can lead to some difficult, if not absurd, situations.

> *Case study*
> In an IR35 defence worked by Accountax, the personal service business was unable to obtain a copy of the agency/end-user contract. The inspector obtained a copy and claimed it contained clauses that showed IR35 applied. The personal service business wished to refute this and asked for copies of the clauses in question. The inspector refused on the grounds that the agency/end-user contract was confidential and he could not release it! The ability to complete form P35 accurately would seem to depend, at least in part, on the contractor's psychic powers. Absurd.

8.33 But there are other factors. Whenever an IR35 challenge is defended, it is wise, even at an early stage, to consider what the likely arguments will be if the case goes to the Tax Tribunal on appeal.

8.34 It is the author's view that the Tax Tribunal will tend to apply a good dose of common sense and try to avoid absurd conclusions where there is an option to do so. This is particularly the case where losing the appeal would result in substantial extra tax or national insurance. In brief it is not impossible to get the benefit of the doubt when a plausible and robust argument is presented.

8.35 Why indeed should a worker have his tax and national insurance liabilities determined by a contract he has never seen or had any influence over and one that he has not signed? It is likely to be perceived as grossly unfair that the worker's own position can be influenced by such a contract. To add insult to injury, IR35 liabilities will be determined after the year has finished and hence any deductions required to be paid over will be retroactive.

8.36 Although it is commonly accepted that there is no equity in tax it is submitted that HMRC would be going too far if it attempts to impose fiscal liabilities on the contractor by primary reference to the agency/end-user contract.

8.37 *Crucial question 3: is the agency/end-user contract relevant?*

8.37 To make matters even worse, what would happen where the personal service business did in fact see the agency/end-user contract and tried but failed to have certain clauses improved, removed or clarified? Perhaps the personal service business formally lodges its concerns and objections with the contract to the agency and end user but to no avail. Not only is the personal service business not a party to the contract but it is now on record as saying that it objects to some of the clauses it contains. Is the Tax Tribunal still going to suggest that the worker is bound by this agency/end-user contract? It is thought not.

8.38 To extend the argument let it be assumed that both personal service business/agency and agency/end-user contracts are to be taken into account. What if the personal service business/agency contract deals with, say, the correction of defective work but the agency/end-user contract is silent on this issue? Which contract carries more weight and why?

8.39 If the personal service business/agency contract says that the worker will have freedom as to how the contract works are carried out, ie there is a lack of control, but the agency/end-user contract says the worker will be under the control of the end user (a commonly encountered clause) then again, which contract is to take precedence and why?

8.40 All these impossible questions can be neatly avoided if the agency/end-user contract is disregarded as it should be. There is the added complication that there may be as many as five or six parties in the chain, not just three. If HMRC maintain all contracts in the chain are relevant should they not be examining all the contracts? They seldom do.

Again if all the contracts in the chain are relevant why does HMRC not ask to see any contract the worker (usually a director) has with his own personal service business? They almost never do.

8.41 HMRC's view seems to be that, where there are inconsistencies, then what happens 'in reality' takes precedence, but this flies in the face of their hypothetical contract approach. In any event, contracts (real or even imaginary) are concerned with rights and obligations and not just with whether those rights and obligations are called upon in practice. For example, the right to send in a substitute may never be put into practice but the right can still exist; the obligation to correct defective work may never be tested in practice because no defective work is actually carried out, but the obligation still remains. So there could now be an absurd situation where HMRC would be asking the Tax Tribunal to appraise contradictory terms, some of which the personal service business has not even signed up to. Presumably, the Tax Tribunal would also be asked by HMRC to second guess what rights and obligations might or might not exist in an imaginary contract, not based purely on reality and practice but also on what could be quite untested and theoretical. Surely this is an impossible task. In other words, the hypothetical terms are so open to interpretation and assumption that no one can prove that their view of the hypothetical terms is any more sound than the next person's.

The fact that HMRC have indicated (in their illustration in Charlotte) that the broader business background will be taken into account is a different point altogether, and has nothing to do with hypothetical terms, but is concerned with real-life instances of being 'in business'.

Existing case law

8.42 There already exists a number of cases where an individual has claimed rights (usually employment law rights) against a third party end user with whom he or his service company did *not* have a contract. The decisions have not all gone the same way.

The main cases can be split between workers who had a limited company and those who did not.

8.43 In the 1978 case of *Winter v Westward TV Ltd* (unreported), the worker tried to claim he was really an employee of the client despite the use of his own limited company to contract himself out. He failed. The Employment Appeals Tribunal described as 'almost impossible' the suggestion that in a three-party chain a hypothetical relationship between the worker and the end user could be implied. They said any such hypothesis would be 'invalid'.

8.44 The Court of Appeal in the *Abbey Life v Tansell* ([2000] IRLR 387) case in 1999 confirmed that the director of a personal service business which contracted via an agency to an end user was within the definition of 'worker' for the purposes of the Disability Discrimination Act 1995, but said it was going too far to imagine that there was a hypothetical contract of employment between the worker and the end user.

8.45 In 2001 the case of *O'Murphy v Hewlett Packard* ([2002] IRLR 4) was heard in the employment tribunal. This case decided that the worker, who was a director of his own service company, was to be treated as an employee of the end user. It was clear on the facts that the company owned by the worker had been inserted as an administrative convenience and that the contract it had entered had few, if any, hallmarks of a genuine contract for services.

However, the decision in this case was appealed and a hearing took place in the Employment Appeal Tribunal in 2002 and the original decision was reversed. This case still serves to remind practitioners that it is certainly not beyond Tribunals to 'ignore' the personal service company and consider a direct relationship between the client and the worker, even without taking into account the IR35 legislation.

8.46 Turning to cases where workers did not have their own personal service businesses, a trend can be seen. In the 1998 case of *Serco v Blair*, (EAT/345/98) the Employment Appeal Tribunal decided that a contract with the end user could not be implied, and this was followed in *Costain Building & Civil Engineering Ltd v Smith* [2000] ICR 215. A contrary decision was reached in *Motorola Ltd v Davidson* [2001] IRLR 4, where the worker was held to be an employee of the end user.

8.47 This latter case is unusual in that the main argument put forward by Motorola was the control criterion, yet it was easily established on the facts that Motorola controlled Davidson. The judgment makes for some interesting reading

8.47 *Crucial question 3: is the agency/end-user contract relevant?*

and it is very difficult to understand why Motorola did not argue the *Costain* and *Serco* principle, that is to say, they simply did not have a contract with the worker. In the *Motorola* case, the tribunal felt restricted to consider the one status test advanced (ie control), but may well have come to a different conclusion had the case been argued more comprehensively.

8.48 An agency case for a non-incorporated worker is *Montgomery v Johnson Underwood* ([2001] EWCA Civ 318) which was heard by the Court of Appeal in 2001. In this case the worker, a receptionist, worked for an agency at an end user's premises. She was there for over two years. Having been dismissed for making private telephone calls in the office she took out an action against both the agency and the end user. As a preliminary point her status had to be determined. The conclusion was that she was not employed by either the agency or the end user because she was not sufficiently controlled, nor was there mutuality of obligations.

8.49 What can be gathered from these cases? First, it must be remembered that in all of these cases the workers themselves wanted to be treated as an employee of the end user, and one assumes that IR35 at-risk workers will want to resist such an outcome at all costs—at least in the first instance.

Secondly, it is arguable that the *Motorola* case was not comprehensively argued, and in the *O'Murphy* case the contract was very poorly drafted and the worker was clearly controlled.

8.50 Nothing can be taken for certain in tribunal proceedings, but overall it seems the tribunals are generally unwilling to imply contractual relations between third parties, whether the worker is incorporated or not. Where sound contractual relations are entered into with the agency, particularly where it can be demonstrated that there is little control or mutuality, HMRC will take no comfort from the above cases.

8.51 Although the case law has not always been consistent there are several decisions that state that implying hypothetical contract terms is, as in the *Winter v Westward TV* case, 'almost impossible' and an 'invalid' approach. This can only help to underline the fact that, so far as IR35 is concerned, the contract to concentrate on is the one the personal service business enters into. Of course these cases were decided before IR35 came into force and they cannot overrule statutes which came after them. However, if HMRC are going to argue that there is a disguised employee situation, this case law can only help to show that the courts are generally reluctant to make such a finding. Unfortunately, IR35 requires a hypothetical contract to be inferred from the circumstances and arrangements and this is inescapable. Non-IR35 case law shows how difficult it can be implying hypothetical contracts and this perhaps underlines once again that IR35 as written is at best difficult to apply with any certainty.

Summary

8.52 There are many technical and common-sense justifications to disregard the agency/end-user contract and to reject HMRC's interpretation of the legislation and

Crucial question 3: is the agency/end-user contract relevant? **8.52**

the need to see the agency/end-user contract. However, in practice all contracts in the chain tend to be considered by the courts.

HMRC, in FAQs, Contract, 2 and 8 (available on HMRC's website at http://www.hmrc.gov.uk/ir35/contract.htm) express the view that all the contracts in the commercial chain need to be taken into account but the detailed arguments in this chapter demonstrate the weaknesses with this approach.

The relevance of the agency/end-user contract was brought up in the *F S Consulting Ltd* Special Commissioners' decision of 2002 and *Usetech Ltd v Young* in 2004. These decisions are considered in Chapter 11 below.

Chapter 9

Crucial question 4: is the personal service business an agency within ITEPA 2003, Pt 2, Ch 7?

9.1 There is a further threat. This is found in ITEPA 2003, ss 44–47. There are equivalent provisions for national insurance found in the Social Security (Categorisation of Earners) Regulations 1978, SI 1978/1689.

If this legislation applies, the consequences can be as devastating in terms of tax and national insurance as they would be under IR35.

Some advisers have been unaware of the potential application of the agency rules to the personal service sector. This chapter explains what the problem is and how it should be addressed and avoided.

The agency trap

9.2 In essence ITEPA 2003, s 44 says that if business A supplies worker B to a client C, then business A will be acting as an agency. There are very few escape strategies.

9.3 Under ITEPA 2003, s 47(3), all forms of payment made by company A to worker B in these circumstances will have to suffer PAYE and national insurance deductions unless the payments have already been treated as employment income, in which case the appropriate deductions should already have been made.

9.4 It does not matter if company A is not registered as an agency, or that it does not consider itself to be an agency. It is a question of fact as to whether it has supplied a worker. Nor does it matter whether or not the worker is personally named.

9.5 In the author's extensive practical experience of contract reviews in the context of IR35, it is quite clear that many personal service businesses are doing nothing more than supplying the director to the next party in the commercial chain. Often the director is named as the 'authorised personnel' or 'nominated consultant'. It is even often stated at the outset of the contract that the personal service business will supply personnel.

The personal service business is thus acting as an agency *itself* and falls within the agency regulations. The exemption for incorporated workers at Pt 2, Ch 7 is of

Crucial question 4: is the personal service business an agency? **9.12**

no assistance because the agency 'trap' has merely trickled down from the legitimate agency to the personal service business.

9.6 Partners and staff at Accountax have personally handled cases where both HMRC and former Contributions Agency officers have tried this precise line of attack. There has been a noticeable increase in the use of the agency legislation by HMRC. It is increasingly being applied to composite companies who do not realise they are effectively acting as agencies.

9.7 Although the agency regulations are not easy to understand, they can certainly be interpreted in such a way as to justify their application to personal service businesses.

HMRC clearly believe that this is a technically legitimate argument.

9.8 Furthermore, the flow chart in the internal manuals at ESM 3032 previously directed tax officers to consider the agency argument where the straight IR35 challenge could not succeed. In other words, tax officers were having their specific attention drawn to the possibility of an agency challenge. Thankfully, HMRC have now excluded the agency argument from ESM 3032; nonetheless this does not mean tax officers will not consider the argument. The author understands that a specialist unit has been set up within HMRC to focus on the agency regulations.

9.9 For background information it is worth mentioning a little-known case from 1992, called Revenue Decision Four (RD4) (which was briefly mentioned in *Tax Bulletin 2* (http://www.hmrc.gov.uk/bulletins/tb2.htm)), although the decision is now obsolete. The decision states that a challenge was made to a director of a company who was attempting to extract funds from his company via consultancy fees. This in itself should not overly concern practitioners in the context of IR35 as it is a fairly commonplace technical argument. What is disturbing is that HMRC's challenge was not that the consultancy fees were really disguised director's remuneration, but that the company was acting as an agency *itself* within the agency regulations. HMRC's interpretation was upheld.

9.10 The agency trap is a very real threat to tens of thousands of small personal service businesses who merely supply a consultant (usually the director—the worker) to a client. When coupled with HMRC's new focus on Pt 2, Ch 7 and the success it has had with RD4, it would be an unwise practitioner who fails to address this issue.

It seems s 47(3) could apply to dividends, as 'remuneration' includes all forms of payment. Certainly, HMRC will consider this line of attack.

How can the agency trap be avoided?

9.11 There are really only two possibilities of avoiding the agency trap.

Demonstrate that the strict terms of ITEPA 2003, Pt 2, Ch 7 have not been met

9.12 In essence ITEPA 2003, s 44 merely says that if company A supplies worker B to client C then company A will be acting as an agency, and PAYE and

9.12 *Crucial question 4: is the personal service business an agency?*

national insurance deductions will have to be made from all forms of payment made to the worker. It is, however, first necessary to consider carefully ITEPA 2003, s 44 as these provisions lay down certain criteria which must be satisfied before the section applies.

9.13 Section 44(1)(*a*) provides that the worker must render, or be under an obligation to render, personal services to a client. Unfortunately, even where there is an unfettered substitution clause, this subsection can still be satisfied because it includes de facto personal service as an alternative to an obligation to provide personal service.

9.14 In other words, the existence of a right of substitution will not defeat this subsection where personal service is in fact given. Internal and former contributions agency instructions and guidance state that even where a former substitute is sent, in practice this should not defeat s 44(1)(*a*) in itself, particularly where a substitute is sent only very occasionally. Another argument open to the authorities is that those occasions when a substitute is sent can be severed from occasions when personal service was given and the latter will still be caught by the agency rules and the national insurance regulations equivalent.

9.15 Section 44(1)(*a*) goes on to say that the worker must be 'subject to, or to the right of, supervision, direction or control as to the manner in which he renders those services'. This subsection, it should be noted, concentrates on the 'how' by referring to the 'manner' in which the services are rendered.

9.16 It should be carefully observed that the subsection is worded in such a way that supervision, direction and control are all alternatives to each other. Control is generally accepted as having the quality of a significant degree of interference, whereas mere supervision and direction operates at a lower level. As such, the subsection can be applied in cases were the interference of the agency does not amount to full control but still amounts to supervision or direction.

9.17 In the case of traditional labour agencies (as opposed to personal service business deemed agencies), HMRC do accept that it is possible for an agency supplied worker not to be under the supervision, direction or control of another person, but practitioners can expect strong resistance, particularly in the case of unskilled or semi-skilled workers.

9.18 Unfortunately, s 44(1)(*c*) does not state that the supervision, direction or control has to be exercised by the agency or any other specific named party. As such, it may apply irrespective of the identity of the person or business which supervises, directs or controls or who has the right to supervise, direct or control the worker.

9.19 In the context of IR35 workers, the scope for control is likely to be limited, but mere supervision or direction may well be present and difficult to resist. This is especially so in light of contract clauses which refer to the worker having to 'comply with all rules and regulations in operation' etc.

Crucial question 4: is the personal service business an agency? **9.25**

9.20 So the first strategy to defeat the agency rules is to show that the worker is not subject either to supervision, direction or control or the right of supervision, direction or control by any third party 'as to the manner' in which the services are provided. This, quite simply, will be a straight question of fact by reference to the contract terms and practical arrangements if different.

Demonstrate that 'services' and not 'personnel' are being supplied

9.21 It may be possible to show on the facts that s 44(1)(*a*) does not apply because the personal service business is not acting as an agency because it is undertaking services as opposed to supplying mere workers. Again, this will be a question of fact.

9.22 Accountax has reviewed many contracts in respect of IR35 only to find that the contract quite clearly spells out that a person or consultant or authorised personnel, often named in a schedule, is being provided, as opposed to commercial services being undertaken. To put this into context, it is the difference between Fred Bloggs Computer Services Limited contracting to 'supply a consultant at £50 per hour', which would indicate a potential agency position, and contracting to 'undertake Oracle DBA programming at a rate of £50 per hour', which would be the provision of a service, and not caught by the agency rules.

In the late 2001 Court of Appeal decision in *Jobsin Co Uk Plc v Department of Health*, ([2001] EWCA Civ 1241) the court drew the distinction between providing computer services and providing personnel. This was not an IR35 case—it was concerned with tendering regulations in public service contracts but the point is still made. The crucial question to be asked, said the court, was 'what is being provided?' This very neatly highlights the importance of the contractual obligation to provide 'services' or 'personnel'.

9.23 Sometimes contracts are not quite clear on exactly what is being provided and, even with highly paid specialist IT and engineering contractors, it is not uncommon for there to be no written contract at all.

9.24 In these circumstances reference to the invoices raised may lead to clarification of precisely what is being supplied. If an invoice reads, 'To professional fees in respect of Oracle DBA programming for a total of 35 hours at £50 per hour' then it is fair to say that such wording indicates the undertaking of a service. If, however, the invoice reads, 'To professional fees for the supply of Fred Bloggs for 35 hours at £50 per hour' then such wording would indicate an agency relationship.

9.25 Although the strict contractual terms should carry most weight, other correspondence or invoices which indicate that a worker only is being supplied, as opposed to the undertaking of commercial services, at best muddy the waters and could at worst be used as hard evidence that in truth the personal service business is a deemed agency under ITEPA 2003, Pt 2, Ch 7, with all the disastrous fiscal ramifications which follow on from such a conclusion, courtesy of s 47(3).

A further minor complication is that if the agency rules are deemed to apply (as opposed to IR35) there may well be ramifications for claiming travelling expenses

9.25 *Crucial question 4: is the personal service business an agency?*

as the rules relating to 'agency workers' and 'temporary workplaces' are interpreted narrowly by HMRC.

Summary

9.26 There is a potential trap for personal service businesses in ITEPA 2003, Pt 2, Ch 7. In the past HMRC have tended not to pursue the agency argument, but it is certainly open for them to do so. For HMRC's current views and approach to the agency rules, see ESM 2000 onwards.

9.27 It can be demonstrated that the agency rules do not apply by showing that the strict criteria laid down in subsection (1) are not met, but this may not be an easy task. The only certain way to avoid an agency challenge is to show that, both contractually and in respect of supporting paperwork and invoices, a worker is not being supplied but that the personal service business is undertaking commercial services.

9.28 HMRC may not pursue the agency argument to the bitter end, but if they can show a requirement for personal service then they have at the same time demonstrated that the first criteria of IR35 has been met.

9.29 There is little evidence that HMRC have actively pursued personal service companies under the agency legislation. If they do, the consequences of having travelling expenses disallowed (on the basis that agency workers have permanent workplaces not temporary ones), the impact could be great and practitioners need to be aware of the risks. The agency trap is something that those using umbrella companies should be particularly aware of (see Chapter 10).

Chapter 10
Crucial question 5: do composite companies defeat IR35?

Background

10.1 The use of composite or single-person companies proved very attractive for contractors. Composite companies provided the same tax advantages of having a limited company, but removed the hassle and administration of running a company. The risks associated with IR35 were somewhat removed from the contractor, as they did not themselves have the responsibility of checking contracts etc.

10.2 The basic structure of a composite company is where an administration company or scheme provider forms a number of companies, provides corporate director and company secretarial functions and prepares business accounts, board minutes, dividend vouchers, etc. Each of these companies would have mulitple shareholders (the contractors), who are often not directors. The contractors then receive the tax advantages of being a shareholder, but without the adminstration burden. The composite provider charges the shareholders a fee for the services it provides.

10.3 HMRC were concerned that contractors were able to reap the tax advantages of providing services though a limited company, without being subject to any of the negative aspects of running a company. Increasing numbers of companies were also flouting the rules to try to become more attractive to contractors. Lastly, and more importantly for HMRC was that the continuation of composite companies meant a significant loss to the exchequer.

The managed service company (MSC) rules

10.4 In essence, the MSC rules are aimed at companies that 'promote and facilitate' the use of companies to supply the services of an individual. This includes (but is not limited to) composite companies and single person companies. The legislation is contained in ITEPA 2003, Part 2, Chapter 9 and s 688A, and is underpinned by various statutory instruments. A list of primary and secondary legislation, together with associated documents, can be found on HMRC's website (http://www.hmrc.gov.uk/employment-status/legislation.htm).

10.5 In order to get around these draconian rules, many scheme providers originally attempted to re-brand themselves as accountancy services in order to take

10.5 *Crucial question 5: do composite companies defeat IR35?*

advantage of a perceived exemption for accountants in the MSC rules. However, the draft legislation was amended and the so-called accountants' exemption is now somewhat illusory. Those scheme providers who have done little other than badge themselves as accountants are likely to be on the end of expensive litigation.

10.6 The effect of the MSC rules is that the company engaging the contractors should have operated the deemed payment calculation on the dividends paid out to the individuals. The composite company will then be liable for the tax and national insurance on all dividend payments. The MSC rules were introduced for income tax purposes with effect from 6 April 2007, but apply from 6 August 2007 for national insurance purposes.

10.7 The MSC rules take precedence over the personal service company provisions (ITEPA 2003, s 48(2)(*aa*)). To the extent that the two codes overlap, the IR35 rules are therefore effectively switched off so far as the worker is concerned.

10.8 With the introduction of the transfer of debt provisions (ITEPA 2003, s 688A, and supporting Regulations), companies cannot simply close the company when they are faced with a large tax bill as the liability can be transferred onto the directors of the companies, and, other parties in certain circumstances.

10.9 It is not possible to assess how broadly HMRC are going to try and apply the MSC rules as, at the time of writing, no test cases have been before the Tax Tribunal (or its predecessors, the Commissioners), but there are bound to be some.

'Umbrella' companies

10.10 Providing the companies are correctly set up, umbrella companies (ie where the contractor is an employee of the company, offsetting certain expenses against the money generated) and commercial contractors are still outside the scope of the MSC rules.

10.11 For many contractors, these structures will not however offer the same financial rewards as working through your own limited company (lack of dividends). However, users of umbrella companies should be aware of the potential for challenge by HMRC under the agency provisions (see **9.29**).

Summary

10.12 Composite companies are now caught by the MSC rules and as such they no longer provide any tax savings for contractors.

Umbrella structures can work to defeat IR35, but only if those running them understand and apply the law correctly.

Contractors should choose very carefully. The new MSC rules bring in very considerable dangers for those working through ill thought out mass marketed schemes.

Chapter 11
Analysing IR35 case law

IR35—the cases

11.1 IR35 has been with us now for over nine years and many cases were heard by the Commissioners (ie prior to the introduction of the Tax Tribunals from 1 April 2009), some of which proceeded on appeal to the High Court. It is worth remembering that, although previous Commissioners' decisions may be persuasive evidence in later cases, they do not form legal precedent. However, they are noteworthy as examples of lines of argument.

Battersby v Campbell (2001) Special Commissioner Dr N Brice Ref SPC 189

11.2 The taxpayer was a computer analyst and programmer. In 1988 he established a limited company of which he and his wife were sole directors. In 1994, the company obtained a contract through an agency with a bank. In 1999, the bank consolidated all of its self-employed contractors through a limited company who then paid the contractors.

11.3 The agreement included the clear intention that this was not an employer/employee relationship. It also stated that the service company was responsible for all sickness, disability and pension arrangements; absence had to be notified to the bank in advance; responsibility for the quality, quantity and performance of the work rested with the bank; normal hours of work were seven hours a day, five days a week and that the taxpayer had to use the bank's mainframe computer system situated at the bank's premises. In April 2001, the taxpayer accepted a position with the bank as an employee.

11.4 The issue to be decided was whether the taxpayer would have been regarded as an employed earner if his contract had been with the bank and not with the service company. The relevant authorities had established the principle that the question of whether a person was employed under a contract of service or a contract for services was a question of fact. The factors pointing towards a contract of service were stronger than those pointing to a contract for services and, therefore, it was held that if the taxpayer's contract had been with the bank, he would have been regarded for the purposes of the 1992 Act as employed by the bank. IR35 applied.

11.5 *Analysing IR35 case law*

11.5 The appellant defended himself in this case. That is he had no professional advocate speaking on his behalf. His defence was that it was common in the computer industry for enhancement work to be undertaken by self-employed contractors; he took the risks of a self-employed person; the bank could reduce his earnings without notice; his company was not part of an 'umbrella' company and that he was a director of his own company; and finally, that people who supplied their services through service companies were not 'tax fraudsters'.

11.6 In making her decision, Dr Brice, the presiding Special Commissioner, said that she had sympathy with Mr Battersby's assertions that he was not a tax fraudster but the fact that he was running his business correctly did not mean that the IR35 regulations did not apply.

11.7 Unfortunately, the rest of Mr Battersby's defence was not very strong. The appellant did not present any case law, nor did he challenge any of the Revenue's case law. Although there were factors which indicated self-employment, in that he had the right to send a substitute, there was no control over the methods he used and there was a clear intention that it was a contract for services, these arguments were not put forward and, therefore, the Special Commissioner had to make a decision based on the facts and legal submissions presented.

F S Consulting v McCaul (Inspector of Taxes) (2002) Special Commissioner Dr N Brice SpC 138

11.8 The taxpayer S was a computer consultant conversion specialist and the sole director and shareholder of a limited company. The company and an agency T Ltd entered into a contract for the company to supply services to a client, B plc. S was the named consultant. A substitute could be proposed but B plc would have to approve the substitute. The contract could be terminated without notice on the grounds that S was incompetent or by T Ltd with four weeks' notice. Between April 2000 and June 2001 the taxpayer provided his services to his company who provided them to B plc. S worked in a project team of seven, five of whom were employees of B plc. S did not act as a team leader and could not decide which employees formed the project team. He could advise the employees but could not tell them what to do. His working hours were flexible and he recorded his time on a timesheet which had to be signed by a representative of B plc. S had to give notice and get permission for leave.

11.9 It was held that:

1. the phrase 'arrangements involving an intermediary' to be found in regulation 6 of the Social Security Contributions (Intermediaries) Regulations, SI 2000/727 was wide enough to include arrangements involving both an intermediary and a non-intermediary; the phrase was not 'arrangements with an intermediary' which would exclude arrangements with a non-intermediary; and
2. the principle had been established that the question of whether a person was employed under a contract of service or a contract for services was a question of fact, in each case to be determined having regard to all the relevant factors. In this

case, the factors pointing towards a contract of service were stronger than those pointing to a contract for services. Focusing on the actual contractual arrangements rather than their form, had the arrangements taken the form of a contract between S and B plc, S would have been regarded as an employee of B plc.

11.10 In this case the appellant *was* represented. The arguments put forward were first, that according to the legislation, the end-user contract could not be taken into account; secondly, as the contract was between T Ltd and the company, S could not be held to be an employee of B plc because B plc paid T Ltd and not S or his company; and thirdly, that as T Ltd did not exercise supervision, direction or control over S, he could not be an employee of T Ltd.

11.11 The Special Commissioner dismissed the third argument on the basis that neither S nor T Ltd was making the appeal.

11.12 Dr Brice then decided that the legislation did allow her to take the end-user relationship into account and said that reference to arrangements involving 'an intermediary' was wide enough to include arrangements involving a 'non-intermediary'. It is thought that Dr Brice's remarks have been misinterpreted (including by the author in the previous edition of this book).

11.13 One explanation is that reference had to be made to the non-intermediary, as a contract necessarily requires two parties, and one of those parties must be a non-intermediary. The personal service company (the intermediary) cannot contract with itself and so the arrangements with the non-intermediary have to be taken into account. Perhaps this is all Dr Brice was saying. She did not refer to arrangements with the client or deemed employer, and in fact, according to the judgment, she did not go on to consider the upper contract.

The relevance of the upper contract was also called into question in *Usetech Ltd v Young (HMIT)* [2004] EWHC 2248—see later.

11.14 This case could arguably have been disputed more comprehensively. The Revenue relied to some extent on out-of-date case law, but this was not challenged. There were also factors pointing to this being a contract for services as neither B plc nor T Ltd had any right of control over the methods S used in doing the work, S had the right to send a substitute, albeit that this right was fettered by the need to get B plc's permission and there was a clear intention that this was to be a contract for services.

11.15 However, it appears from the published decision that, as none of these points were raised by S or his representative and the Revenue's arguments were not successfully refuted, the Special Commissioner had to make her decision based on the evidence and legal arguments presented.

G S Ltd v Gregory (2002) Special Commissioner Mr Sadler SpC— unpublished preliminary hearing

11.16 In August 2002 Accountax represented a design engineer contractor who had been subject to an IR35 enquiry.

11.17 *Analysing IR35 case law*

11.17 At a preliminary hearing it was argued by Accountax that the section 8 Notice of Decision (NIC IR35 assessment) should be discharged on the basis that it did not refer to a specific time period and was therefore invalid. The defect in the assessment could not be corrected under TMA 1970, s 114 on the Court of Appeal authority of *Baylis v Gregory* [1987] STC 22. The Special Commissioner accepted the argument. If the Revenue wanted to pursue IR35 it would have to do so on the basis of correctly worded assessments. This technical victory appears to be the first win for a contractor at the Specials and should remind all practitioners to check assessments very carefully.

The name of G S Ltd is anonymised.

Synaptek Ltd v Young (Inspector of Taxes) [2003] EWHC 645 (Ch) [2003] STC 543

11.18 *Synaptek Ltd v Young* was heard on appeal in the High Court in February 2003. The appeal originated from a decision made by the General Commissioners in 2002.

The General Commissioner's decision

11.19 Synaptek Ltd, a company which had traded since 1990, had contracted through an agency to perform IT services which were ultimately for the benefit of the Benefits Agency in Longbenton. In this case, the chain consisted of Synaptek Ltd who contracted with NESCO (an agency) who in turn contracted with EDS who had a contract to supply services to the Benefits Agency.

The General Commissioner held that if there had been a contract between the taxpayer and EDS it would have been a contract of service. IR35 applied.

11.20 The taxpayer represented himself at the General Commissioners. Being an ex-police officer he did have experience in court hearings. He produced good-quality bundles and gave his evidence clearly and well. Unfortunately, he relied too heavily on comments made by Burton J during *R* (*on the application of Professional Contractors Group Ltd and Others*) *v IRC* ([2001] EWHC Civ 1945 which, as they were not made in connection with the actual case in hand, do not form legal precedent. The taxpayer also produced a list of over 40 differences between himself and permanent employees of EDS.

11.21 Some of the case law relied upon by the Revenue was out of date. They argued that the taxpayer did not have to be in the same position as that of a normal employee, but as he was in the same position as a temporary employee of EDS, then IR35 applied. There were also some fundamental indicators that this was a contract for services, such as the right of substitution and lack of control.

It is interesting to note that the 'end user' in this case was found to be EDS and not the Benefits Agency.

11.22 Synaptek Ltd had many factors which pointed to its being 'in business on its own account' and had, in fact, won a small-business award. The director put forward evidence to show that the company was being run as a genuine business, that he was not controlled and that the company could send a substitute to do the work. However, the General Commissioners found that the particular contract in question, on balance, was caught by IR35.

11.23 The taxpayer appealed to the High Court on the following grounds.

- That the fact that Synaptek was in business on its own account was a very strong indicator of the contract being one for services on the authority of *Davies (Inspector of Taxes) v Braithwaite* [1931] 2 KB 628 and that this factor had not been given sufficient weight by the General Commissioners.
- That the General Commissioners had misdirected themselves in law when they considered whether there was sufficient mutuality of obligations for a contract of service to exist.
- That there was a right of substitution and again the General Commissioners had misdirected themselves in law in not considering this to be incompatible with a contract of service.
- That the General Commissioners had misplaced reliance on the case of *F S Consulting Ltd v McCaul* [2002] STC (SCD) 138.

High Court decision

11.24 Mr Justice Hart decided that there was not sufficient reason to interfere in the decision made by the General Commissioners and dismissed the appeal. He had the following to say on the four pertinent points.

In business on own account

11.25 Mr Justice Hart did not see anything in the judgment of *Davies (Inspector of Taxes) v Braithwaite* which suggested that, where a person was in business on his or her own account, any contract entered into by them would automatically be a contract for services. Therefore, although it was an important contextual factor, it was up to the General Commissioners to assess how much weight should be attributed to it.

Mutuality of obligations

11.26 Although the appeal was not successful on these grounds some interesting points were brought out. First, the Revenue agreed that if there was no obligation on the agency to provide work for the entire period of the notional contract there was not sufficient mutuality of obligations for a contract of services to exist. This is a departure from their usual stance that there must simply be work and payment for mutuality to be present.

11.27 Secondly, the judge distinguished between mutuality beyond the contract and mutuality within it, making the point that when considering a particular contract one looks at whether there is mutuality of obligations for the duration of the contract

11.27 Analysing IR35 case law

and not simply whether there is an obligation to offer and accept work when the contract is over.

11.28 In the case of *Synaptek Ltd* there was a clause in the contract which stated that there was an obligation on the client to 'allocate work' to Synaptek for the duration of the contract. Mr Justice Hart felt that this, together with a four-week notice period (which he argued would serve no purpose were mutuality of obligations not to be present), meant that there was sufficient mutuality of obligations.

Right of substitution

11.29 There was a clause in the contract with Synaptek Ltd which stated that:

> 'In the interests of continuity the Company shall use its best endeavours to procure that the Services are provided by the Company Employee personally but may with the consent of the Client substitute alternative personnel subject to procuring that such alternative personnel are bound by the terms of this agreement.'

11.30 It was argued on behalf of the taxpayer that this gave Synaptek Ltd the right to send a substitute which would, in itself, mean that the contract was outside of IR35.

11.31 Mr Justice Hart considered the clause together with the authority in *Express and Echo Publications Ltd v Tanton* [1999] IRLR 367, which is the leading pronouncement on substitution and concluded that:

> 'In the present case the provision in question (cl 9A of the NESCO agreement) does not give Synaptek any *right* to perform the services by anyone other than Mr Stutchbury. The effect of the contract is that, unless and until agreed otherwise, the services do have to be performed personally by Mr Stutchbury.'

11.32 Essentially, this means that the clause amounted to a limited right of delegation more akin to that in *McFarlane v Glasgow City Council* [2001] IRLR 7. Therefore, it was for the General Commissioners to decide how much weight to attach to this factor.

Misplaced reliance on F S Consulting Ltd v McCaul [2002] STC (SCD) 138

11.33 It was argued on behalf of the appellant that the General Commissioners had placed too much reliance on the case of *F S Consulting Ltd v McCaul* and had therefore misdirected themselves.

11.34 In the stated case the General Commissioners did make the point that the facts in the case bore 'a close similarity' to *F S Consulting Ltd v McCaul* and that the legal principles in that case were a useful guide in deciding *Synaptek*.

11.35 It was argued on behalf of the appellant that the facts of the present case were substantially different and it was therefore a misdirection to apply the principles as set out in *F S Consulting Ltd v McCaul*.

11.36 Mr Justice Hart concluded that the General Commissioners had not misdirected themselves and had not placed too much reliance on *F S Consulting*. He said that had the stated case suggested that the General Commissioners believed the facts of *Synaptek* to be indistinguishable from those in *F S Consulting*, there may well have been a powerful argument for saying that the Commissioners had misdirected themselves, but that this argument did not have the same force where, as was the case here, the Commissioners had merely referred to a 'close similarity' in the facts of the two cases.

11.37 HMRC have taken the view that this case weakens the substitution argument in IR35 and, following the case, have started to suggest that, for IR35 purposes, a right of substitution can only be of more weight than the other factors where it is in fact utilised. However, it is worth remembering that Mr Justice Hart said that the clause in the contract did not actually equate to a true right of substitution and it was this that made it possible for the General Commissioners to regard it as simply one of many factors to be considered. It should also be noted that, in the stated case, the General Commissioners themselves stated that the clause was a strong indication of self-employment.

11.38 HMRC have also taken the view that, following this case, any contract which has a termination period must have the prerequisite amount of mutuality of obligations. There is a certain amount of logic to this argument and it seems fair that where there is a significant period of notice, any argument that there is a total lack of mutuality of obligations would be weakened. It should be noted, however, that HMRC have been very slow to acknowledge the fact that their barrister conceded that there had to be an obligation to offer work for the entire period of the notional contract for mutuality of obligations to exist, not merely work which is done for payment.

11.39 One final point regarding this case was that it raised awareness of a very fundamental difference between the General Commissioners and the Special Commissioners, under the jurisdiction and procedural rules which applied before the introduction of the Tax Tribunals. When the Special Commissioners gave their decision they were required (under SI 1994/1811, reg 18) to provide a statement of facts found and the reasons for the determination. The General Commissioners, on the other hand, merely had to give a decision. This made it much harder to try and show that they had misdirected themselves, especially in an area as grey as IR35.

11.40 It should also be noted that, as in *Battersby v Campbell* [2001] STC (SCD) 189, the director of Synaptek Ltd represented the company at the initial appeal. This would seem to suggest that professional representation is valuable from the outset in these cases as it is the Commissioners who find the facts and make the decision; the higher courts can merely review the decision.

11.41 *Analysing IR35 case law*

Lime-IT Ltd v Justin (Officer of the Board of Inland Revenue) (2002) Special Commissioner Dr John F Avery Jones CBE SpC 342

11.41 Accountax represented the taxpayer in this case and it was the first IR35 case to be won by the taxpayer at the Special Commissioners.

11.42 F was the sole shareholder and director of L Ltd, an information technology company, formed on 4 April 2000. On 17 April 2000 L Ltd entered into a contract with an agency, E, to provide IT services to M Ltd, the end user. The contract was for the provision of specific projects, such as introducing a new e-mail system, organising remote access, etc, and had an estimated completion date of 10 April 2001. It was estimated that L Ltd would need to provide a consultant for around 37 hours per week in order to complete the services on time; however, the hours actually worked varied considerably from this. The terms of the contract allowed for L Ltd to send a substitute consultant. This clause was specifically negotiated by F so that should she wish to work on other contracts she could. The clause did allow for M Ltd to reject the substitute but only on reasonable grounds. The agreement between E and M Ltd was drawn up to reflect the terms of the agreement between L Ltd and E. During the term of the contract to provide services to M Ltd, L Ltd provided services to four other clients. The services were carried out from one of M Ltd's offices and partly from F's home, where she had an office containing four computers dedicated to the business of L Ltd.

11.43 The Revenue was of the opinion that IR35 applied and accordingly raised a formal decision which was appealed by the taxpayer. The standard IR35 issue under appeal was whether, had the arrangements in the instant case taken the form of a contract between F and M Ltd, she would be regarded as employed under a contract of service.

11.44 It was held that: the basic test of whether someone was employed or self-employed was to ask whether a person was 'in business on his own account' and three conditions had to be satisfied in order for a contract of service to exist. First, the servant must have agreed that in consideration of a wage or other remuneration he would provide his own work and skill in the performance of some service for his master. Second, the servant must have agreed, expressly or impliedly, that in the performance of that service he would be subject to the other's control in a sufficient degree to make that other master. Third, the other provisions of the contract must be consistent with its being a contract of service. In the instant case, there was very little evidence to suggest an employment relationship. In essence M Ltd was contracting for a particular IT job from a small business in the way one would expect an IT consultant to be engaged. Accordingly, on the hypothesis that F had contracted directly with M Ltd, she would not have been employed under a contract of service; she would have been in business on her own account and IR35 did not apply.

11.45 Obtaining evidence from the end user is something HMRC have always been keen to do and is endorsed by various courts and tribunals, but it is believed that it is only necessary if the terms of the contract are varied from the day-to-day arrangements. In this particular case there was no evidence from the end user, and the Special Commissioner, Dr Avery Jones, said 'in future cases on this legislation (and its income tax equivalent) the Special Commissioners will wish to explore at a preliminary hearing whether it is possible to obtain evidence from the client'. HMRC have interpreted this to mean that they must obtain evidence from the end user in every IR35 case before they can give an opinion. This is clearly not what Dr Avery Jones said.

11.46 There were several factors in this case which pointed to F being in business on her own account. She had a dedicated office containing four computers which were used specifically for the services provided to M Ltd. L Ltd advertised its services via its website and undertook four other contracts during the M Ltd contract. Travel between M Ltd's sites was at the expense of the appellant. In this case these factors were important in helping the Special Commissioner reach his decision.

11.47 There was no control by M Ltd as to the manner in which F carried out her activities. While this was accepted by the Special Commissioner, he agreed with the contention of Mr Williams (brought in from the London Regional Advocacy Unit to represent the Revenue) that 'control may not be particularly important when dealing with an expert'.

11.48 While the Special Commissioner did not see liability insurance as a particularly important factor he did highlight the financial risk resulting from invoicing as a pointer towards self-employment. He said 'the fact of invoicing and the 30-day (or even 10-day, if that is what was subsequently agreed) terms for payment, even ignoring the actual delays in payment, seem to me to point towards self-employment'. Unfortunately, HMRC still fail to accept this argument.

11.49 The Revenue tried to play down the fact that F supplied her own equipment, as she was not contractually obliged to do so and even suggested that the desk and telephone provided by M Ltd were slight pointers towards employment. Of this, Dr Avery Jones said 'an employee does not normally provide a laptop but a self-employed person may do so if it makes the work easier to do, regardless of any contractual requirement. I do not regard the provision of a desk and telephone at M Ltd as particularly significant'.

11.50 F had specifically negotiated a substitution clause in the contract between L Ltd and E and even though this right had never been exercised, Dr Avery Jones said that 'it is a strong indicator of self-employment' and then went on to quote Lord Justice Peter Gibson in the 1999 Court of Appeal case, *Express and Echo Publications Ltd v Tanton*.

11.51 The contract stated that F was obliged to work a 37-hour week and it was the Revenue's argument that this obligation was the same as any employee of M Ltd. In reality F worked varied hours and Dr Avery Jones said 'the variations in the number of hours actually worked is more indicative of self-employment'. He went on to say, in situations such as this where what happens in reality differs from the contractual terms, one should look beyond the terms of the contract.

11.52 It is also worth pointing out that at the beginning of the hearing the inspector who had been handling the case handed over a two-page written apology saying

11.52 *Analysing IR35 case law*

that he was not happy with the way he had handled the case and with the guidance currently available he would have tackled the situation differently. Although the handling of the case is not relevant to the appeal and has no influence on the decision, it does reflect badly on the Revenue. The taxpayer received financial compensation from the Revenue in this case.

11.53 *Lime-IT Ltd v Justin (Inland Revenue Officer)* [2003] STC (SCD) 15 remains an important IR35 case. For the first time the taxpayer was represented by specialists, and in his judgment Dr Avery Jones made it clear that taking an overview there was 'very little to suggest an employment relationship'.

11.54 Regrettably, HMRC have continued to make formal decisions and force the inconvenience and expense of a contentious appeal on taxpayers when HMRC's case is, at best, weak.

11.55 When faced with a high-profile Commissioners' hearing many taxpayers back down and there is evidence, both empirical and anecdotal, that HMRC play on this. *Lime-IT Ltd v Justin* stopped the rot and reversed the trend.

Tilbury Consulting Ltd v Gittins (2004) STC (SCD) 72

11.56 *Tilbury Consulting Ltd v Gittins* was heard in October 2003 and was the fourth IR35 case to be heard at the Special Commissioners. Accountax represented the taxpayer. A preliminary point was heard by Dr Nuala Brice and the substantive issue was heard by His Honour Stephen Oliver QC.

The background

11.57 This case originated from request by the director of Tilbury Consulting Limited for an opinion on his contract from the Revenue. Mr Tilbury sent in copies of his contract and explained that Ford had outsourced part of its IT function to an agency. It was with this agency that Tilbury Consulting Limited had contracted. The local tax office replied explaining that they would need to ask Ford some questions before they gave an opinion and Mr Tilbury gave his permission for it to do this.

11.58 The answers to these questions showed that there was no control by Ford over how the work was done and that they would accept a substitute but only via the agency, because this is where their contract actually lay. There was a corresponding clause in the contract between Tilbury Consulting Limited and the agency which allowed a substitute to be sent by Tilbury Consulting Limited.

11.59 The Inspector, Mrs Gittins, then issued the opinion that this contract did indeed fall within the IR35 legislation and that, in effect, Mr Tilbury was a disguised employee of Ford. The taxpayer was told that he could accept this opinion, reject it, or request a formal decision against which he could appeal.

11.60 In the meantime the inspector wrote again to Ford, without informing the director that she was doing so, and challenged some of the information provided in the initial responses. The response she received backed up the original statements.

11.61 The director decided that he wanted some certainty and asked for a formal notice of decision to allow him to appeal. This was issued and an appeal was made with an election that the appeal be heard by the Special Commissioners.

The preliminary issue

11.62 A preliminary hearing was held in this case to decide whether the Revenue should be allowed to summons the person at Ford, who had already answered two sets of questions, to give evidence at the substantive hearing.

11.63 The application for a witness summons is usually *ex parte*, which means that the other side do not have the right to make representations. However, in this case the taxpayer was permitted to make representations.

11.64 The taxpayer objected on two grounds. First, that the Revenue had already obtained sufficient evidence, and secondly, that by forcing a witness to attend, the Revenue was jeopardising the delicate commercial relationship between the company and Ford. The Revenue argued that having the witness at the hearing meant that the Special Commissioner could ask questions to obtain the facts.

11.65 The Special Commissioner considered both arguments and decided that, in the interests of natural justice, the Revenue should be allowed to call the witness. It is interesting to note that, having gone through this process, the Revenue subsequently decided to call two different people as witnesses.

11.66 Unusually for a preliminary hearing, the judgment was published, as it was felt that this was an area where guidance would be helpful. It is important to remember, however, that the guidance provided was in connection with the calling of witnesses at an appeal hearing and not, as the Revenue subsequently tried to claim, that in an IR35 case the inspector should be allowed to interview the end client.

The substantive appeal

11.67 The main arguments for the appellant (Tilbury Consulting Limited) were that there was a right of substitution which flowed through the chain of contracts, there was a lack of control over the manner in which the services were provided, there was an element of financial risk from invoicing and an instance of an invoice which was paid late and there were many differences between Mr Tilbury and an employee of Ford.

11.68 The Revenue was represented by one of the Inspectors from the new Regional Appeals Units. These are an extension of the London Appeals Unit (which represented the Revenue in *Lime-IT v Justin*) and are made up of Inspectors who have been specifically trained to take cases to the Commissioners. The appellant was represented by Accountax.

11.69 *Analysing IR35 case law*

Construction of the contract

11.69 The Revenue argued that the first step in establishing whether IR35 applied was to assume that Ford had taken Mr Tilbury on directly. The second step would be to establish what the terms would have been had they done this. This meant that they could ignore the terms in the written contracts and the day-to-day arrangements and construct a completely new hypothetical contract.

11.70 The Revenue's argument, that one starts with the assumption that the worker is taken on directly and then works out what the contract terms would have been, may seem untenable on first hearing but looking at the legislation, which has long been felt to be badly worked, it is actually perfectly possible. FA 2000, Sch 12 (now ITEPA 2003, Pt 2, Ch 8) says (see s 49(1)) that IR35 will apply where there is personal service, and:

> '(b) The services are provided not under a contract directly between the client and the worker but under arrangements involving a third party ('the intermediary'), and
> (c) the circumstances are such that, if the services were provided under a contract directly between the client and the worker, the worker would be regarded for income tax purposes as an employee of the client.'

11.71 It had always been assumed by those in practice that this meant one had to look at the terms that were actually in place at the time and then remove the intermediary (service company) and possibly the agency. This creates a hypothetical contract, but the terms of that contract are the real terms that were in place.

11.72 Looking at the legislation it is possible to see how the Revenue had come to its opinion. However, had the Revenue been correct it would make it almost impossible for anyone to decide whether they were outside of IR35 or not.

11.73 Fortunately, the impossible situation that this would place taxpayers in was not lost on His Honour Stephen Oliver QC, the Presiding Special Commissioner. During the hearing he remarked that this interpretation would lead to a 'sea of unreality' where the Revenue could invent terms which supported an employer/employee relationship.

11.74 This comment did not make it into the judgment, but Mr Oliver made his view very clear by stating that the legislation calls for a two-stage exercise:

1 find the facts as they existed during the period covered by the decision; and
2 then assume that the worker was contracted to perform services to the client and to determine whether *in light of the facts found* the worker would be regarded as an employee of the client.

11.75 In other words, the hypothesis of IR35 is to place the worker in the shoes of the intermediary; it is not to invent a whole new set of terms and conditions. Since 2000, when the legislation was passed, the author has maintained this is the correct approach—and this has now been judicially confirmed.

Substitution

11.76 The Revenue put forward two arguments as to why substitution was not effective in this case. The first was that Ford would only accept a substitute from the agency and not directly from Tilbury Consulting Limited and therefore, as it was the hypothetical relationship between Tilbury Consulting and Ford that one was concerned with, there was no right of substitution in that relationship. The Inspector claimed repeatedly that Ford were only interested in the personal service of Mr Tilbury.

11.77 However, under cross-examination, the Revenue's witness from Ford agreed that so long as the work was done, Ford did not mind whether it was done by 'Tom, Dick or Harry'.

11.78 This case also provided the Revenue with an opportunity to test their new theory on substitution and IR35, which has been borne out of the decision in *Synaptek Ltd v Young* [2003] STC 543. The Revenue interpretation of this case is that, where there is a qualified right of substitution in an IR35 case, but this right is not exercised, it is not the knockout blow that it would usually be but is simply one of the factors to be considered.

11.79 Both of these arguments would seem to have been rejected by the Special Commissioner who found as a fact that Tilbury Consulting Limited could send a substitute to the agency and that the agency could send a substitute to Ford. This fact was then among the most important in his conclusion which he found to be inconsistent with an employment relationship.

Other factors

11.80 There were other factors which were put forward by both sides, including the fact that the director's pass was a different colour to that of an employee and that he was unable to use the staff gymnasium.

11.81 The Revenue also brought out evidence that had he fallen ill whilst on Ford's premises, the director would have received first aid from the Ford medical team, as would any employee of Ford. However, it was brought out in evidence that this would have been the case had the director simply been a visitor to the offices and therefore this point seemed of limited value to the argument.

11.82 The issue of mutuality of obligations was brought up but was not part of the main argument for either side. It is worth mentioning, however, that when the case of *Montogmery v Johnson Underwood Ltd* [2001] EWCA Civ 318 was referred to by the appellant's advocate, the inspector dismissed the whole case on the grounds that the judges in the Court of Appeal had clearly got mutuality of obligations wrong and had been confused about the points made in *Ready Mixed Concrete (South East) Ltd v Minister of Pensions and National Insurance* [1968] 2 QB 497. This argument did not seem to carry much weight with the Special Commissioner.

11.83 *Analysing IR35 case law*

The judgment

11.83 It is hard to see from the judgment how much weight has been attributed to these various minor factors, because with this judgment there was a shift away from the 'picture painting' balancing exercise favoured by the Revenue and a return to the purist approach which asks whether any of the terms are fundamentally inconsistent with a contract of employment. This is one of the most important features of this case.

11.84 In these situations, if it were simply a matter of weighing up the number of factors for and the number against, the contractor will often lose. However, the return to the principles as outlined in the *Ready Mixed Concrete* case, that for there to be a contract of employment there must be an irreducible minimum, means that far more contracts would be found to be outside of IR35.

The Revenue's view

11.85 The Revenue has largely sought to disregard this decision for various reasons.

11.86 One of the problems that they had at the appeal was that it quickly became apparent that the agency in this case were not merely supplying bodies, but had actually taken over part of Ford's IT function and had project-management responsibilities. Essentially, this meant that in making their decision the Revenue had arguably picked the wrong 'client'.

11.87 This is borne out by the judgment, and early indications are that the Revenue will claim that this was a simple case of mistaken identity and, therefore, the case has very little to add to the question of IR35.

11.88 However, this is clearly not the case. The fact that the wrong client was picked is part of the reason why the appeal succeeded, in so far as it meant that Ford did not have the necessary control over Mr Tilbury. This in itself is a very important point, as it reinforces the argument that, even in IR35 situations, there must be the required control present in order for the relationship to be caught.

11.89 The judgment also points to substitution being a factor 'inconsistent with an employer/employee relationship'. This has nothing to do with who was selected as the client but is a fundamental point in status law and it is pleasing to see it reaffirmed.

11.90 It should be noted that when the issue of who was client was raised at the hearing the Revenue admitted that, knowing what they knew now, perhaps the wrong party had been selected. The inspector then went on to say that had the client co-operated more and allowed the Revenue access to the end user, this mistake could have been avoided.

11.91 During the hearing the inspector suggested that the taxpayer had somehow misled the Revenue as to the identity of the end user and therefore contributed to the

Analysing IR35 case law **11.99**

mistake. However, the appellant's advisors pointed out that in one of the very early letters to the inspector, the representatives of the appellant explained that the function had been outsourced to the agency. As such the Special Commissioner saw little in the Revenue's arguments and they were rejected.

11.92 *Tilbury* is an important IR35 case. It re-emphasised the fundamental approach to status issues and exposed the weakness of several of the Revenue's interpretations of the legislation.

Future Online v S K Faulds (Inspector of Taxes) (2004) Special Commissioner His Honour Stephen Oliver QC SpC 406

11.93 In this case, the taxpayer was represented by JSA Services Ltd, a well-known firm in the contracting world. The Revenue was represented by the Regional Appeal Unit.

11.94 R was a joint shareholder and director of FOL, a company which provided computer consultancy services. From July 2000 through until the end of May 2003, FOL had a contract with ECL (agency) to provide services to EDS. The job had been advertised on the internet and R sent his details. He was contacted by ECL and attended an interview the next day with an EDS contractor where he was offered a contract.

11.95 EDS had an agreement with the Department of Work and Pensions (DWP) to install the Child Support Reform (CSR) programme.

11.96 The contract between FOL and ECL was to provide the services of R (or such other consultant of FOL that FOL may provide in accordance with a 'substitution' clause at 1.4) to EDS and was initially for three months.

11.97 Clause 1.4 of the FOL/ECL contract allowed FOL to provide a substitute consultant with the written consent of EDS. Hours worked in excess of 37.5 per week were to be agreed in advance by EDS. There was a four-week notice period on the contract between FOL and ECL.

11.98 The agreement between ECL and EDS was in the form of a purchase order issued by EDS which set out the relevant details (eg payment, job description, location, duration, line of reporting etc). It also made it clear that ECL undertook to require that the contractor 'comply with any reasonable terms and conditions specified in relation to any particular purchase order'.

11.99 The purchase order dated 21 July 2000 was for the 'Professional services of R to work as a systems engineer' and the purchase order dated 12 December 2000 was for the 'Professional services of R to act as a systems test team leader based at EDS Longbenton'. It also stated that 'any hours worked over the standard 7.5 hours a day must be with the prior agreement and authorisation of the EDS project manager' and that 'all work to be carried out in accordance with the instructions from Simon Young or nominee'. Later Purchase Orders contained the same requirements,

11.99 *Analysing IR35 case law*

although the purchase order dated 5 June 2001 differed slightly in that the services were described as 'Build Manager'.

11.100 After a few weeks R was 'promoted' (to use his own words) to 'Build Manager', with responsibility for a specific phase of the project for which R was given no specific guidance as to the carrying out of the work.

11.101 R assembled a team and interviewed some 160 staff members on behalf of EDS. R allocated work between team members and ensured the objectives were met.

11.102 R was part of the organisational structure of EDS and His Honour Stephen Oliver QC was satisfied that throughout the period that R worked for EDS, he was part and parcel of the organisation.

11.103 The EDS project line manager allocated work to R and his team following meetings. R attended weekly meetings to report on progress and each night and each morning R reported to the EDS programme manager.

11.104 It was argued on behalf of R that the agreement/purchase orders between ECL and EDS were nothing to do with him, as he was not party to them. It was also argued that, despite the contract between FOL and ECL requiring authorisation to work more than 37.5 hours a week, R regularly did so without prior authorisation. The Special Commissioner accepted that while there was a strict legal obligation on R to obtain prior approval, it was not EDS's practice to require this of him and that had EDS wished to insist on the strict position, they could have done so but on giving reasonable notice to R.

11.105 R did carry out some of the work from his home using his own laptop and 'remote access' to the EDS local network. R understood he was the only person on the CSR project to have remote access from home.

11.106 The Special Commissioner said that neither R nor FOL had any *right* to send a substitute, all they could do was offer, but EDS was not obliged to accept. The purchase orders from EDS specifically requested the services of R and, as EDS had to give written consent for FOL to send a substitute, it was fairly clear that personal services was required.

11.107 His Honour Stephen Oliver QC accepted that R had a large measure of control over how he conducted the testing procedure; but there was a test manager with overall direction and responsibility for testing procedures. That is, there was a right of control. He found that in law, although not in practice, there was control over the work, as the purchase order required R to carry out work in accordance with instructions. It was also in the FOL/ECL agreement that R had to obtain permission to work additional hours and that R was required to adhere to EDS's rules and regulations.

11.108 It was also found that, although R's work involved an especially high level of skill and independence of judgment, EDS were able to control how the work was to be done through their organisational structure. It was the Special Commissioner's conclusion that there was sufficient control to make EDS 'master' and that had there been a contract between R and EDS the contract would have been one of service.

11.109 It was argued by Mr Allen that the actual obligations between EDS and R were so limited that they fell short of the 'irreducible minimum of obligation on each side' required to create a contract of service. His Honour Stephen Oliver QC referred to *Nethermere (St Neots) Ltd v Gardiner* [1984] ICR 612; however, I do not believe he has followed that slavish approach. He found in this case that, until termination of the agreement by EDS, there was an obligation on EDS to provide paid work at a place of work and a corresponding obligation on EDS for the provision of R's services to the end user. That, coupled with R's obligation to conform with EDS's rules and working practices, was enough to show that mutuality of obligations did exist between R and EDS and that they were well above the irreducible minimum. He found that there was an obligation on EDS to provide work; there was an obligation on R to provide his services personally and that there was an obligation on R to conform with EDS's rules and working practices. Therefore, there was mutuality of obligations. He has not given a specific definition of what mutuality of obligations is; he has just said that because these factors were present there was mutuality of obligations sufficient to create a contract of service.

11.110 On the facts there seems little if any doubt that not only was this the right decision, but all Special Commissioners hearing the case would very likely come to the same conclusion. R was in effect a manager at EDS with few real trappings of self-employment.

The case proceeded on appeal to the High Court (*Future On-Line Ltd (a firm) v Foulds* [2004] EWHC 2597 (Ch)) (see **11.132**), where FOL's appeal was dismissed. The court held, *inter alia*, that the Special Commissioner had been right to consider all the circumstances in which R performed services for EDS as well as the actual contractual terms. In addition, the Special Commissioner had been entitled to find on the facts that in carrying out his work, R was part and parcel of the EDS organisation and that, had a contractual relationship existed between EDS and R, it would have been one of employer and employee.

11.111 This case illustrates the importance of considering how a contractor acts in practice, as well as what his contract says. There was nothing in his contract saying he would recruit 160 people on behalf of EDS, yet this is what happened in reality. Accountax had reviewed this file and suggested the contractor was caught by IR35. I regret to note that we were correct.

Ansell Computer Services Ltd v Richardson (HM Inspector of Taxes) (2004) Special Commissioner Graham Aaronson QC SpC 425

Background

11.112 Mr Ansell was a specialist defence industry software contractor operating through his personal service company via an agency. The end users were Marconi and BAe. The Revenue was represented by Mr Gleig of the Regional Appeals Unit;

11.112 *Analysing IR35 case law*

the taxpayer by Accountax; and the Special Commissioner was Graham Aaronson QC.

The facts

11.113 Although Mr Ansell worked on specific defence projects, his contracts were regularly renewed and in effect rolled from one year to the next. He worked with a team of software specialists, some permanent employees and others freelance contractors. He showed very few of the classic 'in business on own account' factors the Revenue normally equates with genuine self-employment, yet his appeal succeeded.

Why the appeal succeeded

11.114 The Special Commissioner identified five main reasons why the appeals should succeed. Readers will be familiar with one, two and four, but may be slightly surprised to see three and five. The first and second reasons given were that Marconi and BAe 'were under no obligation to keep Mr Ansell in work throughout the ... respective engagements' and that Mr Ansell had no obligation to 'put in a particular amount of work, whether each day or each week or in aggregate during his period of engagement'. On the evidence there was an overriding maximum number of hours Ansell could be used, but with no guarantee of a minimum number of hours. Effectively this is saying that there was a lack of mutual obligations and follows the concession by Revenue Counsel in *Synaptek Limited v Young* [2003] EWHC 645 that in an IR35 context the mutual obligations have to subsist for the entire period of the notional contract.

11.115 In *Ansell*, Accountax argued strongly that where there is an absence of mutuality of obligations there cannot in law be a contract of employment. The Special Commissioner was referred to Longmore LJ's judgment in *Montgomery v Johnson Underwood Ltd* [2001] EWCA Civ 318 where it was said 'whatever other developments this branch of the law may have seen over the years, mutuality of obligations and the requirement of control on the part of the potential employer are the irreducible minimum for the existence of a contract of employment'. The Special Commissioner said: 'Given this clear statement by Longmore LJ, I see considerable force in Mr Smith's submission.'

11.116 The third reason for deciding IR35 did not apply was the simple fact that Mr Ansell could take time off without seeking permission from the end user. This effectively amounted to one aspect of a lack of control. HMRC cannot complain: they successfully argued the same principle when trying to prove self-employment in *Barnett v Brabyn* 1996 [STC] 716.

11.117 The fourth factor concerned substitution. Mr Aaronson acknowledged that the taxpayer had 'the ability to withdraw and suggest a substitute individual'. The evidence of Marconi/BAe and the taxpayer was that this was genuine, despite the Commissioner noting that 'it was very unlikely that the situation would in fact arise'. This is important because HMRC continually attempt to play down the substitution factor where substitution does not actually happen in practice. Substitution did not happen in *Ansell* (and in the Marconi period the substitution clause was relatively weak) yet the possibility of substitution was still held to be important as an anti IR35 factor.

11.118 Finally, the Special Commissioner identified as important many of the 'practical matters' that differentiated Mr Ansell from regular employees. These included a lack of sick and holiday pay and a lack of membership of the company social club. This again is an important point. HMRC argues that such benefits are a consequence of employment status labels; not a determinant of employment status and they say, the only reason Mr Ansell received no benefits was because the parties did not treat him as an employee! As such, argued the Revenue, these factors are of no relevance in determining status. The Special Commissioner did not buy that. He said that negotiating away such benefits in order to retain flexibility and independence was part of the commercial process that Ansell and Marconi/BAe genuinely considered when deciding the nature of their relationship.

Why the Revenue failed

11.119 The Special Commissioner noted that the documents relied upon by Mr Gleig for the Revenue were in the form of mere amendments to purchase orders and were 'barely legible and cryptically expressed'. Mr Aaronson preferred to rely on the contract entered into by the taxpayer company with CDL (the agency) and the oral evidence of the witnesses. He noted that it was significant that the Ansell/CDL contract contained a clause whereby CDL said it would enter into an agreement with the end user that reflected the terms of the Ansell/CDL contract and in particular the substitution clause. In fact this never happened, but the right of substitution was inferred from the lower contract and the evidence of the witnesses. The Revenue's argument that Marconi/BAe wanted Mr Ansell the man and Mr Ansell only as opposed to the provision of software services was unsustainable.

11.120 The Revenue strongly argued that Mr Ansell showed few of the classic 'in business' factors normally (in their view) needed to indicate a genuine self-employed relationship. On the facts they were right. For example, Ansell had no PIT cover and did not have multiple clients and did not provide much by way of equipment or premises. Yet the Special Commissioner said that a subjective approach had to be taken and in the case of a specialist software consultant working on secret projects in secure premises, one would not expect to see the typical entrepreneurial traits that others might exhibit. As such, the 'in business on own account' test developed in *Market Investigations Ltd v Minister of Social Security* [1968] 3 All ER 732 was of little practical assistance in the present case.

Usetech Ltd v Young (Inspector of Taxes) [2004] EWHC 2248 (Ch)

11.121 H was skilled in the production of design drawings of oil wells, rigs and similar equipment and was the sole director and shareholder of a limited company. In 2000 an agency, NES, entered into a contract for the company to supply services to a client, ABB. The Revenue was of the opinion that IR35 applied and that the

11.121 *Analysing IR35 case law*

payments received by the taxpayer company were to be treated for national insurance and income tax purposes as if they had been personal income of H from employment with ABB.

11.122 The taxpayer company appealed against the Revenue's decision and the Special Commissioner dismissed its appeal. The taxpayer company appealed to the High Court, contending that the Special Commissioner had erred in law in that the relationship could not be one of employer and employee given the fact that the contractual provisions between the taxpayer company and NES entitled the taxpayer company to provide the services of a substitute in place of H and because ABB had not been obliged to provide work for H to do, although in fact it did so, there was therefore insufficient mutuality of obligations for an employer/employee relationship to exist.

Substitution

11.123 The NES/Usetech contract contained a substitution clause which enabled H to send a substitute subject to prior written consent from NES—such consent not to be withheld if the proposed replacement had the necessary skills, qualifications and abilities in the reasonable opinion of the Client. This clause was absent in the NES/ABB contract.

11.124 A representative from ABB gave evidence at the Special Commissioners indicating that it was ABB's intention to secure H's services. If he had become unavailable, for example because of prolonged illness, ABB would have heeded his recommendation of a replacement, but the replacement would have been interviewed and taken on by ABB only if he was considered suitable. ABB would have regarded his being taken on as a new contract, as opposed to a continuation of H's services.

11.125 In light of this evidence the Special Commissioner concluded that in reality ABB required H's services. The right of substitution was not a sham—a suggested substitute would be given some weight but Mr H and [Usetech] could not dictate, at will who would perform the work: it had to be Mr H. The Special Commissioner viewed the 'right' of substitution to be largely illusory.'

11.126 Mr Justice Park agreed with the Special Commissioner's conclusion that the inclusion of a substitution provision in the Usetech/NES contract did not mean the appeal should be allowed, but put the matter rather differently. He said there is logically a prior question which ought to be considered—would there have been any right of substitution at all in the notional contract between H and ABB which the IR35 provisions require to be assumed? The High Court thought not and rejected the argument that H did not know and had no means of knowing that there was no corresponding substitution clause in the NES/ABB contract.

11.127 It was pointed out that if Usetech had speculated about the NES/ABB contract the likely speculation would have been that there would be no substitution clause. Usetech took no steps to request or require NES to include such a clause in the upper contract. (This is a healthy reminder to readers never to assume that the terms of an agency contract are reflected in the upper agency/end client contract!)

Mutuality of obligations

11.128 The Special Commissioner did not accept that there was a lack of mutuality of obligations. He considered that the requirement of mutuality might 'be satisfied by the obligation, on the one hand, to work and, on the other, to remunerate'. It is worthy of note that this is also what the Revenue consider to be mutuality of obligations.

11.129 Despite agreeing with the decision of the Special Commissioner, Mr Justice Park disagreed with the Special Commissioner's interpretation of mutuality and stated:

> 'I would accept that it is an over-simplification to say that obligation of the putative employer to remunerate the worker for services actually performed in itself always provides the kind of mutuality which is a touchstone of an employment relationship. Mutuality of some kind exists in every situation where someone provides a personal service for payment, but that cannot by itself automatically mean that a relationship is a contract of employment: it could perfectly well be a contract for freelance services.'

11.130 In determining whether or not mutuality of obligations were present, consideration was given to whether ABB were obliged to provide any work to H. It was argued that ABB were under no obligation to provide work for H. This was rejected on the basis of the minimum hours provision in the NES/ABB contract. The agreement between NES and ABB specified an hourly rate, and also specified 'Minimum Hours: 37.5 hours'. The High Court held the effect of this condition was that ABB agreed with NES that it would provide a minimum of 37.5 hours of work a week for H. Even if it failed to do that, it would plainly have to pay NES for 37.5 hours.

11.131 The appeal was dismissed. However, Mr Justice Park mentioned that he did not necessarily agree or disagree with the decision of the Special Commissioner, but rather his job was to consider the two grounds of appeal submitted by the appellant, both of which had failed to convince him.

Future On-Line Limited v S K Foulds (HM Inspector of Taxes) [2004] EWHC 2597 (Ch)

11.132 This case was an appeal against the decision dated 31 March 2004 of Special Commissioner Mr Stephen Oliver QC (see **11.110**). The case was heard before Sir Donald Rattee (sitting as a judge of the High Court). Mr J Antell appeared on behalf of the taxpayer and Mr A Nawbatt appeared on behalf of HMRC.

11.133 *Analysing IR35 case law*

The facts

11.133 R was an IT specialist with particular expertise in testing computer systems. From 1997 he had been employed as a consultant by the appellant Future On-Line Limited (FOL), a company whose issued shares were owned equally between R and his wife. From 1 July 2000 until 30 May 2003, R worked with a company called EDS pursuant to two contracts.

One contract was between FOL and a computer services agency called Elan to provide the services of R to EDS (or such other consultant as FOL and EDS might agree). The second contract was between Elan and EDS and Elan undertook to supply the services of various contractors to EDS on submission of 'a purchase order' in respect of the contractor EDS required. EDS submitted a series of such purchase orders to Elan for the 'professional services' of R.

11.134 R provided his services to EDS as required by the two contracts and purchase orders. The work was in relation to the installation of a computer system referred to as the Child Support Reform Programme pursuant to a contract between EDS and the Department of Work and Pensions.

11.135 The Special Commissioner found IR35 to apply and fees paid by the client to the service company were to be treated not as income of the company, but as earnings of the individual subject to income tax under Schedule E (as was) and National Insurance Contributions.

The appeal

11.136 The taxpayer submitted two grounds of appeal the first of which was based on a new argument not heard before the Special Commissioner. The new argument was that it was wrong to regard EDS as the client for the purposes of the conditions in paragraph 1(1) of Schedule 12 to the Finance Act 2000 and the client for that purpose was Elan not EDS. This would mean the hypothetical contract for the purposes of IR35 would be between FOL and EDS, which on the facts found by the Special Commissioner would make it impossible for condition (c) of paragraph 1(1) of Schedule 12 to apply. Mr Antell argued that Elan could properly be said to be a client because R provided his services for the purpose of Elan's agency business.

11.137 Sir Donald Rattee rejected this submission and said it was clear that it was EDS who required the services of an IT specialist for the purposes of its business of supplying computer systems to its customers. Sir Donald Ratee pointed out that Elan was in the business of a recruitment agency and it could not sensibly be said that R performed those services for the purpose of the business of Elan.

11.138 The appellant's second ground of appeal was that the Special Commissioner had placed too much emphasis on the 'part and parcel' test and when applying that test failed to distinguish between part and parcel of the EDS team who was assembled to carry out the project and being part and parcel of EDS itself.

11.139 Mr Antell relied on a *dictum* of Mummery J in *Hall (Inspector of Taxes) v Lorimer* [1992] 1 WLR 939 where he made it clear that the 'part and parcel of the organisation test' was only one factor that in some cases might be relevant, whereas in this case he submitted the Special Commissioner placed far more significance upon it and used it as an overall test to determine whether R could be said to be employed by EDS.

11.140 Sir Donald Rattee said it was clear from the Special Commissioner's decision that he was not treating the part and parcel test as a test of employment in its own right, or as anything other than one feature of all the circumstances he was properly considering. Sir Donald Rattee stated 'He regarded it only as confirming the conclusion which he had reached on the other factors of the case. This he was perfectly entitled to do'.

11.141 Further Sir Donald Rattee dismissed an argument that the Special Commissioner had failed to distinguish between part and parcel of the EDS business and part and parcel of the EDS CSR Project team. Mr Antell relied on the decision under appeal in *Hall v Lorimer* which the Special Commissioner said 'Being one of a team to produce a programme does not in my view lead to the conclusion that in the taxpayer's case he is part and parcel of the organisation ... a violinist in an orchestra may be part and parcel of the orchestra for the performance being given but it does not follow that he is part and parcel of the organisation which runs or manages the orchestra.'

11.142 Sir Donald Rattee concluded that this criticism was not justified in the present case and it was clear from the Special Commissioner's decision that he found R to be an integral part of the EDS business.

11.143 The taxpayer failed to make good any of the criticisms of the Special Commissioner's decision and the appeal was dismissed.

Netherlane Limited v York (2004) Special Commissioner Dr John F Avery Jones SpC 457

Background

11.144 In this case the taxpayer was represented by A D Robertson FCA CTA. The Revenue were represented by Mike Faulkner, HM Inspector of Taxes.

11.145 This was an appeal to the Special Commissioners against a Revenue decision that the circumstances of the arrangements between Mr M J Renshaw and AMP UK (Formerly NPI) for the performance of IT services from 6 April 2000 to 23 February 2001 were such that the 'IR35' legislation applied to National Insurance Contributions. The Special Commissioner was Dr John F Avery Jones CBE.

11.146 R was the joint shareholder and sole director of Netherlane Limited (NL), a company providing IT services. NL contracted through RML (an agency) on a series of six-month contracts to provide IT maintenance and support services to NPI.

11.147 *Analysing IR35 case law*

11.147 R had never seen the contract between RML and NPI, the terms of which were incorporated into the lower contract between NL and RML. The Special Commissioner accepted that R was unaware of these terms, but as the appellant entered into the lower contract incorporating its terms he took it as R having agreed to its terms.

11.148 R's work consisted of leading a team that supported and maintained two NPI mainframe computer systems. Users would report faults and R would categorise these faults in relation to severity before passing them on to a member of his team to take action.

11.149 The six-monthly contracts did not coincide with any particular aspect of the work and there were always problems to fix at the beginning and end of each contract.

11.150 R submitted fortnightly statistical reports to Mr Clark of NPI, who would also be informed immediately if any urgent faults were not fixed, R as a last resort would discuss poor performance of his team to Mr Clark and would even discuss salary reviews of members of the team with management.

Mutuality of obligations

11.151 The appellant submitted that there was no obligation on the parties to renew the contracts at the end of each six-month term. The Commissioner found it irrelevant that there was no obligation to enter into another contract on termination of each one. The Commissioner pointed out that this may be relevant in an umbrella contract with breaks between the work where the employer is free not to offer work and not to pay, as in *Carmichael v National Power Plc* [1999] 1 WLR 2042.

11.152 In this case, NPI were obliged to pay a rate for each working day throughout each of the contracts with the appellant having to give four weeks' notice to terminate the contract subject to working the first six weeks of each contract. This effectively tied R into the first six weeks and last four weeks of each contract thus creating mutuality.

11.153 The Commissioner stated 'The reality was that there was plenty of work requiring R's services in managing the team supporting and maintaining the computer system, and this factor points towards an employment relationship.'

Control

11.154 The upper contract provided that R had to 'obey any lawful instructions given by NPI and work a seven-hour day at NPI's office in Cardiff'. R was left to arrange how his team would work, but he reported to Mr Clark fortnightly and kept Mr Clark informed about serious computer problems.

11.155 Dr Avery Jones stated 'R was similar to a senior employee who was not told how to do his work but made regular reports on the state of the work. Clearly some control over R was necessary as he was in charge of a team of NPI's employees.'

Personal service

11.156 The lower contract contained a substitution clause requiring RML's consent (not to be unreasonably withheld); however the upper contract only allowed RML to propose a substitute who needed to be approved in writing. The Commissioner refrained from implying the terms of the lower contract into the IR35 hypothetical contract on the basis that RML did not agree to such a term with NPI.

11.157 The Special Commissioner highlighted that 'even if the same provision has been in the hypothetical contract it would not have amounted to a right of substitution; it was no more than a possibility envisaged by the contract to which NPI might or might not have agreed.'

The decision

11.158 Dr Avery Jones placed a high degree of importance on the day-to-day practices of R. Using the standing back and painting a picture approach he considered whether R would be an employee under such a hypothetical contract.

11.159 Using this approach the Special Commissioner highlighted the following factors as being important: R was the person in charge of a team in the sense of having management responsibility for the team; R was carrying out continuous support and maintenance work rather than a specific assignment. R was paid a daily rate and could therefore earn more by working longer hours; R did not work for other clients; and that the arrangement would terminate on four weeks' notice, all of which pointed towards an employment relationship.

11.160 In considering the factors that pointed away from employment he mentioned the absence of any usual employee fringe benefits (although in practice R had a normal holiday entitlement), and the method of payment against invoices and worksheets.

11.161 The factors Dr Avery Jones considered unimportant were the provision of equipment, and the lack of control over how R did his work. In weighing up the aforesaid factors Dr Avery Jones came to the conclusion that R would clearly be an employee. The appeal was dismissed.

Useful information

11.162 Dr Avery Jones was critical about the presentation of the case, namely that there was a lack of any real evidence. He said 'What was required was oral evidence to put some flesh on the upper level contract.'

11.163 The Special Commissioner was disappointed by the parties' witness statements and thought he had been given a survey of employment law, rather than a detailed description of the type of work done.

11.164 *Analysing IR35 case law*

11.164 The appellant made a case that it was the Revenue's responsibility to obtain all the facts themselves; however, Dr Avery Jones said this was a misunderstanding of the law and 'It is not for the Revenue to go looking for facts that are in the taxpayer's knowledge.'

Island Consultants Limited v HMRC (2007) Special Commissioner Dr John F Avery Jones SpC 618

Background

11.165 This case was heard at the Special Commissioners by Dr John F Avery Jones CBE. Accountax represented the taxpayer. The appeal concerned the work performed by H as director and shareholder of Island Consulting Limited which contracted with Spring Limited, an IT agency, who in turn contracted with Severn Trent Water (STW) in connection with a project for a new computerised billing system known as Target.

11.166 H was one of the external consultants who provided expertise that was not available in-house. The issue is whether if H had contracted with STW, he would have been an employee of STW.

11.167 STW contracted with Spring Limited on the following terms:

'[Spring's] method and timing of work is its own but [Spring] shall procure that the Executive shall:

- Comply with all reasonable requests of [STW] for information and statements as to progress as the case may require
- Co-operate with any of [STW's] personnel concerned with or other company appointed in connection with the project and
- Comply with all health and safety requirements and/or policies of [STW].'

11.168 Neither Spring nor Island were entitled to benefits such as holiday entitlement or sick pay. Either party could terminate the contract on four weeks' notice. STW had no obligation to use or continue to use the services of Spring Limited. The appendix specified H's name along with a daily rate of pay.

11.169 There was a continuous succession of contracts for three-month periods (or in two cases six-month periods). Contracts were often renewed at the last minute by the project manager approaching H. H hoped the contracts would be renewed, but did not expect this. The project manager would have been upset if H had not renewed and would have applied moral pressure to encourage him to do so.

11.170 Spring Limited contracted with Island on the following terms (H was named as the individual who will provide the services): 'Island may propose a replacement for the individual but any such replacement shall take place provided the Client (STW) is satisfied that the proposed replacement has the necessary qualifications, skills and experience and is suitable to perform services for the Client.'

11.171 Spring had the right to terminate the contract on 14 days' notice for a contract between eight and 26 weeks. The services were to be performed at STW's premises for four days per week (32 hours), but management could request a fifth day if required.

Facts

11.172 H generally worked five days a week, occasionally six and even seven if the IT conversion task needed to be performed over the weekend. His hours varied from five to 12 hours a day. He mainly worked on site but sometimes he would write a report at home, or co-ordinate conversion tasks at home, usually from 8pm to 10pm and sometimes weekends. H was free to decide the times he attended, the hours worked in a day and when he took breaks. Absences were agreed with the project manager out of courtesy.

11.173 H reported to the project manager who did not have IT expertise, but could judge the work by whether or not targets were being met. H was expected to correct errors at his own expense—the project manager was not aware of this—but H said it happened during conversion when there were file errors.

11.174 H did not manage other people at STW. H was provided with a desk and a laptop including a dial-in from his home. He used his own computer and scanner on three or four occasions.

11.175 H had an ID badge identifying him as a contractor. He could use the staff canteen and car park. He received no holiday pay, sick pay or pension rights.

11.176 Island billed Spring monthly accompanied by a timesheet. For three months' invoices Island's VAT registration number was not included on the invoice leading to late payments. This took six months to resolve.

11.177 H personally performed all the duties during the period under appeal. In 2003, H met with the project manager and had a document signed which confirmed the working arrangements. The document was signed by the project manager and stated that 'The contractor has the right to send a substitute to carry out the services in the contract in the place of (H).' The document went on to say that the contractor could subcontract the services to another party and that STW agrees to these rights providing that the substitute or subcontractor has the skills to carry out the services specified in the contract.

11.178 In 2005, the project manager signed another document presumably at the Revenue's request. This document said that STW would be prepared to *consider* a suitable replacement worker at the appellant's request.

11.179 On the day of the hearing under oral examination STW's project manager changed his witness statement. Having gone away and thought about it he had decided that he would not accept a substitute. This shows that no matter how prepared you are to take your case to the Special Commissioners it can all boil down to

11.179 *Analysing IR35 case law*

evidence on the day. HMRC called STW's project manager as a witness. This highlights the importance of calling end client witnesses yourself.

11.180 The Commissioner believed this to be the true relationship, as it was in accordance with the Spring and STW contract. It also represented the reality that it was a sensitive project and they contracted with the appellant for H's services on the basis of his special skills. Another person would find it difficult to pick up the project in the middle without H's direction.

The decision

11.181 The appeal was dismissed for the following reasons: Four weeks' notice would be needed as the provision of the Spring–appellant contract was not replicated in the upper contract, so could not form part of the hypothetical contract.

11.182 Not much control is expected for an expert like H, as stated in Lord Parker's judgment in *Morren v Swinton and Pendlebury Borough Council* [1965] 1WLR 576. H could be asked where to work. There was some control over when to work as some conversion services had to be performed outside normal hours of computer use. H would have to comply with all reasonable requests of STW for information and statements as to progress. H would have to co-operate with other personnel working on the project. There was something just short of contractual control over the number of days worked, but if more days were required H agreed to it. The Commissioner considered the totality of these factors to amount to sufficient control, though rather less than one would expect for a normal employee.

11.183 On mutuality of obligations the Commissioner decided the fact that there was no obligation to renew the contract after each three- (or six-) month period may be relevant to determine whether someone is employed during breaks in work, as in *Carmichael v National Power* [1999] 1 WLR 2042. Nonetheless, the Commissioner decided, as in *Cornwall County Council v Prater* [2006] EWHC Civ 102, that it was sufficient that within each contractual period there was an obligation on STW to provide work and pay the agreed rate. There was an obligation for four days' work a week, subject to the possibility of STW terminating the contract on four weeks' notice. The Commissioner said that the reality was that this was a five-year project and there was plenty of work requiring H's continuing services. STW was obliged and did provide and pay for work during each separate contractual period.

11.184 The Commissioner decided there was no right of substitution. It was decided that the most that STW agreed to was that they would consider a request. The Commissioner states 'In practice this would require considerable scrutiny by STW'.

11.185 Accordingly, the Commissioner concluded that the hypothetical contract would have the necessary irreducible minimum to constitute an employment contract.

11.186 Dr Avery Jones then dealt with the need to stand back and look at the arrangements as a whole as in *Hall v Lorimer*. He concluded that standing back and considering the position as a whole, the factors predominantly pointed towards employment, although a somewhat unusual one. He decided the only factors pointing away from employment were the longer payment terms than normal for an employee, which is not important; and the intention of the parties, which is not directed to the hypothetical situation.

11.187 Dr Avery Jones pointed out that the number of separate contracts would normally point away from employment, and there was a risk of the contracts not being renewed; however he stated 'while the project needed his services and he was satisfactorily performing his duties, this was not a real commercial risk, and it is inherent in IR35 that one must consider the contracts separately, because one starts with the actual contracts'.

First Word Software Limited v HMRC (2007) Special Commissioner Dr N Brice SpC 652

11.188 In this case the taxpayer was represented by Accountax. The Revenue was represented by Graham Conway of the Regional Appeals Unit. The case was heard by Special Commissioner Dr Brice.

11.189 N was the sole director and shareholder of First Word Software Limited (FWS), a company which provided computer consultancy services. From 4 September 2000 to 31 January 2002, FWS contracted with Plexus who in turn supplied FWS to Reuters.

11.190 The case came before the Special Commissioners because HMRC were of the view that the circumstances were such that, if the services had been performed under a contract between N and Reuters, N would be regarded as an employee of Reuters and subject to National Insurance Contributions and PAYE under the IR35 legislation.

11.191 N designed a solution for Reuters' problem with the migration of human resources and payroll systems and would report weekly to the Reuters manager. Reuters told FWS that they wanted the work done by a specific date and FWS was expected to manage its own project and was responsible for delivery, quality and timescales.

11.192 N on behalf of FWS led a project team of 20, most of whom were contractors. The project was carried out at Reuters London premises, but N also did some work at his office at home and on the train journey home using his personal laptop. N did not invoice Plexus for work carried out at home or on the train.

11.193 FWS could send a substitute, if the client was happy with them, although N never used a substitute. FWS had professional indemnity insurance, employer's liability insurance and public liability insurance. FWS did not provide services to others, but was free to do so. N was identified as a contractor in Reuters' telephone directory. N did not receive holiday or sick pay or any pension benefits; he was paid for the hours he worked and no more.

11.194 *Analysing IR35 case law*

Personal service

11.194 Dr Brice found that Mr Akins did in fact do the work personally, but the intention of the parties was that the appellant could assign the obligations and benefits of its agreement with Plexus so long as the assignee was acceptable to Reuters. Dr Brice stated 'In other words, the intention of the parties was Mr Atkins was not obliged to perform the services personally.'

11.195 This demonstrates that the correct test in IR35 cases is not whether or not the worker has a right to send a substitute but whether or not the worker is personally obliged to perform the services. Although a right of substitution remains a clear demonstration of a lack of personal service it is not the sole test.

Control

11.196 When considering control Dr Brice paid particular attention to control as to the manner in which the services were provided.

11.197 Dr Brice stated 'N was engaged to provide "a small piece of a large jig saw" and the way in which that was done was left to him'.

11.198 The Special Commissioner went on to say 'the manager did not control N in the way he worked in the way that an employer controls an employee, even a senior professional employee.'

11.199 HMRC often argue that control as to the manner is irrelevant when considering a professional as they should know how to do the work, like a senior employee. Dr Brice's statement confirms that even in the case of a professional, control as to the manner is important.

Mutuality of obligations

11.200 On mutuality of obligations the Commissioner found that had N been unable to work during the period of the agreement, then Reuters would not have to find him other work to do and would not have to pay him. Reuters were under no obligation to continue to make work available for the duration of the 2000 agreement. Dr Brice held that these arrangements point to the conclusion that N was not an employee of Reuters.

11.201 Dr Brice's comments demonstrate that mutuality of obligations is more than simply remuneration for work done (HMRC's view) and that mutuality of obligations is highly important in IR35 cases.

Datagate Services Limited v Revenue and Customs Commissioners (2007) Special Commissioner Adrian Shipwright SpC 656

11.202 In this case, Datagate Services Limited (DS) was represented by John Antell and HMRC by Michael Faulkner of the Regional Appeals Unit. The Special Commissioner was Adrian Shipwright.

Background

11.203 B had a wide range of experience in the design and development of computer software and was the sole director and shareholder of DS.

11.204 DS entered into a contract with TPS who in turn had an arrangement with MBDA for the supply of services. TPS entered into a three-month arrangement with MBDA in January 2001 which was extended until September 2004.

11.205 The work had to be carried out by a particular person for security reasons. There was a right to provide a substitute, so long as suitable security clearance was obtained.

11.206 There was no provision for a minimum amount of hours and B could take time off. B arrived when he liked and could leave when he liked; however he tended to arrive after 9.30am and leave before 4pm to suit his lifestyle.

11.207 The DS/TPS contract was non exclusive and DS could provide services to third parties. The contract also stated the parties' intention to remain independent and not create an employer/employee relationship.

Decision

11.208 The Special Commissioner followed *Ansell* and held that the correct approach was to look at the picture as a whole and determine whether or not B was in business on his own account and was not a person working as an employee in someone else's business. In doing so the onus of proof is on the taxpayer.

11.209 The Special Commissioner took the unusual approach of considering each of the factors listed in HMRC's Manuals.

11.210 It was held that there was no ultimate right of control on the part of MBDA. Further, the Special Commissioner commented that even if there was an ultimate right of control this was because of the security requirements and not anything akin to that under employment law.

11.211 MBDA had discretion in deciding whether or not to renew the engagement. There was nothing in the documents requiring personal service and the documentation allowed for a substitute to be provided or helpers engaged.

11.212 Financial risk was considered to be an essential part of being in business on your own account and the fact that B ran the risk of not having his engagement continued satisfied this requirement.

11.213 B was able to profit from sound management by organising his work effectively so as to save himself time. The basis of payment was a fee base, which the Commissioner found to be entirely consistent with self-employment. Further there were no employee-type benefits such as holiday and sick pay.

11.214 Analysing IR35 case law

11.214 There was no requirement for B to work exclusively for MBDA, he was not integrated into MBDA as an employee and was given self-contained projects. The Special Commissioner found that the number, or continuation of engagements did not give rise to employment status. The intention of the parties was also of importance.

11.215 Standing back and looking at the picture as a whole, the Special Commissioner found that B was in business on his own account and was not a person working as an employee in someone else's business on the hypothetical requirements that the legislation requires.

MKM Computing Limited v HMRC (2007) Special Commissioner Charles Hellier SpC 653

11.216 In this case, MKM was represented by Qdos Consulting and the Revenue by Mrs C D Cumming, Inspector of Taxes. The Special Commissioner was Mr Charles Hellier.

11.217 E was the sole director and owner of 50% of the shares of MKM. E worked for MKM and contracted with Proactive Appointments Limited (an agency) who agreed to make E's services available to London General Holdings Limited (LGL).

11.218 The rapidly changing demands of LGL's clients led to peaks and troughs in the demand for the services of analysts and programmers. MKM filled this demand by supplying the services of E, who was a skilled analyst programmer. MKM advertised in the yellow pages, had its own notepaper and website, and provided E with a laptop computer.

11.219 In considering whether or not E would be an employee under the hypothetical contract Mr Hellier paid particular attention to the three main factors of MacKenna J's test in the case of *Ready Mixed Concrete*, namely personal service, control and mutuality of obligations.

Personal service

11.220 The Proactive/LGL contract contained a substitution clause whereby the substitute had to be mutually acceptable. The lower contract did not contain a clause relating to substitution. MKM however prepared a document in 2002 stating that MKM had the right to send a substitute as long as the substitute possessed the necessary skills qualifications and experience. This document was signed by the director at LGL.

11.221 When questioned in court the same director of LGL stated that he would expect any substitute to be provided by Proactive and not MKM which would constitute a new contract with the agency. The director then said it would have been relevant if the substitute was sent by MKM rather than Proactive, as MKM may have communicated its knowledge giving the substitute an advantage.

11.222 Mr Hellier found the director of LGL 'more convincing than the statement quoted above signed by him on 5 June 2002' and that his oral insistence that a substitute would be subject to a new contract indicated he did not regard MKM as having even a limited right of substitution. This was despite a contractual term to the opposite effect. The Special Commissioner commented '…the most that (E) had was an expectation that LGL would consider favourably a substitution introduced by him'.

11.223 Despite the above Mr Hellier concluded that LGL's management regarded the arrangement as being for the supply of E's services only. That was who they interviewed, and who later they knew; that was who they thought they would get. Whilst they would consider any proposed substitute they did not regard themselves as being bound to do so, and even if a proposed substitute were interviewed and found acceptable they did not regard themselves as bound to accept him.

Mutuality of obligations

11.224 MKM were under no obligation to accept work at LGL and LGL were under no obligation to offer MKM any work, both parties could also terminate the contract upon giving four weeks' notice. Nonetheless, Mr Hellier adopted the approach that mutuality of obligations was met by an obligation on E to work and an obligation on LGL to remunerate him.

11.225 The Special Commissioner found that a four-week notice period meant LGL were required to pay MKM for four weeks, even if the project had ended early. Further when LGL's computer system back-ups were running late and MKM invoiced for this time, Mr Hellier held this to be evidence of LGL's obligation to pay for work not done.

Control

11.226 E was not subject to control as to the manner in which the services were performed. Nonetheless, Mr Hellier stated that E was subject to the kind or control which in the context of a professional employee would be sufficient to say that LGL was E's master.

11.227 Under the hypothetical IR35 contract Mr Hellier held that there would have been a right to require E to undertake a project in co-operation with other persons at LGL and to adapt his work to ensure effective progress as determined by internal discussions. The Special Commissioner commented:

> ' that right in my view would be sufficient in the case of a professional skilled person to say that LGL had a right to control what (E) did and, generally when he did it. Or to say that he was so subject to LGL's control (albeit exercised through guidance and discussion rather than command) as to make LGL his master.'

11.228 *Analysing IR35 case law*

Conclusion

11.228 Mr Hellier looked at the various 'in business factors' and decided that these factors overall pointed gently away from employment, but not vigorously so. In conclusion the Special Commissioner held that none of MacKenna J's conditions were failed, and that it is possible for the notional contract to constitute one 'of service'.

Larkstar Data Ltd v HMRC (2008) General Commissioners; High Court [2008] EWHC 3284 Ch

11.229 Unusually this case was heard before the General Commissioners. The General Commissioners do not tend to be legally qualified and the hearing is less formal. The taxpayer represented himself which is probably why he failed to opt for the Special Commissioners. The Revenue was represented by Inspector Anthony Mear of the regional Appeals Unit.

Background

11.230 R was the sole director and majority shareholder of Larkstar Data Ltd (LD). In August 2000, LD entered into an agreement with TPS (an agency) for the provision of consultancy software services to MBDA.

11.231 The work consisted of an open-ended series of contracts for work done on a particular project. At the commencement there was no means of knowing how long the project would take. The detailed requirements of the project unfolded as the project progressed.

11.232 B was paid an hourly rate, there was no provision for sickness, paid holiday, pension bonuses or any employees' rights and privileges such as car parking, and sports facilities.

11.233 The work had to be done at MBDA's site because of security requirements. B was encouraged to work during MBDA's core hours, but was free to decide when to work outside these hours. B would negotiate with MBDA the next stage of the unfolding project, but would not be controlled in how he did his work.

11.234 B was deliberately set apart by MBDA from their company structures so he could independently analyse, test and criticise their systems. For security reasons, B was not allowed to use his own equipment for testing MBDA's systems.

11.235 B occupied no post and had no title; his badge described him as a contractor. B worked only on a particular project under a series of five contracts. When the project ended, or if it had been terminated prematurely, the engagement ended. There was no obligation on MBDA to provide further work beyond each contract, and, if it had been offered B was under no obligation to do it.

11.236 Under B's contract he could provide an alternative suggestion to provide the services; however any substitute would be checked for skill level and security clearance before being considered.

Decision

11.237 In reaching their decision the General Commissioners followed the agenda for distinguishing between employment and independent subcontractors contained in the explanatory leaflet published by the Special Commissioners.

Personal service

11.238 Each of the series of contracts allowed a substitute to be provided subject to rigorous security procedures. B was one of only 1,000 individuals who held his level of security clearance, and this restricted the possibility of providing a substitute. In practice, it had never happened. The Commissioners found this factor to be neutral.

Control

11.239 When considering control, the Commissioners took into account whether or not the client could control what, where, when and how the work was done.

11.240 The nature of the work was specified in outline only; each contract provided a framework within which change could and did take place. B could and did advise as to the priority of tasks and made good suggestions as to the equipment used. B had more freedom than an employee as to what was to be done and this pointed towards him being an independent contractor.

11.241 The work had to be done at the site designated by the client for security reasons and because of this had no relevance to the issue of employment and independence.

11.242 B was encouraged to work the core hours, but was free to decide when to work outside of those hours. On its own, the Commissioners found this to be a neutral factor.

11.243 B was not controlled as to how he did his work. This indicated that B was an independent contractor.

Mutuality of obligations

11.244 The Commissioners considered whether the client was obliged to offer work and whether B was obliged to do the work. The Commissioners found there was no obligation either way; this indicated that B was an independent contractor.

Other factors

11.245 In total, the General Commissioners considered 16 other factors indicating that some factors carried more weight than others. The General Commissioners found that the most compelling of the 19 factors were:

11.245 *Analysing IR35 case law*

- control under 'what';
- whether the worker gets paid for sickness and holidays and what the pension arrangements are; and
- whether, and under what conditions, the contract can be terminated by the client.

11.246 The above factors all pointed towards B being an independent contractor and therefore B was not caught under the IR35 legislation. These factors were not usually considered fundamental by the Special Commissioners who usually placed more reliance on personal service, control as to how the services are performed and mutuality of obligations. Despite LD's victory this highlights the danger of having your case heard by the General Commissioners.

HMRC subsequently took the case to appeal before the High Court ([2008] EWHC 3284 Ch) on four separate grounds that the General Commissioners had erred in law. The judge, Sir Donald Rattee, did not accept HMRC's arguments on all of them. However, he held that the Commissioners misdirected themselves on the law when considering the questions of control and mutuality of obligations, and made one finding of fact (ie that Mr Brill was only encouraged to work core hours) that was unjustified by the evidence before them. The taxpayer's appeal was therefore remitted back to the General Commissioners for re-hearing by a different panel.

Alternative Book Company Limited v HMRC (2008) Special Commissioner Michael Tildesley OBE SpC 685

11.247 This case was heard before the Special Commissioners in January 2008. The taxpayer was represented by John Antell and HMRC by Susan Jones and Colin Williams, HM Inspectors of Taxes. The Special Commissioner was Michael Tildesley OBE.

Background

11.248 S was the sole director and shareholder of Alternative Book Company Limited (ABC). S was a skilled IT consultant who provided his services to NCM through a series of two connected contracts. The first was a contract between ABC and Computer People Limited (an agency), to perform services for NCM (the lower level contract). The second was a contract between the agency and NCM to supply the services of ABC using S (the upper level contract).

11.249 The issue in dispute was whether S would have been an employee of NCM had he contracted directly with NCM under the hypothetical contract presupposed by the IR35 legislation.

11.250 S worked for NCM full time averaging 36 hours per week from 1998 to 2005, he showed little evidence of marketing his services or taking active steps to find alternative work during the period of his engagement.

11.251 S performed his services at NCM's Cardiff offices which was necessary to work on the mainframe computer of NCM. NCM provided S with a computer terminal, desk, chair and phone at its premises. S performed a small amount of work at home, but this was out of choice in order to demonstrate his commitment to the job. S was expected to work during the core hours of 9.30am to 11:30am and 2.00pm to 3.30pm.

11.252 S was paid hourly and could only increase his income by working extra hours at the weekend. S invested no capital in the project and payments were guaranteed under the contract on production of timesheets and made at regular pre-defined intervals.

11.253 It was the mutual intention of the parties that this contract was one for services and not of service. Neither party wished to create an employer/employee relationship, and there was a clause to this effect in the contract.

Personal service

11.254 The 2000 contract contained no substitution clause. A subsequent contract six months later included a substitution clause, but enabled NCM to refuse the substitute on any reasonable grounds. However S had told HMRC in a meeting that the clause had been inserted as its omission would have been a stronger pointer towards the work falling within IR35. NCM's representatives gave evidence indicating that in practice NCM would either tolerate S's absence or terminate his contract and find somebody else.

11.255 The Special Commissioner held that under the hypothetical IR35 contract there would be a requirement for S to provide his services personally. The substitution clause was too fettered and at its highest was no more than a right to nominate another worker. Further the Special Commissioner added that the substitution clause was window dressing and had no practical effect on how the contract would operate.

Control

11.256 Although it was argued that S had freedom as to how the services were carried out, a meeting with HMRC and evidence from NCM's representatives painted a different picture. NCM confirmed that S was required to make formal progress reports every month to the project manager. The quality assurance team would carry out testing and acceptance checks on S's work and he would be expected to rectify any errors (NCM would pay S to rectify errors). Further, S could be over-ruled by a full-time senior member of staff, and NCM had the final say on S's standard of work.

11.257 The Special Commissioner held that the controls exercised over S were the same as those for NCM's employees and consistent with a contract of service.

Mutuality of obligations

11.258 There was no guarantee that ABC would be offered further work, but in practice new contracts were always offered and S did not look elsewhere to line up

11.258 *Analysing IR35 case law*

future work. The contracts could not be terminated without notice if there was no work for S.

11.259 The Special Commissioner held that mutuality was satisfied by the obligation upon S to perform services and upon NCM to pay him for those services throughout the period of the fixed-term contracts. NCM was required to provide work for 36 hours per week under the contracts which could only be terminated early by four weeks' notice or on exceptional grounds.

Mutual intention of the parties

11.260 A disputed issue in this case was whether or not the mutual intentions of the parties are relevant in IR35 cases. The intention of the parties is often disregarded by HMRC. The Special Commissioner addressed this issue and stated that the intention will have to be considered in the analysis of a hypothetical contract. The weight to be attached to mutual intention would vary from case to case and its evidential weight would depend on whether or not that intention has been translated into actual substantive arrangements of self-employment.

Other areas

11.261 The Special Commissioner found that S was not exposed to significant financial risk from his engagement with NCM. S was part of the scenery at NCM and there was no compelling evidence that S was in business on his own account.

Decision

11.262 It was held that the hypothetical IR35 contract would have the necessary irreducible minimum to constitute an employment contract. The relationship between NCM and S was overwhelmingly one of employment.

Dragonfly Consulting Limited v HMRC [2008] EWHC 2113 (Ch)

The facts

11.263 B was the director and owner of 50% of the shares in Dragonfly Consulting Limited (DCL). B was a highly skilled IT systems tester, and during the relevant period he worked almost exclusively for the AA on three IT projects.

11.264 DCL did not provide B's services directly to the AA, but did so through an agency, DPP International Limited (DPP). The AA entered into an agreement with DPP to supply consultancy services and temporary staff and DPP in turn entered into an agreement with DCL who provided the services of B.

11.265 B worked mainly at the AA's premises, although during the second project B could access the AA's computer from home, and during the same period paid

£400 for a training course for the benefit of the AA project. The cost of the training was not reimbursed by the AA.

11.266 When working at the AA's premises B was provided with a desk and computer and worked alongside other employees and contractors. He wore a pass that differentiated him as a contractor rather than an employee. Towards the end of the relevant period B provided, at his own expense, a special chair to help with his back problems.

11.267 B was invited to the project Christmas party and was able to use the on-site canteen (the Special Commissioner's decision failed to mention that B paid for the Christmas party and did not receive the benefit of subsidised canteen prices like other employees).

11.268 At home and at his own expense B had an ISDN telephone line installed to access the AA's mainframe computer. B also had a designated office with a desk, two laptop computers (although not bought specifically for the AA project), fax, scanner and office furniture.

Special Commissioner's decision

11.269 In January 2008, the Special Commissioner, Charles Hellier agreed with HMRC that, for IR35 purposes, B should be treated as an employee. When considering what terms the hypothetical contracts between the AA and B would have contained the Special Commissioner found as follows:

- There would be a series of contracts each with a fixed term. There would be no requirement for the AA to offer a renewal and no obligation for B to accept any offer of an extension.
- Each contract would be terminable before the end of its fixed term by 28 days' notice in writing by either party.
- Each contract would be terminable by written notice if B's performance was unsatisfactory.
- Each contract would be for the services of B. The contract would provide that B could send a substitute, but only if the AA had given notice that that particular substitute was acceptable in place of B for such a period as it should specify.
- In relation to control, up until 2 January 2002, B should undertake the tasks allocated to him with a specified but reviewable timeframe and should accept AA's reasonable directions in relation to what he was doing (rather than how he did it). Thereafter, the arrangements were that B should do work allocated to him within the framework of the project timetable and be subject to the guidance of the team and its managers.
- Payment would be made for the number of days on which B worked at the relevant daily rate.
- In relation to the first and third project, B would have been required to work most of his time at the AA's premises. For the second project, he would have been required at the AA's premises to the extent necessary to do the testing properly.

11.269 *Analysing IR35 case law*

- There would have been no provisions for pension, holiday pay or sick pay.
- There would have been no provisions for appraisal.

11.270 The Special Commissioner considered whether under the notional contracts, B would have been an employee. He approached this question by reference to the guidance in the *Ready Mixed Concrete* case. The Commissioner found as follows:

Personal service

11.271 The contracts would have been for the personal service of B in return for remuneration. The AA would only have accepted (and paid for) a substitute if the substitute's presence and person had been expressly agreed by it, and the AA would not have acted as if it was bound to accept any substitute for B even one who, when offered, was found to be acceptable. This very limited right of substitution is not inconsistent with employment and does not point strongly away from it.

Control

11.272 The right of the AA to direct through the operation of the team and guidance of the team manager was enough, in the case of a skilled professional man, to be able to say that there was sufficient control.

Mutuality of obligations

11.273 The Special Commissioner concluded that the mutuality condition was satisfied by an obligation to work in return for an obligation to remunerate. Further he added that a requirement to make work available (or to pay when it was not) was a significant pointer (a touchstone) towards employment.

11.274 Nonetheless, the Special Commissioner did highlight that the notional contract would have obliged AA to pay B only for work done. This was seen to be a pointer away from, or put a doubt over, whether it was a contract of employment. However in these circumstance it was not in the Special Commissioner's view a serious doubt because it was compensated by the fact that work was always available to the 'tail end charlies' and that it was known that it would be available during the period of the contract.

High Court Appeal

The grounds of appeal

11.275 DCL contended that the Special Commissioner erred in law in four respects:

- He wrongly concluded that the right of substitution within the notional contract would not have been inconsistent with employment.

- He wrongly concluded that the notional contracts would have contained provisions conferring upon the AA a sufficient right of control to justify the conclusion that the contracts would have been contracts of service.
- He wrongly concluded that the intentions of the parties were irrelevant.
- He wrongly directed himself that the relevant dividing line lay between being in business on one's own account on the one side, and employment on the other side. He failed to allow for the fact that a person may be self-employed without necessarily being in business on his own account. The law recognises the concept of 'worker' status. The Special Commissioner evaluated the circumstances without taking into account the fact that an individual might be a worker rather than an employee.

The decision
Personal service

11.276 Mr Justice Henderson found it clear that DCL did not have an unqualified right as against DPP to provide a substitute to perform the services for the AA, but could only do so with DPP's prior written consent. Mr Justice Henderson had no doubt that a limited right of substitution in these terms would have been compatible with the existence of a relationship of employment between the AA and B. His Honour went on to say that in order to displace such an inference, it would be necessary to find an express provision in the contract between DPP and the AA permitting substitution at the unfettered discretion of DPP.

11.277 Nothing groundbreaking has been established from Henderson J's *dictum* on personal service. His Honour has merely reiterated that substitution must be unfettered and that the terms of an 'upper' agency to end client contract must reflect the 'lower' agency to limited company contract. In this case the 'upper contract' contained no provisions on substitution; further the substitution clause in the 'lower contract' was fettered in the respect that B would first require prior written consent from DPP.

11.278 His Honour pointed out that the situation was quite different from the extreme and unqualified right of substitution which the Court of Appeal considered in *Express & Echo Publications Limited v Tanton* [1999] ICR 693. Despite this, Henderson J did not go as far to say that the only acceptable form of substitution would be a blanket clause, as was found in the *Express & Echo* case.

Control

11.279 Mr Justice Henderson concluded that on the strength of the oral evidence, the Special Commissioner was fully entitled to conclude that B's performance of his duties was subject to a degree of supervision and quality control which went beyond merely directing him when and where to work. In the case of a skilled worker, you do not expect to find control over how the work is done. Conversely, in the case of a self-employed worker in business on his own account you would not normally

11.279 *Analysing IR35 case law*

expect to find regular appraisal and monitoring of the kind attested to by the witnesses who gave oral evidence.

11.280 In light of the above Henderson J stated:

> 'The weight and significance to be attached to this evidence was a matter for the Special Commissioner, and in my view it was open to him to conclude that the nature and degree of the control by the AA under the hypothetical contract was on balance a pointer towards employment.'

11.281 It is clear from this statement that His Honour was unwilling to interfere with the Special Commissioner's findings of fact. His honour provided no guidance on the correct approach to take when considering control and simply said it was open for the Special Commissioner to attach the relevant weight to the evidence at hand.

The intention of the parties

11.282 Henderson J pointed out that the intention of the parties cannot prevail over the true legal effect of the agreement between the parties. His Honour did recognise that in a borderline case a statement of the parties' intention may be taken into account and may tip the balance one way or another, but in the majority of cases such statements will be of little assistance in characterising the relationship between the parties. Further, His Honour pointed out the increased difficulty in the context of IR35 legislation, where the contract is hypothetical and therefore there is no actual contract in respect of which the parties' could have stated their intentions. Nonetheless, Henderson J did not rule out the possibility that there may be borderline IR35 cases where intentions could be of real assistance.

11.283 The Special Commissioner in the lower court stated 'the intention of the parties as regards to whether or not there was to be an employment seems irrelevant'. Henderson J read this as a conclusion that the question of intention is irrelevant in the circumstances of the present case, rather than as a proposition of law that statements of intention can never be relevant for the purposes of the hypothetical contract. In this respect there was no error of law in his conclusion.

11.284 In light of this decision, perhaps the intentions of the parties could tip the balance of an IR35 case where there are equal numbers of pointers towards and away from employment.

Worker status

11.285 Counsel for DCL pointed out that in certain statutory contexts, such as the Working Time Regulations 1998 there is a special definition of 'worker' which includes not only employees under a contract of employment, but also an intermediate category of people who are neither in business on their own account nor employees. It was suggested that the Special Commissioner's analysis was impaired by his failure to consider the possibility that B might have fallen into a third intermediate category of this nature.

11.286 Mr Justice Henderson was unable to accept this submission. His Honour agreed with Counsel for HMRC that such categories only have meaning and relevance in particular statutory contexts in which they are found. Henderson J stated 'In the context of IR35, the only distinction that matters is whether the notional contract would be a contract of service or not'.

Conclusion

11.287 The appeal failed on all grounds and was therefore dismissed.

Appeals units

11.288 Finally, it is worth mentioning that HMRC now have a number of regional Appeals Units staffed by experienced advocate inspectors. Prior to the introduction of the Tax Tribunals from 1 April 2009, these inspectors took more complex General Commissioners appeals and most Special Commissioners appeals.

11.289 Readers who have had cases referred to the Appeals Unit need not be overly concerned, as these are relatively small units with limited staff resources under considerable pressure. In the author's experience, the inspectors are pragmatic and reasonable and often bring a healthy dose of common sense to bear and will drop cases where justified. They have the ability to stand back and re-evaluate a case where the original case worker might have become too embroiled to have a fully objective opinion.

Summary

11.290 After a disappointing start in *Battersby v Campbell* and *F S Consulting v McCaul* the taxpayer scored three important victories in *Lime-IT v Justin*, *Tilbury Consulting v Gittins* and *Ansell v HMRC*. These victories were short lived and were followed by a string of five successive losses for the taxpayer. *Synaptech* and *Usetech* both reached the High Court and were useful in developing some aspects of IR35, in particular mutuality of obligations. *Dragonfly* also reached the High Court, but again the taxpayer was unsuccessful. The recent victories in *First Word Software*, *Datagate* and *Larkstar* have helped restore faith on the part of the taxpayer (although HMRC did take the *Larkstar* case to the High Court—but the appeal was remitted back to the General Commissioners on errors of law, and will therefore be heard a second time). These decisions show that IR35 appeals can and do succeed, but nothing can be taken for granted.

Chapter 12

Should an HMRC contract review be requested?

12.1 In its press release of February 2000, the Revenue announced that it was offering a service to taxpayers whereby they could obtain a formal Revenue review of the IR35 status of their contract. The Revenue stated that it would reply within 28 days and would give an opinion as to whether the contract was caught by, or escaped from, IR35. HMRC has assured the taxpaying public time and again that they are not attempting to impose any particular status and will offer a contract review in a neutral customer service led manner. Practitioners' experience and certainly those of the author do not bear this out.

12.2 Under this service, HMRC undertakes to review signed contracts only, rather than hypothetical drafts (but it is noted that they will be happy to consider hypothetical contracts when it comes to enforcing IR35). Contracts should be submitted to a central HMRC IR35 Unit (IR35 Unit, HM Revenue & Customs, North East Metropolitan Area, Fountain Court, 119 Grange Road, Middlesbrough, TS1 2XA), or by e-mail to IR35@hmrc.gov.uk.

12.3 This service remains available for those who wish to use it, but would it be wise? The first published figures (June 2000) from HMRC showed that 53% of the contracts supplied were within IR35 and the balance were not. To some extent this removed some of the fears within the industry that HMRC would automatically apply IR35 to as many contracts as possible. The author's latest information is that HMRC are now 'passing' around only 35% of contracts. This seems low. Not only are contracts becoming more IR35-proof as time goes by, contracts reviewed by Accountax enjoy a pass rate of around 60%. The gap between 30% and 60% causes concern. In common with many other advisers, the author's view is that there is little point in sending a contract to HMRC for review for several reasons.

12.4 IR35 was introduced as a financial expedient by the Treasury; it was estimated that almost half a billion pounds would be raised through extra tax and national insurance with the implementation of IR35. As such it seems, at least, questionable whether HMRC are entirely neutral or objective in implementing the review service as they have much to gain from IR35. While this may seem a little cynical, evidence, both anecdotal and actual, bears out this concern. Many practitioners will recall the Revenue's and Contribution Agency's attack on self-employment in the construction industry during the late 1990s. This was rarely conducted in a true spirit of neutral fact finding and application of the correct law. Several websites contain examples of contracts submitted to the Revenue for review which resulted in something of a knee-jerk reaction, with the Revenue stating the contracts were caught by IR35. When challenged with robust argument, the Revenue changed its mind on many of these initial judgments. It should be noted, however, that had the taxpayer accepted the initial judgment then the Revenue would have been happy to have treated the contract as caught by the legislation. This is disturbing.

12.5 Submitting a contract to HMRC for their opinion arguably sends a message of weakness. Unwittingly, the message may be interpreted as a lack of conviction and such a course of action could be interpreted as showing a lack of real confidence or certainty in the case.

12.6 The Revenue has failed time and again to turn contract reviews around within its published 28-day target. Accountax dealt with one particular case where the client submitted a contract to the Revenue for review in March but did not receive an initial response until September. In this case the Revenue could not meet a 28-week target let alone 28 days and in the meantime the client felt that she was left in limbo and in a very invidious position. Without any explanation the same client then received a second opinion from a quite different tax office, leaving her with the belief that the Revenue's contract review service was a farce, with the left hand not knowing what the right hand was doing.

12.7 There are undoubtedly highly skilled technical experts within HMRC, who have a valuable role to play in respect of tax status generally and IR35 in particular. However, the reality is that the overwhelming majority of contract reviews are carried out at district level by local status inspectors and their employer compliance teams who may not necessarily share the same depth of technical understanding as their head office colleagues. This leads to HMRC opinions often based on a misunderstanding of case law and often in ignorance of the more recent legal precedents. HMRC's internal guidance is still selective in respect of the case law it cites, with several important cases having been omitted completely. This results in superficial decisions that are often based on an outdated interpretation of the law. The author has received many comments from inspectors around the country who claim they have not received proper support and training in the more technical aspects of status. Indeed one tax inspector commented to the author that IR35 was unfair to the Revenue. This was, he said, because well-briefed practitioners had all the up-to-date case law and specialist advice at their fingertips and had the technical advantage over the Revenue's foot soldiers who have been burdened with IR35. The inspector concerned was supplied with a free copy of this book and confirmed in writing that it was very useful!

12.8 The standard of contract reviews is also extremely variable across the country. When giving evidence in the judicial review case brought by the Professional Contractors Group in March 2001 (*R (on the application of the PCG) v IRC* [2001] EWHC Admin 236), the PCG's leading barrister Geoffrey Barling QC pointed out, in open court, that two Revenue offices in different parts of the country had reviewed an identical contract but had come to opposite

12.8 Should an HMRC contract review be requested?

conclusions as to whether the contract was caught by IR35. This might suggest to some that the fate of a contract review will be determined by which inspector happens to be given the file in which particular tax office, and this cannot be satisfactory. Indeed, Mr Justice Burton in the High Court found such inconsistencies to be 'deeply alarming', although some inconsistency is probably inevitable in the real world.

12.9 HMRC's standard contract review report letter is written in a stencilled format, whereby it is *already assumed* that certain direct employment factors have been established. A note at the end of the relevant instruction reminds inspectors to send such a standard letter only if it actually fits the facts! There are instances of so-called contract reviews where HMRC have not read the contracts properly, their response letters referring to clauses in the contracts which do not exist. Sham contract reviews are no better than sham contracts.

12.10 It might seem too obvious to state that a contract submitted for an HMRC review which is deemed to be caught by IR35 leads inevitably from a contract review to an IR35 compliance investigation. This is happening more and more. When this happens it is of course open to the taxpayer to inform HMRC that he no longer wants an HMRC opinion and that he will complete form P35 as he sees fit. However, HMRC have confirmed, in writing, that where a contract review is requested by the taxpayer and HMRC find the contract to be within IR35 and the taxpayer does not apply the legislation to the contract, then HMRC will treat the matter as a compliance issue (see Frequently Asked Questions, Compliance, Q2, on HMRC's website at http://www.hmrc.gov.uk/ir35/faq.htm). In other words an innocent customer service contract review will transform into an enquiry. This is a very disturbing development.

It can clearly be seen that there are many disadvantages both practical and technical, in submitting a contract for an HMRC IR35 review. The consensus is to avoid contract reviews.

12.11 As stated above, HMRC's contract review system is still in place and following submission of the contract and any supporting background information HMRC may offer an opinion. On the basis that HMRC's opinion is accepted, that is the end of the matter. HMRC's standard letter offers the applicant an opportunity to disagree with its opinion, whereby the taxpayer is invited to submit further information or arguments in support of his claim that the contract falls outside IR35. This further information may convince HMRC to change their view, but if a stalemate is reached then, subject to one important exception, HMRC will issue a formal decision stating that the contract is caught by IR35. Again, there will be an opportunity to try to convince the inspector to change his mind through technical correspondence, but it is unlikely that he will do so at this stage.

12.12 If the practitioner is determined to continue disputing HMRC's view it will be necessary to obtain from the inspector a Section 8 Notice of Decision. This will give a formal charge to national insurance, effectively stating that the contractor is caught by IR35, against which an appeal can be made. This appeal can then be taken to the Tax Tribunal for a contentious hearing and this is dealt with in Chapters 15–18.

12.13 The one exception mentioned above is the quite bizarre situation where HMRC may request specific additional information from the taxpayer which he cannot obtain. Typically, this is found in the classic personal service business/agency/end-user chain where the inspector wishes to see the contract between the agency and the end user. Much more often than not, the personal service business will not have access to, nor will it be able to obtain, this contract. After all it contains confidential commercial information between other third parties.

In these circumstances inspectors have refused to give a formal decision, leaving the taxpayer in a quite unsatisfactory position. In one case dealt with by Accountax not only did the inspector refuse to make a formal decision, he went so far as to withdraw his earlier informal opinion. It is understood that head office advice is that a formal decision should not be given unless the inspector has seen all contracts in the chain. However, there is evidence that at area level status inspectors are prepared to make a decision on the information placed before them. See the case study at **8.1**. The mechanics of obtaining a formal decision are also considered in Chapter 16 below.

12.14 It should be noted that, where an HMRC opinion on a contract is sought, due pressure should be kept on HMRC should it fail to comply with its published target of 28 days for the review turnaround. The average overworked status inspector, who may not particularly enjoy IR35 work will be happy to let a contract review dispute drag on until such time as he has the time and resources to address the case. As a strategic consideration, wherever possible it is wise to make HMRC work to the contractor's timetable, or at least to its own published targets. There is an element of 'he who shouts loudest' here and, as with construction industry status disputes in the late 1990s, there will be many a case won by the simple expedient of continuing to put the inspector under pressure to account for his actions and opinions.

In short, and as discussed elsewhere in this book, the name of the game is to avoid a drawn out dispute with HMRC. If by pushing and probing, the inspector drops the case then the client has been represented well.

12.15 It is necessary to read critically the actual wording of an HMRC opinion. In a case Accountax dealt with in Spring 2001 the inspector said that having reviewed the contract and surrounding background information the whole picture 'suggested' the client escaped IR35. Experienced practitioners will at once spot the danger. Use of the word 'suggested' rather than something less equivocal perhaps leaves the door open for an HMRC challenge by a different inspector or a change of mind by the first. This woolly wording leaves the client in a very difficult position.

On speaking to the inspector on the telephone it was immediately acknowledged that the wording from the client's point of view would be unsatisfactory but that the letter was written on the basis of standard wording encouraged by head office. It was agreed that a further exchange of correspondence would be necessary to clarify that, in the inspector's opinion, the IR35 legislation did not apply. This exchange of correspondence was swiftly carried out and the client now has a much more satisfactory and straightforward letter saying she escapes IR35.

There is an important lesson to be learnt here: even where it is possible to obtain a favourable contract review one should ensure that the wording leaves no room for subsequent argument.

12.16 *Should an HMRC contract review be requested?*

Summary

12.16 There seems little worth, both strategically and practically, of incurring the time, fees and trouble of obtaining an HMRC contract review. Requests for an HMRC contract review can lead to drawn-out correspondence and, effectively, a quasi-investigation.

IR35 is a financial expedient. It is not concerned with 'employment rights' for disguised employees or anything else. When tax inspectors are asked to provide a contract review opinion they sometimes take head office advice. But this advice is not necessarily focused on providing a neutral customer service. It is concerned with advising the inspector whether HMRC can win a contentious appeal if the contract in question ends up at the Commissioners.

Most, if not all, commentators agree that seeking an HMRC contract review has little to commend it and it is understood that very few people now go down this route. Anyone determined to do so would be well advised to review HMRC's Employment Status Manual, which contains a whole section of guidance on its approach to providing opinions on contracts (ESM3280–ESM3313).

Obtaining a professional contract review from an independent firm of tax advisers might still be wise. In the event that there is an IR35 failure, it is important for the client to be able to show that he took reasonable steps to clarify his position, as this may mitigate or even eradicate penalties.

Chapter 13

Appraising a case, interest penalties and directors' personal liability and can IR35 be reversed?

13.1 Perhaps the hardest task for the practitioner is to take a wider view of his client's position, particularly where the client has been with the practitioner for many years. A full and objective appraisal of the terms of the working relationship and in particular the contract will now become necessary. It is time to stand back and judge the merits of the case as a whole and whether there is a realistic chance of success at the Tax Tribunal.

13.2 The emphasis will of course be on the trinity of substitution, control and mutuality of obligations, together with an appraisal of the worker's financial risk, 'bigger picture' and modus operandi. Even at this stage the astute practitioner will be weighing up other relevant factors: will the contractor be a strong witness, will the inspector, if called, be a strong witness, is the paperwork and documentation in order?

13.3 Each case will have its own nuances and peculiar features. Few cases are the same on the facts. Ultimately, a subjective weighing up of the case has to be made in conjunction with the contractor.

It needs to be decided whether the contractor wants to play safe and accept that IR35 applies or would rather put his arguments forward if challenged and take his chances. If it is decided that there are no relevant engagements then the 'no' box is ticked on the P35. If a challenge comes and HMRC's view prevails the consequences for the worker and his business are as follows.

Interest charges

13.4 Interest will be charged from the date the deductions should have been handed over, under SI 2003/2682, reg 82(2).

Penalties

13.5 Finance Act 2007, s 97 and Sch 24 introduced a new penalty regime, replacing the previous penalty rules and practices. The new penalty regime for

13.5 *Appraising a case, interest penalties and directors' personal liability*

incorrect (or to be precise, 'inaccurate') tax returns etc, or failure to notify HMRC of tax under-assessed, affects income tax, corporation tax, VAT, PAYE and other returns, for periods from 1 April 2008 which are due to be filed after 31 March 2009. If inaccuracies extend over a period straddling the 'old' and 'new' regimes, practitioners will need to take account of the different methods by which penalties are charged and potentially mitigated. An awareness of the old penalty regime may therefore still be necessary for some time yet.

The 'new' regime

13.6 Under the FA 2007 penalty regime, the level of penalties will generally be higher than in the past. The legislation introduces four categories of behaviours ranging from genuine mistake and misinterpretation to deliberate concealment, and the level of penalties imposed are apportioned accordingly. It is noted under the new penalty regime that while the onus is on HMRC to establish the level of mistake (and thus the appropriate level of penalty), the taxpayer is under an obligation to notify HMRC upon noticing a mistake—even if it is HMRC's fault in the first place!

13.7 Perhaps the best approach to resist penalties in an IR35 defeat is to argue that IR35 is very much concerned with a technical area of tax. HMRC have lost as many cases in court as they have won, thus showing that the whole area is somewhat grey. Just because an IR35 case has been lost does not mean that the contractor was culpable. Losing an IR35 argument is not the same as cooking the books!

13.8 Finally, it is considered that any formal penalty determination the inspector makes (if agreement on the level of penalty cannot be reached) has to be proved by HMRC on appeal at the Commissioners to a *criminal* level; that is, beyond a reasonable doubt. This is because, under European law, a financial penalty is seen as punitive and hence carries a higher burden on the Crown. Normally the burden of proof at the Commissioners is a mere balance of probabilities.

The 'old' regime

13.9 Under the penalty regime that preceded the FA 2007 provisions, in theory there could be a penalty equal to a maximum of the duties at stake (under TMA 1970, s 98A(4)), although in practice this would never be implemented.

13.10 At the judicial review hearing (*R (on the application of the PCG) v IRC* [2001] EWHC Admin 236) HMRC's leading barrister confirmed, in open court, that if 'all reasonable steps' had been taken HMRC would not seek penalties. This was consistent with its view stated in HMRC leaflet IR109. This helped clarify HMRC's earlier statement on penalties issued in March 2001.

13.11 There is no definition of what 'all reasonable steps' means, but no doubt a robust argument can be advanced for the personal service business which has taken professional advice, attended courses and genuinely made an effort to fall outside the rules. Certainly, doing nothing and ignoring IR35 is not reasonable. HMRC have confirmed that taking 'all reasonable steps' does not require the contractor to seek

an HMRC contract review although in light of the new penalty regime an independent contract review by a firm of tax advisers would be wise.
HMRC have issued the following helpful 'penalty statement' on their website (http://www.hmrc.gov.uk/ir35/faq_qanda/compliance_q1.htm):

> 'An employer might fail to meet its obligations to file a correct return because of a genuine misunderstanding about the rules. This would be taken into account, along with the effort made by the employer to establish whether a contract is subject to the IR35 rules, when considering penalties.'

13.12 Penalties imposed under this regime can always be mitigated, and even if they are exigible they are unlikely to be more than 15–25% of the duties at stake. Penalties are abated by reference to the extent that any irregularity is disclosed, the extent to which the taxpayer co-operates with HMRC, and the overall size and gravity of the case. Whether the penalty ends up at nothing, 10% or 20% will also be down to the skills and experience of the contractor's representative. In any event, rumours of 100% penalty loadings are fantasy, and personal service businesses with a good case should not back down simply because there might be a small penalty if the case is eventually lost.

Personal liability

13.13 Some personal service businesses may be tempted to ignore IR35, and, should a liability eventually materialise, ensure the company is without assets whereby HMRC go begging; the contractor then starts another limited company the next day. This will not work and, indeed, it probably amounts to evasion. Accordingly, such a course of action should never be attempted or advised.

13.14 While the liability is initially that of the business, not the contractor personally, the director can be held personally responsible. This is because there are powers to serve a Notice of Personal Liability on a 'culpable officer' (in accordance with Social Security Administration Act 1992, s 121C) where he knowingly failed to make the necessary deductions.

13.15 There is a right of appeal and the onus is on HMRC to prove their case (SSAA 1992, s 121D(4)). If HMRC do so there is a real risk of imprisonment, as well as a fine.

13.16 While it is considered unlikely that many directors will be pursued, it is not impossible; and contractors who intend to abuse companies may be in for a big shock. Indeed criminal proceedings may be instigated in accordance with SSAA 1992, s 115.
There are also criminal offences of fraudulently evading income tax (FA 2000, s 144) and NICs (see SSAA 1992, s 114). These provisions were not designed with IR35 in mind, but are drawn widely enough to apply to service companies.

13.17 So far as PAYE income tax is concerned, HMRC have powers under the Income Tax (Pay As You Earn) Regulations 2003, SI 2003/2682, reg 72 whereby in

13.17 *Appraising a case, interest penalties and directors' personal liability*

certain limited circumstances they can pursue the individual personally. A detailed review of these powers is outside the scope of this book, but practitioners and contractors should understand that where HMRC can show the contractor deliberately failed to make the deductions he should have made then personal liability can be transferred.

13.18 In the author's experience HMRC have never successfully transferred an IR35 liability to a contractor despite making threats to do so. Readers may recall the *Usetech* IR35 case where the hearing was held in Bill Hood's (the contractor's) front room as he was ill. Bill had ticked the box to say he was caught by IR35, but subsequently changed his mind and argued he was not caught. Despite losing his case and despite prolonged HMRC threats to pursue him personally, it never happened.

Can IR35 be 'reversed'?

13.19 What if, on the basis of poor advice, or no advice at all, the taxpayer accepts that IR35 applies and pays the duties on the 'deemed salary'. Can the amounts paid be reclaimed?
Subject to one important condition the answer is 'yes'. This condition is that only where a 'deemed salary' has been calculated can there be a possible payment. Where an actual salary has been paid this cannot be reversed.

13.20 There are two methods of reclaiming IR35 tax and national insurance paid in error. The first is to make an 'error or mistake' relief claim under TMA 1970, s 33. This method requires HMRC to agree that a mistake was made and only if it is satisfied will it make a repayment. If it does not accept the mistake the matter must be referred to the Tax Tribunal for adjudication. This can be a relatively lengthy process.

13.21 The alternative method is for the taxpayer to submit a revised or supplementary form P35 showing no liabilities due. He is, in effect, reassessing his position under a self-assessment regime. The repayment should automatically follow even if HMRC want to take issue with the claim. This second method should avoid the lengthy delays likely to be encountered in the first method.

13.22 Reclaiming the IR35 duties will have a knock-on effect as corporation tax will increase, as there is no longer a deduction for the deemed salary. Most contractors, if not all, will be better off with a reclaim, but professional advice should be taken in all cases.

Summary

13.23 Individual cases need to be weighed up and clients need to be aware that penalties may become due if no action is taken in consideration of IR35. Personal liability for the director of the personal service business cannot be ruled out. Reclaiming IR35 duties paid in error on a deemed salary is also possible under the s 33 route or the supplementary P35 route.

Chapter 14
How HMRC will target IR35 cases

14.1 There are several possible ways in which an IR35 challenge may arise.

1. Ticking the 'service company' box on Form P35

14.2
Question 6 of the 2007/08 Employers Annual Return (form P35) was amended by HMRC in light of the Managed Service Company legislation.
The revised question 6 asks 'are you a Service Company?' If the 'yes' box is ticked it goes on to ask 'have you operated the Intermediaries Legislation (sometimes known as IR35) or the Managed Service Company Legislation?'

14.3 Much ambiguity has been caused by the terminology '*Service Company*'. HMRC have since clarified that the term 'Service Company' relates to limited companies, limited liability partnerships and general partnerships within the range of the Intermediaries legislation (IR35) or the managed service company legislation.
They have also issued guidance on answering the questions. The first question should be answered 'yes' if:

- an individual personally performs services for a client and the services are provided not under a contract directly between the client and the worker but under arrangements involving the limited company, limited liability partnership or general partnership (the service company);
- the limited company, limited liability partnership or general partnership's (the service company) business consists wholly or mainly of providing the services of individuals to clients.

The second question should only be answered 'yes' if income has been treated as deemed employment income and PAYE/National Insurance has been deducted in accordance with the Managed Service Company or Intermediaries legislation (IR35).

HMRC have stated there will be no penalties for ticking the wrong box. Equally, HMRC have stated they will not use the answers to question 6 to risk profile individual companies for a compliance review.

14.4 Despite HMRC's assurances, if a contractor admits to having had personal service income within IR35 by ticking the relevant box, he is potentially alerting

14.4 *How HMRC will target IR35 cases*

HMRC to the fact that he should be paying the appropriate deductions from the deemed salary. It is an easy exercise for HMRC to link the P35 with the contractor's personal tax return in order to see that the correct deductions have been made.

14.5 On the other hand, by ticking 'no' in box 6 particularly where the contractor's personal service business operates in an IR35 at-risk area, for example, computer consulting, HMRC may wish to satisfy itself that the intermediaries' legislation does not apply.

14.6 Whether or not HMRC wish to devote the necessary resources to linking such documents in all cases is doubtful. However, HMRC have invested heavily in IT in recent years and the benefits of this will no doubt trickle through to compliance activities before too long.

2. Examination of the taxpayer's self-assessment return

14.7 There is a new provision on the self-assessment Tax Return requiring taxpayers to make an entry for the total amount of income derived from services performed through a service company.

Similarly to the new P35 question there has been much debate as to whether or not HMRC will use this information to risk profile individual companies for a compliance review. Further there has also been debate as to whether or not this question is actually *ultra vires* on the basis that it will not assist HMRC in the task of establishing a person's taxable income (or gains); or help them to establish a person's liability to tax.

14.8 HMRC operate a sophisticated system of risk assessment when processing tax returns. If it is shown that a personal service business is paying a high level of dividends to its shareholders together with a low salary, then it is almost certain that such a scenario will present a possible and worthwhile IR35 challenge for HMRC.

14.9 Again, whether HMRC wish to devote sufficient time and resources to linking personal tax returns to possible personal service companies is doubtful, but, without question, the computer technology is available to do this.

3. Routine compliance visits

14.10 As part of its normal compliance routine HMRC will send out PAYE auditors to examine the books and records of businesses. Tax officers have now been alerted to look for IR35-type situations and this will become just another aspect of routine compliance.

14.11 HMRC adopted a similar approach during their status attack on the construction industry in the late 1990s and what was ostensibly a routine books and record review often became very focused on the issue of tax status. It is understood that tax officers have been told to pay particular attention to IR35. Practical advice on how to deal with an actual challenge is given in Chapter 15.

Information and inspection powers

14.12 New HMRC powers were introduced in Finance Act 2008, scheduled to take effect from 1 April 2009 (FA 2008, Sch 36). The powers allow HMRC officers to issue notices to provide information or produce documents 'for the purpose of checking the taxpayer's tax position'. This includes the introduction of provisions allowing HMRC officers to inspect business premises.

14.13 A 'check' for these purposes could be anything from a short telephone call to a detailed investigation into a person's financial affairs over a number of years. The new rules mean that HMRC's information powers are no longer related to enquiry notices. In some cases, HMRC officers will be able to request information and inspect records before the relevant tax return is filed. In addition, HMRC can give information notices if they discover or have reason to suspect that tax has not been assessed, or that tax has been understated, or that excessive tax relief has been given. Whilst there is a right of appeal against information notices, this right does not extend to information or documents forming part of the taxpayer's 'statutory records', or to an information notice issued by the First-tier Tribunal.

14.14 HMRC's information and inspection powers are intended to be used on the basis of risk. It is therefore possible that the powers may be used in cases where, for example, the 'Service Company' box in an individual's self-assessment return has been completed.

4. Submission of a contract review to HMRC

14.15 Chapter 12 deals with the issue of submitting a contract to HMRC for review. It is the consensus of many professional advisers that submission of a contract to HMRC can only increase the chances of an IR35 challenge. Real life experience shows that a request for a contract review can, where HMRC's view is disputed, slowly slide into what can only be described as quasi-IR35 investigation. This has now been acknowledged by HMRC.

5. Powers under TMA 1970, s 16

14.16 Under TMA 1970, s 16, HMRC have powers to serve a notice on agencies requiring the agency to give full details of all payments made to personal service businesses.

14.17 This is an extremely effective power, as it would enable HMRC to go direct to the larger agencies and in one fell swoop require the agency to reveal details of hundreds, possibly thousands of personal service businesses.

14.18 HMRC will then take the appropriate files and cross-check the details given to see which entries have been filled in on the P35 and also cross-check with the tax returns, which will show the extent to which salary is being sacrificed for dividends.

14.19 *How HMRC will target IR35 cases*

14.19 It was believed that the larger agencies would be the primary targets of this approach, but it seems that HMRC have not been active in this area.

6. Informants

14.20 Practitioners and personal service businesses alike should never underestimate the sheer volume of anonymous letters received by HMRC on an almost daily basis in which one taxpayer attempts to spill the beans on another. This was very noticeable during the construction industry status challenge in the late 1990s, where a contractor who had decided to operate PAYE would complain to HMRC via the Business Anti-Fraud Hotline about a competitor who was not operating PAYE.

14.21 While the IR35 sector is not the same as the construction industry, informants' letters do trigger a certain number of HMRC investigations.

7. Random enquiries

14.22 These will trigger very few IR35 challenges, but the possibility of a challenge remains.

8. Research teams

14.23 A previous Annual Report of HMRC revealed some poor results in certain areas of compliance. Concerns with yield are widespread and this has led to more focused campaigns based on risk-assessed analysis. This can only increase the chances of an IR35 challenge.

9. Schemes advertised as 'Avoiding IR35'

14.24 HMRC's Special Civil Investigations teams have become involved in IR35 cases. The SCI team looks at schemes which present themselves as a means to evade or avoid tax. HMRC have confirmed that 'it is likely that schemes advertised to "Avoid IR35" will consequently attract their attention, and may lead to an investigation' (see General Frequently Asked Questions, compliance, 4, on HMRC's website at http://www.hmrc.gov.uk/ir35/faq_qanda/compliance_q4.htm). As a result, taxpayers involved in offshore EBT (Employee Benefit Trust) schemes, for example, are probably running a higher risk of challenge. This is not to say that such schemes are illegal or ineffective, but they will attract HMRC attention and enquiry. Indeed many 'provocative' websites exist either offering dubious tax savings or suggesting that quite extraordinary levels of expenses can be claimed.

Summary

14.25 Not a lot can be done about these sources of an IR35 challenge. Forms P35 should always be filled in correctly as should tax returns.

14.26 One way or another there is a realistic possibility that an IR35 challenge will be at least *considered* by HMRC for perhaps 1% or 2% of all personal service business per year. Whether it then decides to take the challenge any further will depend on its risk assessment, workloads and other factors.

14.27 If a challenge arises it should be remembered that there is absolutely no legal obligation whatsoever on a personal service business or its directors or shareholders to attend a compliance visit and answer verbal questions put to it by HMRC. Refusing to attend a meeting is not a lack of co-operation by the taxpayer—it is his right. This is a very commonly misunderstood aspect of tax investigations, and the personal service business is entirely at liberty to insist that any questions are put to it in writing. Attending meetings with professional assistance is a very time-consuming and expensive process. In the heat of the moment questions and answers can easily be misunderstood. Even sophisticated experienced contractors may misunderstand questions being put to them and, in a bid to end an HMRC interview as soon as possible, sometimes say the first thing that comes into their head. This is a perfectly natural reaction, particularly from those who are a little nervous or inexperienced in dealing with the authorities. These considerations are dealt with in Chapter 15.

14.28 If, on the other hand clear, written questions are put to the taxpayer and clear written answers given in return there is a greater possibility that the questions will be better understood and given proper consideration and that the replies will be more reliable and detailed. This makes for a better quality of evidence should the dispute proceed on appeal to the Tax Tribunal.

Chapter 15
HMRC interviews and IR35 strategies

15.1 HMRC envisage that the majority of compliance activity on IR35 will be undertaken by the staff in employer compliance units. Following the Contributions Agency merger, these units contain a mixture of compliance cultures. On the one hand there are the former staff of an agency charged with protecting the interests of the contributor; on the other the tax inspector redressing loss to the Exchequer. Within HMRC, there have been various forms of employer compliance staff: PAYE-only auditors, staff specialising in dealing with benefits-in-kind, Construction Industry Scheme auditors and staff carrying out full inspections in all areas.

15.2 In terms of a compliance visit to inspect the records of a personal service business, the approach may vary depending upon the experience and background of the inspector. To its credit, HMRC have now standardised the format and scope of employer compliance inspections. These now encompass all the relevant areas of PAYE, national insurance, benefits in kind, statutory sick pay, statutory maternity pay, working families' tax credit, disabled persons' tax credit, student loan deductions and the Construction Industry Scheme. And now IR35, of course. A visit can be exhaustive, and exhausting.

15.3 This chapter assumes that the personal service business has been selected for an employer compliance inspection as above.

The start of the inspection

15.4 Prior to the introduction of HMRC's new information and inspection powers (see below), the first indication was a standard letter (commonly form ECR105) indicating the name of the employer compliance unit (usually, but not always, located where the PAYE scheme is dealt with) and the officer wishing to call to inspect the client's records. Included with this letter there would be copies of HMRC's factsheets EC/FS 1 or EC/FS 2 (for larger employers) and EC/FS 3, setting out certain of the rights and obligations taxpayers under review have, and indicating how the review will take place.

Following the information and inspection powers introduced in FA 2008, HMRC's power to enter business premises and inspect business documents is placed on a proper legislative footing. At the time of writing, the extent to which the new powers will give rise to a change in the above inspection procedures remains to be seen. The following is therefore based on HMRC's procedures at the time of writing.

15.5 HMRC do not need to give a reason for undertaking inspections, and generally speaking they will not. However, the reason for the inspection may be evident from the information sought (for example requests for contracts). It will also be reluctant to cancel the inspection unless there is a good reason to do so, for example, the business is going into liquidation with little chance of any dividend to preferential creditors. If the personal service business has ceased trading, or is insolvent, HMRC should be informed immediately, otherwise the next step is to decide how the inspection can best be handled.

15.6 Depending upon the volume of paperwork, it may be quite convenient to provide HMRC with the records, rather than have them visit to carry out an inspection. HMRC's standard letter provides for the records to be inspected at your business at a time that suits you. Generally, they will want to see a complete tax year for which a P35 has been submitted (as they will be checking the accuracy of the return), but they may only request a 12-month sample period. The advantages of this approach will become more evident throughout this chapter. A disadvantage is that the inspector will be under far less pressure than he would be if attending the client's premises to carry out a full inspection in one day, the records will be thoroughly analysed and every discrepancy or uncertainty picked up and queried.

15.7 If a visit is acceptable, the compliance officer will have suggested a date, or range of dates, within which the visit can take place. Typically, an inspection will take a half to a full day, perhaps slightly less for the average 'one-man service company' as the records will not be complex. If the business operates from home, and this is where the inspection takes place, two officers are likely to attend, for reasons of Health and Safety. Even if not, it is becoming more common for an inspection to be conducted by an employer compliance officer and one administrative assistant, who will carry out the more basic compliance checks.

15.8 Regarding the authority these officers have, as mentioned new information and inspection powers were introduced in FA 2008. The powers contained in the primary legislation (FA 2008, Sch 36) were expected to be introduced by secondary legislation with effect from 1 April 2009. The provisions were intended to replace the information powers in the Income Tax (Pay As You Earn) Regulations, SI 2003/2682, reg 97 ('Inspection of employer's PAYE records') which, generally speaking, gave inspection powers to 'authorised officers of the Board' who would be trained and experienced in dealing with this type of work. The FA 2008 information powers were also intended to replace previous corresponding powers (within the Social Security (Contributions) Regulations 2001, SI 2001/1004 at para 26 of Sch 4) for national insurance purposes. The officer should carry some confirmation of this fact, and HMRC employees carry identity cards. It is perhaps worth noting that 'an officer of Revenue and Customs' may carry out inspections under the new powers regime, and that the term 'authorised' from in previous powers has been dropped in the new legislation.

15.9 Under the pre-FA 2008 regime, the powers conferred by SI 2003/2682, reg 97 were limited to records relating to the calculation or payment of 'emoluments'. Specifically, they did not cover the following:

15.9 HMRC interviews and IR35 strategies

- Purchase invoices, although these were sometimes requested during a review. These needed only be provided if they related directly to 'emoluments' (including benefits in kind).
- Sales invoices, which may have been requested to determine fees received by the service company.
- Contracts between the service company and the agency, or any other party.
- Self-assessment returns (which should remain the same under the new regime as they do not pertain to 'business records' – see **15.10** below). An officer should not have questioned an entry on the director's self-assessment return without first opening a formal section 9A enquiry. This did not preclude him from investigating a matter that had an implication for both the self-assessment return and the client as an employer. For example, during an employer compliance inspection, the officer may have stated that a taxpayer submitted a P11D return for his company car, but had not returned the benefit on his SA return, and asked why this was so. The officer was effectively making enquiries into the taxpayer's return, despite not having followed the necessary formalities. Even if an enquiry was opened in this informal manner, it was still open to the taxpayer to ask the Commissioners to direct that the enquiry be closed. This was something of significant concern within HMRC, as a direction to issue a closure notice would preclude HMRC making any more enquiries into the return in question.
- CTSA returns. Similarly, the officer's enquiries had to be focused on the area under review—the employer's statutory obligations—as opposed to straying into querying items in the accounts.

15.10 HMRC's 'new' (FA 2008) information and inspection powers are more widely drawn, and are seemingly geared towards a single aligned compliance checking procedure to cover more than one tax. The power for HMRC officers to inspect business premises extends to business records as well. 'Business records' are those relating to the carrying on of the business, and which form part of the statutory records. HMRC have powers to determine exactly what constitutes a 'statutory record' for these purposes. Employers should therefore be prepared for the possibility that a requested inspection by HMRC may cover additional areas of the business, such as VAT.

15.11 Although there is no obligation to attend a meeting with HMRC, many HMRC officers are unaware of this, having met little resistance to a meeting request in the past. It is sometimes found that an officer will become insistent, and develop a strident attitude when a meeting request is refused.

As an example, during a previous contentious dispute handled by Accountax, the inspector threatened verbally to obtain directions from the Commissioners to compel the client to meet with the inspector. A swift written response to the inspector pointing out that he could not seek directions to force a meeting made him realise the irrational and futile stance he was taking. Meetings cost money in lost income and professional fees. Off the cuff kneejerk answers rarely provide reliable evidence. This has all been explained to HMRC. Still HMRC pursue personal meetings, but these should be avoided as a general rule.

15.12 As mentioned above, HMRC have standardised the procedural aspects of inspections, bringing together the various facets of employer compliance activities into a common approach. There is currently a standard questionnaire completed at each review that directs the officer through an interview with the client. This is usually how each review commences. It directs the officer to areas of potential problems. In a face-to-face meeting, HMRC will expect these questions to be answered. However, there is no obligation to attend a meeting or answer verbal questions put by HMRC.

15.13 HMRC will see a meeting as an opportunity to gather background information, to understand the operation of the business, and plan effectively how they will undertake the review of the business records. In reality, this is one of the likely points at which IR35 issues will first emerge, and an alert officer will already be taking note of salient points that can, and will, be used later in argument.

15.14 As is human nature, the officer will be looking for pieces of the jigsaw to complete the picture that the risk analyst has already begun. This person is a 'disguised employee'. That is why the case has been selected for review. Make no mistake that the intention of the officer, unless the contrary is strongly argued, will be to bring the company within IR35.

At the risk of criticising HMRC, it should be asked how many times HMRC have reviewed a PAYE workforce and strongly argued that the workers should be *self-employed*? Probably never. That is not their job. The officer's remit is to ensure compliance with the legislation. If a company can be brought within IR35, it is his duty to do so.

15.15 The innocuous questionnaire can provide the compliance officer with entirely the wrong impression, and all the ammunition needed for an IR35 argument. There is a real danger, particularly with the layman, that questions will be misinterpreted, answers will carry thoughtless connotations with employment and the compliance officer's mindset will gradually and irreversibly be established. And this is before a single contract is reviewed.

15.16 It is imperative that the interviewee is not drawn into the HMRC officer's world. The officer will not be communicating on the same level; the representative being interviewed will not be controlling the interview; the pressure of being interviewed in this manner may lead to misleading, even wrong answers against the favour of the business, particularly if the questions are leading; and the compliance officer is likely to be looking only for evidence of 'disguised employment'.

15.17 There is a strong argument to be made that no discussion at all should be had with HMRC, and that HMRC should be asked to put all matters in writing; this is any taxpayer's entitlement. It is easy to imagine how difficult this might be when faced with two HMRC officers, feeling under pressure to act co-operatively. But there is nothing uncooperative in establishing the officers in a suitable room, with the records, and respectfully requesting any questions be put in writing at the end of the inspection. HMRC's officers have a burden to act with courtesy and not to overstep the mark.

15.18 *HMRC interviews and IR35 strategies*

Factsheets and Codes of Practice

15.18 Employer Compliance activity was previously conducted under HMRC's Code of Practice 3 (COP3) which explained the purpose of the visit. Leaflet IR109 was issued at the end of an employer compliance review if irregularity was discovered and explained how an agreement could be reached. This was subsequently replaced by a series of factsheets (EC/FS 1 to 5) which amalgamate the contents of COP3 and IR109.

HMRC are expected to publish new Codes of Practice on compliance checks to coincide with the introduction of its new information and inspection powers in FA 2008. At the time of writing, final versions of the Codes have not been published, and the factsheets currently in operation are therefore discussed below.

15.19 HMRC will usually start with recent periods, say, 12 months or so. If earlier records are subsequently requested, this is the first sign that there may be a problem, and the officers may be quantifying the liability going back over a number of years. Similarly, if the officer pounces on a particular contract, or asks for information relating to a specific item outside the usual extent of the review, he already has his target in mind, and alarm bells should be ringing. The clear indicator that the officer believes that the regulations have not been complied with is the issue of factsheet EC/FS 4. Factsheet EC/FS 4 is provided to the employer at the time risk is confirmed or identified as an irregularity that suggests a penalty offence has been committed.

15.20 HMRC's instructions to staff on the issue of factsheet EC/FS 4 are published on HMRC's website (http://www.hmrc.gov.uk/manuals/echmanual/ECH8027.htm). However, a significant section of these instructions is not in the public domain due to exemptions in the Freedom of Information Act 2000. The information stated on HMRC's website is as follows:

Issue of Factsheet EC/FS 4

It is appropriate to issue factsheet EC/FS 4 (penalties) if the employer/contractor requests one or when an irregularity which may lead to a recovery is discovered or a penalty offence has been committed.

 (This text has been withheld because of exemptions in the Freedom of Information Act 2000)

 You should, **(This text has been withheld because of exemptions in the Freedom of Information Act 2000)**

- make sure the employer/contractor is aware that they do not need to co-operate (ECH 8028)
- issue factsheet EC/FS 4 to the employer or contractor
- record in the notes of meeting
  - what was said
  - the date of issue
  - to whom factsheet EC/FS 4 was issued, and
  - at what point in the meeting it was issued.

It is important that

- the employer/contractor is made aware that they do not have to co-operate
- the employer/contractor is given the opportunity to maximise the penalty abatements described in the factsheet, but that, the
- factsheet is not issued before irregularity is discovered (except on request) as this may antagonise the employer or contractor whose PAYE or CIS performance is satisfactory.

15.21 The issuing of factsheet EC/FS 4 is a useful indicator, as it will be the first thing that occurs when an irregularity is suspected, before questioning takes place. This is an important point for HMRC, as every taxpayer should be given the opportunity to minimise penalties. From the point of view of a business under investigation it also indicates that answers to the subsequent questions need to be measured and carefully thought through. Moreover, it can serve as the point at which an unrepresented client can say to HMRC: 'I would now like to seek professional advice before proceeding, please put any questions to my accountant in writing', thus avoiding the pitfalls identified above.

15.22 Another important development in this area is HMRC's recent concern that some of their tax-geared penalties may be found to be 'criminal' for the purposes of Article 6 of the ECHR.

As a public body, HMRC are under a duty to comply with the Human Rights Act 1998. Eventually, this means that the taxpayer is entitled to a 'fair trial'—including the right not to self-incriminate and the right to silence.

The officer may issue a standard letter to the service company inviting co-operation with his review, but drawing attention to the above rights. If he does, this indicates that the officer has not only a loss of tax and NIC in mind, but possibly the addition of a penalty as well. If this occurs, the cautious advice at **15.21** above is particularly important.

If the factsheet is not issued, or is issued after the event (which is not uncommon), there is a justifiable argument on customer service grounds that HMRC have failed to comply with their own guidance.

Contracts

15.23 An HMRC officer is bound to request sight of the contract(s) in considering whether IR35 applies. Although HMRC are giving written opinions elsewhere based solely on what is in the contract, they have always favoured a full fact-finding exercise when considering employment status issues. In terms of IR35, ESM 3325 states:

> 'When deciding what the employment status would have been in a direct engagement, it is necessary to take into account all of the relevant features of the relationship, including all contracts in the chain between the worker and the client.'

15.24 The officer will want to ask some questions about the contracts, not only for the reason of taking into account all relevant features, but also to determine

15.24 *HMRC interviews and IR35 strategies*

whether any of the clauses are a sham. More on this later. The information sought at this stage is likely to be fairly minimal, and will be just enough for the officer to make the broadest of judgments.

15.25 If the officer then feels that he has enough information to form an opinion that the contract is caught by IR35, he will say so. The aim is to gain agreement, to negotiate the additional tax and national insurance due and to collect the money. The whole process remains informal, and, in the interest of administrative convenience for both parties, HMRC prefer to deal on this basis.

15.26 In accepting the informal opinion of the officer, a taxpayer is effectively bowing to his superior knowledge of IR35 and employment status issues. However, the taxpayer should not be surprised if the officer has had little or no formal training in the area of employment status.

Employment and special status inspectors

15.27 Employment status training in HMRC ('categorisation' as the Contributions Agency used to call it), has only recently been given anywhere near the priority it deserves. It is a complex area; a wrong decision can cost hundreds of thousands of pounds, even for a moderately sized company. The decision-making process is also technically involved and can only be effectively conducted by standing back and looking at each case from a position of neutrality. HMRC have a dedicated internal guidance manual on virtually every subject imaginable, from the conduct of the officer himself through to how to deal with a complaint against him. However, the dedicated manual on employment status was not produced until October 2000. Prior to this, guidance was only deemed to warrant several paragraphs in other manuals.

15.28 HMRC, to their credit, have now put resources into dedicated employment status teams, and provided training and the above-mentioned guidance manual to the staff of these teams. However, this technical knowledge is taking time to filter through to the front-line staff, who may have been dealing with status for many years.

15.29 In the case of a routine compliance review, it is unlikely that the officer will be a member of one of the employment status teams. In recognising employment status as a specialism, the specialist knowledge has been invested in specific HMRC staff, those that are usually called upon only when a dispute arises or an issue is beyond the ability of the officer dealing with a particular case. The officer conducting a routine review may not have the knowledge and training accurately to make a contentious or borderline decision. An adverse decision should therefore be challenged, and the compliance officer will seek a more experienced opinion.

15.30 The next step is typically for the specialist status team to become involved. It is these teams who are undertaking the contract opinions, and they are much more experienced in their field than the average compliance officer. There will undoubtedly be a request for a further meeting, unless the original officer has undertaken a very thorough fact-finding exercise and the status inspector can make an immediate judgment based on those facts.

15.31 It is an interesting point that when HMRC used to give an opinion on the status of a worker, it was called a 'decision'. Similarly, the Contributions Agency used to make 'rulings'. This is despite the fact that neither opinion was binding, or had any force in law and neither carried a right of appeal. But it is easy to see how there was a compulsion to accept an opinion, if it were given as a 'ruling'. Thankfully, this presumption is discontinued, and HMRC recognise (at ESM 3284) that taxpayers are 'at liberty to adopt their own alternative view' to HMRC's when considering status.

This has led to greater impartiality of approach by HMRC, as an obviously biased opinion would rightly be ignored, and the status inspector will usually describe the next meeting as an impartial fact gathering exercise.

15.32 Again, the best course of action here is for matters to be put in writing, but HMRC will want to resist this approach, claiming that this prolongs matters, that meetings are more effective and so on. It should be pointed out to the inspector that a written dialogue ensures that questions are properly understood, thoughtfully and accurately answered, and the matter is properly recorded for both parties to rely on as evidence.

15.33 When conducting a meeting with a status inspector, it is usually found that there is little in the way of contentious argument during the meeting. HMRC's preferred approach is to take all the information away from the meeting, and come to a considered opinion after weighing up the whole picture. A good status inspector may challenge answers to questions if he feels they are unrealistic or conflict with other information held, but essentially he is conducting the initial interview to establish fact, not argue a case.

15.34 In 'ordinary' (ie non-IR35) status issues there are two sides to the argument. The engager and the worker both have a story to tell, and both stand to gain or lose by the decision made. It is therefore important that both sides are party to the debate, as either party may appeal against a formal assessment.

This is not so with IR35. Only the personal service business is in the frame. This means that the status inspector may have only one side to the argument, and not exactly a neutral side, and he will need to take extra care to make sure he is getting the correct information. This extra care is already hinted at in HMRC's IR35 chapters of the Employment Status Manual. ESM 3355 reads:

> 'Many contracts contain clauses that appear to give a right of substitution. It seems likely that many of these clauses have only been inserted to try and break the requirement for personal service and change the contract from one of service to one for services. Normally a client requires the services of a particular worker and a substitute would not be acceptable so there must be doubts about the validity of such clauses. Where a contract contains a substitution clause you may need to ensure that there is a genuine right. You should only accept that such a right exists where there is an explicit right for a substitute to be sent and that this right has been accepted by the client. A service

15.34 *HMRC interviews and IR35 strategies*

> company/agency contract may contain a genuine right but this clause may be cut down by what the client says. Their agreement would be with the agency and, although such a right may be given to that agency, it would not necessarily be given by the client to the service company or, more importantly, to the worker.'

The same instruction goes on to say:

> 'You should not accept that a right of substitution exists just because the contract is in the name of the service company. A right of substitution is only likely to exist where the client does not care from one day to the next for the duration of the contract who turns up to carry out the work, provided that whoever does so is suitably qualified and experienced.'

Effectively this starts with the premise that all substitution clauses are a sham, unless it can be proved otherwise. This is a departure from HMRC's usual approach, but it is indicative of the extra vigilance they are exercising over IR35 as a status issue.

15.35 HMRC's approach to status used to involve completing a green pamphlet known as the Status Fact Finder (AF301). Although still favoured by some, the 'newer generation' of status inspectors, particularly former Contributions Agency staff, prefer the more fluid approach of a less regimented discussion in order to gain an insight into the business and the terms on which the worker has been engaged.

15.36 It may be found that, underlying the claimed neutral approach, the status officer gives away his true attitude to the engagement with the words he uses. Many fact-finding exercises are riddled with bias, as the object of the exercise is to police the frontier of employment/self-employment and bring as many over the border into employment as possible.

Look out for the status officer calling the client 'the employer' and the worker 'the employee' (of the client). It may sound unlikely but this often happens. 'Who do you work for?' is a question commonly asked by the status inspector. 'The personal service business', the worker should reply!

Throughout the interview the status inspector will, subconsciously or otherwise, focus on the factors indicating employment and not on those indicating self-employment. The balance needs to be redressed by bringing *all* the factors to the forefront of his attention and making sure appropriate weight is given to them.

Factors the inspector will consider

15.37 There is a non-exhaustive list of factors HMRC will consider at ESM 0515. When considering these factors the inspector is likely to ask the following questions.

What is the client's business?

15.38 Initially the inspector will want to get a background to the business engaging the worker, to determine how the worker fits into the organisation. This not only provides the inspector with a useful insight into the likely relationship between both parties, it also provides the foundation for a 'part and parcel' argument. Although recent case law indicates that this test will not necessarily be determinative, HMRC still consider it to be a factor, although they do recognise it has limitations.

Endeavour to shift the focus to the business relationship with the client (usually the agency), and make sure the inspector gives as much attention to the features that disassociate the businesses.

In the unlikely case that this argument forms the basis of a challenge by HMRC, draw the inspector's attention to his own instructions at ESM 0545:

> 'Another example might be a mechanic, with a contract to maintain a firm's office equipment, who was called in by the firm from a base elsewhere when repairs were needed. In both cases those concerned provide services for the firm yet they are not an integral part of it.'

This example can be compared quite effectively with many IR35 computer consultants.

The instructions add:

> 'Although it can be very difficult to decide whether a person works as an integral part of an organisation, the comments of the Presiding Special Commissioner, Stephen Oliver QC, in the case of *Future Online Ltd v Foulds* (SpC 406) are a useful guide. At paragraph 31 of his decision he says:
>
>> "Finally, I am satisfied that Mr Roberts, throughout the time he worked for EDS, was part and parcel of the organization. In the particular circumstances of the present arrangements Mr Roberts was well integrated into EDS's structure assembled to carry through the CSR project. He had a manager to whom he was accountable. Mr Roberts in turn worked as part of a team managing other people. He was involved in discussions as to work allocation with EDS's project line manager. He was expected to be available to advise and assist other members of the team. He attended meetings with interested parties alongside other EDS managers. Although Mr Roberts' role in the organization will not necessarily be determinative, it is clear that in the present circumstances he was an integral part of the EDS organization dedicated to the CSR project."'

The instructions continue:

> 'However, a distinction has to be made between being part of a team and being an integral part of an organisation. A musician for example may be part and parcel of an orchestra but it does not follow that he/she is an integral part of the organisation that runs the orchestra.'

Are other workers doing the same job?

15.39 HMRC may ask whether a comparison can be made to other workers doing the same job who are employees of the client. This line of questioning is outside the

15.39 HMRC interviews and IR35 strategies

scope of the personal service business' reasonable knowledge as an independent contractor, who has not seen the employment contracts of his client's employees! Remember it is the terms and conditions that decide the status, not the job title or even the duties. It should be borne in mind that ESM 0501 states that:

> '... where there is a dispute the Revenue cannot simply assert that individuals are employees because of their job title.'

15.40 HMRC may also ask whether the worker was formerly an employee of the client. The justification for the IR35 legislation has always been that an employee could leave work on a Friday and return on Monday carrying out the same job through a service company, paying less tax and national insurance. Make sure that the inspector fully appreciates the changes in terms and conditions that come about as a result of working through a service company. If these terms and conditions demonstrate the worker is not a disguised employee of the client, it is irrelevant what the previous terms and conditions might have been.

How did the worker get the job?

15.41 The inspector will be looking for the typical employment scenario of a prospective employee responding to an employer's advertisement or offer of work. Make the inspector aware of any advertising undertaken, and any training needed to undertake the contract.

Is the worker in business on his own account?

15.42 HMRC see this as one of the fundamental tests of self-employment. It is also likely to be highly relevant in the case of a service company. In setting up a service company and engaging an accountant, the first steps towards being in business have been taken. Most service companies go beyond this, setting up office facilities at home, buying a computer or other expensive equipment, possibly giving up a company car and buying a private car—a significant investment. Then there are VAT registrations, liability insurances, stationery, advertising etc.

It will be very tempting for the status inspector, in looking 'behind' the service company to the interface between the worker and the engager, to overlook all of these factors. Make sure that they are forcefully advanced. As HMRC's employment status manual reads at ESM 0514 regarding the 'in business on own account test': 'This goes to the heart of the matter'.

Control

15.43 Control over the work done has always been top of HMRC's list of factors pointing towards employment. The inspector will be seeking to establish the extent to which control has been exerted over the worker. His instructions direct him to consider:

- control over what work is done;
- control over where the work is done;

- control over when the work is done; and
- control over how the work is done.

If the contract is specific on this point, and there is no right of control over the worker, make sure this is pointed out to the inspector.

In reality what, where and when are usually dictated by the nature of the job itself. Do not let the inspector make the mistake of assuming that because the personal service business is contracted to perform a particular task when the office is open at the client's premises, there is control.

15.44 HMRC's usual tack in discussing this point is to ask hypothetical questions, and a common example is:

> 'If you were asked to stop doing the work you are currently undertaking and do something else, would you do so?'

Particular caution should be taken with this type of question. Remember that it is the right of control that is important, not how accommodating the personal service business is when fulfilling the contract. The personal service business may well be willing to oblige certain requests, but if ultimately there is a right to refuse to do so, this is the crux of the matter.

It is generally better to avoid such hypotheses altogether. Direct the status inspector back to the terms and conditions of the contract where necessary. Remember also the fundamental test in *Staples v Secretary of State for Social Services* (2001, unreported) as covered in **5.121**.

15.45 The status inspector will place great emphasis on the administrative side of the contract, such as the requirement to report to a manager and complete timesheets, and will view these as an indicator of control. On the contrary, the fact that regular progress reports have to be made and accurate time sheets completed may be a result of the *lack* of control exerted over the personal service business. The fact is that most employees do not complete timesheets, because of the inherent trust in their relationship with their employer and the control that they are under. Be sure to point this out, and emphasise the business efficacy of progress reports.

Personal service

15.46 At long last HMRC have recognised that the requirement for personal service is fundamental to a contract of employment. If the worker is not required to carry out the work personally, he is not an employee. Substitution clauses present HMRC's biggest problem in terms of IR35, and they will seek to break as many of them as possible.

The internal instructions on IR35 form part of the Employment Status Manual. The manual (at ESM 3012) confirms that IR35 does not introduce any new tests, and the normal guidance concerning employment status in the other parts of the manual should be applied. The guidance does not therefore comment on aspects of deciding employment status, with one very notable exception at ESM 3355 (Considering the evidence: ineffective or sham substitution clauses). The guidance has already been

15.46 *HMRC interviews and IR35 strategies*

reproduced earlier in the chapter, and directs the status inspector to put the onus back onto the personal service business to prove that the substitution clause is *not* a sham.

15.47 Unfortunately for HMRC, it is not incumbent upon the personal service business to prove the contract is a genuine one, it is up to HMRC to prove that it is not. Authorities are reluctant to start overturning contractual arrangements without very good reason. If the status inspector asks for proof that the right is genuine, and this can be easily done by reference to other documentation, then do so. Otherwise, if HMRC have reason to challenge the validity of a clause, it is up to them to do so on their evidence, not a preformed assumption.

Another common attitude adopted by the status inspector when faced with a right of substitution is to ask how many times a substitute has actually been sent. Of course, if a substitute has been used, this is undeniable evidence that the right is genuine. If substitution has not taken place, the inspector may place less weight on the clause in forming an opinion. This is wrong. The client has only to establish that a right exists, not to show that the right has ever been exercised. Make sure the inspector appreciates this.

Yet another attack on the clause is to ask who would actually be sent if the right of substitution were to be exercised. Again, it is suggested that this point is irrelevant, and the inspector should be referred to the case of *McMenamin v Diggles* [1991] 1 STC 419 (see Chapter 5).

Finally, the status inspector will be looking for a fetter on the substitution right, either within the contract or otherwise. Does the client realistically expect that anybody could turn up to do the work? As HMRC's internal guidance (at ESM 3355) says:

> 'A right of substitution is only likely to exist where the client does not care from one day to the next for the duration of the contract who turns up to carry out the work.'

This statement has been roundly criticised as not reflecting the current case law.

Whether or not the client (ie the engager in this context) has this carefree attitude to the substitution clause does not supersede any actual right to send a substitute, if it is in the contract. Remember also that a reasonable degree of prescription on the grounds of skills and experience is acceptable.

15.48 The above are some examples from the author's experience of HMRC's attempts to undermine the right of substitution. Other lines of argument will undoubtedly emerge. At all times the status inspector should be brought back round to whether the contract obliges personal service. If it does not, it cannot be a contract of service.

Provision of equipment

15.49 In the scenario of a typical one person computer consultancy carrying out IT work on the client's premises using the client's equipment, the status inspector will probably think he is going to have a field day. HMRC's interpretation is that the provision of equipment points to a contract of employment, and he will see the engager as supplying the necessary tools to do the job. The status officer's questions will be focused on the IT equipment used, the office facilities available, and any other items provided by the engager.

In the wider sense of the IT contractor's business, he may have his own office facilities at home, a car used to travel between the site of the contract and his base (a significant piece of machinery!), a laptop, mobile telephone and various other items of equipment that are essential to his ability to operate. And let us not forget the main tool of the trade that our imaginary IT contractor possesses, in which he has invested, and on which his business stands or falls—his brain. As we have seen earlier, the provision of labour or skills is an acceptable form of self-employment, and this was underlined firmly in *Hall v Lorimer* [1004] STC 23 (see Chapter 5). The cost of training and keeping up to date can be substantial, and investment in this area funded by the personal service business must be made clear to the inspector.

15.50 HMRC will want to focus in on the day-to-day work carried out on the engager's premises—but they must be made aware of the wider picture of the whole business.

15.51 Another point worth making, if it is relevant, is that the nature of the work often dictates the equipment, location and facilities that can be used. For example, an IT contractor working on a bank's secure systems is sometimes confined to the equipment that can be used.

Financial risk

15.52 This is another topic where a biased slant can lead a status inspector to overlook whole areas of financial risk. The inspector will ask if money could be lost on the contract. Usually, this will only happen if the engager or agency does not pay the fees, with the inspector then getting the answer he predicted.

15.53 The reality is that stepping into the world of the personal service business involves losing much of the financial security associated with employment. Here is a list of possible elements of financial risk, most of which apply to the average personal service business.

- no rights to statutory payments such as any sick pay, holiday pay or redundancy;
- investment in assets (car, computer) that may or may not yield a return depending on the success of the personal service business;
- advertising costs;
- faulty work may have to be corrected at the cost of the personal service business;
- risks of having no contract;
- unpaid invoices;
- meeting costs of own travel arrangements;
- accountancy costs;
- professional liability indemnity insurance costs;
- training costs;
- administrative costs;
- short notice of termination without compensation.

15.53 *HMRC interviews and IR35 strategies*

These are just some examples, there are many more costs incurred by service businesses that the inspector will probably overlook. It is not just a case of whether the client wins or loses on a particular contract without considering all the risk that has been undertaken in gaining the contract in the first place. Draw these costs and financial risks to the inspector's attention and ask for them to be taken into consideration.

In the case of *Lime-IT Ltd v Justin* SpC ([2003] STD (SCD) 15), Dr Avery Jones said 'the fact of invoicing and the 30 day (or even 10-day, if that is what was subsequently agreed) terms for payment, even ignoring the actual delays in payment, seem to me to point towards self-employment'.

Opportunity to profit

15.54 The flipside of financial risk is the opportunity to profit from the sound management of the personal service business.

15.55 The average status inspector will interpret the opportunity to profit as representing the dividing line between being paid hourly (for example) and being quoted a fixed price for a job. As many personal service businesses charge by the hour, the status inspector will equate this with employment, and this again features prominently in many IR35 decisions by HMRC.

If the business is paying by the hour, the inspector will question how profits can possibly be increased. Thankfully, *Hall v Lorimer* provides a ready-made answer. Regarding Mr Lorimer ([1994] IRLR 171 at 174 para 13, Nolan LJ quoting Special Commissioner's judgment):

> 'He has the opportunity of profiting from being good at being a vision mixer. According to his reputation, so there will be a demand for his services for which he will be able to charge accordingly. The more efficient he is at running the business of providing his services, the greater is his prospect of profit.'

The same will be true of any consultant working in any industry. The success, and therefore the profit, of his business is dependent on the demand for his services, which in turn will depend upon the skill and ability with which he fulfils his contracts.

15.56 There is no case law to support HMRC's contention that hourly paid workers are likely to be employees. If you are a professional adviser it is possible that you charge by the hour yourself, and this is a useful point which the inspector will have to consider.

Mutuality of obligation

15.57 The status inspector will not raise the issue of mutuality of obligation, and the extent of his knowledge is likely to be that it is irrelevant anyway. He may be able to quote from HMRC's internal guidance at ESM 7180 which reflects on Waite LJ's comments in *McMeechan* ([1997] IRLR 353 at 360 para 41):

'When it comes to considering the terms of an individual, self-contained, engagement, the fact that the parties are not to be obliged in future to offer—or to accept—another engagement ... is neither here nor there.'

However, the *McMeechan* interpretation of mutuality was criticised in the more recent Court of Appeal decision in *Montgomery v Johnson Underwood Ltd* ([2001] EWCA Civ 318)

15.58 This is such an important and fundamental point that the status inspector cannot be allowed to gloss over the matter without ensuring that the facts are at least recorded and agreed, even if the significance is not appreciated. The status inspector may not fully comprehend the importance of the facts, as internal HMRC guidance has in the past instructed that mutuality of obligation can 'confuse the issue'.

This view can be rebutted, especially if supported by the above quote, by explaining that the Court of Appeal has directly undermined this in the more recent case of *Montgomery v Johnson Underwood Ltd*. In that case Brooke LJ referred to Waite LJ's comments ([2001] IRLR 269 at 275), and decided that the concept of a minimum of mutual obligations could not be dispensed with:

'If, therefore, Waite LJ's judgment in McMeechan is being interpreted as meaning that this line of authority has lost its potency today, that interpretation of it should not be followed.'

Reference should also be made to Mr Justice Burton's criticism of HMRC's position on mutuality of obligation in the Judicial Review of IR35 (*R (on the application of Professional Contractors Group) v IRC* [2001] STC 629 at 651. In the EAT case of *Stuncroft Ltd v Havelock* ([2002] All ER (D) 292 (Jan)), Judge Wilkie agreed that the absence of mutuality of obligations was 'a knockout blow'.

15.59 It is unlikely that the status officer will be willing or able to entertain any debate on this particular subject, other than to play down its significance. But it should be ensured that any lack of mutuality, especially if explicitly written into the contract, is noted by the status inspector.

Entitlement to holiday pay, sick pay etc

15.60 HMRC, in their internal instructions, quite rightly point out that entitlement to statutory benefits follows employment status, not the other way round. In terms of IR35 of course there will be no statutory benefits from the engager, and HMRC may be tempted to skirt over this issue.

However, the lack of holiday pay, sick pay and the other trappings of employment has been taken into account by the courts in the past, and is further evidence of the risk associated with operating a personal service business. Again, make sure that the status inspector includes this as a factor in his appraisal of the engagement.

Termination

15.61 The status inspector will be looking for a right of 'dismissal' with a period of notice, which can be found in many employment contracts, as

15.61 HMRC interviews and IR35 strategies

evidence that a 'disguised employment' exists. If he does not find such a right exists, he will determine this factor to be non-conclusive (in accordance with ESM 0546).

15.62 HMRC's instructions do not give any weight to the financial risk inherent in cases where the contract can be terminated at short notice, or even with no notice at all. Unless there is breach of contract, this is inconsistent with employment, and could be further evidence of a lack of mutuality of obligation.

15.63 In each of the above cases, ensure that the status inspector notes and appreciates the alternative points of view, or no significance at all will be attached to the matter.

Exclusivity

15.64 The nature of the work undertaken by many personal service businesses involves working for one client at a time. Many contracts allow freedom to undertake other work, providing this does not interfere with the performance of the contractual obligations.

15.65 The status inspector will view a requirement for exclusive services as an indicator of employment, although the actual HMRC instructions are far from conclusive. If there are exclusivity clauses within the contract, draw the status inspector's attention to his own instructions at ESM 0555:

> 'However, exclusive services clauses are not only found in contracts of employment. They may also appear in contracts for services. A self-employed individual running an agency for an insurance company may be precluded from selling any other company's policies. Similarly an author may agree to write for only one publisher.'

Parallels can be drawn between the insurance agent in HMRC's example and the personal service company, particularly where intellectual property rights rest with the engager, or a conflict of interests can arise in the competitive IT industry.

15.66 Also, do not let the status inspector confuse rights with practicalities. He may ask whether other contracts could feasibly be undertaken, and the response may be that they could not. But underlying the answer may be practical considerations—perhaps the current contract is lucrative, or conveniently local. The relevant point is whether there is a right to take other contracts. If there is no mutuality of obligation, or if there is a right to terminate a contract without notice, the personal service business is at liberty to move to another contract at will. Sensible business management may make this unlikely, but that is not the point.

15.67 Ensure that the status inspector is also aware of successive contracts with different clients, as this points away from employment.

Intention of the parties

15.68 HMRC accept (as stated at ESM 0554) that in borderline cases, the intention of the parties may be decisive:

> 'When you have gathered all the facts, you should stand back and look at the bigger picture. If you consider that the case is borderline, you should then, and only then, look at the intention of the parties. Where there is mutual intention for a contract of employment or for a contract for services, that will determine the status of the worker.'

In the 1999 Court of Appeal case of *Express Echo Publications Ltd v Tanton* ([1999] ICR 693), Peter Gibson LJ said 'One starts with the common intention of the parties that Mr Tanten should not be an employee but should be self-employed'.

This is a vital point, and a very useful argument to use against the status inspector. If a good debate is made against employee status, you will often hear the status inspector admit that this is 'a very difficult decision' or 'a very narrow case'.

Bearing in mind the above instruction, if a good enough argument can be formulated to get the status inspector to concede his opinion is borderline, the intention of the parties is decisive. It almost goes without saying that both parties intend to avoid an employer/employee relationship—that is one of the main reasons for the existence of a personal service business, and more often than not this can be found explicitly stated within the contract.

Notes of interview

15.69 Following any meeting with HMRC, it is important to request a copy of HMRC's notes of the meeting. These should be drafted by the interviewer as soon as practicable after the meeting, so there should be no delay in providing them.

15.70 The meeting record will provide an insight into how the status inspector has perceived and interpreted the information given to him. If there are factual inaccuracies, it is obviously imperative that the officer is put right immediately. If any aspect of the notes imply a bias towards IR35 which is unreasonable or does not hold with the facts, again, the officer should be put straight and the fact that a neutral position is advocated by HMRC should be pointed out.

If the case becomes contentious and ends up before the Tax Tribunal, HMRC will use the original notes of the meeting as evidence, and if these have been disagreed and challenged at an early stage rather than waiting until the hearing, this lends more weight to the challenge.

In the case of *Parade Park Hotel and another v HMRC* [2007] STC (SCD) 430, the Special Commissioner said that unsigned notes of interview will be given very little weight. Readers should be fully aware of the consequences of signing inaccurate notes of meeting—if the notes are not agreed, do not sign them!

15.71 *HMRC interviews and IR35 strategies*

Developments in tactics

Information notices

15.71 Practitioners have noted that HMRC have shown a marked increase in their willingness to use their statutory powers under TMA 1970, s 20 ('Power to call for documents of taxpayers and others') in IR35 cases.

15.72 This can be seen in cases where information is needed from the end-user client, but the end user is reluctant or unable to provide that information. This may also be the case where the taxpayer or its director (because strictly speaking it is the company that is the appellant) refuses or is unable to provide information.

15.73 Subject to certain limitations and conditions, TMA 1970, s 20 allows HMRC to seek information and particulars both from the taxpayer and third parties. A Section 20 Notice is not the same as the old style 'Commissioners' Precepts' practitioners may have been familiar with. A Section 20 Notice is an inspector's notice that merely requires ratification by a Commissioner. Because the application for ratification is a private matter between HMRC and the Commissioner it is *ex parte* and the taxpayer and his agent have no right to attend or make verbal representations.

15.74 Clearly, in cases of large investigations involving fraud, one can understand the merits and sense in making the application *ex parte*, but in the run of the mill IR35 case it does nothing other than deny the taxpayer the right to put forward his side of the story. Arguably, this is contrary to natural justice and may amount to a breach of human rights. Section 20 Notices do not require an assessment to be under appeal.

15.75 HMRC have confirmed in their manuals that any written representations the practitioner wished to give to the inspector will be read out by the inspector at the meeting. There is little doubt that some inspectors will present such written representations with limited vigour.

15.76 Under the precept system an inspector could raise an assessment which, once appealed, would then be subject to a directions hearing where the Commissioners would consider requiring the production of information. Such a hearing would be in open court and the practitioner could make verbal representations and see that fair play was done.

15.77 Given a choice between raising formal assessments, where the taxpayer can then dictate or at least influence the conduct of the case, or pursuing a Section 20 Notice, which in some ways freezes out the agent, it is disappointing, but of little surprise, that inspectors increasingly seem to prefer to go the Section 20 route.

15.78 Although HMRC seek the taxpayer's 'co-operation' they are using their statutory powers under s 20 where they do not get the co-operation they want. This is the case even in cases of contract reviews, not full compliance enquiries.

15.79 Under the new information powers in Finance Act 2008 as mentioned earlier in this chapter, HMRC will have the power to request information without the need for Commissioners' approval, not only for documentation already in the taxpayer's possession, but to include creation of explanatory information by the taxpayer such that HMRC deem relevant. These powers would replace s 20(1) and similar provisions for third-party information would be introduced to replace those of s 20(3). While it is noted that there will be a right of appeal against such notices, the effect of such an appeal (and its success in comparison to s 20 Notice appeals) is a matter of waiting to see how narrowly the Tribunals will interpret what is and what is not relevant.

End-user evidence

15.80 Following HMRC defeats in *Lime-IT Ltd v Justin* ([2003] STC (SCD) 15) and *Tilbury Consulting Ltd v Gittins* ([2004] STC (SCD) 72) there has been a noticeable shift in the way HMRC approach IR35 cases. Information and statements will be sought from representatives of the end user. Unfortunately, this information may be given by human resources rather than procurement and might often muddy, rather than clarify, matters. Of even greater significance is the fact that HMRC will tend to obtain this information after formal assessments have been issued. From a self-assessment perspective this is very unsatisfactory, as the evidence or views of the end user might well be highly relevant in deciding whether IR35 applies or not. Yet the taxpayer never gets to see this information unless the case is about to be heard by the Tax Tribunal! The court commented on the virtually impossible position of the taxpayer in the IR35 appeal *Ansell Computer Services Ltd v Richardson (HMIT)* SpC [2004] STC (SCD) 472 (SpC 425).

Customer service or compliance enquiry

15.81 HMRC have previously given categoric assurances that where a taxpayer requests a contract review under the customer service initiative, if HMRC's 'caught by IR35' opinion is not accepted by the taxpayer, that will not lead to the taxpayer being enquired into. However, HMRC have now changed their policy, despite the FAQs not telling the full story. If a taxpayer now rejects the HMRC's 'caught' opinion, once the filing date for form P35 has passed HMRC will treat the refusal to accept their opinion as an act justifying a compliance enquiry. The old assurance has gone. When challenged on this, HMRC have responded that 'the position has moved on and an enquiry is justified'. When again challenged as to how the position has moved on HMRC have responded by saying that the taxpayer has not accepted their 'caught' opinion! Practitioners beware.

A new approach to substitution

15.82 Despite case law that clearly states a substitution clause will be effective in defeating employed status, for example the *Express Echo* case, HMRC seem to have adopted their own approach.

15.83 *HMRC interviews and IR35 strategies*

15.83 HMRC specialists have confirmed to Accountax that substitution is merely another factor to be taken into account. As such they will try to play it down, but the law is not on their side.

15.84 HMRC will often attempt (and succeed) in getting the end user to concede that the contractor could not decide 'from one day to the next' to send any substitute he wished. Most end users will confirm this, but this is not the test.

15.85 As substitution is a central factor (and HMRC know this) they will increasingly focus on either playing it down, or will present unrealistic scenarios to the end user in a bid to get confirmation that a substitute could not be sent.

Conclusion

15.86 Handling an IR35 enquiry, particularly a face-to-face meeting, is a major aspect of defending a client. Practitioners should note an increased preference for HMRC to use its statutory information powers. Where HMRC have obtained statements or information from a third party this should be requested at an early stage to appraise the evidence.

Summary

15.87 To be forewarned is to be forearmed. Compliance officers will concentrate on the above areas, many of which are fundamental to IR35 'disguised employee' status. But they must operate within the law at all times.

Questions on IR35 disguised employee status should be answered in writing and the contractor should not get involved in a technical verbal argument with the officer.

Areas which are important, such as mutuality of obligations may not even be raised by the officer. If the contractor is represented by his accountant this and other factors which are relevant but which have not been raised should be discussed and included in any notes of meeting.

Chapter 16
Appeal formalities and strategies in an unresolved IR35 dispute

Making an appeal

16.1 It would be hoped that a robust presentation of the available arguments in Chapters 3, 7 and 8 will result in HMRC backing down, but this will not always be the case. Despite cogent technical argument and possibly attendance at meetings with HMRC, the practitioner may find that the dispute cannot be agreed. As was seen in the last chapter, there is ample evidence that HMRC will doggedly pursue cases that are either very weak (*Lime-IT Ltd v Justin* [2003] STC (SCD) 15) or misconceived (*Tilbury Consulting Ltd v Gittins* [2004] STC (SCD) 72) This approach was seen again in the more recent cases of *Lewis v HMRC* ([2006] STC (SCD) 253) and *Parade Park Hotel v Revenue and Customs Commissioners* ([2007] STC (SCD) 430).

In these circumstances HMRC will raise, or may already have raised, formal IR35 decisions to force the matter to the next stage. That is not to say that the raising of such formal decisions necessarily means further arguments cannot be advanced; indeed, formal NIC decisions (and Regulation 80 Determinations under the Income Tax (Pay as You Earn) Regulations, SI 2003/2682) are sometimes raised at an early stage. But it now has to be assumed that deadlock has been reached and, despite the best efforts of all concerned, agreement cannot be secured.

16.2 If it has not yet done so, HMRC will issue a formal Section 8 Notice or, in the case of a traditional status dispute, a Regulation 80 Determination. Strictly, both Section 8 Notices and Regulation 80 Determinations should be raised if HMRC wish to pursue both national insurance and tax. It is therefore necessary to lodge an appeal if HMRC's view is to be disputed.

16.3 In ESM 3296 the whole focus of the procedure is via a Section 8 Notice with little mention of a Regulation 80 Determination. It seems HMRC may only raise the Section 8 Notice but then treat any Commissioners' decision as binding for tax purposes also. However, this is unwise. First, the NIC legislation in respect of IR35 is worded differently from the tax legislation, so it is difficult to see how an NIC decision could automatically be binding from a tax point of view. Secondly, the appellant taxpayer may *not* accept an NIC determination as binding for tax purposes whatever HMRC might think is expedient.

16.4 *Appeal formalities and strategies in an unresolved IR35 dispute*

16.4 As such, a second hearing could be forced. This can be avoided if a Regulation 80 Determination is made at the same time as the Section 8 Notice, whereby appeals can be lodged against both and heard at the same time by the same Commissioners. This appeal must be in writing and must state the grounds of appeal. In a typical case this might be:

> Dear Sir,
>
> Re F Bloggs Computer Services Ltd
>
> We are in receipt of your Section 8 Notice/Regulation 80 Determination relating to the above client for the year 20XX/XX and wish to appeal.
>
> Our grounds of appeal are that you have failed to apply the correct law to the full facts of this case and as such it is our view that our client is not caught by the intermediaries' legislation and that IR35 does not apply.
>
> Please ensure that all duties are immediately postponed, and please acknowledge safe receipt of this appeal.
>
> We will write further in due course explaining our client's further arguments.
>
> Yours faithfully

16.5 Practitioners should note that an appeal must be made within 30 days of the date of the notice of assessment. However, many practitioners are unaware that if they fail to make a timely appeal they have a right to lodge a late appeal under TMA 1970, s 49. HMRC must agree to the admission of a late appeal if:

- a written request is made for HMRC to agree to the late appeal;
- HMRC are satisfied that there was a reasonable excuse for the late appeal; and
- HMRC accept that the late appeal was made without unreasonable delay after the reasonable excuse ended.

Where a late appeal is necessary, it should therefore state both the reason the appeal is being made late and that it has not been delayed unreasonably thereafter. For example, a serious illness would normally be accepted as reasonable grounds for lodging a late appeal, but if following recovery from the illness the delay continues unreasonably thereafter the benefit of the late appeal provisions will probably not be given.

It should be noted that where the inspector refuses to accept the late appeal on the grounds that the excuse is not reasonable or that the delay continued unreasonably thereafter, he must refer the late appeal to the Tribunal in order that they may consider whether or not to accept it (TMA 1970, s 49(2)(*b*)). In other words, the inspector himself does not have the last word on refusing a late appeal. In the author's experience many inspectors seem unaware that if they reject a late appeal they must refer the matter to the Tribunal.

16.6 When listening to a late appeal application the Tribunal are only determining whether or not the late appeal itself should be accepted. They are not hearing and determining the main subject matter of the appeal, ie whether IR35 applies or not. Prior to the introduction of the Tax Tribunal system, the overwhelming majority of Commissioners were anxious to have a full and fair hearing and it was unusual for them to reject an application for a late appeal. In most cases the inspector himself will accept the late appeal and will tend to refer only the most extreme cases of delay to the Tribunal.

In truth the inspector knows that the Tribunal are more likely than not to accept the late appeal if it goes before them and as such he will tend to accept the late appeal in order to avoid an unnecessary and expensive hearing before the Tribunal. The Tribunal would not thank the inspector for 'forcing' late appeal hearings when common sense would indicate the Tribunal would allow it. The Tribunal probably have better things to hear.

16.7 However, practitioners should also note that it tends to be the same accountants who regularly fail to get their appeals in on time and it is strategically unwise to get a reputation, both with the inspector and Tribunals, of being the accountant who is always chasing his tail and leaving everything to the last minute. Interestingly, the author has noted on many occasions that it is mysteriously the same accountants who always manage to suffer postal delays, letters not delivered and a history of weak and desperate excuses. Practitioners should ensure they do not get this kind of reputation.

16.8 At the time of making the appeal it is necessary to advise the inspector that any duties charged need postponing. Many accountants lodge the appeal but fail to lodge a postponement application. If a postponement application is omitted the normal collection procedures will continue and the client will wonder what is going on. The suggested letter above illustrates a postponement application as well as the appeal. It is of course not possible to have a postponement application without an appeal. Postponing the duties will not stop HMRC charging interest if duties are ultimately payable. A Section 8 Notice itself does not bring any duties into charge (unlike a Reg 80 Determination). This is because a Section 8 Notice is a formal decision not an actual assessment. A postponement application is essential where a Reg 80 Determination has been issued.

The Tax Tribunals

16.9 A major reform of the tax appeals system took place during 2009. The Tax Tribunals were introduced from 1 April 2009, replacing the General and Special Commissioners, as well as the VAT & Duties and Section 706 Tribunals. The previous roles of the General Commissioners and Special Commissioners that many practitioners were familiar with therefore ceased to exist from the above date, although members of existing Tribunals (apart from the General Commissioners) were generally transferred to the new Tribunals.

16.10 The 'new' system comprises a 'First-tier Tribunal' (Tax Chamber) and a Finance and Tax 'Upper Tribunal'. Practitioners will generally become more familiar with the former Tribunal than the latter, as most tax cases will initially be dealt with by the First-tier Tribunal. The Upper Tribunal hears appeals on points of law from the First-tier Tribunal, although a small number of complex tax appeals

16.10 *Appeal formalities and strategies in an unresolved IR35 dispute*

may be transferred from the First-tier Tribunal to the Upper Tribunal. Appeal hearings of the First-tier Tribunal are available locally, utilising the pre-existing network of Tribunal hearing centres across the country.

16.11 The First-tier Tribunal consider both simple and complex cases on wide-ranging issues. Nearly all tax appeals are initially heard by the First-tier Tribunal, although a small number of complex cases selected by the Tribunal President may start in the Upper Tribunal. Practitioners should note that they are entitled to represent clients in both the lower and upper tribunals even if they are not professionally qualified. Cases are allocated between various procedural categories (ie 'Default Paper', 'Basic', 'Standard' or 'Complex' cases). In certain circumstances, complex cases may be transferred from the First-tier Tribunal to the Upper Tribunal if appropriate (eg if a case involves an important or complex issue, or where the finding of fact is subsidiary to points of law).

16.12 The First-tier Tribunal will generally be staffed by a legally qualified judge supported by wing members (similar to employment tribunals). The wing members are likely to be people with appeals experience. The Upper Tribunal will generally be presided over by one qualified judge who may be either a current High Court judge or a Special Commissioner.

Internal reviews

16.13 HMRC have implemented a new system of 'internal reviews' to coincide with the new Tax Tribunals. Internal reviews broadly provide an alternative means for taxpayers and HMRC to resolve disputes, rather than a tribunal hearing. HMRC's view is that internal reviews provide simpler and more consistent appeals-handling procedures, and 'a less costly and more effective way to resolve disputes without the need for a tribunal hearing'.

16.14 If an appeal has been submitted to HMRC and the issue cannot be settled, the taxpayer can notify the appeal to the Tribunal. Alternatively, the taxpayer may ask HMRC to review the point at issue, or HMRC may offer the taxpayer a review (TMA 1970, s 49A). If the taxpayer asks for a review, HMRC must respond by stating their original view within 30 days, or possibly a longer period if this is reasonable. If HMRC offer a review, the taxpayer has 30 days in which to accept. Otherwise, HMRC's original view generally stands (s 49C). If a review takes place, HMRC may uphold, vary or cancel their original view of the matter, and notify the taxpayer of their conclusion within the following 45 days, or other agreed period (s 49E). If HMRC's review is unfavourable, the taxpayer may notify the appeal to the Tribunal within 30 days, or outside this period with the Tribunal's permission.

16.15 HMRC have described internal reviews as 'an important safeguard' for taxpayers. However, as the name suggests, internal reviews are conducted from within HMRC, albeit by a different officer from the one who made the decision. Practitioners could perhaps be forgiven for being concerned that internal reviews may be less than impartial, such that the process is treated with scepticism by some.

At the time of writing, the practical use of internal reviews in the context of IR35 appeals remains to be seen.

Getting the appeal listed for hearing

16.16 A feature of the new appeals regime is that it is independent of HMRC, who previously controlled listings and some case management aspects under the General Commissioners appeal system.

16.17 Under the Tax Tribunals regime, taxpayers and advisers will generally lodge their appeals directly with the Tribunal via a central processing centre, without involving HMRC in the application process. The Tribunal will then arrange a hearing to decide the appeal.

The 'lost art' of advocacy

16.18 Historically (ie in the days of the Commissioners, prior to the introduction of the Tax Tribunals), many appeal listings were concerned with what used to be called 'delay' hearings. In the pre-self-assessment era taxpayers would often be behind with their accounts, often by several years. There would typically be several years' assessments, the subject of estimated assessments, which were under appeal. Eventually (and often HMRC can only be accused of excessive patience) HMRC would become anxious to bring matters up to date and list the open appeals, along with many other similar cases, at a regular meeting of the Commissioners. This would be called a delay hearing.

16.19 Often the outstanding accounts would come in prior to the date of the hearing and the inspector would then consider the accounts and either agree them and determine the profits under TMA 1970, s 54 or would raise queries on the accounts. Cases where the accounts had arrived would either be removed completely from the list of cases to be considered by the Commissioners or the inspector would tell the Commissioners the accounts had been received and would request the Commissioners to adjourn the appeal *sine die* (without day). In other words remove the appeal from any future listings.

In such cases there was little point in the taxpayer's accountant turning up at the hearing as the listing had either already been removed or would be adjourned as a mere formality.

16.20 However, the effect of this system was that the accountants rarely appeared at the Commissioners and as such they would fail to develop any familiarity or experience of meetings, even in the context of simple matters. On the other hand, HMRC would appear at the Commissioners on a very regular basis, seeing the same Commissioners and liaising with the Clerk. A competent, well-organised inspector would have had many opportunities to make his mark with the Commissioners. It should be stressed immediately that the Commissioners were entirely independent of HMRC. Yet the party who appeared regularly before the Commissioners and who had a long history of performing professionally in

16.20 *Appeal formalities and strategies in an unresolved IR35 dispute*

front of them must have had some kind of advantage. The same is true, of course, of the new Tax Tribunals.

16.21 Sometimes accounts would not be sent in on time or the extra time the Commissioners gave to the accountant to produce the accounts may have lapsed. In these circumstances the accountant would have to turn up at the hearing and explain to the Commissioners why he or his client needed yet more time to submit the accounts and he would be in the unenviable position of having to ask for the Commissioners' 'indulgence' yet again.

16.22 The majority of practitioners therefore had little experience of the Commissioners and when they did have some experience it was normally when they were asking for more time because they, or their clients, had not done what they should have done. It is little wonder the profession does not enjoy a tremendous reputation for advocacy. It was therefore generally the inspector who tended to force the issue by making the listing of an open appeal to the Commissioners.

However, under the new Tax Tribunals system, practitioners are expected to approach the Tribunal Service to arrange for cases to be heard. This should at least enhance awareness of appeals procedures. Further information on the appeals process is contained in HMRC's Factsheet 'HM Revenue & Customs decisions— what to do if you disagree', which is available via the HMRC website (http://www.hmrc.gov.uk/factsheets/hmrc1.pdf).

16.23 Whilst the appeals process under the Tribunals regime forces the practitioner's hand to some extent, contacting the Tribunals Service to request an appeal hearing does at least show to the client that the practitioner is taking a positive approach.

16.24 In addition, it sends a clear message to the inspector that the accountant is prepared to turn up at the Tribunal hearing. Not only does this show the inspector that the taxpayer means business, it can also result in the inspector having to respond to the accountant's moves and, to some extent at least, work to his timetable.

How a hearing is arranged

16.25 For direct tax cases such as IR35 disputes, an appeal must first be lodged with HMRC before an appeal hearing can be arranged before the Tribunal.

The Tribunals Service website includes a 'Venue Finder' search facility to enable appellants to find the Tribunal venue nearest to where they live (http://www.tribunals.gov.uk/qasvenuefinder.aspx). Previously, the many Clerks to the Commissioners were listed in *Tolley's Tax Office Directory*, and future editions will no doubt list the Tribunal venues as well. Alternatively, a call to the inspector who 'deals with' Tribunal hearings with the direct question 'where is the nearest Tribunal venue?' will usually provide the information needed. It might also take the inspector by surprise. The telephone number for general enquiries to the Tribunals Service is 0207 566 1270.

16.26 A suggested letter to have an appeal hearing arranged under the previous Commissioners regime might have read as follows:

Dear Sirs,

Re Fred Bloggs Computer Services Ltd Tax District ref: XYZ

Our client has under appeal an assessment on his income under Section 8 of the 1999 Social Security Contributions (Transfer of Functions etc) Act. HMRC alleges our client's income is that of a disguised employee under the IR35 intermediaries' legislation. Our client maintains the intermediaries' legislation does not apply and that he is running a genuine independent business.

Following a long technical argument we have not been able to reach a settlement with HMRC. Our client has instructed us to contact you in order to request an appeal hearing as soon as possible.

We have asked HMRC to draw up a draft Statement of Agreed Facts which will no doubt assist the Commissioners on the day.

Please note it is our normal practice to provide the Commissioners with copies of all the case law and statute upon which we rely. We will furnish you with a list of case law references well before the hearing.

At this stage we anticipate calling two witnesses but will confirm this nearer the hearing. We anticipate our client's case will take around two hours to present.

As our client is the appellant and with the burden of proof being on him, we respectfully request that we address the Commissioners first on the day.

We now look forward to hearing from you with a couple of alternative dates for the hearing. Our client is anxious to have the matter laid down as soon as possible.

Yours faithfully

When requesting the hearing, a copy of the Notices/Determinations and the appeal would be enclosed, to show the Clerk that an appeal had been properly lodged with HMRC. A copy of the letter would be sent to the inspector dealing with the case.

Under new Tax Tribunals regime, a Tax Appeals Processing Centre in Birmingham will process appeals from taxpayers. Whilst no standard form of appeal was available at the time of writing, it is envisaged that a multi-purpose appeal from will eventually be available for download on a new Tax Tribunal website. The appeal notification should be sent to the processing centre, where the appeal will be categorised (dependent on its complexity) and either resolved in writing or a Tribunal hearing arranged.

What does an appeal notification to the Tribunals Service say? It sends a clear signal that the taxpayer is taking the initiative in taking the case forward. This will put pressure on the inspector and is, therefore, strategically worthwhile.

Furthermore, by implication HMRC and the Tribunal now know that the Tribunal Procedure Rules are understood by the taxpayer's representative, which can only increase the credibility of the practitioner. The references to witnesses, case law etc show a full understanding of the procedures in a contentious case and in particular with reference to the statement of facts.

It will be noted from the above letter that the right to address the Commissioners first on the day was requested. There were very sound procedural reasons for doing this as will be explained later. Under the previous Commissioners' regime, as any

16.26 *Appeal formalities and strategies in an unresolved IR35 dispute*

hearing before the Specials would be more formal the appellant was automatically expected to speak first. At the time of writing, the protocol for hearings before the Tax Tribunals has not been established, but if the facility to speak first is available, it may be worthwhile taking the opportunity to do so.

As mentioned, a copy of the hearing application should be sent to HMRC for their information and action on the draft statement of agreed facts. If directions are agreed this will usually require HMRC to draft the statement.

The above approach establishes a confident attitude and demonstrates an understanding of the basic procedures and considerations involved in a contentious appeal.

16.27 At this stage it is not unknown for HMRC to request a further meeting to discuss the case and sort out details relating to witnesses and documents. Unless there is a clear indication that the inspector is about to concede and wants to reach a face-saving compromise of some kind, such meetings should be resisted.

16.28 It is also possible that the inspector might apply to the Tribunal for directions in order that documentation he should have sought earlier can now be reviewed! A request for 'directions' can be a time-buying exercise by HMRC, and should be resisted in most cases.

16.29 The more astute inspector will see this pre-hearing meeting as an opportunity to probe the taxpayer and his accountant with a view to obtaining details of their precise arguments, witnesses and the case law they will use on the day. As the finer details of case law references etc are exchanged only seven days before the hearing the inspector could be trying to get advance knowledge of the strengths of the taxpayer's case and indeed the advocacy skills of the practitioner. In short, the unwary practitioner might end up giving his hand away well in advance of the time he has to, and this will probably be to the detriment of the taxpayer, his client, whom he is meant to be representing.

16.30 It might be thought that a genuine attempt to resolve the dispute without the need to go to the Tribunal is a good thing, and so it is. But practitioners should be wary of the inspector who offers a last-minute meeting, ostensibly to see if the case can be settled. They may find that in the process the client's detailed case has been given away in advance with the inspector pressing ahead with the appeal hearing anyway. Be warned.

16.31 Several alternative dates may need to be put forward for the appeal hearing, because the date of the hearing has to be convenient to all parties including the inspector, the taxpayer, the practitioner, the witnesses and not least the Tribunal.

It can be difficult to arrange an appeal hearing when the movements of all of these persons have to be taken into account and it can be exacerbated by hearings during busy holiday periods etc. Indeed, historically it was sometimes necessary to organise an appeal hearing three or four months in advance.

Where a case is particularly complicated or where the number of witnesses to be called is excessive it is possible that the hearing will spill over into a second day. In these circumstances it may prove even more difficult to arrange two consecutive days when all the parties involved in the hearing, will be available.

A note on calling HMRC's bluff

16.32 During a long and complex technical argument it is easy for both sides to become entrenched in their views and arguments, and, it has to be said, personalities sometimes come into play. The practitioner may feel that he is on a slippery slope that will inevitably lead to a contentious hearing. In some cases both sides will take a very assertive approach where an early hearing is threatened, despite the fact that the case could, with a bit more willingness on both sides, be settled amicably.

16.33 In other cases, despite providing the inspector with the facts, relevant case law and reasoned arguments, it is simply impossible to make progress. In this type of situation the practitioner has to take the initiative and proceed to a Tribunal hearing. However, this should not be threatened unless there is the resolve to see the matter through.

> *Case study*
> In a case under the previous Commissioners' regime, HMRC pulled out of an IR35 appeal very shortly before the hearing. They then wrote to the Clerk saying the dispute had been settled by 'agreement'. We pointed out that the case had been conceded by HMRC, not simply 'agreed'.

16.34 Although many cases which are laid down for a hearing are settled shortly before the case goes ahead, it would be very unwise to call HMRC's bluff. A listing of a case should only be sought where the taxpayer and his representative are prepared to turn up on the day.

16.35 Tactically, pushing for a hearing may result in HMRC backing down, but this is not something to be relied upon. If the practitioner develops a reputation with the local tax office or the local Tribunal that he is constantly requesting and then pulling out of contentious appeal hearings, this cannot enhance his reputation. On the other hand, if it is made clear that there is a real willingness to go to the Tribunal, then without question the inspector will know that he is dealing with somebody who is serious, and not someone merely calling HMRC's bluff.

16.36

> *Case study*
> Accountax has had considerable success in getting HMRC to drop cases simply by pushing HMRC when HMRC's workload is high. Appeals Unit staff in particular do not want to appear before the Tribunal unprepared and if put under sufficient pressure may simply concede the case.

Doing the pre-hearing homework

16.37 Having written to the Tribunals Service to have the appeals laid down it is very important at this stage to stand back and again reconsider the strengths and weaknesses of the case as a whole. During the course of the inquiries the

16.37 *Appeal formalities and strategies in an unresolved IR35 dispute*

practitioner may have taken a very proactive approach but it now has to be accepted that for whatever reasons, the arguments have failed and it has not been possible to convince the inspector of the merits of the taxpayer's arguments. The challenge now is to convince the Tribunal, on a balance of probabilities, that the appeal should be upheld. Particular attention should be given to the available evidence and, where available, witness statements.

16.38 Convincing the Tribunal is not the same as trying to win the argument with HMRC. Many inspectors still like to be completely satisfied before they will concede. Indeed, practitioners may know of instances of inspectors who are 95% 'satisfied' but who still decline to accept the explanations and arguments put forward.

16.39 However, it must be stressed that at the Tribunal the burden of proof is nothing more than the balance of probabilities. In numerical terms this means 51%. If the arguments and explanations are probably correct the appeal should succeed. For example, if there are three Tribunal members involved in an appeal hearing, it is therefore necessary only to convince two out of the three to the tune of 51% to win the case. This is a standard of proof which falls far short of the inspector's own subjective 'being satisfied'.

16.40 Where a hearing has been laid down it is perhaps worth reminding the inspector that the standard of proof at the Tribunal is nothing more than convincing a majority of them on the balance of probabilities. The author has experienced long drawn out disputes with HMRC and as the date of the hearing approached, the inspector, often in conjunction with his senior line manager (who may well be taking the case for HMRC), looks again at the arguments. It is then realised that although the inspector may still not be satisfied himself, the Tribunal may very well be. In these circumstances the senior officer may intervene with a view to closing the case down or coming to some kind of compromise settlement.

16.41 It goes without saying that the case should never have come this far unless there is real confidence that on the balance of probabilities it is felt the appeal can be sustained. In the author's experience, it is in the few weeks leading up to the hearing itself when a great deal of extra detail can be gleaned from the file. As preparation of the detailed appeal presentation gets underway there will undoubtedly be discovered minutiae which may prove very helpful, and sometimes unhelpful, to the contractor's case.

Summary

16.42 At this stage it is vitally important to revisit the entire history of the arguments so that the appeal can be prepared and presented properly. This requires very careful attention to detail, particularly in respect of documentation, witnesses and briefing of the client. These topics are covered in detail in Chapter 17 'Preparing for an appeal hearing'. The new Tax Tribunal rules need to be understood from 1 April 2009.

Chapter 17
Preparing for an appeal hearing

Introduction

17.1 Without question the overwhelming majority of practitioners will be anxious when taking an appeal to the Tribunal; particularly for the first time. Indeed, they will be nervous or at least galvanised even if they have taken many such cases. This is normal and perfectly rational, and it should not in itself dissuade a conscientious practitioner from representing his client (and thereby avoiding the higher fees that are likely to be charged by a specialist tax consultant with experience of presenting appeals). Indeed, there is a school of thought which says that if the advocate is not at least a little anxious about the 'big day' then he is probably not taking it seriously enough.

17.2 Some of the advice on preparing for an appeal offered in this section might seem not worth worrying about, but in the author's experience every extra point is worth scoring. Bearing in mind the onus on the taxpayer is a mere balance of probabilities, anything which can get one step nearer the winning line has to be worth taking. The advice offered is based on the author's practical experience of conducting appeals in the real world.

17.3 Despite the high stakes and the prospect of either an outright win or an outright loss (in status/IR35 cases there is rarely a middle ground) the good news is that the proceedings on the day will be generally slow-paced, quite informal and, if proper preparation has been carried out, an enjoyable and educational experience.

> *Case study*
> At a recent IR35 appeal before the Tax Tribunal regime, after both sides had finished, the Special Commissioner said 'This is where I stand and imperiously leave the court ... but I have too much to carry so leave in your own time'. Such informality makes for an enjoyable experience at the tribunal.

The most important of these factors is the slow-paced nature of the proceedings. There will be plenty of time to 'think on your feet' while Tribunal members are making notes or reading from the bundles of evidence. If an assistant is taken by the practitioner, which is highly recommended, the assistant can organise the paperwork, which will take even more pressure away.

17.4   *Preparing for an appeal hearing*

17.4   In short, the whole process, while demanding, is well within the skills range of the ordinarily competent professional adviser. The key is preparation and understanding the rules, then having the courage to proceed in a confident manner.

Before the hearing

17.5   It is normal practice before a contentious appeal that certain administrative formalities are attended to. These are designed simply to make the case run more smoothly on the day and are to the benefit of HMRC, taxpayer and Tribunal alike. Under the previous appeals regime, where a hearing was before the Special Commissioners, these pre-hearing formalities were more likely to be laid down by way of a 'directions' order, where a formal timetable was ordered in respect of statements of facts, documents, witness details etc. The new First-tier Tribunal is empowered to make similar directions. Any correspondence between you and the court or indeed between the inspector and the court should be immediately copied to the other side. Sadly Accountax have encountered several inspectors who fail to observe this basic professional courtesy.

Sometimes it is necessary to 'buy time' and a familiarity with the procedural rules can assist.

> *Case study*
> In a case Accountax recently worked on, the appellants were under extreme pressure to comply with a direction that required them to complete a great deal of work in a very limited timeframe. However, it was discovered that HMRC had not fully complied with the previous direction which meant that technically the clock had not started running for the appellants to deal with the next direction. Correspondence ensured which ultimately bought the clients an extra two months of preparation time. It should be noted that this was not an exercise in semantics—a genuine issue was spotted and corresponded on.

Agreed statement of facts

17.6   The statement of facts is an agreed declaration between HMRC and taxpayer that certain facts are not 'in dispute'. Although there is no obligation on either HMRC or taxpayer to come to such an agreed statement, indeed it is sometimes impossible, in the majority of cases an agreed statement is expected by the Tribunal.

17.7   The reason why such a statement of facts is important and desirable is that it will speed matters up considerably on the day of the appeal hearing. This is because facts have to be 'proved' and if it is necessary to prove every fact by formal evidence to the Tribunal it makes for a very long hearing indeed. Although historically some panels of Commissioners were prepared to admit 'facts' relatively informally, it will be appreciated that it would be a drawn out and quite unnecessary process to go through matters which are not in dispute in the first place.

17.8   At its simplest a statement of facts consists of the name of the taxpayer and the assessments under appeal. This, however, is exiguous to say the least. A more detailed statement of facts would state, for example, when the taxpayer started trading, what he does, what correspondence has been entered into and what meetings have been attended. In the case of tax status disputes generally, detail might be given regarding the terms and conditions in the contract, the rates of pay etc. In an IR35 dispute agreed facts could include what salary or dividends have been taken or what money has been invested in training or equipment.

It will be appreciated that a statement of facts can vary from the brief bare bones to a fully detailed account of facts established and agreed throughout the course of HMRC's enquiries leading up to the appeal hearing.

17.9 The advantage of such a statement is obvious—matters are clarified and agreed in advance saving time on the day of the hearing. But there are some potential disadvantages in agreeing a statement of facts. For both HMRC and the taxpayer once a statement of facts is formally agreed it cannot be resiled from at a later stage.

If, for example, it is agreed that all the terms and conditions of a working relationship were contained in the written contract HMRC would not be able to go behind this agreed fact at the hearing and seek to establish if there were any other oral terms. Likewise, if the taxpayer concedes in a meeting that he has never funded any training courses, it would not be open to him to come up later with details of courses he claims he funded himself.

Whether there is a legal case to say that a fact has been agreed in 'error' and should therefore be ignored is not something either side would want to put to the Tribunal, as their patience would be severely tested. The danger is in agreeing as a fact something which cannot later be disputed, because both sides are prohibited from doing so. If in doubt do not agree a fact. If it is felt that there is something to add or explain about a 'fact' do not agree it.

Quite simply, having agreed a fact the practitioner will be denied the opportunity to adopt a different view later. This is not to say that the taxpayer should be reserving his right to change his position on a whim. It is more a case of ensuring he is not restricting himself from arguing what the real facts are on the day.

Facts which are not in dispute should be agreed in a written statement in advance. Facts which are in dispute should never be agreed in advance. Instead the determination of the Tribunal should be sought on the day, by evidence.

17.10 A statement of facts is not a list of arguments or contentions. Practitioners should be very cautious about agreeing as a fact something HMRC are merely alleging. Statements of agreed facts should be just that—agreed facts and nothing else. Any contentious interpretations or arguments are to be aired on the day, backed up by evidence, and either accepted or rejected by the Tribunal.

Case study
The inspector drafted a 120-paragraph statement of facts, about 100 of which were not facts at all. Accountax responded by trimming the statement to 22 facts. This upset the inspector, who then trimmed it further to just six facts. The Special Commissioner noted in court that it took him less than 30 seconds to read. In the end, the statement was virtually useless but it would have been harmful to agree as fact what was no more than HMRC contention.

17.11 *Preparing for an appeal hearing*

17.11 In the author's experience, the inspector will sometimes try to put a fact into a statement which would not be strictly relevant to the appeal, even though it is still a fact. For example, the taxpayer may have a history of poor tax compliance or may have been investigated by HMRC in the past, where irregularities were found in the accounts or tax return. If this is the case then although such detail is 'fact' it is not relevant to the proceedings under appeal and it should not be put in the statement.

If it was agreed in the statement of facts that the taxpayer was previously investigated and irregularities were discovered this would undoubtedly be unhelpful to the taxpayer and would be referred to by the inspector in an effort to discredit the taxpayer.

If, on the other hand, such a fact is not agreed in a statement of agreed facts then the inspector would find it much harder to introduce and use against the taxpayer. It might look as if he was being perhaps 'petty' in dragging up the past. Indeed, the practitioner would explain to the Tribunal that the past is not germane to the proceedings under appeal. But without doubt it will be harder to argue this if the taxpayer's fiscal history has been incorporated into the statement of agreed facts. Facts should only be included if they are relevant to the appeal and if there is no wish to dispute them.

Who should prepare the statement of facts?

17.12 The author's view is that the initial draft should be prepared by HMRC. Although the taxpayer is the appellant and therefore carries the onus of proof, it is nonetheless HMRC who are trying to challenge the status quo. If HMRC feel the IR35 intermediaries' legislation applies then it is not unreasonable for HMRC to take on the initial task of preparing the draft statement of facts. Usually this is a task HMRC will tend to deal with in any event. This is because historically they have tended to take the initiative as the taxpayer and his professional representative will have little if any experience of such matters.

An inexperienced practitioner might agree a statement of facts not entirely to his clients' advantage, if the statement is presented to him as a *fait accompli*. It must be remembered that it takes both parties to agree a statement. It is not a question of imposing a statement on the other side—it has to be agreed through a process of amendment, re-drafting and possible further amendment before it can be signed off by both parties.

There is an interesting possible strategic advantage in actually requesting HMRC to draft a statement of facts for the taxpayer's approval. This is that the HMRC inspector will not want to be told what to do or when he should be doing it.

Under standard directions the Tribunal will expect a draft statement to be agreed and possibly initially drafted by the appelant.

> *Case study*
> The author advised a practitioner in a status dispute during the Commissioners' era and when it was clear the matter was going to go to hearing HMRC were asked to produce an initial draft statement of facts. The inspector, who no doubt had countless other files to worry about was reluctant to draft a statement. A reminder was sent to the inspector pointing out that an agreed statement would speed matters up on the day and would in any event be expected by the Commissioners. A copy of the letter was sent to the Clerk.

The inspector was unhappy at being chased and dug in deep and again refused to issue the draft statement. A second reminder was sent and copied to the Clerk who was by now concerned that the inspector seemed to be unco-operative.

Shortly before the hearing HMRC backed down from the appeal and a statement of facts was never produced. In a telephone conversation with the Clerk, it was made clear to the author that the Clerk, and one can only assume the Commissioners, were unimpressed by HMRC's dilatoriness and apparent lack of co-operation.

17.13 The lesson to be learned is that by putting HMRC under pressure to draft a statement of facts, which can be a difficult time-consuming matter if done thoroughly, the inspector may well drag his feet. Part of the reason for this is that inspectors do not like taxpayers' representatives suggesting to them what they should be doing. Inspectors like working to their own timetable and may therefore become entrenched in their unwillingness to draft a statement. If this gets back to the Tribunal they will not be impressed. A small point perhaps, but one which can only help the taxpayer. Previously, at the Special Commissioners it was likely that the directions would require HMRC to produce the draft statement of agreed facts. A similar approach is likely in the Tax Tribunals regime.

17.14 In the above case study practitioners should imagine what the reaction of the Commissioners would have been had the case gone ahead without a statement of facts? They would not have been pleased with the situation. If correspondence could then be adduced to show that the taxpayer had requested a statement of facts several times but the inspector had refused to co-operate this would tend to work against the inspector.

Of course it does not mean that the taxpayer will automatically win just because the inspector has dragged his feet over a statement of facts. It will, however, register in the minds of the Tribunal, who expect very high levels of professionalism and efficiency from HMRC at all times.

The question for determination

17.15 Although it is not strictly a 'fact' it is common for the question the Tribunal are being asked to determine to be added to the statement, or provided separately. It has to be remembered that the Tribunal may have no prior knowledge of the case, except perhaps for an advance sight of the agreed statement of facts. They are coming to what could be a highly technical appeal and may not fully understand what it is that they are being asked to determine.

This is not a criticism of the Tribunal—it is in fact a criticism of the parties to the appeal (ie HMRC and the taxpayer), for not making it clear. Failing to make clear exactly what the point at issue is, and the determination being sought, is a typical failing of the accountant advocate.

It therefore makes sense to give *advance* warning to the Tribunal, as to precisely what they are being asked to determine. The question for determination can be usefully appended to the statement of facts.

Skeleton arguments will be exchanged before the hearing. This is a fairly detailed

17.15 *Preparing for an appeal hearing*

summary of each side's case, legal authority, etc. Under the previous Commissioners regime, the skeletons were given to the Tribunal usually one to two weeks before the hearing.

17.16 In an IR35 dispute the question to be determined could be along the lines of:

> 'Whether the intermediaries' legislation in ITEPA 2003, Part 2, Ch 8 (ss 48–61) applies to the engagements entered into by Fred Bloggs Computer Services Ltd for the year 20XX/20XX.'

In the more traditional status dispute, the question to be determined might be phrased:

> 'Whether XYZ Construction Ltd was engaging workers under a contract of services for the year 20XX/20XX.'

Having the question for determination clearly spelt out can only help. Following the introduction of the Tax Tribunals in April 2009, it remains to be seen whether this becomes standard procedure in any event.

Administrative procedures

17.17 Previously, it was customary and courteous to supply to the Commissioners and the inspector, at least seven days prior to the hearing, a list of case law references, statute, documents and details of witnesses. The protocol under the Tax Tribunals regime is not known at the time of writing, but it seems likely that similar procedures will apply.

This is a good time for the practitioner to remind the Tribunals Service, if necessary, that he wishes to speak first at the hearing. This should already have been indicated when submitting the hearing application and is referred to in Chapter 16, although it may be that formal directions have already dealt with this.

17.18 The Tribunals Service should also be reminded that on the day of the appeal hearing full copies of all relevant documents and case law decisions will be supplied to the Tribunal. There is nothing more irritating for the Tribunal than finding that insufficient copies of documents have been prepared for all concerned. Surprisingly, this was an error the inspector often made in the Commissioners' era, and it shows a lack of care in preparation, which can only harm one's case.

> *Case study*
> At a General Commissioners' hearing on a tax status dispute in late 2001, Accountax prepared documentation running to 234 pages. Copies were available for all persons present. On the other hand the inspector's documents ran to only four pages and he had not prepared copies for anyone, not even the Commissioners. He had to read his own documents then hand them to the Commissioners who had to look over each other's shoulders. This is a prime example of bad preparation. HMRC lost the hearing.

So far as the inspector is concerned it was again customary, and indeed wise, to give him a list of case law references, statute, documents not already in the inspector's possession and witness details at least seven days prior to the hearing. If it is not already clear he should be reminded what the taxpayer's main contentions are, but the practitioner is not obliged to go into detail nor is he required to give away all his evidence in advance. The Tribunal may cater for this via formal directions.

17.19 The reason it is wise to give this information, especially documentation, to the inspector seven days prior to the hearing is that there should be no surprises at the hearing.

If there are any such surprises (by either side) the other side would be entitled to ask for either a brief adjournment to look at the new evidence or, in the case of substantial documentary evidence, an adjournment to another day. The Tribunal will not grant this lightly and if they do, they will not be impressed by the party who introduced the new evidence. It is difficult enough arranging a full day appeal hearing without the extra aggravation of having to re-arrange it because one party has tried to deny the other side access to a document.

17.20 It should be noted that the Tribunal are empowered to issue clear directions that both sides have to exchange all documentary evidence upon which they seek to rely, including witness statements and detailed legal arguments called 'skeletons'.

17.21 Practitioners should note that producing a document in advance as an 'agreed' document does *not* mean that its *contents* are agreed.

17.22 It must be stressed that different tax inspectors and Tribunal members will take their own approach to these administrative formalities and what they expect of the practitioner.

For example, in the pre-Tribunal regime the author dealt both with Clerks who by profession were coroners and who generally demanded a higher degree of formality as well as with Clerks who adopted a more informal approach.

A wise practitioner will therefore consider the specific Tribunal members he is dealing with and adapt his approach accordingly. There is no merit in insisting on a particularly formal or informal approach when it is clearly contrary to what the Tribunal expect.

17.23 Dealing with these formalities in an efficient and professional manner will not win the case for the appellant but his credibility will be enhanced from the outset. If this gets him 1% nearer to the magical 51% then it would be foolish not to take it.

17.24 It may be found that once the extensive case law has been detailed and witnesses to be called have been confirmed the inspector may start to feel a little uncomfortable, particularly if this information is revealed only shortly before the hearing. It is clearly better to win the argument without the need of going to the Tax Tribunal if at all possible, but it has to be said that many inexperienced tax officers may not have given proper attention to the case law and may end up in the unenvi-

17.24 *Preparing for an appeal hearing*

able position of having to carry out substantial research when the hearing is only a few days away.

Case study
In a tax status case prior to the introduction of the new Tax Tribunals, the inspector was telephoned by the author. It was explained that as deadlock had been reached the best way to proceed would be by having formal assessment that could be appealed. The author explained he would then contact 'Beryl'. This confused the inspector. He was told Beryl was one of the listing clerks at the Special Commissioners. The inspector expressed concern that the case would go to the Specials. He conceded the case shortly afterwards without issuing any assessments. It is interesting to note that a search of the case law database revealed that the inspector concerned had never been to the Specials as either an advocate or witness.

17.25 It should be noted that when presenting HMRC with a list of case law references the practitioner is *not* obliged to provide details of the specific passages to be quoted nor is he obliged to give the inspector copies of the case law. Essentially, both sides should be aware of the court judgments and HMRC certainly have the technical resources to obtain copy judgments.

In other words, it is not the practitioner's job to make life easy for HMRC by doing HMRC's homework for them. By the practitioner playing fair but hard, HMRC may be forced into a situation where they would rather drop the case than proceed.

Case study
In a previous technical tax dispute under the Commissioners' regime, HMRC alleged that an associate dentist had ceased one profession and commenced another when she started her own surgery. This resulted in a significant extra tax charge. The only justification the inspector put forward was that her internal instructions made it clear that in these circumstances the cessation and commencement rules applied. Accountax argued that, in the particular circumstances of the case, there was no cessation and commencement and advised the inspector that witnesses would be called and further case law would be adduced at the contentious appeal hearing which had been arranged.

Accountax made it clear that further details of witnesses, contentions and case law etc would not be given to the inspector until seven days prior to the hearing. The inspector explained that she was part-time and this would not give her much time to prepare her case and that she would have to seek an adjournment. Accountax reminded the inspector that this was a contentious appeal hearing, not a mere 'delay' hearing and that any application for an adjournment would be vigorously opposed.

One week later Accountax received a letter from the inspector confirming that she now felt the matter was not clear-cut and would therefore drop her arguments. Note that if this appeal had been heard by the Specials, directions would have required the disclosure of documents etc at an earlier stage. The Tax Tribunal have a power to give directions, either on application by one of the parties to the appeal, or on their own initiative.

It should be noted that the above case was won, not simply because of the technical arguments *but because the inspector was put under pressure* and had to work to a very tight timetable. This assertive approach, without doubt, helped get the case closed down.

It is of course a judgment in each case as to whether all evidence, case law, witness statements and documents should be given to the inspector well in advance of the appeal hearing. On the one hand the inspector may review his opinion and concede. On the other hand the practitioner may be doing his client a massive disservice by giving away all his evidence in advance.

What needs to be done

17.26 The most important thing to remember is that the onus of proof lies with the taxpayer and hence with the practitioner as his representative.

To show that the appeal should be upheld, facts have to be established and legal argument advanced. Facts are 'proved' in a variety of ways. First, there may already be an agreed statement of facts, whereby certain issues are not in dispute and are taken as read.

Secondly, the practitioner will have to establish facts by evidencing them and this can be done either through documentary evidence or oral evidence. Having established the facts it is then a matter of showing *precisely how* the law applies to those facts by detailed reference to case law judgments. Chapter 5 deals with the major case law decisions. Essentially, the practitioner has to show why his arguments are preferable, on the balance of probabilities, to the inspector's.

Opinions count for nothing

17.27 Although the Tribunal will have a very well-developed sense of fair play and justice they can only uphold the appeal on the basis of evidence. Clear evidence of fact and legal precedent taken from case law decisions are the two most important factors the Tribunal will take into account.

It is no use the taxpayer complaining about the legislation being 'unfair' any more than the practitioner making vague submissions that, in his opinion, the taxpayer is not a disguised employee. This kind of assertion will carry no weight.

The practitioner must focus on establishing facts by reference to evidence and then refer to detailed case law to support his case. Quoting a précis or one-paragraph summaries of case law decisions is a waste of time. Quoting the words that judges have actually used is the most devastating weapon in the practitioner's armoury.

For example, simply suggesting that having the right to send a substitute is an important indication of self-employment is nothing more than an opinion. On the other hand, supporting this assertion with the celebrated quotation from Lord Justice Peter Gibson in the *Express and Echo* case ([1999] IRLR 367 at 370 para 31—'where, as here, a person who works for another is not required to perform his services personally, then as a matter of law the relationship between the worker and the person for whom he works is not that of employer and employee') will result in an important legal point being made effectively.

17.27 *Preparing for an appeal hearing*

Case study
In a contentious appeal in the West Country (under the pre-Tax Tribunal regime) concerning tax status of construction workers the inspector relied heavily on the HMRC publication IR56 ('Employed or self-employed?—A guide for tax and National Insurance'). This document explained HMRC's approach, in a rather simplistic manner, to tax status. At the hearing one of the Commissioners asked the inspector whether the booklet IR56 carried any force of law. The inspector admitted that it did not. The Commissioner made the point that simply reading out IR56 did not advance the inspector's argument because the publication was nothing more than HMRC's opinion and, therefore, had no legal weight. On the other hand, every legal submission made by Accountax was backed up with a quotation from a leading case law authority. The taxpayer won the appeal.

Documentation

17.28 At this stage it would be hoped that a statement of facts has been finalised and copied to the Tribunal.

17.29 It is recommended that the practitioner now prepares two bundles of documents to be called Bundle A and Bundle B. These bundles will contain all of the necessary paperwork to be presented to the Tribunal at the hearing. This is assuming the Tribunal have not already made directions which make it clear what documents have to be prepared and when.

Bundle A

17.30 This bundle will contain all of the non-legal paperwork, including relevant correspondence, copies of the assessments under appeal and any other documentary evidence to be put forward, for example, copies of invoices raised and notes of meetings or telephone conversations.

Each bundle should have a clear and attractively designed header sheet detailing the names of the parties, the date of the hearing and the assessments under appeal. The practitioner should put in the effort to make sure the header sheets look professional.

At the front of Bundle A there should be a clear index and it is imperative that all pages are clearly numbered. Some documents may be photocopied landscape rather than portrait style and as such they will need numbering in a different corner. Do not overlook these administrative formalities.

17.31 The contents of a typical Bundle A might read as follows:

	Folio
Correspondence to HMRC dated 14 July 2007 requesting contract review	1–2
Response from HMRC dated 17 December 2007	3–4
Further correspondence to HMRC dated 22 December 2007	5–6

	Folio
Further correspondence from HMRC dated 6 February 2008	7
Section 8 Assessment dated 1 April 2008	8–9
Appeal against the Section 8 Assessment dated 20 April 2008	10–11
Further correspondence from HMRC dated 16 May 2008	12
Further correspondence to HMRC dated 28 May 2008	13
Note of Telephone Conversation dated 1 June 2008	14
Notes of Meeting dated 7 June 2008	15–19
Further correspondence to HMRC dated 18 June 2008	20–21
Correspondence to Clerk to the General Commissioners dated 29 June 2008	22
Contract for Services dated 31 March 2007	23–27
Copies of earlier contracts	28–38
Copy Invoices	39–41
Copy Public Liability and Professional Indemnity Insurance Certificates	42–47
Copy Business Stationery	48–49
Copy letter from Computer Agency	50–51
Copy website print out and advertisements	52–57

Bundle B

17.32 This bundle will contain all of the case law authorities to be brought to the attention of the Tribunal together with copies of the relevant statutes or statutory instruments relating to the appeal. Once again it is important that a clear index is prepared and all pages are clearly numbered. It is also recommended that after the index page there is a further sheet giving a separate list of the relevant case law and the years in which the cases were heard. Again, a header page should be included, as with Bundle A.

17.33 A typical Bundle B would contain the following:

	Folio
Full index of case law decisions with references	1
ITEPA 2003, Part 2, Chapter 8 and Social Security Contributions (Intermediaries) Regulations 2000	2–8
Section 8 Notice of Decision	9–10
Case law decisions in full	11–216

Practitioners will appreciate this is only an example of a typical Bundle B in a tax status or IR35 dispute.

17.34 *Preparing for an appeal hearing*

17.34 The importance of numbering the bundles in a clear fashion cannot be over-estimated and the Tribunal will not appreciate badly photocopied paperwork. Careful preparation must not be skipped. There is only one chance at the Tribunal to present the case effectively.

> *Case study*
> Several years ago Accountax was involved in a contentious Commissioners appeal, where the inspector had not produced sufficient copies of his own bundle of documents nor checked the quality of the photocopies contained in the bundle. A remarkably similar failing is noted at **17.18** above. The General Commissioners had difficulty not only reading over each other's shoulders but could not decipher a particular enclosure because it was badly photocopied.
> Accountax had prepared ample copies of its own bundles and the document that was difficult to read was common both to the inspector's bundle and that of Accountax. Accountax pointed this out to the Commissioners who then referred to the Accountax bundle and expressed dissatisfaction with the paperwork produced by the inspector.

17.35 Preparing the paperwork properly will not on its own win the case but it will aid presentation and create a good impression. Once again, if careful preparation of documents gets the taxpayer just 1% nearer to the winning line then it is something that should be undertaken without hesitation.

17.36 It is not always clear which documents should go in one bundle or the other. For example, the inspector's decision and notice under Section 8 could perhaps go in both bundles, as could the basic legislation. As far as is possible it is wise to separate the general correspondence from the more legal documentation to be found in Bundle B.

17.37 It is unhelpful to include in Bundle A copies of documentation which add nothing to the proceedings. As it may be necessary to go through each of these documents and formally admit them in evidence anything which is genuinely superfluous should be left out. The process of introducing documents and other evidence is explained in Chapter 18.

17.38 So far as Bundle B is concerned, this should contain the case law to be relied on. In a typical IR35 or traditional tax status dispute it may be necessary to refer to between ten and 15 case law decisions. On average each case is perhaps 20 pages long and therefore Bundle B can be over 200 pages long, and that is without taking into account the other enclosures such as the statutes and statutory instruments.

17.39 It is not particularly difficult to prepare the bundles but care must be taken and sufficient time must be allowed to do the job properly. The majority of practitioners will delegate the photocopying of the bundles to a junior member of staff, but it is worth checking that everything is correctly numbered and that there are sufficient copies for everybody.

17.40 Although there is no hard and fast rule, in the author's experience the best way to collate bundles is by the use of extra-long treasury tags. This is more effective and convenient than paper clips, staples or loose sheets. As many as eight to ten sets of Bundles A and B will be required for the hearing, as every person present should have one.

It might be suggested by HMRC, that one agreed master Bundle containing both side's documents is collated and paginated. This no doubt makes the paperwork a little easier to handle on the day. The Tribunal may formally direct this.

The practitioner's own documents

17.41 As well as having the bundles mentioned above, the practitioner will also have his own set of notes. These documents will contain arguments and various bullet points to act as an aide memoire during the proceedings as well as being a list of the questions to be asked of the witnesses. If an assistant is taken, he can hand out the bundles and this will take away some pressure from the practitioner leaving him free to concentrate on the appeal itself.

17.42 These notes will contain the opening address to the Tribunal, and should be nothing more than a short summary of what the case is about, together with a copy of the questions to be put to the various witnesses, questions to be put to HMRC's witnesses in cross-examination, legal submissions and a final summary. (The actual presentation of the case is discussed in considerable detail in Chapter 18.)

Clarifying what determination is being sought

17.43 It is very important not to lose sight of what it is the Tribunal are being asked to determine. During the course of an appeal the Tribunal may become overwhelmed with potentially hundreds of pages of photocopied documents and it is recommended that occasional reference is made to the point to be determined.

Witnesses

17.44 Long before the case gets to the Tribunal, stock should have been taken of the reliability and quality of the witnesses to be called on behalf of the taxpayer, including the taxpayer himself. Indeed, in many ways the most important witness will be the client. It will also be necessary to consider HMRC's witnesses and plan ahead for their cross-examination. The actual process of examination of witnesses and the cross-examination of HMRC's witnesses is explored in greater depth in Chapter 18.

It is possible to serve a potential witness with a witness summons under The Tribunal Procedure (First-tier Tribunal) (Tax Chamber) Rules, thus ensuring attendance at the hearing, see **17.54** below.

17.45 There tend to be two kinds of witness. The first type of witness can be relied upon to turn up on time at the Tribunal, wear smart clothes, treat the Tribunal members, as well as the inspector, with respect. This witness will consider questions

17.45 *Preparing for an appeal hearing*

carefully and will answer slowly and clearly. He will not start an argument with HMRC, nor will he ramble when answering questions. This is a good witness.

The second kind of witness is determined to have his 'day in court' and 'give a piece of his mind'. He cannot be relied upon to remain calm or to show the necessary respect to the Tribunal. Such witnesses tend not to take on board guidance they are given and often become their own worst enemy.

17.46 If a witness is likely to be a poor witness the practitioner should think very carefully about calling him at all. Not only will a bad witness fail to advance the practitioner's case but, more importantly, after he has been examined by the practitioner the inspector will have the opportunity to cross-examine him. The 'bad' witness can easily be discredited and provoked by an experienced inspector, potentially damaging the taxpayer's case.

> *Case study*
> If it is felt that a witness can give helpful evidence it is wise to call that witness yourself rather than let HMRC call him. In a recent case Accountax made the mistake of allowing HMRC to call a witness who subsequently gave evidence quite contrary to his earlier position. It would have been preferable in hindsight not to have let HMRC call him.

> *Case study*
> Some years ago the author was involved in a case concerning NICs on payments made to certain Catholic nuns. Although the matter did not get to court, because the Contributions Agency (as they then were) dropped the case we were quite prepared to call the nuns as witnesses. The CA recognised that the nuns would make impeccable witnesses and rightly dropped the case, not least it is assumed because of the publicity that would have ensued.

17.47 Of course this goes both ways. The inspector who is presenting the case on behalf of HMRC may be painfully aware that the technical skills of the investigating officer or inspector are limited. The officer may have little or no experience of taking part in contentious appeals with the prospect of being closely cross-examined. Coupled with this if the officer has not handled the case particularly well and there is a risk that any shortcomings would be exposed in front of the Tribunal it is not unheard of for HMRC to refuse to call the officer as a witness. This can be the case even where the officer concerned has been involved with the case from the outset.

> *Case study*
> In a contentious Commissioners' appeal under the pre-Tribunals regime, the inspector taking the case refused to call the officer who, from the outset, had handled the case. The officer had made many fundamental mistakes and was likely to be given a robust cross-examination. In the circumstances the inspector taking the case was left without his major witness, but wanted to protect the officer from being shown in a poor light. The Commissioners were unimpressed that HMRC failed to call the inspector who had dealt with the case from the beginning and this helped Accountax in winning the appeal hearing. Calling an inspector might add little to the evidence of the actual appeal but can be very important where costs are being claimed.

17.48 Having decided, hopefully, that the witnesses to be called on behalf of the taxpayer will be credible and punctual two things must be clearly explained to them. The first is the general order of proceedings: the layout of the room where the hearing will take place and an idea as to who the various personnel are and what their function is. For those practitioners who are not familiar with this Chapter 18 gives the necessary information.

Having given the client some general guidance as to what happens on the day attention should be turned to the questions that he will be asked when he is examined, that is to say when he is called as a witness. It is perfectly permissible to go through this process before the hearing, and the practitioner can rest assured that the inspector representing HMRC will go through the same process with any other inspector or person he intends to call as his witnesses.

17.49 What must not happen is the putting of words into the mouth of the witness, either before the hearing or by the process of asking leading questions, during the hearing. There is also a danger that over-rehearsed questions and answer sessions will appear stilted and artificial and will not impress the Tribunal. The questions asked should be open, in order that the client can effectively 'tell his story' in his own words.

It is important to remind the client, several times, and once shortly before the hearing, that he should answer the question but then remain silent.

Case study
In a recent appeal it became very clear that one of HMRC's witnesses was unhappy with the draft witness statement HMRC had prepared on his behalf. Words had been attributed to the witness which he had not said. This reflected badly on HMRC. Witness statements are living documents and they will be drafted and changed but the starting point should be an accurate record of what the witness actually said when interviewed, not what HMRC wished he had said.

17.50 In the event that any answer is too brief then either the practitioner or indeed Tribunal members themselves may ask the witness to expand upon the information he has given. This is particularly the case in cross-examination, where an experienced advocate will ask the witness an awkward question and will then remain silent after the witness has given his initial response. This is in the hope that the 'pregnant pause' will lead the witness into saying something else beyond his initial answer which may be incriminating.

17.51 In preparing the witness it is important that all the questions he will be asked are fully understood. If he does not understand the wording of the questions, the time to clarify this is before the hearing.

17.52 The full procedures of a Tribunal hearing are explained in Chapter 18, but it is worth mentioning at this stage that after the examination of the taxpayer's witnesses has finished the inspector will have the opportunity to cross-examine them to test the accuracy and truth of the information given. Cross-examination can be very testing. Whereas the examination of the witness can be a fairly pedestrian and gentle conversation, cross-examination will be more focused on inconsistencies or weaknesses in the evidence given, and a competent inspector will wish to expose any such weaknesses. Cross-examination can sometimes border on the hostile and can certainly be very brusque in nature. In cross-examination leading questions are allowed.

Briefing of the witness must include a warning that cross-examination can be difficult but that the key to dealing with this successfully is to listen to the question carefully and to answer slowly and clearly and not to rush into a confrontation with the inspector.

> *Case study*
> In 2000, the author appeared as a witness for the plaintiff in a High Court libel action. He was cross-examined by the shadow Attorney-General, Sir Edward Garnier QC who suggested that the evidence given was not credible. In an exchange a question was put along the lines of 'are you seriously trying to suggest that …'. The answer given was a straightforward unequivocal and calm 'yes'. Nothing more, nothing less. The barrister had nowhere to go and ran out of steam. The plaintiff won and received substantial damages.

Witness summons

17.53 Any person can be called as a witness if it is felt that the person's evidence will be helpful. But what happens if the practitioner wishes to have the opportunity of cross-examining the inspector who has worked the case and HMRC refuse to call him as a witness?

17.54 Under the Tribunal Procedure (First-tier Tribunal) (Tax Chamber) Rules 2009, it is possible to serve a witness summons on any person (rule 16), and this includes tax officers and inspectors. It is necessary to apply to the Tribunal Service explaining why it is necessary to serve a witness summons and the Tribunal will, if satisfied, approve the witness summons.

The power to issue a witness summons should not be underestimated.

> *Case study*
> At a contentious tax status dispute in 2001 Accountax served a witness summons on a tax officer who had carried out the initial PAYE compliance review. In examination he was forced to concede that he had not even examined the contract terms and conditions and that in fact he had 'not carried out the review thoroughly or properly'. This evidence was very damaging to HMRC. The taxpayer won the appeal.

17.55 The usual justification for a witness summons is that the person concerned has been heavily involved in the case and may have important evidence to give. If a witness fails to comply with a witness summons without good cause, he is committing an offence.

Case study
In the IR35 appeal *Tilbury Consulting Ltd v Gittins* SpC [2004] STD (SCD) 72 (SpC 390), Accountax tried to argue against a witness from Ford being called as a witness or summonsed, on the basis that it would cause commercial harm to the contractor. Dr Brice decided the summons should be issued in the interests of justice. In the event HMRC called a different witness from Ford and lost at the substantive hearing. The lesson is: if you want a witness summons you are likely to get one.

17.56 The only witness the practitioner is likely to want to summons will be an inspector who has been involved in the case and whose evidence may be beneficial to the client's appeal. It should go without saying that most reasonable inspectors are prepared to give evidence voluntarily and the Tribunal members may raise their eyebrows where an inspector has refused to do so other than for the fact that a witness summons was issued to him. Equally, a witness summons can be issued against the client, although it would be a foolish client who refuses to give evidence on a voluntary basis at his own appeal, unless he would be a very poor witness indeed.

Case study
In a tax status case heard by the General Commissioners in 2000, the initial inspector of taxes had formed the view that the worker was self-employed. His colleague who took the case over adopted a different view and came to the conclusion that the worker was employed. Several years earlier Customs and Excise had visited the worker, who had his own established business, and concluded that the services he provided to the putative employer were part and parcel of his normal business trading activities and VAT should have been charged. HMRC refused to call the second inspector to give evidence. Accountax applied for and served a General Commissioners witness summons on the VAT inspector and the original inspector voluntarily gave evidence. It was left too late to serve a witness summons on the second inspector, who refused to give evidence.

The refusal by the second inspector to give evidence was extraordinary and must have had some influence on the General Commissioners' appraisal of HMRC's case. The initial inspector explained in a very straightforward and honest manner why he felt the worker was indeed self-employed and the VAT inspector did the same. In an unusually long written decision the General Commissioners explained that they had found unanimously in favour of self-employment and made several references to the quality of the witnesses called and the evidence given.

17.57 It should be borne in mind that HMRC officers should only be called when they can give valuable evidence that goes to the heart of the appeal. There is very limited value in calling an inspector merely to expose his failings. The Tribunal's function is not to hear complaints!

17.58 It will not have escaped the attention of the sharper practitioner that although a witness summons can be used very effectively against HMRC, sometimes there is more to be gained by letting HMRC withhold one of their main or

17.58 *Preparing for an appeal hearing*

most obvious witnesses. The Tribunal will draw their own conclusions from such an unusual, and arguably unprofessional, stance.

The reader may wish to refer to an article in *Taxation* 14, February 2002 where the author comments on the procedural complications of calling witnesses.

Summary

17.59   The key to a successful Tribunal hearing is preparation, preparation and more preparation. Having taken the step of getting the case listed (see Chapter 16) the biggest danger facing the practitioner is not a lack of familiarity with appeal hearings but the giving of insufficient time and resources to the preparation of the case. This should never be underestimated. In the author's experience seven to ten working days are required, and the work must start well in advance of the hearing.

17.60   Bundles of documents must be carefully prepared, indexed and numbered. Full case reports are available from most university libraries or from the various professional accountancy bodies or the internet.

17.61   Witnesses have to be considered carefully and fully briefed but not overprepared. Although the taxpayer has probably never been to the Tribunal before and will almost inevitably be nervous a great deal can be done to calm his nerves by going through the procedures in advance. In this respect Chapter 18 will be particularly useful.

17.62   A witness summons should always be considered where a key witness, often a tax officer, is reluctant to give evidence voluntarily. There can, however, also be a tactical advantage to be gained in letting HMRC *not* call an obvious witness.

17.63   In summary, it must be remembered that preparation is all and full familiarity with the administrative procedures and requirements will get the preparation off to a flying start.

Chapter 18
Presenting an appeal

18.1 This chapter gives guidance on what to expect at the appeal hearing in order to assist the practitioner who is not familiar with such proceedings. It is also very important to explain to the client what will happen on the day. Those practitioners who have never been to an appeal hearing should learn a great deal from this chapter.

18.2 The procedural rules for hearings changed with the introduction of the new Tax Tribunals from 1 April 2009, and the consequent phasing out of the General and Special Commissioners. Having said that, the following updated guidance seems likely to remain sound in relation to the order of proceedings and documentation.

Location

18.3 Appeal hearings before the First-tier Tribunal tend to be heard in Regional Tribunal Centres (similar to employment tribunals), which are based in major cities. The Tribunals Service have indicated that there is an available network of 130 hearing centres across the country, with the facility to use privately hired venues.

18.4 The general rule is that all Tribunal appeal hearings must be held in public. However, in exceptional circumstances an application can be made for the Tribunal to direct that all or part of the appeal be heard in private (eg to protect a person's privacy, or to maintain the confidentiality of sensitive information).

18.5 The First-tier Tribunal (Tax Chamber) Rules 2009 lay down the administrative formalities pertaining to the listing of a hearing. The Tribunal must give the parties to a hearing 'reasonable notice' of the time and place of any hearing. That period of notice must be at least 14 days, unless the parties agree otherwise or in urgent or exceptional circumstances.

> *Case study*
> In a case under the previous Commissioners' regime, the Notice of Hearing not only gave less than the statutory period, but it also failed to identify the year of assessment and failed to include a date stamp. Although a Notice of Hearing for a General Commissioners' case appeared to be issued by the Clerk, it was in fact issued by HMRC. The errors on the Notice were pointed out and HMRC quite rightly immediately agreed to re-issue the Notice. Crucially this bought the clients another month or so to prepare their case.

18.6 *Presenting an appeal*

Representation

18.6 In accordance with the First-tier Tribunal (Tax Chamber) Rules 2009, the taxpayer may appoint anyone to represent them at the appeal hearing, whether legally qualified or not. Written notice of the representative's name and address must be provided in advance to the Tribunal, and to HMRC. Alternatively, the taxpayer may be accompanied at the hearing by another person who may act as a representative or otherwise assist, with the Tribunal's consent.

> *Case study*
> In an IR35 appeal (during the Commissioners' regime) before the Special Commissioner it was made quite clear that the Commissioner did not want to be given a lecture on employment law! He already knew the law and instead wanted the taxpayer's representative, a chartered accountant, to apply the law to the facts established in evidence. This approach is a classic example of what the competent advocate has to do, whether representing HMRC or the taxpayer—apply the law to the established facts with no meanderings.

18.7 HMRC will usually be represented by a senior officer from the local area. Exceptionally, they will be represented by either a barrister or a member of one of HMRC's specialist advocacy units.

18.8 The inspector representing HMRC may have an assistant with him to help with the paperwork. No objection should be made to this. Just as the practitioner will question his own client to draw out the evidence the inspector may question the officer who has dealt with the file, again to draw out 'what was said'. This can be particularly relevant where there is a dispute over the accuracy of notes of interview. HMRC have to be very careful here as the following illustrates.

> *Case study*
> In a 2007 Special Commissioner's status case, HMRC sought to rely on unsigned notes of interview which had been disputed by those interviewed. HMRC however, failed to call the officers involved in the interviews and as such the Special Commissioner was unable to hear their evidence. This damaged HMRC's position. As an aside it should be noted that one of the officers involved was in fact in court, but by this time had left HMRC to work as a tax consultant in the private sector!

18.9 One of the advantages of HMRC being represented by a senior inspector is that the inspector may not be familiar with all of the detail of the file's history. Although one would think that very careful preparation goes without saying, the author has been involved in contentious hearings where the inspector leading for HMRC was not as familiar with the file as he should have been.

The First-tier Tax Tribunal

18.10 The Tax Chamber of the First-tier Tribunal was introduced with effect from 1 April 2009. The Tribunal's judicial personnel comprise salaried and fee-paid judges (including the previous Special Commissioners), and 75 fee-paid non-legal members. The non-legal members are chosen on the basis of experience of tax appeals and/or direct experience of specific businesses. Those who served under the previous General Commissioners' regime were not transferred into the new Tribunal system. However, their experience would probably have been beneficial, and no doubt many of them therefore applied to become non-legal members of the First-tier Tax Tribunal.

18.11 The number of members of the Lower-tier Tribunal who hear a particular appeal can vary. The decision as to the number of members is determined by the Senior President of Tribunals (The First-tier Tribunal and Upper Tribunal (Composition of Tribunal) Order, SI 2008/2835). At the time of writing, the composition of the Tribunals in practice remains to be seen. As the First-tier Tribunal will deal with cases previously heard by the General Commissioners, it seems likely that cases involving no material legal issues will generally be heard by non-legal members, with judges hearing cases with significant legal content. However, it will be interesting to see how Tribunals to hear IR35 cases will generally be comprised in practice.

18.12 Under the previous regime of the Commissioners, three General Commissioners would hear a contentious appeal. The minimum number for a valid quorum was two, with a maximum of five. In the event that only two Commissioners were available to listen to the appeal, the Chairman would have the casting vote.

Case study
Accountax's Matt Boddington was due to represent a client prior to the Tax Tribunal regime at the General Commissioners in Montrose, Scotland. Having forgotten his ID he was refused permission to fly and so drove to Scotland in order not to let the client down. Arriving at the hearing bleary eyed he was faced not with the usual three General Commissioners but just one! One General Commissioner was not a valid quorum. However, common sense prevailed and Accountax and HMRC agreed that just the one Commissioner could hear the appeal and his decision would be deemed to be binding on both parties. This wholly unorthodox but pragmatic approach illustrates what can be achieved in unusual circumstances. The taxpayer won the appeal which made the 800-mile round trip worthwhile.

18.13 Where the Specials heard an appeal there was only a requirement for one Special but occasionally two may have heard the case. This could sometimes lead to a problem where there was a split decision, amply illustrated by the 'settlements' case of Arctic Systems (*Jones v Garnett*), which was ultimately decided in favour of the taxpayer ([2007] STC 1536)).

18.14 Non-legal members of the First-tier Tribunal will withdraw from an appeal hearing where there is a conflict of interest, for example, a Tribunal member could be a director of a computer business which supplies the taxpayer with products.

18.15 Presenting an appeal

18.15 It may pay dividends to do a little research on the region of the Tribunal that will hear the appeal:

> *Case study*
> The author took a contentious appeal hearing under the 'old' Commissioners' regime and shortly beforehand carried out a search on case law to see if the division of Commissioners concerned had been involved in any recent cases which had gone on to the High Court. The search revealed that the Commissioners concerned had dealt with *McManus v Griffiths* ([1997] STC 1089), a tax status case in 1997. The Commissioners had determined the worker was self-employed.
>
> At the hearing, the *McManus* case was quoted and the Commissioners, unsurprisingly, took a real interest in it. The author commented that the Commissioners would no doubt be familiar with the case, yet the inspector seemed oblivious to its relevance. This just added some topical interest and showed that the background to the case was fully appreciated. Not a winning factor per se but a small point in the client's favour perhaps.

The Tax Tribunal judge

18.16 As mentioned above, the judges on the First-tier Tax Tribunal include Special Commissioners transferred from the previous regime. These are legally qualified professionals, including several QCs and academics, who all have at least ten years' post-qualification experience.

In the author's experience of the Tribunal judges in their previous guise of Special Commissioners, they go to some pains to make sure the taxpayer has as much time as is reasonably necessary to present his appeal in the manner he would like. The 'Specials' were known for extending considerable courtesy and patience to the taxpayer. The facilities to hear cases in difficult circumstances were better at the Specials.

> *Case study*
> In a previous hearing at the Special Commissioners, one of the witnesses was partially sighted, one had a speech impediment and two were hearing-impaired but every effort was made to cope with these unusual circumstances and in their usual helpful and efficient manner the clerks made sure the Special Commissioner was aware of the circumstances.

The inspector

18.17 It should be borne in mind that once at the hearing the inspector will be there in the role of advocate, not negotiator, and the practitioner should be aware that the inspector will do whatever he reasonably can to win the case. HMRC do not like losing an appeal hearing any more than the taxpayer, not least because it can affect their credibility with the local Tribunal, particularly if several cases are lost in a short period of time.

The layout of the meeting room

18.18 At the time of writing, the protocol of appeal hearings before the First-tier Tribunal in practice is not clear, but it seems likely that the layout of the appeal hearing room will be based on the Commissioners' regime.

Although it would vary, the traditional layout in a General Commissioners' hearing would typically comprise a top table, where the General Commissioners sat, with the Clerk to one side. Looking towards the top table from the back of the room there would usually be a table on the left where the taxpayer and his representative would sit and a table on the right where the inspector would sit.

Practical experience of the Commissioners' regime was that occasionally the tables would be arranged whereby the taxpayer and his representative sat immediately in front of the Commissioners with the inspector sitting to one side. Unfortunately, such an arrangement is a little off-putting and the taxpayer and his representative may feel that they have been summoned to the headmaster's study to explain themselves! Thankfully, this type of arrangement is unusual and most Commissioners were sensitive to the propriety of a symmetrical layout.

18.19 At the Special Commissioners formal courts were the norm. The top table or 'bench' was raised and a horse-shoe shape was not used. Both taxpayer and HMRC sat in front of the bench and next to each other, with the public behind. The public gallery was often no more than a few spare chairs.

The proceedings

18.20 It should always be remembered that the taxpayer is the appellant and the onus of proof is on him. He has made an appeal against an assessment or notice of decision and, in order for his appeal to succeed, he must show that on the balance of probabilities the assessment should be discharged.

18.21 The Tribunals, Courts and Enforcement Act 2007 provides for 'Tribunal Procedure Rules' to govern the practice and procedure to be followed in the First-tier Tribunal. The procedure rules relating to the First-tier Tax Tribunal (The Tribunal Procedure (First-tier Tribunal) (Tax Chamber) Rules 2009) provide the general framework for appeal hearings. Subject to TCEA 2007 and any other enactment, the Tribunal may regulate its own procedures. No such further regulations or guidance was available at the time of writing on the conduct of appeal hearings before the First-tier Tax Tribunal.

18.22 As mentioned above, the First-tier Tax Tribunal includes judges transferred from the previous Special Commissioners' regime. Historically, cases before the 'Specials' were subject to detailed directions, exchange of witness statements and skeleton arguments and therefore both sides, and the court, were fully aware of the issues and arguments. The First-tier Tax Tribunal rules provide for similar procedures, although very simple and basic cases will be dealt with on the papers with few, if any, formal directions.

18.23 It makes sense that the appellant speaks first at the hearing, because the burden of proof is on him. In addition, tactically it must help his case to do so. By

18.23 *Presenting an appeal*

speaking first as well as last an advantage will be gained, if only in being able to emphasise one's arguments at the outset and at the conclusion of the proceedings. Furthermore, if the appellant speaks first HMRC not only have to worry about making their own presentation after the practitioner has made some forceful points, but will have to try to incorporate some of the issues already raised. In other words, HMRC will have to think on their feet under pressure.

Case study
At a Special Commissioners' 'directions' hearing the inspector forgot that because he had applied for the directions he was obliged to speak first. This completely threw him as he was expecting to speak second, as he would at a full hearing. He was thus unprepared and struggled. The Special Commissioner subsequently accepted Accountax's arguments and refused the inspector's proposed directions.

18.24 Historically, despite the advantages of speaking first and last, many inexperienced practitioners allowed the inspector to go first. This was usually because the practitioner was unsure of the procedures and he felt he might be able to ease his way into the proceedings by sitting back and letting HMRC take the initiative. This was a major tactical mistake. At the 'Specials' it was almost certain that the taxpayer would speak first, and it seems logical that this procedure will be followed in the First-tier Tax Tribunal.

18.25 On the basis that the practitioner speaks first, the usual order of proceedings is as follows:

1 The practitioner addresses the Tribunal and introduces himself and his client.
2 The practitioner offers a very brief summary of the appeal under consideration, and hands out Bundle A only (if the Tribunal do not already have this).
3 The practitioner calls his client and any other witnesses to give evidence. This is called the examination-in-chief. Documents will be referred to such as witness statements, contracts, letters, etc.
4 The inspector has the right to cross-examine the taxpayer and witnesses called on behalf of the taxpayer to test the truth and completeness of their evidence.
5 The practitioner then has a further opportunity to re-examine his witnesses.
6 The Tribunal may well want to ask the witnesses some questions and may do so at any stage.
7 Having dealt with his own witnesses HMRC then repeat the process.
8 HMRC call and examine their witnesses.
9 The practitioner cross-examines them.
10 HMRC may re-examine their witnesses.
11 At this stage both practitioner and HMRC have finished their questions.
12 The Tribunal may ask HMRC's witnesses any questions.
13 At this stage the facts should be known so the practitioner makes legal submissions to support the appeal and summarises his case.
14 The inspector will make his case law submissions and summarise his case.
15 On the taxpayer's behalf the practitioner has a final brief summary.
16 The Tribunal then retire to make their decision.

The whole process is fairly straightforward and logical. There is absolutely nothing to be worried about so long as the case has been prepared carefully.

This summary of the order of proceedings and the various stages is examined in more depth below.

1. Addressing the Tribunal and introducing the client

18.26 Many practitioners do not know what to call the Tribunal members. This point of etiquette is fairly straightforward but is worth learning and committing to memory. They should be called either 'Sir' or 'Madam'.

18.27 The client should be called 'my client' or 'the taxpayer' or referred to by his surname. Overuse of the word 'appellant' may lead to the further use of formal legalese, which is not necessary.

18.28 The HMRC representative should be referred to as 'the inspector' or by his surname. It is also permissible to say 'HMRC' when referring to actions taken by the inspector, for example, 'HMRC wrote to our client on 14 July'. It should be remembered that the inspector is not a policeman. The author has heard references to 'Inspector Black of HMRC said ...', which is quite inappropriate.

18.29 Throughout the entire hearing, with the exception of asking direct questions of the witnesses, the practitioner should direct his remarks *to the Chairman*. It is equally important to remind the client before the hearing that he should address his answers, including those given in cross-examination, not to the person who asks the question but to the Chairman. It is vitally important to make sure that the Tribunal clearly hear what is being said.

18.30 It goes without saying that the taxpayer and his representative should never engage in a verbal battle across the room with the inspector.

18.31 Tribunal members may be acquainted with the inspector and it will therefore be obvious who is the taxpayer's representative. However, as a courtesy it is important that the practitioner introduces himself and his client.

18.32 The respect to be shown to the Tribunal should be reflected in one's attire. It is strongly recommended that a sober business suit and tie is appropriate for men and a business suit for women. Turning up without a jacket or wearing an absurd comedy tie will not lose the case but it might suggest to the Tribunal that the proceedings are not being taken seriously.

> *Case study*
> The author represented a taxpayer in a very important capital gains tax appeal prior to the introduction of the Tax Tribunal, at the General Commissioners. It was a very warm summer's day and the author left the office without taking his suit jacket. Turning up in mere shirt sleeves even in hot weather is not recommended as it gives the appearance of being rather casual. Fortunately the author had with him an assistant who was wearing a suit. Unfortunately, it was

18.32 *Presenting an appeal*

not the same colour as the author's trousers. The view was taken that it would not be too bad if the assistant turned up without a jacket but it would look bad if the taxpayer's main representative was not wearing one. The author entered the hearing carrying boxes of documents wearing a blue jacket with black trousers, said hello to the Commissioners, commented on what a hot day it was and asked if the Commissioners objected to jackets being removed. The Commissioners did not object and the non-matching jacket was hastily dispatched to the back of the chair!

18.33 When standing to address the Tribunal it is very likely that the Chairman will give immediate permission to sit down, on the basis that the proceedings are informal. In these circumstances unless the practitioner particularly wishes to stand (which could be for a very long time), he is then at liberty to sit. By initially standing the practitioner has registered his respect for the Tribunal, which cannot harm his credibility. Interestingly, it is *rare* for the inspector to stand when he first addresses the Tribunal and the contrast in the two approaches will be self-evident.

18.34 Having stood to address the Tribunal the following opening words are suggested:

> 'Good morning. My name is John Brown and I am a partner in Brown and Green Chartered Accountants. I represent the appellant taxpayer here on my right, Mr Fred Bloggs who is a director of Fred Bloggs Computer Services Limited.'

2. *Presenting a brief summary*

18.35 At the time of writing, no hearings have taken place before the Tax Tribunals. However, it may be of interest to practitioners to be aware of the author's experiences under the previous regime of the Commissioners, and useful in terms of presentation technique generally. These are discussed below.

18.36 It was very tempting to launch into a detailed submission without first giving the Commissioners an overview of what the appeal was about. Just as it was important to offer a concise conclusion when wrapping up a case it was equally important to offer a succinct summary at the outset. The Commissioners needed to be given a true idea of the substance of the appeal before witnesses were called or legal arguments started. Following on from the introductions the following summary might have been used:

> 'Before going into the detail of this appeal it might assist the Commissioners to have a brief summary of what this case is all about. [Pause] My client has appealed against what is known as a Section 8 Notice issued by the Inland Revenue for the tax year 2003/04. [Pause] In essence the Section 8 Notice assesses my client as if he were a disguised employee under what are commonly called the IR35 rules. [Pause] This appeal is made on the basis that the taxpayer is not a disguised employee and that he is in fact running a genuine

business and is not caught by the IR35 rules. [Pause] I hope to demonstrate to the Commissioners that the Section 8 Notice should, on the balance of probabilities, be discharged. I will call witnesses and in due course adduce detailed case law in support of this appeal.'

Note that at a Special Commissioner's hearing, an introduction was not necessary as disclosure of documents would already have revealed what the case was about.

18.37 At this point when appearing at the 'Generals' the practitioner's assistant would hand out Bundle A to the Clerk (unless the hearing was at the 'Specials' where it will already have been handed in previously), making sure beforehand that there were sufficient copies for everybody, including HMRC. The Clerk would then distribute the bundles to those present. Tactically, at this stage it would be *unwise* to distribute Bundle B. Instead the Chairman would be informed that the bundle of case law extracts would be handed out when the legal submissions were made. The following case study shows how it could be tactically disadvantageous to hand out Bundle B too early:

Case study
In the run-up to a contentious appeal hearing at the General Commissioners it became obvious that HMRC were not particularly familiar with the case law precedents relevant to the point at issue. Although a list of case law references had been provided to the inspector seven days prior to the hearing the list was particularly long and it was quite likely that the inspector did not have the time to read the full judgments. This placed him at a distinct disadvantage as he would have to try to counter the case law arguments put forward by Accountax as they developed on the day. The author made the mistake of handing out both Bundles A and B at the beginning of the hearing. An early lunch break was called by the Chairman, which lasted for one and a quarter hours. At this stage witnesses were still being called and the legal submissions had not started.

During the lunch break the inspector had ample opportunity to go through Bundle B, where all of the relevant case law extracts Accountax was going to cite and rely upon had been clearly asterisked and highlighted! This gave the inspector a last-minute opportunity to revise his own legal submissions as he now knew in advance what passages would be quoted from the judgments. HMRC still lost but there is a lesson to be learnt. Do not give away information and arguments until you need to.

18.38 The above opening summary would take no more than 60 seconds but it neatly encapsulated the essence of the issue.

Note that regular pauses are very important. At all times the Tribunal must be given ample opportunity to make their notes and to take in what is being said. If they are not given enough time it cannot be assumed that they will ask for a slower pace or to go over something again. Instead, there is the serious risk of simply failing to make the point, and the practitioner cannot afford to do this.

By getting into the habit of making regular pauses this early in the presentation it will be that much easier to carry on in the same manner throughout the course of the hearing.

18.39 *Presenting an appeal*

3. Calling and examining witnesses

18.39 It is important to realise that one of the most powerful forms of evidence is that given by the taxpayer himself. A credible, calm and articulate taxpayer can do himself a great deal of good when asked to give evidence.

> *Case study*
> In an IR35 appeal before the Tax Tribunal regime at the Special Commissioners, the taxpayer was very calm and collected and courteous despite being on the receiving end of some inappropriate questions from HMRC. Our client gave clear and measured responses to the Special Commissioner rather than getting into an argument with HMRC. However, HMRC asked one too many inappropriate questions at which point our client turned away from the Special Commissioner and instead gave HMRC a lecture on the risks and hardship involved in building up a small business. It was still calm and collected but delivered from the heart. It is fair to say that it was a very compelling piece of oral evidence and completely threw HMRC. It clearly impressed the Special Commissioner and the appeal was successful.

The First-tier Tax Tribunal Procedure Rules state that the Tribunal may make directions as to the manner of the evidence or submissions they require, whether these be provided orally at a hearing or by written submissions or witness statement. Subject to such directions, it may be preferable for the taxpayer to give oral evidence, attending the hearing rather than simply sending in a letter. However, documentary evidence from witnesses who cannot attend can be useful, particularly if a sworn statement is produced.

18.40 The Tribunal may admit evidence despite the fact that such evidence would be inadmissible in a civil trial before a UK court of law. In other words, the witness may offer hearsay evidence and the Tribunal are entitled to take it into account, although of course they may not attach much weight to it.

However, 'without prejudice' evidence *cannot* be adduced. Using the phrase 'without prejudice' on a letter or document means that it cannot be used against the person who wrote it. It might be that the practitioner makes a last-ditch effort to avoid a hearing by making an offer in settlement. If this is headed 'without prejudice' then the letter cannot be adduced by the inspector at the hearing (to show the taxpayer's doubts in his own case) should negotiations break down.

> *Case study*
> At a contentious appeal in the Commissioners' era the inspector, who was badly prepared generally, attempted to put a without prejudice letter, sent by Accountax, in evidence. Virtually before he had referred to it his senior colleague apologised to all present for the inspector's mistake. The Commissioners were not impressed. HMRC lost and their lack of understanding of the rules of evidence must have played a part.

18.41 The Tribunal have the power to consent to or require any witness to give evidence on oath. In the author's experience of the previous Commissioners' regime this was rare, except at the Specials. However, where the taxpayer is prepared to give evidence on oath this may be worth pointing out to the Tribunal, as this underlines the *bona fides* of the taxpayer.

18.42 The taxpayer himself, although a witness, will be present throughout the entire proceedings. He would be called by addressing the Tribunal along the following lines:

> 'I would now like to ask my client Mr Fred Bloggs to give evidence to the Tribunal. [Turning to the client] Please give your name and address to the Tribunal.'

This is a fairly simple formality which should be gone through with every witness called. He can then be given a copy of his witness statement and asked if it is his signature and whether he is still happy with the statement.

18.43 The best way to elicit oral evidence from the client, and indeed any other witness, is to ask him a series of questions which he can in broad terms be made aware of earlier. There is no point in over-rehearsing the questions and answers. It is important that your client gives his evidence in his own words. Putting words into the mouth of the client is very unwise.

18.44 The practitioner must not ask his own witnesses what are called 'leading questions'. A leading question is one which anticipates and suggests the required reply. An extreme example might be:

> 'Isn't it correct that you had a *written* contract?'

The question should be:

> 'Did you have a contract?'

This may be followed up with:

> 'What form did the contract take?'

It should be noted that when cross-examining an HMRC witness leading questions *can* be asked just as HMRC can ask the taxpayer and his witnesses leading questions during cross-examination.

18.45 It is now a matter of asking the questions in a clear and methodical manner so that the client's evidence unfolds as a natural conversation. In a typical IR35 or tax status dispute this will work towards establishing what the working terms and conditions of the relationship are. If there are other factors which may help the case, for example, the extent to which the client has invested in equipment or training courses, he should also be asked questions on these points.

18.46 By the time the taxpayer has been examined he should have given convincing, clear and confident evidence on all the major issues. In an IR35 or tax

18.46 *Presenting an appeal*

status dispute the practitioner will want to concentrate on the more important factors, such as the right of substitution, mutuality of obligations, financial risk, control and the client's business organisation and general *modus operandi*.

18.47 The client's oral evidence should be cross-referenced to documentation in Bundle A (or whatever documents have been submitted to the Tribunal in advance of the hearing) wherever possible. For example, the client might give evidence to the effect that he has professional indemnity insurance in place and raises invoices on a business letterhead. Once this point is made the Tribunal should then be referred to the appropriate enclosures in Bundle A.

18.48 Hopefully by now, the client through responding to questions asked has painted a picture of the facts the practitioner is hoping to establish, in a measured and clear manner.

18.49 It is important to suggest to the Tribunal that they formally *find* or accept certain facts. This is because, unless the Tribunal reach a completely perverse conclusion, their factual findings cannot be overturned by a superior court. An astute advocate will always be looking to the Tribunal to accept as *fact* certain contentions and to document them accordingly.

18.50 It is tempting only to draw out the evidence which helps the client's case and to try to ignore those factors which do not assist. This is generally unwise because a well-prepared inspector will expose weaknesses in the taxpayer's case when he has his chance to cross-examine the client. Tactically, it is often better to address weaknesses in the client's arguments and try to play them down rather than to pretend that they do not exist in the first place.

4. Cross-examination of the taxpayer and the appellant's witnesses

18.51 The inspector will now try to test the accuracy and truth of the client's evidence by putting to him a series of questions in cross-examination. Cross-examination will generally be less polite than the examination in chief. The client's integrity and cool will be tested as cross-examination can be quite hostile.

18.52 It is important that the client remains calm and listens carefully to the question that is being put to him. If he does not understand the question then he should say so. He should answer the question and say no more. Sometimes the inspector will ask the same question in several different ways until he gets the preferred answer! Your client must be steadfast. If he has answered the question he is quite at liberty to point this out to the Tribunal.

18.53 There are different techniques of cross-examination. The first is to increase the pace and hostility of the questions being asked in the hope that the witness will become flustered and may then contradict himself or lose his composure. The author has witnessed this at first hand where an inspector was particularly effective in his very assertive style of cross-examination.

The second technique is to take a far more measured and calm approach whereby the witness can be lulled into a false sense of security only to find that he has contradicted something he has said earlier.

It cannot be stressed strongly enough that in either case the witness must listen carefully to the question and think carefully before answering. He should direct his answers to the Tribunal not to the inspector asking him the questions even during hostile cross-examination.

18.54 An example of cross-examination is where the inspector mounts an out-and-out challenge to the earlier evidence given by the witness. If, for example, the witness stated earlier that the entire terms and conditions of his working relationship were contained in a written contract then the inspector might try to show that there were other oral or implied arrangements. If he can establish this, he will then attack the credibility of the witness time and again by referring to his earlier incomplete evidence. This is cruel but fair.

18.55 Another technique of cross-examination is to lessen the weight to be attached to evidence given earlier by the witness. For example, it may have been established that the client invested money from his own pocket in attending training courses. This sounds like helpful evidence of financial investment and being in business. But if the question 'How much did the training course cost?' is asked by the inspector, and the answer is 'Only £30', then the importance of the training course will be diluted considerably. Remember the inspector's role, just the same as the accountant's, is that of an advocate who wants to win. On cross-examination and re-examination it is necessary, more than ever, to be able to remain calm and think on your feet.

5. Re-examination of the taxpayer and his witnesses

18.56 During cross-examination careful notes should be taken of anything the client is saying which is *unhelpful* to his case. This is because, after the inspector has finished cross-examining the witness, there will be a final opportunity for his representative to re-examine him. New evidence cannot be adduced at this stage but matters dealt with earlier can be re-visited. For example, referring back to the inexpensive training course it may be possible to establish the fact that the client funded *several* of these courses. The purpose of re-examination is to undo, wherever possible, any damage inflicted by the inspector during cross-examination.

18.57 This process of calling witnesses, examining them, the inspector cross-examining them followed by a final re-examination is carried out for all witnesses called by the taxpayer's representative and the inspector. The taxpayer's representative will of course have his own opportunity to cross-examine the inspector's witnesses in due course.

18.58 The key to a successful examination of the client is preparation. All of the questions need to be written out and the client needs to be aware in broad terms of the questions he is going to be asked. If the case has been prepared properly there should be no real surprises and there should be an appreciation of the weaknesses in the case, which will give a good idea of the questions the inspector

18.58   *Presenting an appeal*

is likely to raise in cross-examination. The key to dealing successfully with cross-examination is to back up the oral evidence wherever possible by reference to documentary evidence and to ensure at all times that the plain truth is told.

18.59   Where the cross-examination of the client has resulted in little or no damage this should be pointed out to the Tribunal as it underlines the fact that the client's evidence and credibility have not been dented by the inspector.

18.60   The client as the appellant will remain in the hearing throughout the entire process. Other witnesses who have been called may have other engagements and it is customary to ask if the witnesses can leave the proceedings once they have given their evidence.

It should be noted that once the client has been cross-examined, unless the Tribunal wish to raise any further questions, the inspector is not at liberty to re-question the client at a later stage.

6. Questions asked by the Tribunal

18.61   It should be noted that the Tribunal may ask questions of the taxpayer at any time but they will usually only do this where a point needs clarifying. Just as a witness may not fully understand the question being put to him by the inspector so the Tribunal may not fully understand the information given in reply. The witness is most likely to be asked questions after he has been examined and cross-examined. It should be remembered that replies to questions must be given clearly and slowly in order that the Tribunal may take notes and ask any relevant questions.

7. Legal submissions by the practitioner (probably given later after all evidence has been heard)

18.62   Winning the appeal hearing is a two-part process. First, the facts must be established by bringing out evidence, either oral or documentary. Second, legal precedents as established by the courts must be advanced and shown how they apply to the facts. Chapter 5 contains all the major case law decisions. Reference should be made to the skeleton arguments submitted earlier.

This is relatively straightforward if the practitioner has a thorough understanding of what the current case law says. If, for example, it has been established as fact that the client has the right to send a substitute, then attention would be drawn to the *Express and Echo* ([1999] ICR 693) Court of Appeal case of 1999 and a quotation from the judgment of Lord Justice Peter Gibson would be read out to the Tribunal. It will be remembered from Chapter 5 that his Lordship made the very clear statement that where a substitute can be sent then 'as a matter of law the relationship will not be one of employer and employee'.

Another example might be where a lack of mutuality of obligations has been established. Here the practitioner may refer to the judgment of Lord Irvine in the 1999 House of Lords in *Carmichael v National Power Plc* [1999] 1 WLR 2042, when the workers' claim to employed status foundered on the 'rock of absence of mutuality'.

18.63 It is important not merely to recite a long list of case law decisions but to show their *relevance* to the facts established. The practitioner must constantly refer back to the evidence given, particularly where it was not challenged successfully in cross-examination. For example, reference might be made to the Court of Appeal decision in *Montgomery v Johnson Underwood Ltd* [2001] EWCA Civ 318 where, *inter alia*, the court stressed the need for the 'irreducible minimum' which needs to be in place before there can be a contract of service. One of the components of the irreducible minimum was control of the worker sufficient to render her a servant of her master. The relevant passage from the case judgment would be quoted to the Tribunal whereafter they would be reminded that it had already been established in evidence that the worker had freedom as to how and where the job was carried out.

18.64 The practitioner must always highlight the relevance of the case law precedents to the facts as established. The law and the facts need marrying up so their combined worth can be applied in support of the appeal.

18.65 Remember, opinions count for nothing. HMRC booklets contain subjective interpretation which do not carry the force of law. The most effective way of making a point is to quote the words of the judges, preferably from senior courts in well-established and recent case law precedents.

18.66 Do not over-burden the Tribunal with lengthy case law extracts unless it is absolutely necessary.

> *Case study*
> At a contentious tax status appeal during the Commissioners' regime, the inspector insisted not only in referring to an overwhelming amount of case law, much of which was not relevant, but made the mistake of reading out page after page verbatim. Despite the protests of the Chairman he continued to read great extracts aloud. Eventually the inspector was told in no uncertain terms that he was to stop and that the Commissioners would read the judgments for themselves. They then proceeded to do so but it was obvious that they skipped over it. The inspector had made the mistake of not heeding the Commissioners' wishes and also failed to maintain their attention. The taxpayer won.

8. Summarising the taxpayer's case

18.67 This summary should not be too brief as it is meant to pull all the evidence and legal submissions in support of the appeal together. It will be unwise to go over everything in what might already be becoming a long hearing, but all pertinent points should be re-visited.

The emphasis must be on the facts established and those not weakened in cross-examination and the application of the law to those facts as supported by appropriate quotations from the actual judgments.

At this stage it is worth reminding the Tribunal that the standard of proof is nothing more than the balance of probabilities.

Finally, a separate sheet which clearly reminds the Tribunal what decision is

18.67 *Presenting an appeal*

being sought may be handed out, unless it has been incorporated in Bundle A. The Tribunal should be thanked for its attention.

9. The inspector responds

18.68 Most of the hard work has been done by this stage. The facts have been established on the basis of oral and documentary evidence and legal submissions in support of the appeal have been made. Hopefully, HMRC have not exposed too many weaknesses in the client's case during cross-examination.

18.69 The inspector is now likely to make a minor tactical error. As it was traditional for HMRC to speak first (because the accountant is happy for him to do so and because this was often the assumption of the General but not the Special Commissioners) inspectors tend to prepare their appeal brief on this basis. This can have a damaging effect on the inspector's case if he fails to adapt his presentation to the practitioner having spoken first.

> *Case study*
> In an appeal hearing prior to the introduction of the Tax Tribunals, Accountax addressed the Commissioners first in a very long contentious hearing with many witnesses being called. The inspector had prepared his presentation in a style more appropriate to him speaking *first*. The result of this was that when he addressed the Commissioners he effectively trawled over the entire history of the file including many aspects which had already been dealt with exhaustively earlier in the day.
>
> The inspector was soon testing the patience of the Commissioners, who on more than one occasion asked him to move on and to stop repeating the background facts which had already been established. This caused the inspector difficulty as he was effectively reading out a prepared speech from longhand notes. He missed his chance to hold the attention of the Commissioners by offering fresh arguments and HMRC lost the appeal.

As the inspector has already had an opportunity to cross-examine the main witness, ie the taxpayer, he may have little more to add. He is of course at liberty to call his own witnesses (usually other HMRC officers who have been involved in the case). But at this stage there may not be many more facts to establish. In IR35 cases HMRC may call witnesses from the end user.

10. Cross-examining the inspector's witnesses

18.70 The rule here is not to be afraid of taking an assertive approach. If HMRC's witnesses and their evidence can be legitimately discredited then it is in the client's interests to do so. Cross-examination need not be overly polite, though out-and-out aggression is not recommended.

18.71 It is an old adage from the legal profession that one should never ask a question in cross-examination unless the answer is known. This is because a successful cross-examination is about controlling the *pace* and *direction* of the questioning and not being taken by surprise.

18.72 A fertile area of cross-examination is often to be found in a careful look through the file. Any errors by HMRC have to be exposed and exploited. HMRC will exploit any inconsistencies or anomalies in the client's case and the practitioner has to be prepared to do the same.

Furthermore, there must be a willingness to make a point even if this causes the witness some embarrassment. Remember, representing a client at an appeal hearing requires the approach of an advocate. The practitioner is his best hope of success. In an attempt to save the client's business and house the practitioner must represent the client to the best of his ability and if that means making a few waves so be it. It can work to the client's advantage if handled properly.

> *Case study*
> A tax officer involved in a status case had expressed the view on the telephone that in his opinion the workers were 'probably self-employed'. His line manager disagreed and the case eventually proceeded to a contentious appeal hearing. The original officer was called to give evidence and then cross-examined. He was persistently asked why he felt the men were 'probably self-employed'. This was extremely awkward for him, and he tried to avoid answering the question. By the time the question was put to him a third time the Commissioners were clearly expecting an answer. In a fit of pique the officer said 'It's obvious they are self-employed'.
>
> No more questions. This was the time to remain silent and let the point register with the Commissioners. It subsequently did and the taxpayer's appeal was successful.
>
> It would have been easy to ease off, but then nothing would have been gained.

18.73 Experienced tax inspectors will expect robust cross-examination, but both before and after the hearing a professional but friendly attitude should be the order of the day.

18.74 It is of course the Tribunal who will decide the worth of the evidence brought out in examination, cross-examination and re-examination.

> *Case study*
> When being cross-examined by the author at a contentious appeal hearing during the Commissioners' regime, a junior tax inspector was being prompted by his senior colleague who was sitting next to him. This happened several times and a complaint to the Chairman was made. The Commissioners were singularly unimpressed with the inspector's behaviour and in no uncertain terms told the senior inspector this was quite unacceptable. This is exactly the kind of procedural error that can help the taxpayer's case.

18.75 Practitioners should note that it is not permissible, with one exception, to cross-examine a witness who has been summoned. This is because, if a person

18.75 *Presenting an appeal*

attends in obedience to a witness summons that person is the witness of the person who summoned him and it is not possible to cross-examine one's own witness. The one exception is where permission is given to cross-examine where the Tribunal are satisfied that the person summoned is a 'hostile witness'. A hostile witness is a person whose mind discloses a bias adverse to the party examining him (see the author's article on this point in *Taxation*, 14 February 2002).

18.76 If a witness summons is applied for, any questioning of the witness must be carefully worded, as cross-examination will not be permitted unless it can be shown he is a hostile witness. The mere fact that a witness summons has been served does not necessarily mean that the person is hostile.

If, on the other hand, it is possible to have HMRC call the witness in question as an *HMRC* witness then he can be cross-examined in the normal way.

Case study
In a contentious appeal hearing (prior to the Tax Tribunal regime) before the General Commissioners, HMRC were reluctant to call a tax officer to give evidence. However, it was agreed by HMRC that a witness summons was unnecessarily formal and might cause the officer some distress. HMRC therefore agreed to call the witness as their own witness. This involved the inspector who was leading for HMRC simply asking the witness his name and confirmation of his job title in HMRC. There were no more questions and the witness was then cross-examined robustly.

18.77 It should be noted that sometimes a person might actually prefer to be served with a witness summons as this will give him protection from breach of confidentiality. A real life example of this was when Accountax served a witness summons on a VAT inspector who was concerned that if she disclosed confidential information in evidence on a 'voluntary' basis she could be at risk from an interested party.

18.78 There are other niceties in applying for a witness summons, such as giving at least 14 days' notice of the hearing, making appropriate provision for the witness to be paid any necessary expenses of attending the hearing and other formalities which are detailed in the Tribunal Procedure Rules.

18.79 In the final analysis, cross-examination is about exposing weaknesses and inconsistency in the other side's evidence. This attacks the credibility of HMRC's witnesses and in so doing enhances the value of one's own witnesses' evidence. Like everyone else, HMRC make errors. In the recent past Accountax has been sent a head office memo in error (it was meant to go to Milton Keynes Tax Office but was faxed to Accountax); an entire file destined for head office was sent to Accountax in error (the file contained some unprofessional comments on an Accountax employee, which resulted in a written apology from the Chairman of the Board of HMRC); and for several years the complaints handbook has been in the public domain yet an Accountax employee was virtually accused of stealing it (this resulted in a written apology from the HMRC's solicitor's office). Where errors are made they should be exposed where this can help the client, and this can most usefully be achieved in cross-examination of the inspector, and other witnesses called by HMRC.

Presenting an appeal **18.84**

11. Re-examination by HMRC

18.80 Here HMRC will try to undo any damage caused during cross-examination or will try to clarify issues to the advantage of its own case. It should be remembered that re-examination should not introduce any new areas of questioning. If it does there will be a further opportunity to cross-examine the witness on those new questions.

12. Questions by the Tribunal

18.81 It should not be assumed that the Tribunal will only want to test the quality of the evidence or ask questions of the taxpayer or any witnesses called by him. They are quite prepared to question HMRC's witnesses in a robust manner where appropriate. Tactically, if it is felt that the Tribunal are picking up on a particular strand of the argument then it would be wise to re-emphasise such a point in the final summary.

18.82 If, during Tribunal questions, anomalies or inconsistencies are exposed the astute practitioner should again remind them of this at the end of the hearing.

> *Case study*
> At a contentious appeal during the Commissioners' regime, evidence was extracted in cross-examination that the Revenue had handled the taxpayer's affairs very inefficiently. The Commissioners picked up on this and went so far as to observe that the Revenue had seriously messed the taxpayer around.
> To make matters worse the inspector then conceded there had been several 'Revenue cock-ups'. The author won the appeal on behalf of the taxpayer and the Revenue were determined to take the matter on appeal to the High Court. When a transcript of the hearing was produced the inspector's use of the phrase 'Revenue cock-ups' was recorded verbatim by the Clerk. The Revenue decided not to proceed to the High Court and substantial financial compensation was recovered for the taxpayer on the basis that the matter should never have got as far as the Commissioners in the first place.

13. HMRC make their legal submissions (possibly immediately after the appellant's legal submissions)

18.83 Just as the taxpayer makes legal submissions so HMRC have their opportunity. Any submissions made by HMRC which are not backed up by case law quotations should be noted and if HMRC are unable to offer much by way of legal submissions to back up their opinions a note of this should be made for the appellant's final summary.

18.84 The quality of legal submissions varies considerably and it will be quickly noted if the inspector is seeking to rely on out-of-date or superseded case law. If the inspector fails to apply the most up-to-date legal precedents this should be pointed out to the Tribunal in the final summary. Chapter 5 contains details of the major case

18.84 *Presenting an appeal*

law decisions. HMRC will probably cross-refer their submissions to an earlier submitted skeleton argument.

14. HMRC summarise their case

18.85 This is the last chance HMRC have to underline the facts they feel they have established and the application of the law to those facts. The summary is not meant to be a wholesale repetition of everything that has been said before. It is meant to be a reasonably detailed but concise reiteration of the most salient points. An overly detailed summary with needless repetition can suggest desperation and should be avoided by both parties.

> *Case study*
> In a recent case HMRC read out what was clearly a pre-written summary. It had little relevance to the evidence heard earlier and sounded more like a 'wish list'. As this was HMRC's last chance to speak it was a wasted opportunity.

15. The taxpayer's final summary

18.86 This should be not much longer than the opening two-minute summary. The practitioner should remind the Tribunal of the more pertinent facts that have been established, and the most important legal authorities submitted, to show that, on the balance of probabilities, the appeal should succeed. The Tribunal should be reminded of exactly what it is the taxpayer is requesting them to determine and, where appropriate, that the client's evidence has not been weakened by cross-examination and that the case law quoted is more up to date than HMRC's. Again reference can be made to the practitioner's appeal summary, either as a separate page or as part of Bundle A, as it will contain a note of what determination is being sought. Final cross-references to the skeleton arguments may be made.

> *Case study*
> In an IR35 case prior to the Tax Tribunal regime at the Special Commissioners, HMRC in their closing summary effectively introduced several new arguments that had not been raised in earlier submissions. This left Accountax in something of an awkward position as our final response would ordinarily be nothing more than a two-minute summary. Nicola Smith on behalf of the taxpayer had to do the crucial thing that all good advocates do in these circumstances: keep calm, think on your feet and address the points raised. What would have been a two-minute summary became a very effective 15-minute response to HMRC's points.

16. The decision

18.87 Having listened to both sides, the Tribunal will want to retire and consider the evidence. The First-tier Tribunal Procedure Rules allow decisions to be given orally at the hearing. The Tribunal must provide the parties to the appeal a decision notice, normally within 28 days of making its decision. This notice will state the Tribunal's decision, and notifies the parties of any right of appeal against the decision together with the time limit for doing so.

In the author's practical experience of the previous Commissioners' regime, in fact it was usually a question of the Commissioners staying in the room and the taxpayer and inspector leaving.

18.88 At this stage, whilst waiting for the decision, it was customary for the two sides to adopt a more informal approach to each other.

> *Case study*
> Accountax represented a taxpayer in a contentious tax status dispute at the General Commissioners. After the hearing a less formal approach was adopted. The inspector told Accountax that it was the best appeal presentation he had ever seen. The author confirmed the inspector's presentation was the worst he had ever seen!
> The inspector claimed HMRC knew it was likely to lose. In other words everyone's time and money had been wasted. Accountax made a claim for reimbursement of all its fees and this was subsequently paid by HMRC.

18.89 At the time of writing, it remains to be seen how decisions of the Tax Tribunal are generally delivered on IR35 cases. Under the previous regime, the General Commissioners sometimes decided cases quickly, that is to say in less than half an hour, though it could take an hour or more. Although they would discuss the case among themselves they may well have already come to their own individual conclusions. The decision did not have to be unanimous. Special Commissioners' decisions were rarely given on the day. A wait of four to six weeks was common.

18.90 The only other formality following the notification of a decision by the First-tier Tribunal may be a reminder by the Tribunal that, if unhappy with the decision, either party may appeal against it on a point of law to the Upper Tribunal. Before applying for permission to appeal, full written findings of fact and reasons for the decision must be obtained from the Tribunal. Any application for them must be received by the Tribunal within 28 days after the date on which the decision notice was issued. The Tribunal must then send the full written statement of findings and reasons to each party, normally within 28 days of receiving the application. Upon receipt of the statement, permission (or, in Northern Ireland, leave) may then be sought to appeal, by making a written application to the First-tier or Upper Tribunal. This is dealt with in Chapter 19.

Notes on presentation style

18.91 An overly theatrical style or the use of formal and pompous language should be avoided. Do not offer 'humble submissions'; instead say 'it is my view'. Do not use 'if it pleases the Tribunal' or other such phrases. Just use straightforward everyday language.

18.92 *Presenting an appeal*

18.92 The key to an effective presentation at the Tribunal is clarity and a modest pace. Give them time to assimilate the points being made. If Tribunal members are making notes, which is likely to be the case, give them plenty of time. Wait until they have stopped writing before the next point is made.

18.93 If a good point is made, perhaps when examining the client or when cross-examining HMRC's witness, be quite prepared to look directly at the Tribunal and remain silent, so as to emphasise the gravity of the particular point. Indeed, repeat the point to underline it.

For example, the client may have had to correct faulty work in his own time or at his own expense. Let this point sink in and then find some way of repeating it.

18.94 Do not distract the attention of the Tribunal with fine points of dubious worth. It is a well-accepted fact that very little of what is heard is remembered, so concentrate at all times on the important points that will weigh heavily in the client's favour. Establish facts by evidence, make authoritative legal points and link the law to the facts as established.

> *Case study*
> The Tribunal will not thank you for pushing unrealistic arguments. At one stage in the *Tilbury* IR35 appeal the Special Commissioner accused HMRC of 'entering a sea of unreality'. Possible arguments are worth pursing, but desperate arguments should be dropped.

A mistake to avoid

18.95 Do not indicate to the Tribunal during the case that if they find for HMRC the client will express dissatisfaction and appeal. This kind of thinly veiled threat is unprofessional and will do the client's case no favours.

> *Case study*
> In an appeal during the Commissioners' regime, at a General Commissioners' hearing concerning the issuing of a CIS certificate the inspector made the mistake of telling the Commissioners that if they did not find for HMRC, HMRC would be very unhappy and would go to the High Court. The Commissioners were very put out by this outburst and found for Accountax. The case did not go further.

18.96 Other aspects of procedure at the Tribunal are also covered by the Tribunal Procedure Rules. Provisions relating to the use of documents and information, joining of additional parties, and lead cases can all be found in the Rules.

Summary

18.97 The key to a successful presentation is preparation, preparation and more preparation. Careful attention must be given to compiling and numbering Bundles

A and B, briefing the client and any other witnesses as to what they can expect and finally to speak clearly, confidently, slowly and avoid an overly theatrical presentation. Be prepared to cross-examine the inspector and his witnesses in a robust manner and to expose inconsistencies, doubts or errors in the way the case has been handled and the actual facts of the case.

18.98 The practitioner must be constantly aware of the need to link the relevance of the case law with the established facts. Do not assume the Tribunal will automatically do this. This is your job!

18.99 Finally, and this cannot be underestimated, make it clear at the beginning and the end exactly what it is the Tribunal is meant to be determining and what decision is being sought.

A blueprint for an IR35 defence and appeal

18.100 It is suggested that a highly focused approach is made. Where appropriate:

1. Argue that the legislation does not apply *at all* because, for example, the client is not giving 'personal service'.
2. Argue that statutory interpretation requires not a hypothetical contract as such but the placing of the worker in the shoes of the personal service business. Expose the many difficulties of HMRC's interpretation of the hypothetical contract.
3. Establish the full terms and conditions of the personal service business contract with its client, usually an agency. Do not allow HMRC to imply terms that are contrary to the contract. Where possible get 'end-user' confirmation on the important areas of substitution, control and mutuality.
4. Establish all broader factors which show the client has a business mindset and history.
5. Quote from case law in support of all contentions made.

Points 1–5 above need to be followed throughout the technical argument with HMRC during an IR35 challenge. If the dispute cannot be resolved it will be necessary to proceed to a contentious appeal hearing at the Tribunal:

(a) Be wary of attending last-minute meetings with HMRC, where they may attempt to extract in advance the evidence likely to be presented by the taxpayer.
(b) At the Tribunal always *link* the case law to the established facts.
(c) Vigorously cross-examine HMRC's witnesses and expose all weaknesses in HMRC's case, either technical or procedural.
(d) At the Tribunal make sure all documentation is properly prepared and checked and that the client and witnesses know exactly what to expect on the day and consider the merits of having a mock cross-examination.

Chapter 19
What happens after the appeal hearing

If the taxpayer has won

19.1 During the course of the hearing the practitioner, the inspector and the Tribunal would have made detailed notes, in particular in relation to the examination and cross-examination of witnesses.

19.2 If the appeal has been upheld the onus will be on the inspector to mount a challenge. As indicated in the previous chapter, the Tribunal must provide the parties to the appeal with a decision notice, normally within 28 days of making their decision, stating the Tribunal's decision and notifying the parties of any right of appeal. Before applying for permission to appeal, the inspector must obtain a full written statement of findings of fact and reasons for the decision. An application for a full written statement must be received by the Tribunal within 28 days after the date on which the decision notice was issued. The Tribunal must then send the full written statement of findings and reasons to each party, normally within 28 days of receiving the application. Upon receipt of the statement, permission (or, in Northern Ireland, leave) may then be sought to appeal, by making a written application to the First-tier (or the Upper) Tribunal.

19.3 The Tribunal Rules (unlike the Commissioners' regime that preceded them) do not allow appeals to the High Court. The standard route for an appeal from the First-tier Tax Tribunal is to the Upper Tier Tribunal. An appeal from the Upper Tier Tribunal can subsequently be made to the Court of Appeal. Under the new rules non-legally qualified practitioners can appear at both the Lower and Upper Tribunals, whereas previously a non-barrister was unable to take cases beyond the Commissioners.

19.4 An appeal from the First-tier Tax Tribunal to the Upper Tribunal can only be made on a point of law arising from the decision (TCEA 2007, s 11). The written application for permission to appeal must normally be received by the Tribunal no later than 56 days after full written reasons for the decision have been sent. The application must identify the Tribunal's decision to which the appeal relates, the alleged error in that decision, and state the desired result of the application (The Tribunal Procedure (First-tier Tribunal) (Tax Chamber) Rules, SI 2009/273, reg 39).

19.5 Upon receipt of the application for permission to appeal, the Tribunal must first consider whether to review the decision. Subject to that, the Tribunal will send their decision whether to give permission to appeal to the parties. In the event that it refuses permission to appeal, it will state the reasons for doing so, and notify the right to make an application to the Upper Tribunal for permission to appeal within the relevant time limit.

19.6 The Tribunal can only review a decision if it has received an application for permission to appeal, and only if satisfied that there was an error of law in the decision. If a review does take place, the Tribunal will notify the parties of the outcome, unless it decides to take no action following the review. It cannot take any action following a review without first giving the parties to the appeal an opportunity to make representations in respect of the action proposed by the Tribunal (SI 2009/273, regs 40, 41). The 56-day time limit for applications for permission to appeal can also apply from the notification of a change of decision following a review, if later.

19.7 Prior to the Tax Tribunal regime, if the inspector was unsuccessful before the General Commissioners and wished to mount a challenge, he did this initially by 'expressing dissatisfaction' with the Commissioners' decision. He could then require the Clerk to produce a stated case, which was essentially a record of the entire appeal hearing. The procedure was different at the Specials and HMRC's Solicitor's Office would get involved and deal with the formalities.

19.8 Having agreed the stated case, it was then open to the inspector to make a final decision as to whether the case should be put before the High Court, and inevitably he would only do this after having taken head office advice. In the author's experience, inspectors may have threatened to go to the High Court, even before the Commissioner's case had been heard, but more often than not this was nothing more than bluff.

> *Case study*
> In a specific contentious appeal in which the author was involved the inspector made the mistake of advising the Commissioners, half way through his presentation, that if they did not reach the determination the inspector was seeking he would be going to the High Court. This was a major error on the inspector's part as it did nothing to endear him or his case to the Commissioners, who felt that they were being unduly pressured. In the event HMRC lost the appeal, the inspector asked for a stated case but, after taking further head office advice, dropped the matter.

19.9 When the Commissioners completed the stated case the question for the High Court was often framed in non-specific terms such as: 'Were we the Commissioners entitled in law to reach the determination made?'

19.10 In the case of an appeal from the Special Commissioners it was not necessary to ask for a stated case. The appellant had 56 days to lodge an appeal in the High Court. The Special Commissioners' decision was effectively the stated case.

It was not open to the High Court to establish or challenge facts previously found and that was why it was so important that any findings of fact made by the Commissioners during the course of the hearing were accurately recorded. It was

19.10 *What happens after the appeal hearing*

common for experienced inspectors and practitioners, during the course of a hearing, to request that the Commissioners 'find' and record a specific fact which they considered to be highly relevant. A similar approach would seem to be appropriate under the Tribunals regime, which succeeded the Commissioners.

19.11 As mentioned, the Upper Tribunal (Tax Chamber) hears appeals on points of law from the First-tier Tax Tribunal. A small number of cases may also be transferred from the First-tier Tribunal to the Upper Tribunal if the case is considered sufficiently complex or important and where the finding of fact is subsidiary to points of law. Such cases were heard by the High Court under the previous regime. Under the Tribunals regime, it is possible to appeal from the Upper Tribunal to the Court of Appeal, and ultimately to the House of Lords.

If the taxpayer has lost

19.12 Exactly the same procedural considerations apply and again it is important to emphasise that it is too easy for the bitter taxpayer to request a full written statement on the grounds that he has 'nothing to lose'. Unless specific points of law can be identified where, on the balance of probabilities, there is a clear chance of making a successful appeal to the Upper Tribunal, one's losses should be cut.

19.13 Having lost at the Tribunal the inspector has not established a binding legal precedent, other than in respect of the specific appeal for the named taxpayer involved in the hearing. Whilst decisions may be generally reported and carry influence, they are not strict legal precedent.

19.14 The Procedure Rules for both the First-tier and Upper Tribunals include the provision to award costs in appropriate circumstances. Under the previous regime, the General Commissioners had no powers to award costs, but the Special Commissioners could award costs against a party that had acted wholly unreasonably in connection with a hearing.

19.15 The First-tier Tribunal (Tax Chamber) Rules 2009 provide that costs (or expenses in Scotland) may only be awarded in certain specific circumstances. These include if a party to proceedings (or a representative) has acted unreasonably in the Tribunal's view. Costs will be awarded if the case is complex and the taxpayer did not request prior to a hearing that costs or expenses be excluded.

The Upper Tribunal Rules makes similar provision for the award of costs following unreasonable behaviour. By contrast, the costs of taking an appeal to the High Court under the Commissioners' regime were substantial, and it was likely that the losing side would have to pay the other side's costs. Although this may not be a major factor to consider, it would no doubt have played heavily on the mind of the practitioner and his client.

It should be noted that under the new regime costs will be awarded much more often as all that is required is 'unreasonable' conduct not 'wholly unreasonable' conduct as under the old rules.

19.16 It is open to the taxpayer to make a compensation claim to HMRC, effectively a 'complaint' (see **18.88**), but this is not a costs 'order' issued by the

Tribunals. Despite the often heard bravura of the losing party the best advice is to call it a day unless there are very substantial resources and strong legal arguments to present to the High Court. Occasionally funds for a High Court appeal may be offered by the PCG or subject to a fighting fund appeal publicised in *Taxation* magazine.

What lessons can be learnt

19.17 Whether the client wins or loses at the Tribunal the decision will relate only to the years under appeal and as such there will be important lessons to learn. If successful there may nonetheless be lessons to be learned from the weaknesses in the client's arguments, exposed by the inspector perhaps in cross-examination. There may be factors not previously considered and from this there may be scope to re-negotiate clauses in the contract, whereby the client's position will be further strengthened. Such lessons can be applied for the benefit of other clients.

> *Case study*
> At the first day of the *Ansell* IR35 appeal a total of eight HMRC staff attended the hearing. One assumes this was some kind of training exercise for them.

On the other hand, if the taxpayer loses, the practitioner will be painfully aware of the strong points put forward by HMRC that resulted in the defeat. Bearing in mind that contracts can be re-negotiated at any stage HMRC's successful arguments may well give some very strong clues as to what areas of the contract need to be tightened up when the client next comes to re-negotiate his terms and conditions.

19.18 Winning or losing at the Tribunal will also give valuable practical experience to the practitioner, which will stand him in good stead for the next appeal hearing.

Summary

19.19 The real issue is what to do if the taxpayer has lost the appeal. It is a major decision to go on appeal to the Upper Tribunal and possibly beyond, in terms of costs for the personal service business itself (and possibly those of HMRC if the case reaches the Court of Appeal and victory is not achieved).

This also assumes there is a point of law on which an appeal can be made. The likelihood of an onward appeal has been somewhat increased following the introduction of the Upper Tribunal from April 2009.

19.20 Contract terms can always be re-negotiated for the future and lessons can be learnt from the whole appeal process which might well stand the practitioner and his other clients in good stead in the future.

Chapter 20
The advice clients need now

1. Agree and implement a sound written contract

20.1 When the Revenue carried out its status challenge on the construction industry in the late 1990s it had most success with those taxpayers who had become, by their actions, or lack of them, 'easy targets'. For example, where there was no written contract (still frighteningly common even in the specialist knowledge-based sector), it was easy for the Revenue to say that the whole situation needed to be established by asking questions of both the engager and the worker. This would often lead to uncertainty, simply because many of the issues raised by the Revenue in its questions had not been specifically considered by the parties previously.

20.2 In truth, even if there is no written contract there must still be a contract of some kind as there has been an offer and acceptance of work; consideration (value) has passed between the parties and there has been an intention to create a legal relationship. In other words, the three basic requisites for a binding contract are in place.

20.3 The problem with contracts which are not written is that they may lead to a very real uncertainty as to what the verbal or implied terms are. That is not to say that a written contract is not open to interpretation, but it is far more *certain* than a verbal contract. In terms of evidence, at a possible appeal hearing before the Tribunal it is clearly advantageous to start with a comprehensive and well written contract. A contract which is signed and dated. A contract must not be backdated in any circumstances.

20.4 Even when advising clients at the early stages of a dispute it is important to have in the back of one's mind the quality of the evidence to be adduced, and one of the most important pieces of evidence in an IR35 dispute will be the contract. So the first task of any practitioner who is trying to defend his clients from the effects of IR35 is to ensure that a comprehensive and competently worded contract for services is committed to writing and that it is signed, dated and implemented.

2. Maintain due diligence records to show the contract is implemented

20.5 There is an interesting legal debate as to whether the terms of a written contract are the only means by which the IR35 relationship can be examined.

HMRC traditionally argue that the contract wording is irrelevant if it does not reflect the reality of the working relationship. Unquestionably there comes a point when a sham contract will be exposed as such and it will carry little if any weight. But does HMRC have the right to disregard the written contract on the assumption that it *may* not fully reflect the true terms and conditions of the working relationship?

20.6 The case law makes it quite clear that, where the terms and conditions governing the relationship of the parties are laid down entirely in a written contract, HMRC are restricted to an examination of those terms only. This is accepted in HMRC's internal guidance manuals. There is one exception to this rule and that is where the subsequent actions of the parties are such that they have effectively amended or varied the terms of their original contract. *Narich Pty v Commissioner of Payroll Tax* [1984] ICR 286 discussed in Chapter 5 confirms this.

If there is a subsequent variation to the contract then those varied terms have to be considered on their own merits. However, there is a significant difference between parties genuinely varying their terms and parties not implementing them.

20.7 Notwithstanding the approach in *Narich*, it is still desirable to be able to show the inspector that the contract is implemented in practice. The client should be able to hand over to HMRC a copy of the comprehensive written contract for services and at the same time provide a series of mini due diligence reports showing that the contract has been implemented and re-visited. For example, any sensible anti-IR35 contract will have a requirement that the contracting company maintains a business organisation and goes about its work in a businesslike manner. This may include the simple requirement to maintain adequate public and professional insurances and to raise invoices on a proper business letterhead.

20.8 The IR35 defence will be made much easier if the various insurance certificates etc can be produced and shown to the inspector at a moment's notice. The inspector can then be provided with not only a comprehensive anti-IR35 contract but with hard proof that its terms are being implemented in practice.

A simple due diligence checklist which can be carried out perhaps twice a year should be a more than adequate way of demonstrating that the contract is being lived and breathed. Wherever possible get a detailed and specific signed statement from the end user stating their understanding of the terms of the relationship, particularly in relation to personal service, mutuality, control and financial risk.

20.9 It should of course be remembered that contracts are concerned with rights and obligations and sometimes these are not easy to 'prove'. For example, if there is a liability on the contracting company to correct defective work without receiving further fees then this is a burdensome risk. If the contracting company never commits defective work this does not take away its liability—it is just that it has never been called upon.

In these situations inspectors have been known to dismiss the defective work clause as ineffective but this misses the point. If the risk and liability is there then it stands, notwithstanding the fact that the client has not had to implement the clause. Of course, the due diligence record will make a note of any instances of defective work and its correction.

3. Educate the client

20.10 Having helped the client agree and implement a sound anti-IR35 contract for services it is important to ensure he knows exactly what is expected of him if he is to be able to resist an HMRC challenge. He should be encouraged to take professional advice at an early stage if a challenge arises, and absolutely must be briefed on what happens at a contentious appeal hearing should he end up going to one. Preparation is all.

It is vital that the contractor realises that the evidence his end user will give is extremely important at any appeal. So even at an early stage the 'long view' has to be taken, and contractors should recognise this.

Chapter 21
Closing reminders and latest developments

21.1 *IR35 Defence Strategies* is not a book about tax compliance. In fact, in many ways it is quite the opposite. The book offers various strategies and ideas to the proactive practitioner who is *trying* to keep his clients out of IR35 or who needs to go on appeal to the Tribunal. And if all else fails it explains how to win at the Tribunal.

21.2 There have been many cases heard prior to the introduction of the Tax Tribunal regime by the Specials and several by the High Court. There were roughly the same number of successful appeals to the Specials as there were losses. Unfortunately the High Court cases to date have all gone against the contractors.

21.3 It was hoped that, when the *Larkstar* litigation reached the High Court, the first win for the taxpayer would be achieved. However, it subsequently transpired that the case (*Revenue and Customs Commissioners v Larkstar Data Ltd* [2008] EWHC 3284 Ch) produced neither a win nor a loss. The Court held that the General Commissioners had misdirected themselves in law in their consideration of what they found to be the questions of control and mutuality of obligations, and had made a finding of fact regarding control which was unjustified by the evidence before them. The case was therefore remitted back to be re-heard by a new panel of General Commissioners (although at the time of writing it is not known whether the case would be heard by the Commissioners or the new Tax Tribunal).

21.4 However, the above statistics completely mask the many hundreds and possibly thousands of IR35 cases that HMRC have dropped before the courts became involved. It is unwise, in the author's view, to adopt a pessimistic attitude simply because half a dozen contractors have lost. Even the recent and disappointing decision in *Dragonfly Consulting Ltd v Revenue and Customs Commissioners* [2008] EWHC 2113 (Ch) should be seen for what it is: a fact-specific case with some weak contract clauses that might well have gone the other way. Indeed some good things came out of the case, not least the High Court's rejection of HMRC's long-held view that the intention of the parties is not relevant to an IR35 scenario.

21.5 There are many aspects of IR35 deliberately not covered in this book. Partnerships have not been considered for the simple reason that the overwhelming majority of personal service businesses operate as limited companies. It will be these very same limited companies HMRC will target as they seek national insurance lost to the dividend route. Equally, overseas considerations have been left out,

21.5 Closing reminders and latest developments

again because most personal service businesses operate in the UK with UK-registered companies.

21.6 Not all of the arguments in this book will work in every situation but it is hoped that practitioners will, at least, now have a much better understanding of the arguments which are potentially available to them. This is also a good time to stand back and think about the style of language that has become common currency in IR35. Should phrases such as 'personal service business' be so readily used? Do not these words automatically imply an admission that personal service is being given as opposed to the undertaking of a commercial service? One has to be careful.

21.7 Practitioners should be wary of mass marketed, 'one size fits all' IR35 solutions. The 2007 managed service company legislation effectively nullifies such schemes. Some solutions *may* work for some personal service businesses in certain circumstances, but many practitioners are highly suspicious of such arrangements and tend to shy away from them. Such schemes are often shrouded in controversy and based on questionable off-shore arrangements. Indeed, HMRC have confirmed that their Special Compliance Office were taking an active interest in schemes that present themselves as a means to evade or avoid tax (see General Frequently Asked Questions, Compliance, 4, on HMRC's website at http://www.hmrc.gov.uk/ir35/). A much easier approach is to operate as a true business and agree and implement contract terms which are clearly outside IR35.

21.8 The importance of understanding and applying current case law with a view to assisting contractors to negotiate anti-IR35 clauses in their contracts must not be underestimated. IR35-proof contracts are not that difficult to agree but they must not be shams, and where possible a confirmation of arrangements letter should be obtained from the end user.

21.9 HMRC can only investigate a very small number of personal service businesses and they will want to pick on the weaker cases or contractors who offer little resistance.

21.10 If technical argument fails and a Tribunal hearing becomes necessary, most practitioners have the necessary skills to make a good job of representing their clients. The practitioner should establish the facts, apply the case law and have the courage and confidence to go to the Tribunal and win.

The nuclear option revisited?

21.11 In the early days of IR35, many freelancers took the view that if they were going to be taxed and NIC'd like a regular employee then why should they not get the same employment law protections of a regular employee? Of course the answer is an easy one: because IR35 creates a hypothetical relationship between worker and client where there is in fact no actual contractual nexus. A concerted effort by contractors to force employment law rights was called the 'nuclear option' but as many contractors defeated IR35 challenges it was not seriously pursued.

21.12 This still leaves a bitter taste in the mouth of the IR35-caught contractor who ends up with the worst of both worlds. Although beyond the scope of this book, the Court of Appeal decision in *Muscat v Cable & Wireless* [2006] All ER (D) 319 is worth noting. In essence an employee was asked, against his will, to provide his services via a limited company having previously been under PAYE as a regular employee. He was then asked to contract via his limited company, but also via an agency (Abraxas). Ultimately his services were dispensed with and he brought an employment law action on the basis that he was throughout the period an employee of Cable & Wireless. Both the Employment Tribunal and Employment Appeals Tribunal agreed with him and implied a contract of employment. Readers will no doubt be aware that a contract of employment can be implied, written or oral. While the facts of *Muscat* were unusual the Court of Appeal essentially said that an implied contract of employment was the only way to make business sense of the arrangements. Later Court of Appeal cases have cast some doubt on *Muscat* but it does throw up an interesting line of argument.

21.13 In essence, what is the difference between having your own limited company but having an implied contract of employment with the end user on the one hand and being caught by IR35 on the other? Does it mean by definition that in one sense you can never be caught by IR35? The argument is that if you are found by the Tax Tribunal not to be caught by IR35 then that is the end of the matter; you are not caught. If, however, it appears on the facts and law that you are clearly caught by IR35, can you not argue that this conclusion must mean that you are in fact and law a *Muscat*-style 'implied employee'?

21.14 So if you are not caught there is no problem, but if it looks like you are caught perhaps you are not because you should be acknowledged as an implied employee. This line of thought has been called the death of IR35 in some quarters, which might be going too far, but it does show that new arguments are developing all the time. It is understood that the *Muscat* decision caused HMRC some disquiet although the matter has received little HMRC public comment.

What exactly is the issue for determination?

21.15 IR35 and tax status litigation tends to ask whether the freelancer is an employee or self-employed. But as has been mentioned several times in previous chapters the real question is whether or not the contractor is an employee, not whether he is self-employed. The difference is potentially important. A Tribunal is faced with two very different choices at extreme ends of the spectrum when deciding if someone is an employee or self-employed. It might be helpful if there was a middle ground or category of worker that was good enough to show the contractor was not an employee, even though he did not look like a fully fledged self-employed person.

21.16 The answer lies in the Working Time Regulations of 1998. These regulations recognise a category of person technically called a 'Worker' which is a term of art. A Worker is in some ways a hybrid of an employee and a self-employed person.

21.16 *Closing reminders and latest developments*

A Worker is afforded certain employment law rights that a fully self-employed person would not enjoy.

21.17 Although a discussion of the case law on Worker status is beyond the scope of this book suffice to say that a Worker differs from an employee in that a Worker has a lower degree of control compared to an employee. If, therefore a contractor has only weak arguments on personal service and mutuality but a stronger argument on control he might be able to argue that under the hypothetical IR35 contract he would be a Worker rather than (a) a fully fledged self-employed person in business on his own account or (b) a full employee.

21.18 This of course would be good enough because a Worker is not an employee and IR35 asks whether the contractor would be an employee. Having the choice of two options to defeat IR35 (ie Worker or fully fledged status) the Tribunal is now faced with two alternatives to employee status either of which is good enough to win the appeal.

21.19 This argument was put forward in the High Court in *Dragonfly*. However, as it had not been advanced at the Specials, limited reliance could be placed on it. In the event, Mr Justice Henderson rejected the argument on the basis that Worker is a term of art of limited application in the field of employment law. This was certainly and unsurprisingly HMRC's view. While one has to accept what the High Court said, one wonders whether this argument might still be advanced in future cases, especially at the tax tribunal.

21.20 It is certainly an area that needs further exploration. After all, the IR35 rules simply ask whether the worker in its non-technical sense is an *employee*. It seems possible with well-crafted argument to submit that he is something else even if that something else is a concept generated by employment law. In the same way it might be possible to argue that someone is an agency worker which has a distinct meaning from a regular employee. In essence the argument is made to give the Tribunal more options than deciding if the worker is in business on his own account.

21.21 The High Court case of *HMRC v Wright* ([2007] EWHC 526 (Ch)) in 2007 made the cogent point that when dealing with the tax status of subcontractors in the construction industry the question is not whether the subcontractor is employed or self-employed but whether he is an employee or not. The 'or not' could be, one assumes, a Worker or an agency worker and there may indeed be other possibilities. Unfortunately *Wright* was not argued in *Dragonfly* and while the High Court gave the 'Worker argument' little credence in *Dragonfly*, in light of *Wright* it is an argument that might see the light of day again.

Another contract to be considered?

21.22 It is well established that the so-called lower (intermediary/agency) and upper (intermediary/client) contract have both to be considered when constructing the hypothetical contract. In practice, the lower contract is often more comprehensive than the upper contract which indeed may be nothing more than a brief purchase order, and the author's experience is that a comprehensive lower contract can in such cases carry more weight.

21.23 However, is it wise to have a contract of employment or director's service agreement between the director/shareholder of the intermediary—ie 'Fred' in the 'Fred Bloggs Ltd' example? Can such a contract assist in mounting an IR35 defence?

21.24 If such a contract itself contained a right of substitution and a lack of control and other aspects of, say, financial risk would such terms be incorporated into the hypothetical contract under IR35? The legislation requires all contracts (plural) to be taken into account and therefore why not? It is not suggested that such terms will take precedence over the lower or upper contract but surely they must carry some weight?

21.25 It might be questioned why no reference is made to a lack of mutuality clause in **21.24** above? This is because in order to claim travelling expenses the contractor needs to show that he has an over-arching contract of employment and a lack of mutuality suggests the opposite. Of course, an added complication is that by having a strong substitution and lack of control clause the contractor effectively makes himself a non-employee of his own company! This outcome, however, can do no harm in arguing IR35 does not apply. On balance it is thought that an appropriately worded contract between the contractor and his own company can only help.

The future of IR35

21.26 HMRC have introduced many new legislative initiatives in recent years including the managed service company rules, proposed income shifting rules as a follow up to *Arctic Systems* ([2007] UKHL 35) and fundamental changes to the Construction Industry Scheme. It is fair to say that Accountax now works fewer IR35 challenges than in the past but they have far from petered out.

21.27 It is felt that IR35 remains a very live issue and is unlikely to go away any time soon. While it is still on the statute books the proactive practitioner has to do everything he can to win the argument. This will always boil down to getting the facts, applying the correct legal principles and having the courage of your convictions. While the overall number of IR35 challenges is probably down on its peak, that is of no comfort if your client happens to be the person picked on.

Appendix 1
ITEPA 2003 Pt 2 Ch 8

Income Tax (Earnings and Pensions) Act 2003 Part 2 Chapter 8: Application of Provisions to Workers Under Arrangements made by Intermediaries

48 Scope of this Chapter

(1) This Chapter has effect with respect to the provision of services through an intermediary.

(2) Nothing in this Chapter—

    (a) affects the operation of Chapter 7 of this Part, [...]¹

    [(aa) applies to services provided by a managed service company (within the meaning of Chapter 9 of this Part), or]¹

    (b) applies to payments [or transfers to which section 966(3) or (4) of ITA 2007 applies

(visiting performers: duty to deduct and account for sums representing income tax)]².

Notes
1. Added by Finance Act 2007 c. 11 Sch 3(1) para 3 (6 April 2007)
2. Words substituted by Income Tax Act 2007 c. 3 Sch 1(2) para 429 (6 April 2007: for income tax purposes, for the tax year 2007-08 and subsequent tax years and for corporation tax purposes for accounting periods ending after 5 April 2007, subject to savings and transitional provisions specified in 2007 c.3 s.1030(1) and Sch 2).

49 Engagements to which this Chapter applies

(1) This Chapter applies where—

    (a) an individual ("the worker") personally performs, or is under an obligation personally to perform, services [for another person]¹ ("the client"),

    (b) the services are provided not under a contract directly between the client and the worker but under arrangements involving a third party ("the intermediary"), and

    (c) the circumstances are such that, if the services were provided under a contract directly between the client and the worker, the worker would be regarded for income tax purposes as an employee of the client.

    [...]²

(3) The reference in subsection (1)(b) to a "third party" includes a partnership or unincorporated body of which the worker is a member.

(4) The circumstances referred to in subsection (1)(c) include the terms on which the services are provided, having regard to the terms of the contracts forming part of the arrangements under which the services are provided.

(5) In this Chapter "engagement to which this Chapter applies" means any such provision of services as is mentioned in subsection (1).

Appendix 1

Notes
1. Words substituted by Finance Act 2003 c. 14 Pt 7 s 136(2) (10 July 2003: substitution has effect in relation to services performed or due to be performed on or after 10 April 2003)
2. Repealed by Finance Act 2003 c. 14 Sch 43(3) para 1 (10 July 2003: repeal has effect in relation to services performed or due to be performed on or after 10 April 2003)

50 Worker treated as receiving earnings from employment

(1) If, in the case of an engagement to which this Chapter applies, in any tax year—

    (a) the conditions specified in section 51, 52 or 53 are met in relation to the intermediary, and

    (b) the worker, or an associate of the worker—

        (i) receives from the intermediary, directly or indirectly, a payment or benefit that is not employment income, or

        (ii) has rights which entitle, or which in any circumstances would entitle, the worker or associate to receive from the intermediary, directly or indirectly, any such payment or benefit,

the intermediary is treated as making to the worker, and the worker is treated as receiving, in that year a payment which is to be treated as earnings from an employment ("the deemed employment payment").

(2) A single payment is treated as made in respect of all engagements in relation to which the intermediary is treated as making a payment to the worker in the tax year.

(3) The deemed employment payment is treated as made at the end of the tax year, unless section 57 applies (earlier date of deemed payment in certain cases).

(4) In this Chapter "the relevant engagements", in relation to a deemed employment payment, means the engagements mentioned in subsection (2).

51 Conditions of liability where intermediary is a company

(1) Where the intermediary is a company the conditions are that the intermediary is not an associated company of the client that falls within subsection (2) and either—

    (a) the worker has a material interest in the intermediary, or

    (b) the payment or benefit mentioned in section 50(1)(b)—

        (i) is received or receivable by the worker directly from the intermediary, and

        (ii) can reasonably be taken to represent remuneration for services provided by the worker to the client.

(2) An associated company of the client falls within this subsection if it is such a company by reason of the intermediary and the client being under the control—

    (a) of the worker, or

    (b) of the worker and other persons.

(3) A worker is treated as having a material interest in a company if—

    (a) the worker, alone or with one or more associates of the worker, or

    (b) an associate of the worker, with or without other such associates,

has a material interest in the company.

(4) For this purpose a material interest means—

Appendix 1

(a) beneficial ownership of, or the ability to control, directly or through the medium of other companies or by any other indirect means, more than 5% of the ordinary share capital of the company; or

(b) possession of, or entitlement to acquire, rights entitling the holder to receive more than 5% of any distributions that may be made by the company; or

(c) where the company is a close company, possession of, or entitlement to acquire, rights that would in the event of the winding up of the company, or in any other circumstances, entitle the holder to receive more than 5% of the assets that would then be available for distribution among the participators.

(5) In subsection (4)(c) "participator" has the meaning given by section 417(1) of ICTA.

52 Conditions of liability where intermediary is a partnership

(1) Where the intermediary is a partnership the conditions are as follows.

(2) In relation to any payment or benefit received or receivable by the worker as a member of the partnership the conditions are—

(a) that the worker, alone or with one or more relatives, is entitled to 60% or more of the profits of the partnership; or

(b) that most of the profits of the partnership concerned derive from the provision of services under engagements to which this Chapter applies—

  (i) to a single client, or
  (ii) to a single client together with associates of that client; or

(c) that under the profit sharing arrangements the income of any of the partners is based on the amount of income generated by that partner by the provision of services under engagements to which this Chapter applies.

In paragraph (a) "relative" means [spouse or civil partner][1] , parent or child or remoter relation in the direct line, or brother or sister .

(3) In relation to any payment or benefit received or receivable by the worker otherwise than as a member of the partnership, the conditions are that the payment or benefit—

(a) is received or receivable by the worker directly from the intermediary, and

(b) can reasonably be taken to represent remuneration for services provided by the worker to the client.

Notes
1 Words substituted by Tax and Civil Partnership Regulations 2005/3229 reg 138 (5 December 2005)

53 Conditions of liability where intermediary is an individual

Where the intermediary is an individual the conditions are that the payment or benefit—

(a) is received or receivable by the worker directly from the intermediary, and
(b) can reasonably be taken to represent remuneration for services provided by the worker to the client.

54 Calculation of deemed employment payment

(1) The amount of the deemed employment payment for a tax year ("the year") is the amount resulting from the following steps—

Step 1
Find (applying section 55) the total amount of all payments and benefits received by the intermediary in the year in respect of the relevant engagements, and reduce that amount by 5%.

Appendix 1

Step 2
Add (applying that section) the amount of any payments and benefits received by the worker in the year in respect of the relevant engagements, otherwise than from the intermediary, that—

(a) are not chargeable to income tax as employment income, and
(b) would be so chargeable if the worker were employed by the client.

Step 3
Deduct (applying Chapters 1 to 5 of Part 5) the amount of any expenses met in the year by the intermediary that would have been deductible from the taxable earnings from the employment if—

(a) the worker had been employed by the client, and
(b) the expenses had been met by the worker out of those earnings.

If the result at this or any later point is nil or a negative amount, there is no deemed employment payment.

Step 4
Deduct the amount of any capital allowances in respect of expenditure incurred by the intermediary that could have been deducted from employment income under section 262 of CAA 2001 (employments and offices) if the worker had been employed by the client and had incurred the expenditure.

Step 5
Deduct any contributions made in the year for the benefit of the worker by the intermediary to a [registered pension scheme][1] that if made by an employer for the benefit of an employee would not be chargeable to income tax as income of the employee.

This does not apply to excess contributions made and later repaid.

Step 6
Deduct the amount of any employer's national insurance contributions paid by the intermediary for the year in respect of the worker.

Step 7
Deduct the amount of any payments and benefits received in the year by the worker from the intermediary—

(a) in respect of which the worker is chargeable to income tax as employment income, and
(b) which do not represent items in respect of which a deduction was made under step 3.

Step 8
Assume that the result of step 7 represents an amount together with employer's national insurance contributions on it, and deduct what (on that assumption) would be the amount of those contributions.

The result is the deemed employment payment.

(2) If [section 61 of the Finance Act 2004][2] applies (sub-contractors in the construction industry: payments to be made under deduction), the intermediary is treated for the purposes of step 1 of subsection (1) as receiving the amount that would have been received had no deduction been made under that section.

(3) In step 3 of subsection (1), the reference to expenses met by the intermediary includes—

(a) expenses met by the worker and reimbursed by the intermediary, and
(b) where the intermediary is a partnership and the worker is a member of the partnership, expenses met by the worker for and on behalf of the partnership.

Appendix 1

(4) In step 3 of subsection (1), the expenses deductible include the amount of any mileage allowance relief for the year which the worker would have been entitled to in respect of the use of a vehicle falling within subsection (5) if—
 (a) the worker had been employed by the client, and
 (b) the vehicle had not been a company vehicle (within the meaning of Chapter 2 of Part 4).

(5) A vehicle falls within this subsection if—
 (a) it is provided by the intermediary for the worker, or
 (b) where the intermediary is a partnership and the worker is a member of the partnership, it is provided by the worker for the purposes of the business of the partnership.

(6) Where, on the assumptions mentioned in paragraphs (a) and (b) of step 3 of subsection (1), the deductibility of the expenses is determined under sections 337 to 342 (travel expenses), the duties performed under the relevant engagements are treated as duties of a continuous employment with the intermediary.

(7) In step 7 of subsection (1), the amounts deductible include any payments received in the year from the intermediary that—
 (a) are exempt from income tax by virtue of section 229 or 233 (mileage allowance payments and passenger payments), and
 (b) do not represent items in respect of which a deduction was made under step 3.

(8) For the purposes of subsection (1) any necessary apportionment is to be made on a just and reasonable basis of amounts received by the intermediary that are referable—
 (a) to the services of more than one worker, or
 (b) partly to the services of the worker and partly to other matters.

Notes
1. Words substituted by Finance Act 2004 c. 12 Sch 35 para 56 (22 July 2004: substitution has effect from 22 July 2004 for the purpose of making orders or regulations; 6 April 2006 otherwise)
2. Words substituted by Finance Act 2004 c. 12 Sch 12 para 17(2) (22 July 2004: substitution has effect in relation to payments made on or after the appointed day under contracts relating to construction operations)

55 Application of rules relating to earnings from employment

(1) The following provisions apply in relation to the calculation of the deemed employment payment.

(2) A "payment or benefit" means anything that, if received by an employee for performing the duties of an employment, would be earnings from the employment.

(3) The amount of a payment or benefit is taken to be—
 (a) in the case of a payment or cash benefit, the amount received, and
 (b) in the case of a non-cash benefit, the cash equivalent of the benefit.

(4) The cash equivalent of a non-cash benefit is taken to be—
 (a) the amount that would be earnings if the benefit were earnings from an employment, or
 (b) in the case of living accommodation, whichever is the greater of that amount and the cash equivalent determined in accordance with section 398(2).

(5) A payment or benefit is treated as received—

Appendix 1

- (a) in the case of a payment or cash benefit, when payment is made of or on account of the payment or benefit;
- (b) in the case of a non-cash benefit that is calculated by reference to a period within the tax year, at the end of that period;
- (c) in the case of a non-cash benefit that is not so calculated, when it would have been treated as received for the purposes of Chapter 4 or 5 of this Part (see section 19 or 32) if—
    - (i) the worker had been an employee, and
    - (ii) the benefit had been provided by reason of the employment.

56 Application of Income Tax Acts in relation to deemed employment

(1) The Income Tax Acts (in particular, the PAYE provisions) apply in relation to the deemed employment payment as follows.

(2) They apply as if—
- (a) the worker were employed by the intermediary, and
- (b) the relevant engagements were undertaken by the worker in the course of performing the duties of that employment.

(3) The deemed employment payment is treated in particular—
- (a) as taxable earnings from the employment for the purpose of securing that any deductions under Chapters 2 to 6 of Part 5 do not exceed the deemed employment payment; and
- (b) as taxable earnings from the employment for the purposes of section 232.

(4) The worker is not chargeable to tax in respect of the deemed employment payment if, or to the extent that, by reason of any combination of the factors mentioned in subsection (5), the worker would not be chargeable to tax if—
- (a) the client employed the worker,
- (b) the worker performed the services in the course of that employment, and
- (c) the deemed employment payment were a payment by the client of earnings from that employment.

(5) The factors are—
- (a) the worker being resident, ordinarily resident or domiciled outside the United Kingdom,
- (b) the client being resident or ordinarily resident outside the United Kingdom, and
- (c) the services in question being provided outside the United Kingdom.

(6) Where the intermediary is a partnership or unincorporated association, the deemed employment payment is treated as received by the worker in the worker's personal capacity and not as income of the partnership or association.

(7) Where—
- (a) the worker is resident in the United Kingdom [, and]¹
- (b) the services in question are provided in the United Kingdom, [...]²

[...]²

the intermediary is treated as having a place of business in the United Kingdom, whether or not it in fact does so.

[...]³

Appendix 1

Notes
1. Word inserted by Finance Act 2003 c. 14 Pt 7 s 136(3)(b)(i) (10 July 2003: insertion has effect in relation to services performed or due to be performed on or after 10 April 2003)
2. Repealed by Finance Act 2003 c. 14 Sch 43(3) para 1 (10 July 2003: repeal has effect in relation to services performed or due to be performed on or after 10 April 2003)
3. Repealed by Finance Act 2004 c. 12 Sch 42(3) para 1 (6 April 2006: repeal has effect subject to transitional provisions and savings specified in 2004 c.12 Sch.36)

57 Earlier date of deemed employment payment in certain cases

(1) If in any tax year—

    (a) a deemed employment payment is treated as made, and
    (b) before the date on which the payment would be treated as made under section 50(2) any relevant event (as defined below) occurs in relation to the intermediary,

the deemed employment payment for that year is treated as having been made immediately before that event or, if there is more than one, immediately before the first of them.

(2) Where the intermediary is a company the following are relevant events—

    (a) the company ceasing to trade;
    (b) where the worker is a member of the company, the worker ceasing to be such a member;
    (c) where the worker holds an office with the company, the worker ceasing to hold such an office;
    (d) where the worker is employed by the company, the worker ceasing to be so employed.

(3) Where the intermediary is a partnership the following are relevant events—

    (a) the dissolution of the partnership or the partnership ceasing to trade or a partner ceasing to act as such;
    (b) where the worker is employed by the partnership, the worker ceasing to be so employed.

(4) Where the intermediary is an individual and the worker is employed by the intermediary, it is a relevant event if the worker ceases to be so employed.

(5) The fact that the deemed employment payment is treated as made before the end of the tax year does not affect what receipts and other matters are taken into account in calculating its amount.

58 Relief in case of distributions by intermediary

(1) A claim for relief may be made under this section where the intermediary—

    (a) is a company,
    (b) is treated as making a deemed employment payment in any tax year, and
    (c) either in that tax year (whether before or after that payment is treated as made), or in a subsequent tax year, makes a distribution (a "relevant distribution").

(2) A claim for relief under this section must be made—

    (a) by the intermediary by notice to [an officer of Revenue and Customs][1] , and
    (b) within 5 years after the 31st January following the tax year in which the distribution is made.

Appendix 1

(3) If on a claim being made [an officer of Revenue and Customs]¹ [is]² satisfied that relief should be given in order to avoid a double charge to tax, [the officer]³ must direct the giving of such relief by way of amending any assessment, by discharge or repayment of tax, or otherwise, as appears to [the officer]³ appropriate.

(4) Relief under this section is given by setting the amount of the deemed employment payment against the relevant distribution so as to reduce the distribution.

(5) In the case of more than one relevant distribution, [an officer of Revenue and Customs]¹ must exercise the power conferred by this section so as to secure that so far as practicable relief is given by setting the amount of a deemed employment payment—

    (a) against relevant distributions of the same tax year before those of other years,
    (b) against relevant distributions received by the worker before those received by another person, and
    (c) against relevant distributions of earlier years before those of later years.

(6) Where the amount of a relevant distribution is reduced under this section, the amount of any associated tax credit is reduced accordingly.

Notes
1. Words substituted by Commissioners for Revenue and Customs Act 2005 c. 11 Sch 4 para 102(1) (18 April 2005)
2. Word substituted by Commissioners for Revenue and Customs Act 2005 c. 11 Sch 4 para 105 (18 April 2005)
3. Words substituted by Commissioners for Revenue and Customs Act 2005 c. 11 Sch 4 para 103(1)(a) (18 April 2005)

59 Provisions applicable to multiple intermediaries

(1) The provisions of this section apply where in the case of an engagement to which this Chapter applies the arrangements involve more than one relevant intermediary.

(2) All relevant intermediaries in relation to the engagement are jointly and severally liable, subject to subsection (3), to account for any amount required under the PAYE provisions to be deducted from a deemed employment payment treated as made by any of them—

    (a) in respect of that engagement, or
    (b) in respect of that engagement together with other engagements.

(3) An intermediary is not so liable if it has not received any payment or benefit in respect of that engagement or any such other engagement as is mentioned in subsection (2)(b).

(4) Subsection (5) applies where a payment or benefit has been made or provided, directly or indirectly, from one relevant intermediary to another in respect of the engagement.

(5) In that case, the amount taken into account in relation to any intermediary in step 1 or step 2 of section 54(1) is reduced to such extent as is necessary to avoid double-counting having regard to the amount so taken into account in relation to any other intermediary.

(6) Except as provided by subsections (2) to (5), the provisions of this Chapter apply separately in relation to each relevant intermediary.

(7) In this section "relevant intermediary" means an intermediary in relation to which the conditions specified in section 51, 52 or 53 are met.

Appendix 1

60 Meaning of "associate"

(1) In this Chapter "associate"—
- (a) in relation to an individual, has the meaning given by section 417(3) and (4) of ICTA, subject to the following provisions of this section;
- (b) in relation to a company, means a person connected with the company; and
- (c) in relation to a partnership, means any associate of a member of the partnership.

(2) Where an individual has an interest in shares or obligations of the company as a beneficiary of an employee benefit trust, the trustees are not regarded as associates of the individual by reason only of that interest except in the following circumstances.

(3) The exception is where—
- (a) the individual, either alone or with any one or more associates of the individual, or
- (b) any associate of the individual, with or without other such associates,

has at any time on or after 14th March 1989 been the beneficial owner of, or able (directly or through the medium of other companies or by any other indirect means) to control more than 5% of the ordinary share capital of the company.

(4) In subsection (3) "associate" does not include the trustees of an employee benefit trust as a result only of the individual's having an interest in shares or obligations of the trust.

(5) Sections 549 to 554 (attribution of interests in companies to beneficiaries of employee benefit trusts) apply for the purposes of subsection (3) as they apply for the purposes of the provisions listed in section 549(2).

(6) In this section "employee benefit trust" has the meaning given by sections 550 and 551.

61 Interpretation

(1) In this Chapter—

"associate" has the meaning given by section 60;

"associated company" has the meaning given by section 416 of ICTA;

"business" means any trade, profession or vocation and includes [UK property business or]¹ a Schedule A business ;

"company" means a body corporate or unincorporated association, and does not include a partnership;

"employer's national insurance contributions" means secondary Class 1 or Class 1A national insurance contributions;

"engagement to which this Chapter applies" has the meaning given by section 49(5);

"national insurance contributions" means contributions under Part 1 of SSCBA 1992 or Part 1 of SSCB(NI)A 1992;

"PAYE provisions" means the provisions of Part 11 or PAYE regulations;

"the relevant engagements" has the meaning given by section 50(4).

(2) References in this Chapter to payments or benefits received or receivable from a partnership or unincorporated association include payments or benefits to which a person is or may be entitled in the person's capacity as a member of the partnership or association.

Appendix 1

(3) For the purposes of this Chapter—

    (a) anything done by or in relation to an associate of an intermediary is treated as done by or in relation to the intermediary, and

    (b) a payment or other benefit provided to a member of an individual's family or household is treated as provided to the individual.

(4) For the purposes of this Chapter a man and a woman living together as husband and wife are treated as if they were married to each other.

[(5) For the purposes of this Chapter two people of the same sex living together as if they were civil partners of each other are treated as if they were civil partners of each other.

For the purposes of this Chapter, two people of the same sex are to be regarded as living together as if they were civil partners if, but only if, they would be regarded as living together as husband and wife were they instead two people of the opposite sex.][2]

Notes
1. Words inserted by Income Tax (Trading and Other Income) Act 2005 c. 5 Sch 1(2) para 586 (6 April 2005: insertion has effect for income tax purposes for the year 2005-06 and subsequent tax years; and for corporation tax purposes for accounting periods ending 5 April 2005)
2. Added by Tax and Civil Partnership Regulations 2005/3229 reg 139 (5 December 2005)

Appendix 2
SSCBA 1992 s 4A

Social Security Contributions and Benefits Act 1992

(1992 Chapter 4)

[4A.— Earnings of workers supplied by service companies etc.

(1) Regulations may make provision for securing that where—
- (a) an individual ("the worker") personally performs, or is under an obligation personally to perform, services [for another person]² ("the client"),
- (b) the performance of those services by the worker is (within the meaning of the regulations) referable to arrangements involving a third person (and not referable to any contract between the client and the worker), and
- (c) the circumstances are such that, were the services to be performed by the worker under a contract between him and the client, he would be regarded for the purposes of the applicable provisions of this Act as employed in employed earner's employment by the client, relevant payments or benefits are, to the specified extent, to be treated for those purposes as earnings paid to the worker in respect of an employed earner's employment of his.

(2) For the purposes of this section—
- (a) "the intermediary" means—
    - (i) where the third person mentioned in subsection (1)(b) above has such a contractual or other relationship with the worker as may be specified, that third person, or
    - (ii) where that third person does not have such a relationship with the worker, any other person who has both such a relationship with the worker and such a direct or indirect contractual or other relationship with the third person as may be specified; and
- (b) a person may be the intermediary despite being—
    - (i) a person with whom the worker holds any office or employment, or
    - (ii) a body corporate, unincorporated body or partnership of which the worker is a member;

and subsection (1) above applies whether or not the client is a person with whom the worker holds any office or employment.

[(2A) Regulations may also make provision for securing that, where the services of an individual ("the worker") are provided (directly or indirectly) by a managed service company ("the MSC") relevant payments or benefits are, to the specified extent, to be treated for the purposes of the applicable provisions of this Act as earnings paid to the worker in respect of an employed earner's employment of his.

Appendix 2

(2B) In subsection (2A) "managed service company" has the same meaning as it has for the purposes of Chapter 9 of Part 2 of ITEPA 2003.]³

(3) Regulations under this section may, in particular, make provision—
- (a) for the worker to be treated for the purposes of the applicable provisions of this Act, in relation to the specified amount of relevant payments or benefits (the worker's "attributable earnings"), as employed in employed earner's employment by the intermediary [or the MSC (as the case requires)]⁴ ;
- (b) for the [intermediary or the MSC (whether or not fulfilling]⁵ the conditions prescribed under section 1(6)(a) above for secondary contributors) to be treated for those purposes as the secondary contributor in respect of the worker's attributable earnings;
- (c) for determining—
  - (i) any deductions to be made, and
  - (ii) in other respects the manner and basis in and on which the amount of the worker's attributable earnings for any specified period is to be calculated or estimated, in connection with relevant payment or benefits;
- (d) for aggregating any such amount, for purposes relating to contributions, with other earnings of the worker during any such period;
- (e) for determining the date by which contributions payable in respect of the worker's attributable earnings are to be paid and accounted for;
- (f) for apportioning payments or benefits of any specified description, in such manner or on such basis as may be specified, for the purpose of determining the part of any such payment or benefit which is to be treated as a relevant payment or benefit for the purposes of the regulations;
- (g) for disregarding for the purposes of the applicable provisions of this Act, in relation to relevant payments or benefits, an employed earner's employment in which the worker is employed (whether by the intermediary [or the MSC]⁶ or otherwise) to perform the services in question;
- (h) for otherwise securing that a double liability to pay any amount by way of a contribution of any description does not arise in relation to a particular payment or benefit or (as the case may be) a particular part of a payment or benefit;
- (i) for securing that, to the specified extent, two or more persons, whether—
  - (i) connected persons (within the meaning of [section 993 of the Income Tax Act 2007]⁷), or
  - (ii) persons of any other specified description, are treated as a single person for any purposes of the regulations;
- (j) (without prejudice to paragraph (i) above) for securing that a contract made with a person other than the client is to be treated for any such purposes as made with the client;
- (k) for excluding or modifying the application of the regulations in relation to such cases, or payments or benefits of such description, as may be specified.

(4) Regulations made in pursuance of subsection (3)(c) above may, in particular, make provision—
- (a) for the making of a deduction of a specified amount in respect of general expenses of the intermediary as well as deductions in respect of particular expenses incurred by him;
- (b) for securing reductions in the amount of the worker's attributable earnings on account of—

Appendix 2

      (i) any secondary Class 1 contributions already paid by the intermediary [or the MSC][8] in respect of actual earnings of the worker, and

      (ii) any such contributions that will be payable by [that person][9] in respect of the worker's attributable earnings.

(5) Regulations under this section may make provision for securing that, in applying any provisions of the regulations, any term of a contract or other arrangement which appears to be of a description specified in the regulations is to be disregarded.

(6) In this section—

"the applicable provisions of this Act" means this Part of this Act and Parts II to V below;

[…][10]

"relevant payments or benefits" means payments or benefits of any specified description made or provided (whether to the intermediary [or the MSC,][11] or the worker or otherwise) in connection with the performance by the worker of the services in question ;

"specified" means prescribed by or determined in accordance with regulations under this section.

(7) Any reference in this section to the performance by the worker of any services includes a reference to any such obligation of his to perform them as is mentioned in subsection (1)(a) above.

(8) Regulations under this section shall be made by the Treasury with the concurrence of the Secretary of State.

(9) If, on any modification of the statutory provisions relating to income tax, it appears to the Treasury to be expedient to modify any of the preceding provisions of this section for the purpose of assimilating the law relating to income tax and the law relating to contributions under this Part of this Act, the Treasury may with the concurrence of the Secretary of State by order make such modifications of the preceding provisions of this section as the Treasury think appropriate for that purpose.][1]

Notes
1. Added by Welfare Reform and Pensions Act 1999 c. 30 Pt V c.II s 75 (22 December 1999)
2. Words substituted by Social Security Contributions and Benefits Act 1992 (Modification of Section 4A) Order 2003/1874 art 3 (8 August 2003)
3. Added by Social Security Contributions and Benefits Act 1992 (Modification of Section 4A) Order 2007/2071 art 2(2) (24 July 2007)
4. Words inserted by Social Security Contributions and Benefits Act 1992 (Modification of Section 4A) Order 2007/2071 art 2(3)(a) (24 July 2007)
5. Words substituted by Social Security Contributions and Benefits Act 1992 (Modification of Section 4A) Order 2007/2071 art 2(3)(b) (24 July 2007)
6. Words inserted by Social Security Contributions and Benefits Act 1992 (Modification of Section 4A) Order 2007/2071 art 2(3)(c) (24 July 2007)
7. Words substituted by Income Tax Act 2007 c. 3 Sch1(2) para 289 (6 April 2007: for income tax purposes, for the tax year 2007-08 and subsequent tax years and for corporation tax purposes for accounting periods ending after 5 April 2007, subject to savings and transitional provisions specified in 2007 c.3 s 1030(1) and Sch 2)
8. Words inserted by Social Security Contributions and Benefits Act 1992 (Modification of Section 4A) Order 2007/2071 art 2(4)(a) (24 July 2007)
9. Word substituted by Social Security Contributions and Benefits Act 1992 (Modification of Section 4A) Order 2007/2071 art 2(4)(b) (24 July 2007)
10. Definition repealed by Social Security Contributions and Benefits Act 1992 (Modification of Section 4A) Order 2003/1874 art 4 (8 August 2003)
11. Words inserted by Social Security Contributions and Benefits Act 1992 (Modification of Section 4A) Order 2007/2071 art 2(5) (24 July 2007)

Appendix 3
SI 2000/727

Social Security Contributions (Intermediaries) Regulations 2000, 2000/727

Made by the Treasury under SSCBA 1992 ss 4A, 122(1), 175(1A), (2)–(4) and the Inland Revenue under SSC(TF)A 1999 s 8(1)(*m*)

Made	13 March 2000
Laid before Parliament	13 March 2000
Coming into force	6 April 2000

1 — Citation, commencement and effect

(1) These Regulations may be cited as the Social Security Contributions (Intermediaries) Regulations 2000 and shall come into force on 6th April 2000.

(2) These Regulations have effect for the tax year 2000–01 and subsequent years and apply in relation to services performed, or to be performed, on or after 6th April 2000.

(3) Payments or other benefits in respect of such services received before that date shall be treated as if received in the tax year 2000–01.

2 — Interpretation

(1) In these Regulations unless the context otherwise requires–

"arrangements" means the arrangements referred to in regulation 6(1)(b);

"associate" has the meaning given by regulation 3;

"attributable earnings" in relation to a worker shall be construed in accordance with regulation 6(3)(a);

["the Board" means the Commissioners for Her Majesty's Revenue and Customs;][1]

[...][2]

"Class 1A contributions" has the meaning given by section 10 of the Contributions and Benefits Act[3];

"client" shall be construed in accordance with regulation 6(1)(a);

"company" means any body corporate or unincorporated association, but does not include a partnership;

"the Contributions and Benefits Act" means the Social Security Contributions and Benefits Act 1992;

["the Contributions Regulations" means the Social Security (Contributions) Regulations 2001;][4]

Appendix 3

"intermediary" has the meaning given by regulation 5;

"relevant benefit" means any benefit falling within regulation 4 that is provided to the intermediary or to or on behalf of the worker under the arrangements;

"relevant payment" means any payment made to an intermediary or to or on behalf of the worker under the arrangements;

"secondary Class 1 contributions" has the meaning given by section 6 of the Contributions and Benefits Act[5];

"secondary contributor" has the meaning given by section 7 of the Contributions and Benefits Act[6];

"the Taxes Act" means the Income and Corporation Taxes Act 1988;

"tax year" means year of assessment;

"worker" means the individual referred to in regulation 6(1)(a).

(2) References in these Regulations to payments or benefits received or receivable from a partnership or unincorporated association include payments or benefits to which a person is or may be entitled in his capacity as a member of the partnership or association.

(3) For the purposes of these Regulations–

(a) anything done by or in relation to an associate of an intermediary is treated as done by or in relation to the intermediary, and

(b) a payment or other benefit provided to a member of an individual's family or household is treated as provided to the individual.

(4) The reference in paragraph (3)(b) to an individual's family or household shall be construed in accordance with [sections 721(4) and (5) of ITEPA 2003][7].

(5) For the purposes of these Regulations a man and a woman living together as husband and wife are treated as if they were married to each other.

[(6) For the purposes of these Regulations two people of the same sex living together as if they were civil partners of each other are treated as if they were civil partners of each other; and, for the purposes of these Regulations, two people of the same sex are to be regarded as living together as if they were civil partners if, but only if, they would be regarded as living together as husband and wife were they instead two people of the opposite sex.][8]

Notes
1. Definition substituted by Social Security Contributions (Intermediaries) (Amendment) Regulations 2005/3131 reg 4(2) (5 December 2005: substitution has effect for the tax year 2005-06 and subsequent tax years, and applies in relation to services performed, or to be performed, on or after 5 December 2005)
2. Definition repealed by Social Security Contributions (Intermediaries) (Amendment) Regulations 2003/2079 reg 4 (1 September 2003)
3. Section 10 was amended by section 52 of, and paragraph 58 of Schedule 7 to, the Social Security Act 1998 (c. 14), paragraph 10 of Schedule 3 to the Social Security Contributions (Transfer of Functions, etc.) Act 1999 and regulation 4 of SI 1994/667.
4. Definition substituted by Social Security Contributions (Intermediaries) (Amendment) Regulations 2002/703 reg 3 (6 April 2002: substitution has effect in relation to services performed, or to be performed, on or after 6 April 2002 and for the year 2002-03 and subsequent years of assessment)
5. Section 6 was substituted by paragraph 2 of Schedule 9 to the Welfare Reform and Pensions Act 1999.
6. Section 7 was amended by paragraph 7 of Schedule 3 to the Social Security Contributions (Transfer of Functions, etc.) Act 1999.

Appendix 3

7. Words substituted by Social Security (Contributions, Categorisation of Earners and Intermediaries) (Amendment) Regulations 2004/770 reg 35(2) (6 April 2004)
8. Added by Social Security Contributions (Intermediaries) (Amendment) Regulations 2005/3131 reg 4(3) (5 December 2005: insertion has effect for the tax year 2005-06 and subsequent tax years, and applies in relation to services performed, or to be performed, on or after 5 December2005)

3 — Meaning of associate

(1) In these Regulations "associate" –

    (a) in relation to an individual, has the meaning given by section 417(3) and (4) of the Taxes Act[1], subject to the following provisions of this regulation;

    (b) in relation to a company, means a person connected with the company within the meaning of section 839 of the Taxes Act[2]; and

    (c) in relation to a partnership, means any associate of a member of the partnership.

(2) Where an individual has an interest in shares or obligations of the company as a beneficiary of an employee benefit trust, the trustees are not regarded as associates of his by reason only of that interest except in the following circumstances.

(3) The exception is where–

    (a) the individual, either on his own or with one or more of his associates, or

    (b) any associate of his, with or without other such associates,

has been the beneficial owner of, or able (directly or through the medium of other companies or by any other indirect means) to control, more than 5 per cent. of the ordinary share capital of the company.

(4) In paragraph (2) "employee benefit trust" has the same meaning as in [sections 550 and 551 of ITEPA 2003][3].

Notes

1. Section 417 was amended by paragraph 6 of Schedule 17 to the Finance Act 1995 (c. 4).
2. Section 839 was amended by paragraph 20 of Schedule 17 to the Finance Act 1995.
3. Words substituted by Social Security (Contributions, Categorisation of Earners and Intermediaries) (Amendment) Regulations 2004/770 reg 35(3) (6 April 2004)

4 — Meaning of benefit

[(1) For the purposes of these Regulations a "benefit" means anything that, if received by an employee for performing the duties of an employment, would be general earnings of the employment.][1]

(2) The amount of a benefit is taken to be–

    (a) in the case of a cash benefit, the amount received, and

    (b) in the case of a non-cash benefit, the cash equivalent of the benefit.

(3) The cash equivalent of a non-cash benefit is taken to be whichever is the greater of–

    [(a) the amount that would, for income tax purposes, be general earnings if the benefit were general earnings from an employment, and

    (b) the cash equivalent determined in accordance with section 398(2)(b) of ITEPA 2003.][2]

(4) For the purposes of these Regulations a benefit is treated as received–

    (a) in the case of a cash benefit, when payment is made of or on account of the benefit; and

    (b) in the case of an non-cash benefit, when it is used or enjoyed.

Appendix 3

Notes
1. Substituted by Social Security (Contributions, Categorisation of Earners and Intermediaries) (Amendment) Regulations 2004/770 reg 35(4)(a) (6 April 2004)
2. Substituted by Social Security (Contributions, Categorisation of Earners and Intermediaries) (Amendment) Regulations 2004/770 reg 35(4)(b) (6 April 2004)

5 — Meaning of intermediary

(1) In these Regulations "intermediary" means any person, including a partnership or unincorporated association of which the worker is a member–

    (a) whose relationship with the worker in any tax year satisfies the conditions specified in paragraph (2), (6), (7) or (8), and

    (b) from whom the worker, or an associate of the worker–

        (i) receives, directly or indirectly, in that year a payment or benefit that is not chargeable to tax [as employment income under ITEPA 2003][1], or

        (ii) is entitled to receive, or in any circumstances would be entitled to receive, directly or indirectly, in that year any such payment or benefit.

(2) Where the intermediary is a company the conditions are that–

    (a) the intermediary is not an associated company of the client, within the meaning of section 416 of the Taxes Act[2], by reason of the intermediary and the client both being under the control of the worker, or under the control of the worker and another person; and

    (b) either–

        (i) the worker has a material interest in the intermediary, or

        (ii) the payment or benefit is received or receivable by the worker directly from the intermediary, and can reasonably be taken to represent remuneration for services provided by the worker to the client.

(3) A worker is treated as having a material interest in a company for the purposes of paragraph (2)(a) if–

    (a) the worker, alone or with one or more associates of his, or

    (b) an associate of the worker, with or without other such associates,

has a material interest in the company.

(4) For this purpose a material interest means–

    (a) beneficial ownership of, or the ability to control, directly or through the medium of other companies or by any other indirect means, more than 5 per cent. of the ordinary share capital of the company; or

    (b) possession of, or entitlement to acquire, rights entitling the holder to receive more than 5 per cent. of any distributions that may be made by the company; or

    (c) where the company is a close company, possession of, or entitlement to acquire, rights that would in the event of the winding up of the company, or in any other circumstances, entitle the holder to receive more than 5 per cent. of the assets that would then be available for distribution among the participators.

In sub-paragraph (c) "close company" has the meaning given by sections 414 and 415 of the Taxes Act[3], and "participator" has the meaning given by section 417(1) of that Act.

(5) Where the intermediary is a partnership the conditions are as follows.

(6) In relation to payments or benefits received or receivable by the worker as a member of the partnership, the conditions are–

Appendix 3

    (a)   that the worker, alone or with one or more relatives, is entitled to 60 per cent. or more of the profits of the partnership; or

    (b)   that most of the profits of the partnership derive from the provision of services under the arrangements–

        (i)   to a single client, or

        (ii)   to a single client together with an associate or associates of that client; or

    (c)   that under the profit sharing arrangements the income of any of the partners is based on the amount of income generated by that partner by the provision of services under the arrangements.

In sub-paragraph (a) "relative" means [spouse or civil partner][4] , parent or remoter forebear, child or remoter issue, or brother or sister .

(7)   In relation to payments or benefits received or receivable by the worker otherwise than as a member of the partnership, the conditions are that the payment or benefit–

    (a)   is received or receivable by the worker directly from the intermediary, and

    (b)   can reasonably be taken to represent remuneration for services provided by the worker to the client.

(8)   Where the intermediary is an individual the conditions are that the payment or benefit–

    (a)   is received or receivable by the worker directly from the intermediary, and

    (b)   can reasonably be taken to represent remuneration for services provided by the worker to the client.

Notes

1. Words substituted by Social Security (Contributions, Categorisation of Earners and Intermediaries) (Amendment) Regulations 2004/770 reg 35(5) (6 April 2004)
2. Section 416 was amended by Part V of Schedule 17 to the Finance Act 1989.
3. Section 414 was amended by section 104 of, and Part V of Schedule 17 to, the Finance Act 1989. Section 415 was amended by paragraph 6(2)(f) of Schedule 38 to the Finance Act 1996.
4. Words substituted subject to transitional provisions specified in SI 2005/3131 reg 7 by Social Security Contributions (Intermediaries) (Amendment) Regulations 2005/3131 reg 5 (5 December 2005: substitution has effect for the tax year 2005-06 and subsequent tax years, and applies in relation to services performed, or to be performed, on or after 5 December 2005, and is subject to transitional provisions specified in SI 2005/3131 reg 7)

6 — Provision of services through intermediary

(1)   These Regulations apply where–

    (a)   an individual ("the worker") personally performs, or is under an obligation personally to perform, services [for another person][1] ("the client"),

    (b)   the performance of those services by the worker is carried out, not under a contract directly between the client and the worker, but under arrangements involving an intermediary, and

    (c)   the circumstances are such that, had the arrangements taken the form of a contract between the worker and the client, the worker would be regarded for the purposes of Parts I to V of the Contributions and Benefits Act as employed in employed earner's employment by the client.

(2)   Paragraph (1)(b) has effect irrespective of whether or not–

    (a)   there exists a contract between the client and the worker, or

    (b)   the worker is the holder of an office with the client.

(3)   Where these Regulations apply–

Appendix 3

(a) the worker is treated, for the purposes of Parts I to V of the Contributions and Benefits Act, and in relation to the amount deriving from relevant payments and relevant benefits that is calculated in accordance with regulation 7 ("the worker's attributable earnings"), as employed in employed earner's employment by the intermediary, and

(b) the intermediary, whether or not he fulfils the conditions prescribed under section 1(6)(a) of the Contributions and Benefits Act[2] for secondary contributors, is treated for those purposes as the secondary contributor in respect of the worker's attributable earnings,

and Parts I to V of that Act have effect accordingly.

(4) Any issue whether the circumstances are such as are mentioned in paragraph (1)(c) is an issue relating to contributions that is prescribed for the purposes of section 8(1)(m) of the Social Security Contributions (Transfer of Functions, etc.) Act 1999 (decision by officer of the Board).

Notes
1. Words substituted by Social Security Contributions (Intermediaries) (Amendment) Regulations 2003/2079 reg 5 (1 September 2003)
2. Section 1(6) was amended by paragraph 56(3) of Schedule 7 to the Social Security Act 1998.

7 — Worker's attributable earnings – calculation

(1) For the purposes of regulation 6(3)(a) the amount of the worker's attributable earnings for a tax year is calculated as follows:

Step One
Find the total amount of all payments and benefits received by the intermediary in that year under the arrangements, and reduce that amount by 5 per cent.

Step Two
Add the amount of any payments and benefits received by the worker in that year under the arrangements, otherwise than from the intermediary, that–

(a) are not chargeable to income tax [as employment income under ITEPA 2003[2]][1], and
(b) would be so chargeable if the worker were employed by the client.

Step Three
Deduct the amount of any expenses met in that year by the intermediary that under [ITEPA 2003][3] would have been deductible from the [taxable earnings of the employment, within the meaning of section 10 of ITEPA 2003, in accordance with section 327(3) to (5) of that Act][4] if the worker had been employed by the client and the expenses had been met by the worker out of [those earnings][5].

Step Four
Deduct the amount of any capital allowances in respect of expenditure incurred by the intermediary in that year that could have been claimed by the worker [under Part 2 of the Capital Allowances Act 2001 (plant and machinery allowances) by virtue of section 15(1)(i) of that Act (which provides that employment is a qualifying activity for the purposes of that Part)][6] if the worker had been employed by the client and had incurred the expenditure.

Step Five
Deduct any contributions made in that year for the benefit of the worker by the intermediary to [a registered pension scheme for the purposes of Part 4 of the Finance Act 2004][7] that if made by an employer for the benefit of an employee would not be chargeable to income tax as income of the employee [, and any payments made in that year in respect of the worker by the intermediary in respect of any of the Pensions Act levies][8].

Appendix 3

This does not apply to excess contributions made and later repaid.

Step Six
Deduct the amount of secondary Class 1 contributions and Class 1A contributions paid by the intermediary for that year in respect of earnings of the worker.

Step Seven
Deduct–

(a) the amount of any payments made by the intermediary to the worker in that year that constitute remuneration derived from the worker's employment by that intermediary including, where the intermediary is a body corporate and the worker is a director of that body corporate, payments treated as remuneration derived from that employment by virtue of [22(2)]^9 of the Contributions Regulations[...]^9 (payments to directors to be treated as earnings), but excluding payments which represent items in respect of which a deduction was made under Step Three, and

(b) the amount of any benefits provided by the intermediary to the worker in that year, being benefits that constitute amounts of [general earnings]^{10} in respect of which Class 1A contributions are payable, but excluding any benefits which represent items in respect of which a deduction was made under Step Three.

If the result at this point is nil or a negative amount, there are no worker's attributable earnings for that year.

Step Eight
Find the amount that, together with the amount of secondary Class 1 contributions payable in respect of it, is equal to the amount resulting from Step Seven (if that amount is a positive amount).

Step Nine
The result is the amount of the worker's attributable earnings for that year.

(2) Where section 559 of the Taxes Act applies (sub-contractors in the construction industry: payments to be made under deduction) the intermediary is treated for the purposes of Step One of the calculation in paragraph (1) as receiving the amount that would have been received had no deduction been made under that section.

(3) For the purpose of calculating the amount of deductible expenses referred to in Step Three of the calculation in paragraph (1) it shall be assumed that all engagements of the worker under the arrangements involving the intermediary are undertaken in the course of the same employment.

(4) For the purposes of this regulation any necessary apportionment shall be made on a just and reasonable basis of amounts received by the intermediary that are referable–

(a) to the services of more than one worker, or
(b) partly to the services of the worker and partly to other matters.

(5) For the purposes of this regulation the time when payments are received by the intermediary or the worker under the arrangements shall be found in accordance with the rules contained in [sections 18 and 19 of ITEPA 2003, subject to the qualification that the worker shall not be treated, by virtue of Rule 2 in section 18, as receiving a payment prior to the time of its actual receipt.]^{11}

[(6) The reference in Step Three of the calculation in paragraph (1) to expenses met by the intermediary includes expenses met by the worker and reimbursed by the intermediary.

(7) Where the intermediary is a partnership and the worker is a member of the partnership, expenses met by the worker for and on behalf of the intermediary shall be treated for

Appendix 3

the purposes of paragraph (6) as expenses met by the worker and reimbursed by the intermediary.

(8) Where—
   (a) the intermediary provides a vehicle for the worker, and
   (b) the worker would have been entitled to an amount of mileage allowance relief under [section 231 of ITEPA 2003][13] [14] for a tax year in respect of the use of the vehicle if the worker had been employed by the client, or would have been so entitled if the worker had been employed by the client and the vehicle had not been a company vehicle,

Step Three of the calculation in paragraph (1) shall have effect as if that amount were an amount of expenses deductible under that Step.

(9) Where—
   (a) the intermediary is a partnership,
   (b) the worker is a member of the partnership, and
   (c) the worker provides a vehicle for the purposes of the business of the partnership,

(10) Where the intermediary makes payments to the worker that are exempt from income tax [as employment income under ITEPA 2003][15] by virtue of [section 229 or 233 of ITEPA 2003][16] (mileage allowance payments and passenger payments), paragraph (a) of Step Seven of the calculation in paragraph (1) shall have effect as if the intermediary had made payments to the worker that constituted remuneration derived from the worker's employment by the intermediary.][12]

[(11) In this regulation "the Pensions Act levies" means—
   (a) the administration levy referred to in section 117(1) of the Pensions Act 2004;
   (b) the initial levy referred to in section 174(1) of that Act;
   (c) the risk-based pension protection levy referred to in section 175(1)(a) of that Act;
   (d) the scheme-based pension protection levy referred to in section 175(1)(b) of that Act;
   (e) the fraud compensation levy referred to in section 189(1) of that Act;
   (f) a levy in respect of eligible schemes imposed by regulations made under section 209(7) of that Act (the Ombudsman for the Board of the Pension Protection Fund).][17]

Notes
1. Words substituted by Social Security Contributions (Intermediaries) (Amendment) Regulations 2003/2079 reg 6(2)(a) (1 September 2003)
2. I.e. the Income Tax (Earnings and Pensions) Act 2003 c. 1: a definition of "ITEPA 2003" was inserted into section 122(1) of the 1992 Act by paragraph 178(2) of Schedule 6 to that Act.
3. Words substituted by Social Security Contributions (Intermediaries) (Amendment) Regulations 2003/2079 reg 6(2)(b)(i) (1 September 2003)
4. Words substituted by Social Security Contributions (Intermediaries) (Amendment) Regulations 2003/2079 reg 6(2)(b)(ii) (1 September 2003)
5. Words substituted by Social Security Contributions (Intermediaries) (Amendment) Regulations 2003/2079 reg 6(2)(b)(iii) (1 September 2003)
6. Words substituted by Social Security Contributions (Intermediaries) (Amendment) Regulations 2003/2079 reg 6(2)(c) (1 September 2003)
7. Words substituted by Social Security Contributions (Intermediaries) (Amendment) Regulations 2005/3131 reg 8(2) (6 April 2006: substitution has effect for the tax year 2006-07 and subsequent tax years, and applies in relation to services performed, or to be performed, on or after 6 April 2006)
8. Words inserted by Social Security Contributions (Intermediaries) (Amendment) Regulations 2005/3131 reg 6(2) (5 December 2005: insertion has effect for the tax year 2005-06 and subsequent

Appendix 3

tax years, and applies in relation to services performed, or to be performed, on or after 5 December 2005)
9. Word substituted by Social Security Contributions (Intermediaries) (Amendment) Regulations 2002/703 reg 4 (6 April 2002: substitution has effect in relation to services performed, or to be performed, on or after 6 April 2002 and for the year 2002-03 and subsequent years of assessment)
10. Words substituted by Social Security (Contributions, Categorisation of Earners and Intermediaries) (Amendment) Regulations 2004/770 reg 35(6) (6 April 2004)
11. Words substituted by Social Security Contributions (Intermediaries) (Amendment) Regulations 2003/2079 reg.6(3) (1 September 2003)
12. Added by Social Security Contributions (Intermediaries) (Amendment) Regulations 2002/703 reg 5 (6 April 2002: insertion has effect in relation to services performed, or to be performed, on or after 6 April 2002 and for the year 2002-03 and subsequent years of assessment)
13. Words substituted by Social Security Contributions (Intermediaries) (Amendment) Regulations 2003/2079 reg 6(4) (1 September 2003)
14. 1988 c. 1. Sections 197AD to 197AH of the Income and Corporation Taxes Act 1988 were inserted by section 57(1) of the Finance Act 2001 (c. 9).
15. Words substituted by Social Security Contributions (Intermediaries) (Amendment) Regulations 2003/2079 reg 6(5)(a) (1 September 2003)
16. Words substituted by Social Security Contributions (Intermediaries) (Amendment) Regulations 2003/2079 reg 6(5)(b) (1 September 2003)
17. Added by Social Security Contributions (Intermediaries) (Amendment) Regulations 2005/3131 reg 6(3) (5 December 2005: insertion has effect for the tax year 2005-06 and subsequent tax years, and applies in relation to services performed, or to be performed, on or after 5 December 2005)

8 — Worker's attributable earnings – deemed payment

(1) The amount referred to in Step Nine of the calculation in regulation 7(1) is treated, for the purposes of Parts I to V of the Contributions and Benefits Act, as a single payment of the worker's attributable earnings made by the intermediary on the 5th April in the tax year concerned or, as the case may be, on the date found in accordance with paragraphs (4) to (7), and those Parts of that Act shall have effect accordingly.

(2) The worker's attributable earnings shall be aggregated with any other earnings paid to the worker by the intermediary in the year concerned to or for the benefit of the worker in respect of employed earner's employment, and the amount of earnings-related contributions payable in respect of that aggregate amount shall be assessed in accordance with the appropriate earnings period specified in [regulation 8]¹ of the Contributions Regulations[...]¹ (earnings period for directors), whether or not the worker is a director of a company during that year.

(3) Where the intermediary is a partnership or unincorporated association, the amount referred to in Step Nine of the calculation in regulation 7(1) is treated, for the purposes of Parts I to V of the Contributions and Benefits Act, as received by the worker in his personal capacity and not as income of the partnership or association.

(4) If in a tax year–

(a) an amount of the worker's attributable earnings is treated as made under paragraph (1), and

(b) before the date on which the payment would be treated as made under that paragraph any relevant event (as defined below) occurs in relation to the intermediary,

that amount is treated, for the purposes of Parts I to V of the Contributions and Benefits Act, as having been made immediately before that event or, if there is more than one, immediately before the first of them.

(5) Where the intermediary is a company the following are relevant events–

Appendix 3

        (a)   where the worker is a member of the company, his ceasing to be such a member;
        (b)   where the worker holds an office with the company, his ceasing to hold such an office;
        (c)   where the worker is employed by the company, his ceasing to be so employed.
        [(d)   the company ceasing to trade.][2]

(6)   Where the intermediary is a partnership the following are relevant events–

        (a)   the dissolution of the partnership or the partnership ceasing to trade or a partner ceasing to act as such;
        (b)   where the worker is employed by the partnership, his ceasing to be so employed.

(7)   Where the intermediary is an individual and the worker is employed by him, it is a relevant event if the worker ceases to be so employed.

(8)   The fact that an amount of the worker's attributable earnings is treated as made under paragraph (1) before the end of the tax year concerned does not affect what payments and benefits are taken into account in calculating that amount.

Notes
1. Word substituted by Social Security Contributions (Intermediaries) (Amendment) Regulations 2002/703 reg 6(1)(a) (6 April 2002: substitution has effect in relation to services performed, or to be performed, on or after 6 April 2002 and for the year 2002-03 and subsequent years of assessment)
2. Added by Social Security Contributions (Intermediaries) (Amendment) Regulations 2002/703 reg 6(1)(b) (6 April 2002: insertion has effect in relation to services performed, or to be performed, on or after 6 April 2002 and for the year 2002-03 and subsequent years of assessment)

9 — Multiple intermediaries – general

(1)   Regulations 10 and 11 apply where in any tax year the arrangements involve more than one intermediary.

(2)   Except as provided by regulations 10 and 11, the provisions of these Regulations apply separately in relation to each intermediary.

10 — Multiple intermediaries – avoidance of double-counting

(1)   This regulation applies where a payment or benefit has been made or provided, directly or indirectly, from one intermediary to another intermediary under the arrangements.

(2)   In that case, the amount taken into account in relation to any intermediary in Step One or Step Two of the calculation in regulation 7(1) shall be reduced to such extent as is necessary to avoid double-counting having regard to the amount so taken into account in relation to any other intermediary.

11 — Multiple intermediaries – joint and several liability

(1)   Where the arrangements involve more than one intermediary, all the intermediaries are jointly and severally liable, subject to paragraph (3), to pay contributions in respect of the amount of the worker's attributable earnings treated in accordance with regulation 8(1) as paid by any of them–

        (a)   under those arrangements, or
        (b)   under those arrangements together with other arrangements.

(2)   For the purposes of paragraph (1), each amount of the worker's attributable earnings shall be aggregated, and the aggregate amount shall be treated for the purposes of regulation 8(1) as a single payment of the worker's attributable earnings, but so that the

Appendix 3

total liability of the intermediaries to pay contributions in respect of that aggregate amount is not less than it would have been if the arrangements had involved a single intermediary and that aggregate amount had been an amount treated as paid in accordance with regulation 8(1) by a single intermediary.

(3) An intermediary is not jointly and severally liable as mentioned in paragraph (1) if the intermediary has not received any payment or benefit under the arrangements concerned or under any such other arrangements as are mentioned in sub-paragraph (b) of that paragraph.

12. Social Security (Categorisation of Earners) Regulations 1978 – Saving

Nothing in these Regulations affects the operation of regulation 2 of the Social Security (Categorisation of Earners) Regulations 1978 (treatment of earners in one category of earners as falling within another category and disregard of employments) as that regulation applies to employment listed in paragraph 2 in column (A) of Part I of Schedule 1 to those Regulations (earner supplied through a third person treated as employed earner).

Appendix 4
Tax Bulletin 45 extract

February 2000. IR Tax Bulletin Issue 45 Provision of personal services through intermediaries

Would the worker have been an employee if engaged directly by the client?

A broad outline of the new rules was given in a press release dated 23 September 1999. They are intended to apply where a worker supplies his or her services to a client through an intermediary such as a service company or partnership. One of the central questions in deciding whether the new rules apply to an engagement is to establish whether the worker would have been an employee of the client if engaged directly. This article addresses this issue in detail. More details of the proposals can be found on the Inland Revenue website at www.inlandrevenue.gov.uk/ir35. [This can now be found at www.hmrc.gov.uk]

The approach to be adopted

Whether a worker would have been an employee if engaged directly by the client depends on a range of factors, set out in this article. But the final decision is not reached by adding up the number of factors pointing towards employment and comparing that result with the number pointing towards self-employment. The Courts have specifically rejected that approach. In *Hall v Lorimer* Mummery J made the following comment which was quoted with approval by Nolan LJ in the Court of Appeal:

> 'In order to decide whether a person carries on business on his own account it is necessary to consider many different aspects of that person's work activity. This is not a mechanical exercise of running through a checklist to see whether they are present in, or absent from, a given situation ... It is a matter of evaluation of the overall effect, which is not necessarily the same as the sum total of all the individual details. Not all details are of equal weight or importance in any given situation. The details may also vary in importance from one situation to another.'

When the detailed facts have been established the right approach is to stand back and look at the picture as a whole, to see if the overall effect is that of a person in business on his own account or a person working as an employee in somebody else's business. If the evidence is evenly balanced the intention of the parties may then decide the issue (*Massey v Crown Life Insurance Co*).

Establishing the facts

In deciding whether a worker would have been an employee if engaged directly by the client it is firstly necessary to establish the terms and conditions of the engagement. In a simple case involving one intermediary (eg where a worker works through a service company) these will

Appendix 4

normally be established mainly from the contract between the client and the intermediary. It is that contract that will usually reflect the terms that would have applied had the worker been engaged directly by the client. The contract may be written, oral or implied—or a mixture of all three.

Having established the terms and conditions it is then necessary to consider any surrounding facts that may be relevant—eg whether the worker has other clients and a business organisation. In this context other contracts the company has under which the worker's services are supplied and any business organisation of the company which is relevant to the supply of the worker's services will be taken into account as relevant surrounding facts.

Deciding employment status

There is no statutory definition of 'employment'. However, the question of employment status has come before the Courts on numerous occasions. The approach taken by the Courts has been to identify factors which help to determine if a particular contract is a 'contract of service' (employment) or a 'contract for services' (self-employment). Relevant factors are:

Control

A worker will not be an employee unless there is a right to exercise 'control' over the worker. This may be a right to control 'what' work is done, 'where' or 'when' it is done or 'how' it is done. Actual control of this sort is not necessary—it the right of control that is important.

Where a client has the right to determine 'how' the work is done this is a strong pointer to employment. But it is not an essential feature of employment—many 'experts' who are employees are not necessarily subject to such control (for example, ship's captain, consultant brain surgeon, etc).

Equally, a right to determine 'what' work is carried out is a strong pointer to employment. It will normally be a feature whenever a client needs a worker to undertake whatever tasks are required at any particular time or where the worker is required to work as part of a co-ordinated team.

A working relationship which involves no control at all is unlikely to be an employment (*Ready Mixed Concrete (South East) Ltd v Minister of Pensions and National Insurance* [1968] 2 QB 497).

The right to get a substitute or helper to do the job

Personal service is an essential element of a contract of employment. A person who has the freedom to choose whether to do the job himself or hire somebody else to do it for him, or who can hire someone else to provide substantial help is probably self-employed (*Australian Mutual Provident Society v Chaplin* (1978) 18 ALR 385 and *Express and Echo Publications Ltd v Tanton* [1999] IRLR 367). However, this must be viewed in the context of the arrangements overall. For example, a worker may choose to pay a helper to take phone messages and deal with invoicing and general book-keeping work for the intermediary. But this would not be directly relevant when considering an engagement where the worker is engaged to lay bricks for a client.

Provision of equipment

A self-employed contractor generally provides whatever equipment is needed to do the job (though in many trades, such as carpentry, it is common for employees, as well as self-employed workers, to provide their own hand tools). The provision of significant equipment

Appendix 4

(and/or materials) which are fundamental to the engagement is of particular importance. For example, where an IT consultant is engaged to undertake a specific piece of work and must work exclusively at home using the worker's own computer equipment that will be a strong pointer to self-employment. But where a worker is provided with office space and computer equipment that points to employment. The fact that a worker might occasionally choose to do some of the work at home using his or her own computer does not change that (many employees do just that). (*Ready Mixed Concrete (South East) Ltd v Minister of Pensions and National Insurance*).

Financial risk

An individual who risks his own money by, for example, buying assets needed for the job and bearing their running costs and paying for overheads and large quantities of materials, is almost certainly self-employed. Financial risk could also take the form of quoting a fixed price for a job, with the consequent risk of bearing the additional costs if the job overruns. Another example of a financial risk is where a skilled worker incurs significant amounts of expenditure on training to provide himself with a skill which he uses in subsequent engagements. This can be treated in the same way as investment in equipment to be used in a trade, as a pointer to self-employment, if there is a real risk that the investment would not be recovered from income from future engagements (*Market Investigations Ltd v Minister of Social Security* [1969] 2 QB 173).

Basis of payment

Employees tend to be paid a fixed wage or salary by the week or month and often qualify for additional payments such as overtime, long service bonus or profit share. Independent contractors, on the other hand, tend to be paid a fixed sum for a particular job. Payment 'by the piece' (where the worker is paid according to the amount of work actually done) or by commission can be a feature of both employment and self-employment.

Opportunity to profit from sound management

A person whose profit or loss depends on his capacity to reduce overheads and organise his work effectively may well be self-employed (*Market Investigations Ltd v Minister of Social Security*). People who are paid by the job will often be in this position.

Part and parcel of the organisation

Establishing whether a person becomes 'part and parcel' of a client's organisation can be a useful indicator in some situations. For example, someone taken on to manage a client's staff will normally be seen as part and parcel of the client's organisation and is likely to be an employee.

Right of dismissal

A right to terminate an engagement by giving notice of a specified length is a common feature of employment. It is less common in a contract for services, which usually ends only on completion of the task, or if the terms of the contract are breached.

Employee benefits

Employees are often entitled to sick pay, holiday pay, pensions, expenses and so on. However, the absence of those features does not necessarily mean that the worker is self-

Appendix 4

employed—especially in the case of short-term engagements where such payments would not normally feature.

Length of engagement

Long periods working for one engager may be typical of an employment but are not conclusive. It is still necessary to consider all the terms and conditions of each engagement. Regular working for the same engager may indicate that there is a single and continuing contract of employment (*Nethermere (St Neots) Ltd v Gardiner* [1984] ICR 612). Where an engagement is covered by a series of short contracts, or an initial short contract subsequently extended for a longer period, it is the length of the engagement that is relevant, rather than the length of each contract.

Personal factors

In deciding a person's employment status it may sometimes be necessary to take into account factors which are personal to the worker and which have little to do with the terms of the particular engagement being considered. For example, if a skilled worker works for a number of clients throughout the year and has a business-like approach to obtaining his engagements (perhaps involving expenditure on office accommodation, office equipment, etc) this will point towards self-employment (*Hall v Lorimer* (1993) 66 TC 349). Personal factors will usually carry less weight in the case of an unskilled worker, where other factors such as the high level of control exercised by the contractor are likely to be conclusive of employment.

Intention

It is the reality of the relationship that matters. It is not enough to call a person 'self-employed' if all the terms and conditions of the engagement point towards employment. However, if other factors are neutral the intention of the parties will then be the decisive factor in deciding employment status (*Massey v Crown Life Insurance Co* [1978] ICR 590).

Revenue guidance

In most cases the question of whether a worker would have been an employee of the client if engaged directly will be obvious from a careful consideration of the terms and conditions of the engagement and the surrounding facts. However, where a worker is in doubt about whether an engagement would have been employment or self-employment then he may ask for an opinion from the Inland Revenue. Full details of how to contact us can be found on our website at www.inlandrevenue.gov.uk/ir35 [now found at www.hmrc.gov.uk]. In such cases a copy of the relevant contract setting out the full terms and conditions of the engagement will have to be provided, together with details of any fact that he considers relevant to the status position. An opinion will only be given on signed contracts and not on draft agreements.

The terms of contracts used by service company workers who obtain engagements through agencies tend to be of a standard form. Such contracts typically require the worker to work on the client's premises, use the client's equipment, work standard hours, be paid at an hourly rate and be subject to a high level of control. In such cases, the opinion of the IR about the engagement is likely to be that it would be employment.

Where a worker is engaged on this type of contract for a period of one month or more, and cannot demonstrate a recent history of work including engagements which have the characteristics of self-employment (see the third example below) then we will say that the engagement would have been employment and therefore be covered by the new rules. Where the contract is for less than a month, then, although the engagement may still have been one of employment, the status position will be considered on a case by case basis.

Appendix 4

Examples

The examples which follow illustrate the process for deciding whether an engagement is employment or self-employment. These examples are purely illustrative. They do not indicate the IR's view of the employment status of particular groups of workers. The role of the IR is to provide advice and guidance about the employment status resulting from a given set of circumstances, not to impose any particular status. The terms and conditions of any engagement are entirely a matter for the parties involved.

Example 1—Gordon—an IT contractor working through his own service company

FACTS

Job description/control

Client is a large retail concern. The contract was obtained through an agency. The terms and conditions of the engagement are set out in the contracts between the client and the agency and the agency and Gordon's company.

Gordon works as part of a support team for the client's payroll system. The team leader (another IT contractor) tells Gordon what work he is to carry out at any particular time (eg help-desk work, specific maintenance tasks, etc).

COMMENTS

The fact that the engagement has been obtained through an agency has no bearing on whether Gordon would have been an employee or not.

FACTS

Job description/control—cont

The client has the right to tell Gordon 'how' the work should be carried out—although in practice such control is not normally necessary.

Gordon must work a regular forty-hour week on the client's premises.

Payment basis/risk

Gordon's company is paid an hourly rate for Gordon's services. Any extra hours worked (by mutual agreement) are paid at 1.5 times the normal hourly rate. The client makes payment monthly following submission of an invoice by the agency. Gordon's service company invoices the agency.

Holiday pay/sick pay

No sick pay or holiday pay paid under the terms of the inter-company contract.

Length of contract and personal factors

The contract is for six months.

Gordon uses a computer, telephone, fax, etc at home to seek and negotiate contracts for his company.

Gordon has worked through his company for two other clients in the last two and a half years—one for three months and one for two years. Prior to that he was a direct employee of another engager.

Appendix 4

COMMENTS

The extensive right of control that exists here is a very strong pointer to employment. The more important features are the client's ability to shift Gordon from task to task and to specify how the work should be done—but in addition the client can control where and when the work is carried out.

The company is paid an hourly rate for Gordon's services and the only financial risk comes from invoicing. There is no opportunity to profit from sound management of the work covered by the contract. Overall this points to employment.

The engagement runs for six months and holiday pay/sick pay might be expected had there been a direct engagement. But both parties see the actual company/client contract as a contract for services and this is probably why no such payments are made. A minor pointer to self-employment.

Gordon's company has a limited 'business organisation' consisting of an office and associated equipment at his home. This is a pointer to self-employment—but not an overly important one in the context of a six-month contract of this sort.

FACTS

Other factors

The company is contracted to supply Gordon to do the work personally.

All equipment and materials are supplied by the client.

Neither side can terminate the contract early.

There is no restriction imposed by the contract that prevents either Gordon or his company providing services to others during the engagement.

Both parties never intended Gordon to be an employee of the client.

COMMENTS

Both point to employment.

Neutral factor (no right to terminate is common in engagements of this length—whether employment or self-employment).

Mild pointer towards self-employment.

Pointer to self-employment, but will only be relevant if the other factors are neutral.

Overall picture

The engagement is fairly long term and there is an extensive right of control over Gordon. He must carry out the services personally. The client provides equipment and accommodation and there is no significant financial risk to the company.

The only pointers to self-employment are the minimal financial risk (from invoicing), the ability to work for others (again, a minor point) and the existence of a business organisation/work for other clients.

Standing back from the detail therefore the engagement is one which would have been an employment had it been direct between Gordon and the client. The common intention for self-employment does not alter that. Whilst it would have proved decisive in a 'borderline' situation a review of other factors points strongly to employment here. The new rules would apply to the engagement.

Appendix 4

Example 2—Henry—a consultant engineer working through his own service company

FACTS

Job description/control

Client is a large manufacturing company. Under a previous contract Henry has undertaken a broad review of a 15 year old production line and established that significant improvements could be made to the line to increase productivity. Under the current contract Henry is to produce a further report with detailed and costed proposals on the improvements and how they might be carried out with minimum disruption to production.

Henry has a free hand over how his work is carried out and when (although there is a deadline of three months for completion). However, Henry is required to keep the client fully informed about progress and the client can require Henry to modify proposals if any aspect seems unsuitable to them.

Payment basis/risk/opportunity to profit

Henry is paid £70 an hour but there is a ceiling of 300 hours on the work. If Henry takes longer than this he will only be paid extra if unforeseen difficulties arise or the client insists on unreasonable changes. If the work takes less than 300 hours Henry is only paid for the hours worked.

Holiday pay/sick pay

No sick pay or holiday pay paid under the terms of the inter-company contract.

COMMENTS

A specific task has been agreed and the client cannot shift the worker to another task. Henry has the major say over how the work is carried out and when. The clients does have some right to ongoing control over the work in that regular reports are required and changes in Henry's proposals can be sought.

Overall, control is limited.

Henry is being paid an hourly rate and there is no real prospect of his making a loss. Nevertheless he is subject to a ceiling and must complete the work in the time allowed for otherwise he will have to finish the work in his own time without further payment. This is a mild pointer to self-employment.

Pointer to self-employment.

FACTS

Length of contract and personal factors

The contract has a deadline of 3 months.

Henry has worked through his company as an engineer for many years and it is accepted that the company is 'in business'. The company has had many engagements similar to the current one and is generally engaged to provide an 'expert' service by clients with little engineering expertise.

Henry has an office and computer at home which he uses for work extensively.

Equipment

Henry visits the client's factory regularly to examine the production line and processes. The only significant equipment he uses is his own computer (to prepare the report). 70% of the work is done in his office.

Appendix 4

Other factors

Engagement cannot be terminated 'early' other than following a breach of contract.

There is no restriction imposed by the contract that prevents either Henry or his company providing services to others during the engagement.

Both parties intend that the company is engaged to carry out the work and that Henry is not an employee of the client.

COMMENTS

The company has a business organisation and many different clients. This is a significant pointer to self-employment.

Significant and fundamental equipment is provided by the company as is office accommodation. This points to self-employment.

Neutral factor (no right to terminate is common in engagements of this length—whether employment or self-employment).

Mild pointer towards self-employment.

Pointer to self-employment, but will only be relevant if the other factors are neutral.

Overall picture

Henry is a skilled worker who has been engaged to carry out a specific task and control over him is limited. He is paid based on an hourly rate but there is an over-riding limit within which the work agreed must be completed. There is a contract deadline of three months and the company has many other clients. Some important equipment is supplied by the company and the work is mainly carried out away from the client's premises.

Henry would have been self-employed if engaged directly by the client and the new rules will not apply. Even if the contract had been expected to last for a longer period—say, nine months—the other factors would still have led to a conclusion of self-employment.

Example 3—Charlotte—an IT consultant working through her own service company

FACTS

Job description/control

Charlotte's client for this engagement is a software company. She has been engaged for her programming skills to work on a specific project as part of a team developing a new piece of software. She works to the client's project manager who allocates particular sub-programs to Charlotte that she writes. The client expects the project to last for around three months.

The manager specifies the way in which the sub-program is to be structured and can require changes to be made to make the work fit in with other parts of the program as it is developed, to rectify overall design faults, etc.

Charlotte works a set number of hours but actual working times are flexible in line with the company's flexi-time arrangements for its employees. She is required to work at the client's premises.

Payment basis/risk/sick pay/holiday pay

Charlotte is paid £3,600 every four weeks in return for working a 40-hour week. Extra payments are made at the equivalent hourly rate for any additional hours agreed.

Appendix 4

COMMENTS

There is an extensive right of control over Charlotte. The more important features are the client's ability to shift Charlotte from task to task and to specify how the work should be done. In addition the client can control to some extent where and when the work is carried out. But control is not total. Charlotte is engaged to work on a specific project so cannot be told to work on something completely different—and she cannot be required to work elsewhere. Overall, this is a strong pointer to employment.

It is the arrangements between the service company and the client that are important here. The company is paid the equivalent of a salary—with overtime payments—but no sick pay

FACTS

Payment basis/risk/sick pay/holiday pay—cont

Payment is made 14 days after the company has invoiced the client.

No sick pay or holiday pay is paid; under the contract Charlotte has with her company she is paid an on-going, but much lower, salary which includes provision for holiday pay and sick pay.

Length of contract and personal factors

The contract is for 12 weeks—but there is provision for an extension if the project over-runs and all parties agree to the extension.

Charlotte does some work for another client at weekends and has worked for various clients in the past—always through her company and often through employment agencies. Her contracts have usually lasted for between one and three months. Most have been similar to this one but some have involved her in specific tasks for a fixed fee using her own equipment and working at home.

Charlotte has an office at home and a computer and other office equipment that is used for some of her other work. These contribute to her company's business organisation—which she uses to obtain work, keep records, prepare invoices, etc.

Other factors

The company is contracted to supply Charlotte to do the work personally.

All equipment is supplied by the client.

The engagement cannot be terminated 'early' other than following a breach of contract.

COMMENTS

or holiday pay. Although the invoicing arrangements result in a small financial risk this is minor. Overall there is no significant financial risk and no opportunity to profit from sound management of the task. This points to employment.

Charlotte and her company have a 'business organisation'—including an office and associated equipment based at Charlotte's home. She has a variety of clients and all her contracts have been fairly short term.

This is a strong pointer to self-employment.

Both point to employment.

Neutral factor (no right to terminate is common in engagements of this length—whether employment or self-employment).

Appendix 4

FACTS

Other factors—cont

There is no restriction imposed by the contract that prevents either Charlotte or her company providing services to others during the engagement.

All parties intended that the company/client engagement would be self-employment.

COMMENTS

Pointer to self-employment.

Pointer to self-employment, but will only be relevant if the other factors are neutral.

Overall picture

This is a borderline case. On balance, given all the facts, Charlotte would have been self-employed had she been engaged directly by the client. The new rules will not apply to the engagement.

The following point towards self-employment:

– Existing business and a variety of different engagements, some of which would clearly count as self-employed if she had been engaged directly by her client.

– Overall business organisation (office and equipment at home, business like approach to obtaining engagements and carrying them out, etc). Charlotte would clearly be regarded as being 'in business on her own account' for those engagements where she carried out of a specific task for a fixed fee using her own accommodation and equipment.

– Risk from invoicing.

– The lack of an exclusivity clause.

Other factors point to employment:

– There is fairly extensive control over Charlotte. The client can dictate 'what' work is carried out on the project and 'how' the work is done. But control is not total. Charlotte cannot be directed to work on another project or undertake some quite different work. Nor is there control in other areas (eg she subject to the clients normal staff rules/disciplinary procedures).

– There is virtually no financial risk in the engagement and no opportunity to profit from sound management of the task.

– Charlotte must carry out the work herself.

– All equipment and accommodation is provided by the client.

What can then have more significance is the extent to which the individual is dependant upon, or independent of, a particular paymaster for the financial exploitation of his or her talents (see *Hall v Lorimer*). The fact that Charlotte's company is also engaged in contracts which involve carrying out a specific task for a fixed fee, using her own equipment, suggests that it is a genuine business and neither she nor her company rely on a single client for the exploitation of her talents. These factors balance the control and other employment factors that exist in this particular context and put the matter near the borderline where the mutual intention for self-employment becomes decisive.

However, the overall picture would have been rather different had the engagement been longer. For example, had the engagement been for twelve months the 'personal factors' would have been far less significant and the employment pointers would have predominated.

Appendix 4

Just because a person has an established business does not automatically make them self-employed for all engagements (see *Fall v Hitchin* ((1972) 49 TC 433)—also referred to in *Hall v Lorimer*). Also, if she had not also had contracts of a type which would clearly have fallen within the definition of self-employment, employment pointers would have dominated and the contract at issue would have been one of employment. The same could apply to shorter contracts.

Appendix 5

The Tribunal Procedure (First-tier Tribunal) (Tax Chamber) Rules SI 2009/293

Made - - - -	5th February 2009
Laid before Parliament	13th February 2009
Coming into force - -	1st April 2009

CONTENTS

PART 1
Introduction

1. Citation, commencement, application and interpretation
2. Overriding objective and parties' obligation to co-operate with the Tribunal
3. Alternative dispute resolution and arbitration

PART 2
General powers and provisions

4. Delegation to staff
5. Case management powers
6. Procedure for applying for and giving directions
7. Failure to comply with rules etc.
8. Striking out a party's case
9. Substitution and addition of parties
10. Orders for costs
11. Representatives
12. Calculating time
13. Sending and delivery of documents
14. Use of documents and information
15. Evidence and submissions
16. Summoning or citation of witnesses and orders to answer questions or produce documents
17. Withdrawal
18. Lead cases

Appendix 5

PART 3
Procedure before the Tribunal
CHAPTER 1
Starting proceedings and allocation of cases to categories

19. Proceedings without notice to a respondent
20. Starting appeal proceedings
21. Starting proceedings by originating application or reference
22. Hardship applications
23. Allocation of cases to categories

CHAPTER 2
Procedure after allocation of cases to categories

24. Basic cases
25. Respondent's statement of case
26. Further steps in a Default Paper case
27. Further steps in a Standard or Complex case
28. Transfer of Complex cases to the Upper Tribunal

CHAPTER 3
Hearings

29. Determination with or without a hearing
30. Entitlement to attend a hearing
31. Notice of hearings
32. Public and private hearings
33. Hearings in a party's absence

CHAPTER 4
Decisions

34. Consent orders
35. Notice of decisions and reasons

PART 4
Correcting, setting aside, reviewing and appealing Tribunal decisions

36. Interpretation
37. Clerical mistakes and accidental slips or omissions
38. Setting aside a decision which disposes of proceedings
39. Application for permission to appeal
40. Tribunal's consideration of application for permission to appeal
41. Review of a decision
42. Power to treat an application as a different type of application

After consulting in accordance with paragraph 28(1) of Schedule 5 to the Tribunals, Courts and Enforcement Act 2007(**a**), the Tribunal Procedure Committee has made the following Rules in exercise of the power conferred by sections 9(3), 22 and 29(3) of, and Schedule 5 to, that Act.

The Lord Chancellor has allowed the Rules in accordance with paragraph 28(3) of Schedule 5 to the Tribunals, Courts and Enforcement Act 2007.

(**a**) 2007 c.15.

Appendix 5

PART 1
Introduction

Citation, commencement, application and interpretation

1.—(1) These Rules may be cited as the Tribunal Procedure (First-tier Tribunal) (Tax Chamber) Rules 2009 and come into force on 1st April 2009.

(2) These Rules apply to proceedings before the Tribunal which have been allocated to the Tax Chamber by the First-tier Tribunal and Upper Tribunal (Chambers) Order 2008(**a**).

(3) In these Rules—

"the 2007 Act" means the Tribunals, Courts and Enforcement Act 2007;

"appellant" means—

(a) the person who starts proceedings (whether by bringing or notifying an appeal, by making an originating application, by a reference, or otherwise);

(b) in proceedings started jointly by more than one person, such persons acting jointly or each such person, as the context requires;

(c) a person substituted as an appellant under rule 9 (substitution and addition of parties);

"Basic case" means a case allocated to the Basic category under rule 23 (allocation of cases to categories);

"Complex case" means a case allocated to the Complex category under rule 23 (allocation of cases to categories);

"Default Paper case" means a case allocated to the Default Paper category under rule 23 (allocation of cases to categories);

"document" means anything in which information is recorded in any form, and an obligation under these Rules to provide or allow access to a document or a copy of a document for any purpose means, unless the Tribunal directs otherwise, an obligation to provide or allow access to such document or copy in a legible form or in a form which can be readily made into a legible form;

"hearing" means an oral hearing and includes a hearing conducted in whole or in part by video link, telephone or other means of instantaneous two-way electronic communication;

"HMRC" means Her Majesty's Revenue and Customs and includes the Serious Organised Crime Agency when carrying out functions under section 317 of the Proceeds of Crime Act 2002(**b**);

"party" means a person who is (or was at the time that the Tribunal disposed of the proceedings) an appellant or respondent in proceedings before the Tribunal;

"practice direction" means a direction given under section 23 of the 2007 Act;

"respondent" means—

(a) HMRC, where the appellant (or one of them) is not HMRC;

(b) in proceedings brought by HMRC alone, a person against whom the proceedings are brought or to whom the proceedings relate;

(c) a person substituted or added as a respondent under rule 9 (substitution and addition of parties);

"Standard case" means a case allocated to the Standard category under rule 23 (allocation of cases to categories);

(**a**) S.I. 2008/2684. The Order is amended by the First-tier Tribunal and Upper Tribunal (Chambers) (Amendment) Order 2009 (S.I. 2009/196).
(**b**) 2002 c.29.

Appendix 5

"Tax Chamber" means the Tax Chamber of the First-tier Tribunal established by the First-tier Tribunal and Upper Tribunal (Chambers) Order 2008;

"Tribunal" means the First-tier Tribunal.

Overriding objective and parties' obligation to co-operate with the Tribunal

2.—(1) The overriding objective of these Rules is to enable the Tribunal to deal with cases fairly and justly.

(2) Dealing with a case fairly and justly includes—

   (a) dealing with the case in ways which are proportionate to the importance of the case, the complexity of the issues, the anticipated costs and the resources of the parties;

   (b) avoiding unnecessary formality and seeking flexibility in the proceedings;

   (c) ensuring, so far as practicable, that the parties are able to participate fully in the proceedings;

   (d) using any special expertise of the Tribunal effectively; and

   (e) avoiding delay, so far as compatible with proper consideration of the issues.

(3) The Tribunal must seek to give effect to the overriding objective when it—

   (a) exercises any power under these Rules; or

   (b) interprets any rule or practice direction.

(4) Parties must—

   (a) help the Tribunal to further the overriding objective; and

   (b) co-operate with the Tribunal generally.

Alternative dispute resolution and arbitration

3.—(1) The Tribunal should seek, where appropriate—

   (a) to bring to the attention of the parties the availability of any appropriate alternative procedure for the resolution of the dispute; and

   (b) if the parties wish and provided that it is compatible with the overriding objective, to facilitate the use of the procedure.

(2) Part 1 of the Arbitration Act 1996(a) does not apply to proceedings before the Tribunal.

PART 2

General powers and provisions

Delegation to staff

4.—(1) Staff appointed under section 40(1) of the 2007 Act (tribunal staff and services) may, with the approval of the Senior President of Tribunals, carry out functions of a judicial nature permitted or required to be done by the Tribunal.

(2) The approval referred to at paragraph (1) may apply generally to the carrying out of specified functions by members of staff of a specified description in specified circumstances.

(3) Within 14 days after the date that the Tribunal sends notice of a decision made by a member of staff pursuant to an approval under paragraph (1) to a party, that party may make a written application to the Tribunal requiring that decision to be considered afresh by a judge.

(a) 1996 c.23.

Appendix 5

Case management powers

5.—(1) Subject to the provisions of the 2007 Act and any other enactment, the Tribunal may regulate its own procedure.

(2) The Tribunal may give a direction in relation to the conduct or disposal of proceedings at any time, including a direction amending, suspending or setting aside an earlier direction.

(3) In particular, and without restricting the general powers in paragraphs (1) and (2), the Tribunal may by direction—

- (a) extend or shorten the time for complying with any rule, practice direction or direction, unless such extension or shortening would conflict with a provision of another enactment setting down a time limit;
- (b) consolidate or hear together two or more sets of proceedings or parts of proceedings raising common issues, or treat a case as a lead case (whether in accordance with rule 18 (lead cases) or otherwise);
- (c) permit or require a party to amend a document;
- (d) permit or require a party or another person to provide documents, information or submissions to the Tribunal or a party;
- (e) deal with an issue in the proceedings as a preliminary issue;
- (f) hold a hearing to consider any matter, including a case management hearing;
- (g) decide the form of any hearing;
- (h) adjourn or postpone a hearing;
- (i) require a party to produce a bundle for a hearing;
- (j) stay (or, in Scotland, sist) proceedings;
- (k) transfer proceedings to another tribunal if that other tribunal has jurisdiction in relation to the proceedings and, because of a change of circumstances since the proceedings were started—
    - (i) the Tribunal no longer has jurisdiction in relation to the proceedings; or
    - (ii) the Tribunal considers that the other tribunal is a more appropriate forum for the determination of the case;
- (l) suspend the effect of its own decision pending the determination by the Tribunal or the Upper Tribunal, as the case may be, of an application for permission to appeal, a review or an appeal.

Procedure for applying for and giving directions

6.—(1) The Tribunal may give a direction on the application of one or more of the parties or on its own initiative.

(2) An application for a direction may be made—

- (a) by sending or delivering a written application to the Tribunal; or
- (b) orally during the course of a hearing.

(3) An application for a direction must include the reasons for making that application.

(4) Unless the Tribunal considers that there is good reason not to do so, the Tribunal must send written notice of any direction to every party and to any other person affected by the direction.

(5) If a party or other person sent notice of the direction under paragraph (4) wishes to challenge a direction which the Tribunal has given, they may do so by applying for another direction which amends, suspends or sets aside the first direction.

Appendix 5

Failure to comply with rules etc.

7.—(1) An irregularity resulting from a failure to comply with any requirement in these Rules, a practice direction or a direction does not of itself render void the proceedings or any step taken in the proceedings.

(2) If a party has failed to comply with a requirement in these Rules, a practice direction or a direction, the Tribunal may take such action as it considers just, which may include—

(a) waiving the requirement;

(b) requiring the failure to be remedied;

(c) exercising its power under rule 8 (striking out a party's case);

(d) restricting a party's participation in proceedings; or

(e) exercising its power under paragraph (3).

(3) The Tribunal may refer to the Upper Tribunal, and ask the Upper Tribunal to exercise its power under section 25 of the 2007 Act (Upper Tribunal to have powers of High Court or Court of Session) in relation to, any failure by a person to comply with a requirement imposed by the Tribunal—

(a) to attend at any place for the purpose of giving evidence;

(b) otherwise to make themselves available to give evidence;

(c) to swear an oath in connection with the giving of evidence;

(d) to give evidence as a witness;

(e) to produce a document; or

(f) to facilitate the inspection of a document or any other thing (including any premises).

Striking out a party's case

8.—(1) The proceedings, or the appropriate part of them, will automatically be struck out if the appellant has failed to comply with a direction that stated that failure by a party to comply with the direction would lead to the striking out of the proceedings or that part of them.

(2) The Tribunal must strike out the whole or a part of the proceedings if the Tribunal—

(a) does not have jurisdiction in relation to the proceedings or that part of them; and

(b) does not exercise its power under rule 5(3)(k)(i) (transfer to another court or tribunal) in relation to the proceedings or that part of them.

(3) The Tribunal may strike out the whole or a part of the proceedings if—

(a) the appellant has failed to comply with a direction which stated that failure by the appellant to comply with the direction could lead to the striking out of the proceedings or part of them;

(b) the appellant has failed to co-operate with the Tribunal to such an extent that the Tribunal cannot deal with the proceedings fairly and justly; or

(c) the Tribunal considers there is no reasonable prospect of the appellant's case, or part of it, succeeding.

(4) The Tribunal may not strike out the whole or a part of the proceedings under paragraphs (2) or (3)(b) or (c) without first giving the appellant an opportunity to make representations in relation to the proposed striking out.

(5) If the proceedings, or part of them, have been struck out under paragraphs (1) or (3)(a), the appellant may apply for the proceedings, or part of them, to be reinstated.

(6) An application under paragraph (5) must be made in writing and received by the Tribunal within 28 days after the date that the Tribunal sent notification of the striking out to the appellant.

(7) This rule applies to a respondent as it applies to an appellant except that—

Appendix 5

(a) a reference to the striking out of the proceedings must be read as a reference to the barring of the respondent from taking further part in the proceedings; and

(b) a reference to an application for the reinstatement of proceedings which have been struck out must be read as a reference to an application for the lifting of the bar on the respondent taking further part in the proceedings.

(8) If a respondent has been barred from taking further part in proceedings under this rule and that bar has not been lifted, the Tribunal need not consider any response or other submissions made by that respondent, and may summarily determine any or all issues against that respondent.

Substitution and addition of parties

9.—(1) The Tribunal may give a direction substituting a party if—

(a) the wrong person has been named as a party; or

(b) the substitution has become necessary because of a change in circumstances since the start of proceedings.

(2) The Tribunal may give a direction adding a person to the proceedings as a respondent.

(3) A person who is not a party to proceedings may make an application to be added as a party under this rule.

(4) If the Tribunal refuses an application under paragraph (3) it must consider whether to permit the person who made the application to provide submissions or evidence to the Tribunal.

(5) If the Tribunal gives a direction under paragraph (1) or (2) it may give such consequential directions as it considers appropriate.

Orders for costs

10.—(1) The Tribunal may only make an order in respect of costs (or, in Scotland, expenses)—

(a) under section 29(4) of the 2007 Act (wasted costs);

(b) if the Tribunal considers that a party or their representative has acted unreasonably in bringing, defending or conducting the proceedings; or

(c) if—

(i) the proceedings have been allocated as a Complex case under rule 23 (allocation of cases to categories); and

(ii) the taxpayer (or, where more than one party is a taxpayer, one of them) has not sent or delivered a written request to the Tribunal, within 28 days of receiving notice that the case had been allocated as a Complex case, that the proceedings be excluded from potential liability for costs or expenses under this sub-paragraph.

(2) The Tribunal may make an order under paragraph (1) on an application or of its own initiative.

(3) A person making an application for an order under paragraph (1) must—

(a) send or deliver a written application to the Tribunal and to the person against whom it is proposed that the order be made; and

(b) send or deliver with the application a schedule of the costs or expenses claimed in sufficient detail to allow the Tribunal to undertake a summary assessment of such costs or expenses if it decides to do so.

(4) An application for an order under paragraph (1) may be made at any time during the proceedings but may not be made later than 28 days after the date on which the Tribunal sends—

(a) a decision notice recording the decision which finally disposes of all issues in the proceedings; or

(b) notice of a withdrawal under rule 17 (withdrawal) which ends the proceedings.

(5) The Tribunal may not make an order under paragraph (1) against a person (the "paying person") without first—

  (a) giving that person an opportunity to make representations; and

  (b) if the paying person is an individual, considering that person's financial means.

(6) The amount of costs (or, in Scotland, expenses) to be paid under an order under paragraph (1) may be ascertained by—

  (a) summary assessment by the Tribunal;

  (b) agreement of a specified sum by the paying person and the person entitled to receive the costs or expenses (the "receiving person"); or

  (c) assessment of the whole or a specified part of the costs or expenses incurred by the receiving person, if not agreed.

(7) Following an order for assessment under paragraph (6)(c) the paying person or the receiving person may apply—

  (a) in England and Wales, to a county court, the High Court or the Costs Office of the Supreme Court (as specified in the order) for a detailed assessment of the costs on the standard basis or, if specified in the order, on the indemnity basis; and the Civil Procedure Rules 1998(a) shall apply, with necessary modifications, to that application and assessment as if the proceedings in the tribunal had been proceedings in a court to which the Civil Procedure Rules 1998 apply;

  (b) in Scotland, to the Auditor of the Sheriff Court or the Court of Session (as specified in the order) for the taxation of the expenses according to the fees payable in that court; or

  (c) in Northern Ireland, to the Taxing Office of the High Court of Northern Ireland for taxation on the standard basis or, if specified in the order, on the indemnity basis.

(8) In this rule "taxpayer" means a party who is liable to pay, or has paid, the tax, duty, levy or penalty to which the proceedings relate or part of such tax, duty, levy or penalty, or whose liability to do so is in issue in the proceedings;

Representatives

11.—(1) A party may appoint a representative (whether a legal representative or not) to represent that party in the proceedings.

(2) If a party appoints a representative, that party (or the representative if the representative is a legal representative) must send or deliver to the Tribunal and to each other party to the proceedings written notice of the representative's name and address.

(3) Anything permitted or required to be done by a party under these Rules, a practice direction or a direction may be done by the representative of that party, except signing a witness statement.

(4) A person who receives due notice of the appointment of a representative—

  (a) must provide to the representative any document which is required to be provided to the represented party, and need not provide that document to the represented party; and

  (b) may assume that the representative is and remains authorised as such until they receive written notification that this is not so from the representative or the represented party.

(5) At a hearing a party may be accompanied by another person who, with the permission of the Tribunal, may act as a representative or otherwise assist in presenting the party's case at the hearing.

(6) Paragraphs (2) to (4) do not apply to a person (other than an appointed representative) who accompanies a party in accordance with paragraph (5).

(a) S.I. 1998/3132.

Appendix 5

(7) In this rule "legal representative" means an authorised advocate or authorised litigator as defined by section 119(1) of the Courts and Legal Services Act 1990(**a**), an advocate or solicitor in Scotland, or a barrister or solicitor in Northern Ireland.

Calculating time

12.—(1) An act required by these Rules, a practice direction or a direction to be done on or by a particular day must be done before 5pm on that day.

(2) If the time specified by these Rules, a practice direction or a direction for doing any act ends on a day other than a working day, the act is done in time if it is done on the next working day.

(3) In this rule "working day" means any day except a Saturday or Sunday, Christmas Day, Good Friday or a bank holiday under section 1 of the Banking and Financial Dealings Act 1971(**b**).

Sending and delivery of documents

13.—(1) Any document to be provided to the Tribunal under these Rules, a practice direction or a direction must be—
   (a) sent by pre-paid post or document exchange, or delivered by hand, to the address specified for the proceedings; or
   (b) sent or delivered by such other method as the Tribunal may permit or direct.

(2) Subject to paragraph (3), if a party or representative provides a fax number, email address or other details for the electronic transmission of documents to them, that party or representative must accept delivery of documents by that method.

(3) If a party informs the Tribunal and all other parties that a particular form of communication (other than pre-paid post or delivery by hand) should not be used to provide documents to that party, that form of communication must not be so used.

(4) If the Tribunal or a party sends a document to a party or the Tribunal by email or any other electronic means of communication, the recipient may request that the sender provide a hard copy of the document to the recipient. The recipient must make such a request as soon as reasonably practicable after receiving the document electronically.

(5) The Tribunal and each party may assume that the address provided by a party or its representative is and remains the address to which documents should be sent or delivered until receiving written notification to the contrary.

Use of documents and information

14. The Tribunal may make an order prohibiting the disclosure or publication of—
   (a) specified documents or information relating to the proceedings; or
   (b) any matter likely to lead members of the public to identify any person whom the Tribunal considers should not be identified.

Evidence and submissions

15.—(1) Without restriction on the general powers in rule 5(1) and (2) (case management powers), the Tribunal may give directions as to—
   (a) issues on which it requires evidence or submissions;
   (b) the nature of the evidence or submissions it requires;
   (c) whether the parties are permitted or required to provide expert evidence, and if so whether the parties must jointly appoint a single expert to provide such evidence;

(**a**) 1990 c.41.
(**b**) 1971 c.80.

(d) any limit on the number of witnesses whose evidence a party may put forward, whether in relation to a particular issue or generally;

(e) the manner in which any evidence or submissions are to be provided, which may include a direction for them to be given—

   (i) orally at a hearing; or

   (ii) by written submissions or witness statement; and

(f) the time at which any evidence or submissions are to be provided.

(2) The Tribunal may—

(a) admit evidence whether or not the evidence would be admissible in a civil trial in the United Kingdom; or

(b) exclude evidence that would otherwise be admissible where—

   (i) the evidence was not provided within the time allowed by a direction or a practice direction;

   (ii) the evidence was otherwise provided in a manner that did not comply with a direction or a practice direction; or

   (iii) it would otherwise be unfair to admit the evidence.

(3) The Tribunal may consent to a witness giving, or require any witness to give, evidence on oath, and may administer an oath for that purpose.

Summoning or citation of witnesses and orders to answer questions or produce documents

16.—(1) On the application of a party or on its own initiative, the Tribunal may—

(a) by summons (or, in Scotland, citation) require any person to attend as a witness at a hearing at the time and place specified in the summons or citation;

(b) order any person to answer any questions or produce any documents in that person's possession or control which relate to any issue in the proceedings.

(2) A summons or citation under paragraph (1)(a) must—

(a) give the person required to attend at least 14 days' notice of the hearing, or such shorter period as the Tribunal may direct; and

(b) where the person is not a party, make provision for the person's necessary expenses of attendance to be paid, and state who is to pay them.

(3) No person may be compelled to give any evidence or produce any document that the person could not be compelled to give or produce on a trial of an action in a court of law in the part of the United Kingdom where the proceedings are due to be determined.

(4) A person who receives a summons, citation or order may apply to the Tribunal for it to be varied or set aside if they did not have an opportunity to object to it before it was made or issued.

(5) A person making an application under paragraph (4) must do so as soon as reasonably practicable after receiving notice of the summons, citation or order.

(6) A summons, citation or order under this rule must—

(a) state that the person on whom the requirement is imposed may apply to the Tribunal to vary or set aside the summons, citation or order, if they did not have an opportunity to object to it before it was made or issued; and

(b) state the consequences of failure to comply with the summons, citation or order.

Withdrawal

17.—(1) Subject to any provision in an enactment relating to withdrawal or settlement of particular proceedings, a party may give notice to the Tribunal of the withdrawal of the case made by it in the Tribunal proceedings, or any part of that case—

Appendix 5

(a) at any time before a hearing to consider the disposal of the proceedings (or, if the Tribunal disposes of the proceedings without a hearing, before that disposal), by sending or delivering to the Tribunal a written notice of withdrawal; or

(b) orally at a hearing.

(2) The Tribunal must notify each other party in writing of a withdrawal under this rule.

(3) A party who has withdrawn their case may apply to the Tribunal for the case to be reinstated.

(4) An application under paragraph (3) must be made in writing and be received by the Tribunal within 28 days after—

(a) the date that the Tribunal received the notice under paragraph (1)(a); or

(b) the date of the hearing at which the case was withdrawn orally under paragraph (1)(b).

Lead cases

18.—(1) This rule applies if—

(a) two or more cases have been started before the Tribunal;

(b) in each such case the Tribunal has not made a decision disposing of the proceedings; and

(c) the cases give rise to common or related issues of fact or law.

(2) The Tribunal may give a direction—

(a) specifying one or more cases falling under paragraph (1) as a lead case or lead cases; and

(b) staying (or, in Scotland, sisting) the other cases falling under paragraph (1) ("the related cases").

(3) When the Tribunal makes a decision in respect of the common or related issues—

(a) the Tribunal must send a copy of that decision to each party in each of the related cases; and

(b) subject to paragraph (4), that decision shall be binding on each of those parties.

(4) Within 28 days after the date that the Tribunal sent a copy of the decision to a party under paragraph (3)(a), that party may apply in writing for a direction that the decision does not apply to, and is not binding on the parties to, that case.

(5) The Tribunal must give directions in respect of cases which are stayed or sisted under paragraph (2)(b), providing for the disposal of or further steps in those cases.

(6) If the lead case or cases are withdrawn or disposed of before the Tribunal makes a decision in respect of the common or related issues, the Tribunal must give directions as to—

(a) whether another case or other cases are to be heard as a lead case or lead cases; and

(b) whether any direction affecting the related cases should be set aside or amended.

PART 3

Procedure before the Tribunal

CHAPTER 1

Starting proceedings and allocation of cases to categories

Proceedings without notice to a respondent

19. If a case or matter is to be determined without notice to or the involvement of a respondent—

(a) any provision in these Rules requiring a document to be provided by or to a respondent; and

Appendix 5

(b) any other provision in these Rules permitting a respondent to participate in the proceedings

does not apply to that case or matter.

Starting appeal proceedings

20.—(1) Where an enactment provides for a person to make or notify an appeal to the Tribunal, the appellant must start proceedings by sending or delivering a notice of appeal to the Tribunal within any time limit imposed by that enactment.

(2) The notice of appeal must include—
   (a) the name and address of the appellant;
   (b) the name and address of the appellant's representative (if any);
   (c) an address where documents for the appellant may be sent or delivered;
   (d) details of the decision appealed against;
   (e) the result the appellant is seeking; and
   (f) the grounds for making the appeal.

(3) The appellant must provide with the notice of appeal a copy of any written record of any decision appealed against, and any statement of reasons for that decision, that the appellant has or can reasonably obtain.

(4) If the appellant provides the notice of appeal to the Tribunal later than the time required by paragraph (1) or by an extension of time allowed under rule 5(3)(a) (power to extend time)—
   (a) the notice of appeal must include a request for an extension of time and the reason why the notice of appeal was not provided in time; and
   (b) unless the Tribunal extends time for the notice of appeal under rule 5(3)(a) (power to extend time) the Tribunal must not admit the notice of appeal.

(5) When the Tribunal receives the notice of appeal it must give notice of the proceedings to the respondent.

Starting proceedings by originating application or reference

21.—(1) Where an enactment provides for a person or persons to make an originating application or reference to the Tribunal, the appellant must start proceedings by providing an application notice or notice of reference to the Tribunal within any time limit imposed by that enactment.

(2) The application notice or notice of reference must state—
   (a) the name and address of the appellant;
   (b) the name and address of the appellant's representative (if any);
   (c) an address where documents for the appellant may be sent or delivered;
   (d) the name and address of each respondent (if any);
   (e) the facts relevant to the originating application or reference;
   (f) the result the appellant is seeking (if any); and
   (g) the grounds for making the originating application or reference.

(3) If the appellant provides the application notice or notice of reference to the Tribunal later than the time required by paragraph (1) or by any extension of time under rule 5(3)(a) (power to extend time)—
   (a) the application notice or notice of reference must include a request for an extension of time and the reason why the application notice or notice of reference was not provided in time; and

Appendix 5

(b) unless the Tribunal extends time for the application notice or notice of reference under rule 5(3)(a) (power to extend time) the Tribunal must not admit the application notice or notice of reference.

(4) When the Tribunal receives an application notice or a notice of reference it must send a copy of the notice and any accompanying document to any respondent.

Hardship applications

22.—(1) This rule applies where an enactment provides, in any terms, that an appeal may not proceed if the liability to pay the amount in dispute is outstanding unless HMRC or the Tribunal consent to the appeal proceeding.

(2) When starting proceedings, the appellant must include or provide the following in or with the notice of appeal—

(a) a statement as to whether the appellant has paid the amount in dispute;

(b) if the appellant has not paid the amount in dispute, a statement as to the status or outcome of any application to HMRC for consent to the appeal proceeding; and

(c) if HMRC have refused such an application, an application to the Tribunal for consent to the appeal proceeding.

(3) An application under paragraph (2)(c) must include the reasons for the application and a list of any documents the appellant intends to produce or rely upon in support of that application.

(4) If the appellant requires the consent of HMRC or the Tribunal before the appeal may proceed, the Tribunal must stay the proceedings until any applications to HMRC or the Tribunal in that respect have been determined.

Allocation of cases to categories

23.—(1) When the Tribunal receives a notice of appeal, application notice or notice of reference, the Tribunal must give a direction allocating the case to one of the categories set out in paragraph (2).

(2) The categories referred to in paragraph (1) are—

(a) Default Paper cases, which will usually be disposed of without a hearing;

(b) Basic cases, which will usually be disposed of after a hearing, with minimal exchange of documents before the hearing;

(c) Standard cases, which will usually be subject to more detailed case management and be disposed of after a hearing; and

(d) Complex cases, in respect of which see paragraphs (4) and (5) below.

(3) The Tribunal may give a further direction re-allocating a case to a different category at any time, either on the application of a party or on its own initiative.

(4) The Tribunal may allocate a case as a Complex case under paragraph (1) or (3) only if the Tribunal considers that the case—

(a) will require lengthy or complex evidence or a lengthy hearing;

(b) involves a complex or important principle or issue; or

(c) involves a large financial sum.

(5) If a case is allocated as a Complex case—

(a) rule 10(1)(c) (costs in Complex cases) applies to the case; and

(b) rule 28 (transfer of Complex cases to the Upper Tribunal) applies to the case.

Appendix 5

CHAPTER 2

Procedure after allocation of cases to categories

Basic cases

24.—(1) This rule applies to Basic cases.

(2) Rule 25 (respondent's statement of case) does not apply and, subject to paragraph (3) and any direction given by the Tribunal, the case will proceed directly to a hearing.

(3) If the respondent intends to raise grounds for contesting the proceedings at the hearing which have not previously been communicated to the appellant, the respondent must notify the appellant of such grounds.

(4) If the respondent is required to notify the appellant of any grounds under paragraph (3), the respondent must do so—

   (a) as soon as reasonably practicable after becoming aware that such is the case; and

   (b) in sufficient detail to enable the appellant to respond to such grounds at the hearing.

Respondent's statement of case

25.—(1) A respondent must send or deliver a statement of case to the Tribunal, the appellant and any other respondent so that it is received—

   (a) in a Default Paper case, within 42 days after the tribunal sent the notice of the appeal or a copy of the application notice or notice of reference; or

   (b) in a Standard or Complex case, within 60 days after the tribunal sent the notice of the appeal or a copy of the application notice or notice of reference.

(2) A statement of case must—

   (a) in an appeal, state the legislative provision under which the decision under appeal was made; and

   (b) set out the respondent's position in relation to the case.

(3) A statement of case may also contain a request that the case be dealt with at a hearing or without a hearing.

(4) If a respondent provides a statement of case to the Tribunal later than the time required by paragraph (1) or by any extension allowed under rule 5(3)(a) (power to extend time), the statement of case must include a request for an extension of time and the reason why the statement of case was not provided in time.

Further steps in a Default Paper case

26.—(1) This rule applies to Default Paper cases.

(2) The appellant may send or deliver a written reply to the Tribunal so that it is received within 30 days after the date on which the respondent sent to the appellant the statement of case to which the reply relates.

(3) The appellant's reply may—

   (a) set out the appellant's response to the respondent's statement of case;

   (b) provide any further information (including, where appropriate, copies of the documents containing such information) which has not yet been provided to the Tribunal and is relevant to the case; and

   (c) contain a request that the case be dealt with at a hearing.

(4) The appellant must send or deliver a copy of any reply provided under paragraph (2) to each respondent at the same time as it is provided to the Tribunal.

Appendix 5

(5) If the appellant provides a reply to the Tribunal later than the time required by paragraph (2) or by any extension allowed under rule 5(3)(a) (power to extend time), the reply must include a request for an extension of time and the reason why the reply was not provided in time.

(6) Following receipt of the appellant's reply, or the expiry of the time for the receipt of the appellant's reply then, unless it directs otherwise and subject in any event to paragraph (7), the Tribunal must proceed to determine the case without a hearing.

(7) If any party has made a written request to the Tribunal for a hearing, the Tribunal must hold a hearing before determining the case.

Further steps in a Standard or Complex case

27.—(1) This rule applies to Standard and Complex cases.

(2) Subject to any direction to the contrary, within 42 days after the date the respondent sent the statement of case (or, where there is more than one respondent, the date of the final statement of case) each party must send or deliver to the Tribunal and to each other party a list of documents—

  (a) of which the party providing the list has possession, the right to possession, or the right to take copies; and

  (b) which the party providing the list intends to rely upon or produce in the proceedings.

(3) A party which has provided a list of documents under paragraph (2) must allow each other party to inspect or take copies of the documents on the list (except any documents which are privileged).

Transfer of Complex cases to the Upper Tribunal

28.—(1) If a case has been allocated as a Complex case the Tribunal may, with the consent of the parties, refer a case to the President of the Tax Chamber with a request that the case be considered for transfer to the Upper Tribunal.

(2) If a case has been referred by the Tribunal under paragraph (1), the President of the Tax Chamber may, with the concurrence of the President of the Finance and Tax Chamber of the Upper Tribunal (if that is a different person) direct that the case be transferred to and determined by the Upper Tribunal.

CHAPTER 3

Hearings

Determination with or without a hearing

29.—(1) Subject to rule 26(6) (determination of a Default Paper case without a hearing) and the following paragraphs in this rule, the Tribunal must hold a hearing before making a decision which disposes of proceedings, or a part of proceedings, unless—

  (a) each party has consented to the matter being decided without a hearing; and

  (b) the Tribunal considers that it is able to decide the matter without a hearing.

(2) This rule does not apply to decisions under Part 4 (correcting, setting aside, reviewing and appealing Tribunal decisions).

(3) The Tribunal may dispose of proceedings, or a part of proceedings, without a hearing under rule 8 (striking out a party's case).

Entitlement to attend a hearing

30. Subject to rules 19 (proceedings without notice to a respondent) and 32(4) (exclusion from a hearing), each party to proceedings is entitled to attend a hearing.

Appendix 5

Notice of hearings

31.—(1) The Tribunal must give each party entitled to attend a hearing reasonable notice of the time and place of any hearing (including any adjourned or postponed hearing) and any changes to the time and place of any hearing.

(2) In relation to a hearing to consider the disposal of proceedings, the period of notice under paragraph (1) must be at least 14 days except that the Tribunal may give less than 14 days' notice—

(a) with the parties' consent; or

(b) in urgent or exceptional circumstances.

Public and private hearings

32.—(1) Subject to the following paragraphs, all hearings must be held in public.

(2) The Tribunal may give a direction that a hearing, or part of it, is to be held in private if the Tribunal considers that restricting access to the hearing is justified—

(a) in the interests of public order or national security;

(b) in order to protect a person's right to respect for their private and family life;

(c) in order to maintain the confidentiality of sensitive information;

(d) in order to avoid serious harm to the public interest; or

(e) because not to do so would prejudice the interests of justice.

(3) Where a hearing, or part of it, is to be held in private, the Tribunal may determine who is permitted to attend the hearing or part of it.

(4) The Tribunal may give a direction excluding from any hearing, or part of it—

(a) any person whose conduct the Tribunal considers is disrupting or is likely to disrupt the hearing;

(b) any person whose presence the Tribunal considers is likely to prevent another person from giving evidence or making submissions freely;

(c) any person where the purpose of the hearing would be defeated by the attendance of that person; or

(d) a person under the age of eighteen years.

(5) The Tribunal may give a direction excluding a witness from a hearing until that witness gives evidence.

(6) If the Tribunal publishes a report of a decision resulting from a hearing which was held wholly or partly in private, the Tribunal must, so far as practicable, ensure that the report does not disclose information which was referred to only in a part of the hearing that was held in private (including such information which enables the identification of any person whose affairs were dealt with in the part of the hearing that was held in private) if to do so would undermine the purpose of holding the hearing in private.

Hearings in a party's absence

33. If a party fails to attend a hearing the Tribunal may proceed with the hearing if the Tribunal—

(a) is satisfied that the party has been notified of the hearing or that reasonable steps have been taken to notify the party of the hearing; and

(b) considers that it is in the interests of justice to proceed with the hearing.

Appendix 5

CHAPTER 4
Decisions

Consent orders

34.—(1) The Tribunal may, at the request of the parties but only if it considers it appropriate, make a consent order disposing of the proceedings and making such other appropriate provision as the parties have agreed.

(2) Notwithstanding any other provision of these Rules, the Tribunal need not hold a hearing before making an order under paragraph (1), or provide reasons for the order.

Notice of decisions and reasons

35.—(1) The Tribunal may give a decision orally at a hearing.

(2) The Tribunal must provide to each party within 28 days after making a decision which finally disposes of all issues in proceedings (except a decision under Part 4), or as soon as practicable thereafter, a decision notice which—
   (a) states the Tribunal's decision; and
   (b) notifies the party of any right of appeal against the decision and the time within which, and the manner in which, the right of appeal may be exercised.

(3) Unless each party agrees that it is unnecessary, the decision notice must—
   (a) include a summary of the findings of fact and reasons for the decision; or
   (b) be accompanied by full written findings of fact and reasons for the decision.

(4) If the Tribunal provides no findings and reasons, or summary findings and reasons only, in or with the decision notice, a party to the proceedings may apply for full written findings and reasons, and must do so before making an application for permission to appeal under rule 39 (application for permission to appeal).

(5) An application under paragraph (4) must be made in writing and be sent or delivered to the Tribunal so that it is received within 28 days after the date that the Tribunal sent or otherwise provided the decision notice under paragraph (2) to the party making the application.

(6) The Tribunal must send a full written statement of findings and reasons to each party within 28 days after receiving an application for full written reasons made in accordance with paragraphs (4) and (5), or as soon as practicable thereafter.

PART 4
Correcting, setting aside, reviewing and appealing Tribunal decisions

Interpretation

36. In this Part—
   "appeal" means the exercise of a right of appeal against a decision of the Tribunal; and
   "review" means the review of a decision by the Tribunal under section 9 of the 2007 Act.

Clerical mistakes and accidental slips or omissions

37. The Tribunal may at any time correct any clerical mistake or other accidental slip or omission in a decision, direction or any document produced by it, by—
   (a) sending notification of the amended decision or direction, or a copy of the amended document, to all parties; and

(b) making any necessary amendment to any information published in relation to the decision, direction or document.

Setting aside a decision which disposes of proceedings

38.—(1) The Tribunal may set aside a decision which disposes of proceedings, or part of such a decision, and re-make the decision, or the relevant part of it, if—

(a) the Tribunal considers that it is in the interests of justice to do so; and

(b) one or more of the conditions in paragraph (2) is satisfied.

(2) The conditions are—

(a) a document relating to the proceedings was not sent to, or was not received at an appropriate time by, a party or a party's representative;

(b) a document relating to the proceedings was not sent to the Tribunal at an appropriate time;

(c) there has been some other procedural irregularity in the proceedings; or

(d) a party, or a party's representative, was not present at a hearing related to the proceedings.

(3) A party applying for a decision, or part of a decision, to be set aside under paragraph (1) must make a written application to the Tribunal so that it is received no later than 28 days after the date on which the Tribunal sent notice of the decision to the party.

(4) If the Tribunal sets aside a decision or part of a decision under this rule, the Tribunal must notify the parties in writing as soon as practicable.

Application for permission to appeal

39.—(1) A person seeking permission to appeal must make a written application to the Tribunal for permission to appeal.

(2) An application under paragraph (1) must be sent or delivered to the Tribunal so that it is received no later than 56 days after the latest of the dates that the Tribunal sends to the person making the application—

(a) full written reasons for the decision;

(b) notification of amended reasons for, or correction of, the decision following a review; or

(c) notification that an application for the decision to be set aside has been unsuccessful.

(3) The date in paragraph (2)(c) applies only if the application for the decision to be set aside was made within the time stipulated in rule 38 (setting aside a decision which disposes of proceedings), or any extension of that time granted by the Tribunal.

(4) If the person seeking permission to appeal sends or delivers the application to the Tribunal later than the time required by paragraph (2) or by any extension of time under rule 5(3)(a) (power to extend time)—

(a) the application must include a request for an extension of time and the reason why the application notice was not provided in time; and

(b) unless the Tribunal extends time for the application under rule 5(3)(a) (power to extend time) the Tribunal must not admit the application.

(5) An application under paragraph (1) must—

(a) identify the decision of the Tribunal to which it relates;

(b) identify the alleged error or errors in the decision; and

(c) state the result the party making the application is seeking.

Appendix 5

Tribunal's consideration of application for permission to appeal

40.—(1) On receiving an application for permission to appeal the Tribunal must first consider, taking into account the overriding objective in rule 2, whether to review the decision in accordance with rule 41 (review of a decision).

(2) If the Tribunal decides not to review the decision, or reviews the decision and decides to take no action in relation to the decision, or a part of it, the Tribunal must consider whether to give permission to appeal in relation to the decision or that part of it.

(3) The Tribunal must send a record of its decision to the parties as soon as practicable.

(4) If the Tribunal refuses permission to appeal it must send with the record of its decision—

  (a) a statement of its reasons for such refusal; and

  (b) notification of the right to make an application to the Upper Tribunal for permission to appeal and the time within which, and the method by which, such application must be made.

(5) The Tribunal may give permission to appeal against part only of the decision or on limited grounds, but must comply with paragraph (4) in relation to any part of the decision or grounds on which it has refused permission.

Review of a decision

41.—(1) The Tribunal may only undertake a review of a decision—

  (a) pursuant to rule 40(1) (review on an application for permission to appeal); and

  (b) if it is satisfied that there was an error of law in the decision.

(2) The Tribunal must notify the parties in writing of the outcome of any review, unless the Tribunal decides to take no action following the review.

(3) The Tribunal may not take any action in relation to a decision following a review without first giving every party an opportunity to make representations in relation to the proposed action.

Power to treat an application as a different type of application

42. The Tribunal may treat an application for a decision to be corrected, set aside or reviewed, or for permission to appeal against a decision, as an application for any other one of those things.

Patrick Elias
Philip Brook Smith Q.C.
Carolyn Kirby
Nicholas Warren
Douglas J May
Newton of Braintree
Nuala Brice
Mark Rowland
M J Reed

I allow these Rules
Signed by authority of the Lord Chancellor

Bridget Prentice
Parliamentary Under Secretary of State
5th February 2009 Ministry of Justice

Appendix 6

The Tribunal Procedure (Upper Tribunal) Rules 2008 SI 2008/2698

Made	9th October 2008
Laid before Parliament	15th October 2008
Coming into force	3rd November 2008

CONTENTS

PART 1
Introduction

1. Citation, commencement, application and interpretation
2. Overriding objective and parties' obligation to co-operation with the Upper Tribunal
3. Alternative dispute resolution and arbitration

PART 2
General powers and provisions

4. Delegation to staff
5. Case management powers
6. Procedure for applying for and giving directions
7. Failure to comply with rules etc.
8. Striking out a party's case
9. Substitution and addition of parties
10. Orders for costs
11. Representatives
12. Calculating time
13. Sending and delivery of documents
14. Use of documents and information
15. Evidence and submissions
16. Summoning or citation of witnesses and orders to answer questions or produce documents
17. Withdrawal
18. Notice of funding of legal services
19. Confidentiality in child support or child trust fund cases
20. Power to pay expenses and allowances

Appendix 6

PART 3
Appeals and references to the Upper Tribunal

21. Application to the Upper Tribunal for permission to appeal
22. Decision in relation to permission to appeal
23. Notice of appeal
24. Response to the notice of appeal
25. Appellant's reply
26. References under the Forfeiture Act 1982
26A. Cases transferred or referred to the Upper Tribunal, applications made directly to the Upper Tribunal and proceedings without notice to a respondent

PART 4
Judicial review proceedings in the Upper Tribunal

27. Application of this Part to judicial review proceedings transferred to the Upper Tribunal
28. Applications for permission to bring judicial review proceedings
29. Acknowledgment of service
30. Responses
31. Responses
32. Applicant seeking to rely on additional grounds
33. Right to make representations

PART 5
Hearings

34. Decision with or without a hearing
35. Entitlement to attend a hearing
36. Notice of hearings
37. Public and private hearings
38. Hearings in a party's absence

PART 6
Decisions

39. Consent orders
40. Decisions
41. Interpretation
42. Clerical mistakes and accidental slips or omissions
43. Setting aside a decision which disposes of proceedings
44. Application for permission to appeal
45. Upper Tribunal's consideration of application for permission to appeal
46. Review of a decision
47. Review of a decision in proceedings under the Forfeiture Act 1982

After consulting in accordance with paragraph 28(1) of Schedule 5 to, the Tribunals, Courts and Enforcement Act 2007 the Tribunal Procedure Committee has made the following Rules in exercise of the power conferred by sections 10(3), 16(9), 22 and 29(3) and (4) of, and Schedule 5 to, that Act.

Appendix 6

The Lord Chancellor has allowed the Rules in accordance with paragraph 28(3) of Schedule 5 to the Tribunals, Courts and Enforcement Act 2007.

PART 1

Introduction

Citation, commencement, application and interpretation

1.— (1) These Rules may be cited as the Tribunal Procedure (Upper Tribunal) Rules 2008 and come into force on 3rd November 2008.

(2) These Rules apply to proceedings before the Upper Tribunal.

(3) In these Rules—

"the 2007 Act" means the Tribunals, Courts and Enforcement Act 2007;

["appellant" means—
- (a) a person who makes an appeal, or applies for permission to appeal, to the Upper Tribunal;
- (b) in proceedings transferred or referred to the Upper Tribunal from the First-tier Tribunal, a person who started the proceedings in the First-tier Tribunal; or
- (c) a person substituted as an appellant under rule 9(1) (substitution and addition of parties);][1]

"applicant" means a person who applies for permission to bring, or does bring, judicial review proceedings before the Upper Tribunal and, in judicial review proceedings transferred to the Upper Tribunal from a court, includes a person who was a claimant or petitioner in the proceedings immediately before they were transferred;

[…][2]

"dispose of proceedings" includes, unless indicated otherwise, disposing of a part of the proceedings;

"document" means anything in which information is recorded in any form, and an obligation under these Rules or any practice direction or direction to provide or allow access to a document or a copy of a document for any purpose means, unless the Upper Tribunal directs otherwise, an obligation to provide or allow access to such document or copy in a legible form or in a form which can be readily made into a legible form;

"hearing" means an oral hearing and includes a hearing conducted in whole or in part by video link, telephone or other means of instantaneous two-way electronic communication;

"interested party" means—
- (a) a person who is directly affected by the outcome sought in judicial review proceedings, and has been named as an interested party under rule 28 or 29 (judicial review), or has been substituted or added as an interested party under rule 9 (substitution and addition of parties); and
- (b) in judicial review proceedings transferred to the Upper Tribunal under section 25A(2) or (3) of the Judicature (Northern Ireland) Act 1978[3] or section 31A(2) or (3) of the Supreme Court Act 1981[4], a person who was an interested party in the proceedings immediately before they were transferred to the Upper Tribunal;

"judicial review proceedings" means proceedings within the jurisdiction of the Upper Tribunal pursuant to section 15 or 21 of the 2007 Act, whether such proceedings are started in the Upper Tribunal or transferred to the Upper Tribunal;

[…][5]

Appendix 6

"mental health case" means proceedings before the Upper Tribunal on appeal against a decision in proceedings under the Mental Health Act 1983 or paragraph 5(2) of the Schedule to the Repatriation of Prisoners Act 1984;
"party" means a person who is an appellant, an applicant, a respondent or an interested party in proceedings before the Upper Tribunal, a person who has referred a question to the Upper Tribunal or, if the proceedings have been concluded, a person who was an appellant, an applicant, a respondent or an interested party when the Tribunal finally disposed of all issues in the proceedings;
"permission" includes leave in cases arising under the law of Northern Ireland;
"practice direction" means a direction given under section 23 of the 2007 Act;
"respondent" means—

(a) in an appeal, or application for permission to appeal, against a decision of another tribunal, any person other than the appellant who—
    (i) was a party before that other tribunal [; or]6
    [...]6
    (iii) otherwise has a right of appeal against the decision of the other tribunal and has given notice to the Upper Tribunal that they wish to be a party to the appeal;
(b) in an appeal against any other decision, the person who made the decision;
(c) in judicial review proceedings—
    (i) in proceedings started in the Upper Tribunal, the person named by the applicant as the respondent;
    (ii) in proceedings transferred to the Upper Tribunal under section 25A(2) or (3) of the Judicature (Northern Ireland) Act 1978 or section 31A(2) or (3) of the Supreme Court Act 1981, a person who was a defendant in the proceedings immediately before they were transferred;
    (iii) in proceedings transferred to the Upper Tribunal under section 20(1) of the 2007 Act, a person to whom intimation of the petition was made before the proceedings were transferred, or to whom the Upper Tribunal has required intimation to be made.
[(ca) in proceedings transferred or referred to the Upper Tribunal from the First-tier Tribunal, a person who was a respondent in the proceedings in the First-tier Tribunal;]7
(d) in a reference under the Forfeiture Act 1982, the person whose eligibility for a benefit or advantage is in issue; or
(e) a person substituted or added as a respondent under rule 9 (substitution and addition of parties);
[...]8
"working day" means any day except a Saturday or Sunday, Christmas Day, Good Friday or a bank holiday under section 1 of the Banking and Financial Dealings Act 1971.

Notes
1. Definition substituted by Tribunal Procedure (Amendment) Rules 2009/274 rule 5(a) (1 April 2009)
2. Definition repealed by Tribunal Procedure (Amendment) Rules 2009/274 rule 5(b) (1 April 2009)
3. 1978 c.23. Section 25A was inserted by section 19(2) of the 2007 Act.
4. Section 31A was inserted by section 19(1) of the 2007 Act.
5. Definition repealed by Tribunal Procedure (Amendment) Rules 2009/274 rule 5(c) (1 April 2009)
6. Revoked by Tribunal Procedure (Amendment) Rules 2009/274 rule 5(d)(i) (1 April 2009)
7. Added by Tribunal Procedure (Amendment) Rules 2009/274 rule 5(d)(ii) (1 April 2009)
8. Definition repealed by Tribunal Procedure (Amendment) Rules 2009/274 rule 5(e) (1 April 2009)

Overriding objective and parties' obligation to co-operate with the Upper Tribunal

2.—(1) The overriding objective of these Rules is to enable the Upper Tribunal to deal with cases fairly and justly.

Appendix 6

(2) Dealing with a case fairly and justly includes—

    (a) dealing with the case in ways which are proportionate to the importance of the case, the complexity of the issues, the anticipated costs and the resources of the parties;

    (b) avoiding unnecessary formality and seeking flexibility in the proceedings;

    (c) ensuring, so far as practicable, that the parties are able to participate fully in the proceedings;

    (d) using any special expertise of the Upper Tribunal effectively; and

    (e) avoiding delay, so far as compatible with proper consideration of the issues.

(3) The Upper Tribunal must seek to give effect to the overriding objective when it—

    (a) exercises any power under these Rules; or

    (b) interprets any rule or practice direction.

(4) Parties must—

    (a) help the Upper Tribunal to further the overriding objective; and

    (b) co-operate with the Upper Tribunal generally.

Alternative dispute resolution and arbitration

3.—(1) The Upper Tribunal should seek, where appropriate—

    (a) to bring to the attention of the parties the availability of any appropriate alternative procedure for the resolution of the dispute; and

    (b) if the parties wish and provided that it is compatible with the overriding objective, to facilitate the use of the procedure.

(2) Part 1 of the Arbitration Act 1996 does not apply to proceedings before the Upper Tribunal.

PART 2

General powers and provisions

Delegation to staff

4.—(1) Staff appointed under section 40(1) of the 2007 Act (tribunal staff and services) may, with the approval of the Senior President of Tribunals, carry out functions of a judicial nature permitted or required to be done by the Upper Tribunal.

(2) The approval referred to at paragraph (1) may apply generally to the carrying out of specified functions by members of staff of a specified description in specified circumstances.

(3) Within 14 days after the date on which the Upper Tribunal sends notice of a decision made by a member of staff under paragraph (1) to a party, that party may apply in writing to the Upper Tribunal for that decision to be considered afresh by a judge.

Case management powers

5.—(1) Subject to the provisions of the 2007 Act and any other enactment, the Upper Tribunal may regulate its own procedure.

(2) The Upper Tribunal may give a direction in relation to the conduct or disposal of proceedings at any time, including a direction amending, suspending or setting aside an earlier direction.

Appendix 6

(3) In particular, and without restricting the general powers in paragraphs (1) and (2), the Upper Tribunal may—

- (a) extend or shorten the time for complying with any rule, practice direction or direction;
- (b) consolidate or hear together two or more sets of proceedings or parts of proceedings raising common issues, or treat a case as a lead case;
- (c) permit or require a party to amend a document;
- (d) permit or require a party or another person to provide documents, information, evidence or submissions to the Upper Tribunal or a party;
- (e) deal with an issue in the proceedings as a preliminary issue;
- (f) hold a hearing to consider any matter, including a case management issue;
- (g) decide the form of any hearing;
- (h) adjourn or postpone a hearing;
- (i) require a party to produce a bundle for a hearing;
- (j) stay (or, in Scotland, sist) proceedings;
- (k) transfer proceedings to another court or tribunal if that other court or tribunal has jurisdiction in relation to the proceedings and—
  - (i) because of a change of circumstances since the proceedings were started, the Upper Tribunal no longer has jurisdiction in relation to the proceedings; or
  - (ii) the Upper Tribunal considers that the other court or tribunal is a more appropriate forum for the determination of the case;
- (l) suspend the effect of its own decision pending an appeal or review of that decision;
- (m) in an appeal, or an application for permission to appeal, against the decision of another tribunal, suspend the effect of that decision pending the determination of the application for permission to appeal, and any appeal;
- (n) require any other tribunal whose decision is the subject of proceedings before the Upper Tribunal to provide reasons for the decision, or other information or documents in relation to the decision or the proceedings in that tribunal.

Procedure for applying for and giving directions

6.—(1) The Upper Tribunal may give a direction on the application of one or more of the parties or on its own initiative.

(2) An application for a direction may be made—

- (a) by sending or delivering a written application to the Upper Tribunal; or
- (b) orally during the course of a hearing.

(3) An application for a direction must include the reason for making that application.

(4) Unless the Upper Tribunal considers that there is good reason not to do so, the Upper Tribunal must send written notice of any direction to every party and to any other person affected by the direction.

(5) If a party or any other person sent notice of the direction under paragraph (4) wishes to challenge a direction which the Upper Tribunal has given, they may do so by applying for another direction which amends, suspends or sets aside the first direction.

Failure to comply with rules etc.

7.—(1) An irregularity resulting from a failure to comply with any requirement in these Rules, a practice direction or a direction, does not of itself render void the proceedings or any step taken in the proceedings.

Appendix 6

(2) If a party has failed to comply with a requirement in these Rules, a practice direction or a direction, the Upper Tribunal may take such action as it considers just, which may include—

  (a) waiving the requirement;
  (b) requiring the failure to be remedied;
  (c) exercising its power under rule 8 (striking out a party's case); or
  (d) except in mental health cases, restricting a party's participation in the proceedings.

(3) Paragraph (4) applies where the First-tier Tribunal has referred to the Upper Tribunal a failure by a person to comply with a requirement imposed by the First-tier Tribunal—

  (a) to attend at any place for the purpose of giving evidence;
  (b) otherwise to make themselves available to give evidence;
  (c) to swear an oath in connection with the giving of evidence;
  (d) to give evidence as a witness;
  (e) to produce a document; or
  (f) to facilitate the inspection of a document or any other thing (including any premises).

(4) The Upper Tribunal may exercise its power under section 25 of the 2007 Act (supplementary powers of the Upper Tribunal) in relation to such non-compliance as if the requirement had been imposed by the Upper Tribunal.

Striking out a party's case

8.—(1) The proceedings, or the appropriate part of them, will automatically be struck out if the appellant or applicant has failed to comply with a direction that stated that failure by the appellant or applicant to comply with the direction would lead to the striking out of the proceedings or that part of them.

(2) The Upper Tribunal must strike out the whole or a part of the proceedings if the Upper Tribunal—

  (a) does not have jurisdiction in relation to the proceedings or that part of them; and
  (b) does not exercise its power under rule 5(3)(k)(i) (transfer to another court or tribunal) in relation to the proceedings or that part of them.

(3) The Upper Tribunal may strike out the whole or a part of the proceedings if—

  (a) the appellant or applicant has failed to comply with a direction which stated that failure by the appellant or applicant to comply with the direction could lead to the striking out of the proceedings or part of them;
  (b) the appellant or applicant has failed to co-operate with the Upper Tribunal to such an extent that the Upper Tribunal cannot deal with the proceedings fairly and justly; or
  (c) in proceedings which are not an appeal from the decision of another tribunal or judicial review proceedings, the Upper Tribunal considers there is no reasonable prospect of the appellant's or the applicant's case, or part of it, succeeding.

(4) The Upper Tribunal may not strike out the whole or a part of the proceedings under paragraph (2) or (3)(b) or (c) without first giving the appellant or applicant an opportunity to make representations in relation to the proposed striking out.

(5) If the proceedings have been struck out under paragraph (1) or (3)(a), the appellant or applicant may apply for the proceedings, or part of them, to be reinstated.

Appendix 6

(6) An application under paragraph (5) must be made in writing and received by the Upper Tribunal within 1 month after the date on which the Upper Tribunal sent notification of the striking out to the appellant or applicant.

(7) This rule applies to a respondent [or an interested party][1] as it applies to an appellant or applicant except that—

    (a) a reference to the striking out of the proceedings is to be read as a reference to the barring of the respondent [or interested party][2] from taking further part in the proceedings; and

    (b) a reference to an application for the reinstatement of proceedings which have been struck out is to be read as a reference to an application for the lifting of the bar on the respondent [or interested party][2] [...][3] taking further part in the proceedings.

(8) If a respondent [or an interested party][4] has been barred from taking further part in proceedings under this rule and that bar has not been lifted, the Upper Tribunal need not consider any response or other submission made by that respondent [or interested party, and may summarily determine any or all issues against that respondent or interested party][5].

Notes
1. Words inserted by Tribunal Procedure (Amendment) Rules 2009/274 rule 6(2)(a) (1 April 2009)
2. Words inserted by Tribunal Procedure (Amendment) Rules 2009/274 rule 6(2)(b) (1 April 2009)
3. Word repealed by Tribunal Procedure (Amendment) Rules 2009/274 rule 6(2)(c) (1 April 2009)
4. Words inserted by Tribunal Procedure (Amendment) Rules 2009/274 rule 6(3)(a) (1 April 2009)
5. Words inserted by Tribunal Procedure (Amendment) Rules 2009/274 rule 6(3)(b) (1 April 2009)

Substitution and addition of parties

9.—(1) The Upper Tribunal may give a direction substituting a party if—

    (a) the wrong person has been named as a party; or

    (b) the substitution has become necessary because of a change in circumstances since the start of proceedings.

(2) The Upper Tribunal may give a direction adding a person to the proceedings as a respondent or, in judicial review proceedings, as an interested party.

(3) If the Upper Tribunal gives a direction under paragraph (1) or (2) it may give such consequential directions as it considers appropriate.

[Orders for costs

10.—(1) The Upper Tribunal may not make an order in respect of costs (or, in Scotland, expenses) in proceedings referred by or on appeal from another tribunal except—

    (a) in proceedings on appeal from the Tax Chamber of the First-tier Tribunal; or

    (b) to the extent and in the circumstances that the other tribunal had the power to make an order in respect of costs (or, in Scotland, expenses).

(2) The Upper Tribunal may not make an order in respect of costs or expenses under section 4 of the Forfeiture Act 1982.

(3) In other proceedings, the Upper Tribunal may not make an order in respect of costs or expenses except—

    (a) in judicial review proceedings;

    (b) in proceedings transferred from the Tax Chamber of the First-tier Tribunal;

    (c) under section 29(4) of the 2007 Act (wasted costs); or

Appendix 6

  (d) if the Upper Tribunal considers that a party or its representative has acted unreasonably in bringing, defending or conducting the proceedings.

(4) The Upper Tribunal may make an order for costs (or, in Scotland, expenses) on an application or on its own initiative.

(5) A person making an application for an order for costs or expenses must—

  (a) send or deliver a written application to the Upper Tribunal and to the person against whom it is proposed that the order be made; and

  (b) send or deliver with the application a schedule of the costs or expenses claimed sufficient to allow summary assessment of such costs or expenses by the Upper Tribunal.

(6) An application for an order for costs or expenses may be made at any time during the proceedings but may not be made later than 1 month after the date on which the Upper Tribunal sends—

  (a) a decision notice recording the decision which finally disposes of all issues in the proceedings; or

  (b) notice of a withdrawal under rule 17 which ends the proceedings.

(7) The Upper Tribunal may not make an order for costs or expenses against a person (the "paying person") without first—

  (a) giving that person an opportunity to make representations; and

  (b) if the paying person is an individual and the order is to be made under paragraph (3)(a), (b) or (d), considering that person's financial means.

(8) The amount of costs or expenses to be paid under an order under this rule may be ascertained by—

  (a) summary assessment by the Upper Tribunal;

  (b) agreement of a specified sum by the paying person and the person entitled to receive the costs or expenses ("the receiving person"); or

  (c) assessment of the whole or a specified part of the costs or expenses incurred by the receiving person, if not agreed.

(9) Following an order for assessment under paragraph (8)(c), the paying person or the receiving person may apply—

  (a) in England and Wales, to the High Court or the Costs Office of the Supreme Court (as specified in the order) for a detailed assessment of the costs on the standard basis or, if specified in the order, on the indemnity basis; and the Civil Procedure Rules 1998 shall apply, with necessary modifications, to that application and assessment as if the proceedings in the tribunal had been proceedings in a court to which the Civil Procedure Rules 1998 apply;

  (b) in Scotland, to the Auditor of the Court of Session for the taxation of the expenses according to the fees payable in that court; or

  (c) in Northern Ireland, to the Taxing Office of the High Court of Northern Ireland for taxation on the standard basis or, if specified in the order, on the indemnity basis.][1]

Note
1. Substituted by Tribunal Procedure (Amendment) Rules 2009/274 rule 7 (1 April 2009).

Representatives

11.—(1) A party may appoint a representative (whether a legal representative or not) to represent that party in the proceedings.

Appendix 6

(2) If a party appoints a representative, that party (or the representative if the representative is a legal representative) must send or deliver to the Upper Tribunal [...]¹ written notice of the representative's name and address.

[(2A) If the Upper Tribunal receives notice that a party has appointed a representative under paragraph (2), it must send a copy of that notice to each other party.]²

(3) Anything permitted or required to be done by a party under these Rules, a practice direction or a direction may be done by the representative of that party, except signing a witness statement.

(4) A person who receives due notice of the appointment of a representative—

    (a) must provide to the representative any document which is required to be provided to the represented party, and need not provide that document to the represented party; and

    (b) may assume that the representative is and remains authorised as such until they receive written notification that this is not so from the representative or the represented party.

(5) At a hearing a party may be accompanied by another person whose name and address has not been notified under paragraph (2) but who, subject to paragraph (8) and with the permission of the Upper Tribunal, may act as a representative or otherwise assist in presenting the party's case at the hearing.

(6) Paragraphs (2) to (4) do not apply to a person who accompanies a party under paragraph (5).

(7) In a mental health case if the patient has not appointed a representative the Upper Tribunal may appoint a legal representative for the patient where—

    (a) the patient has stated that they do not wish to conduct their own case or that they wish to be represented; or

    (b) the patient lacks the capacity to appoint a representative but the Upper Tribunal believes that it is in the patient's best interests for the patient to be represented.

(8) In a mental health case a party may not appoint as a representative, or be represented or assisted at a hearing by—

    (a) a person liable to be detained or subject to guardianship or after-care under supervision, or who is a community patient, under the Mental Health Act 1983; or

    (b) a person receiving treatment for mental disorder at the same hospital home as the patient.

[(9) In this rule "legal representative" means an authorised advocate or authorised litigator as defined by section 119(1) of the Courts and Legal Services Act 1990, an advocate or solicitor in Scotland or a barrister or solicitor in Northern Ireland.]³

Notes
1. Words repealed by Tribunal Procedure (Amendment) Rules 2009/274 rule 8(a) (1 April 2009)
2. Added by Tribunal Procedure (Amendment) Rules 2009/274 rule 8(b) (1 April 2009)
3. Added by Tribunal Procedure (Amendment) Rules 2009/274 rule 8(c) (1 April 2009)

Calculating time

12.— (1) An act required by these Rules, a practice direction or a direction to be done on or by a particular day must be done by 5pm on that day.

(2) If the time specified by these Rules, a practice direction or a direction for doing any act

Appendix 6

ends on a day other than a working day, the act is done in time if it is done on the next working day.

(3) In a special educational needs case or a disability discrimination in schools case, the following days must not be counted when calculating the time by which an act must be done—

    (a) 25th December to 1st January inclusive; and
    (b) any day in August.

(4) Paragraph (3) does not apply where the Upper Tribunal directs that an act must be done by or on a specified date.

[(5) In this rule—

"disability discrimination in schools case" means proceedings concerning disability discrimination in the education of a child or related matters; and

"special educational needs case" means proceedings concerning the education of a child who has or may have special educational needs.][1]

Note
1. Added by Tribunal Procedure (Amendment) Rules 2009/274 rule 9 (1 April 2009)

Sending and delivery of documents

13.—(1) Any document to be provided to the Upper Tribunal under these Rules, a practice direction or a direction must be—

    (a) sent by pre-paid post or [by document exchange, or delivered by hand,][1] to the address specified for the proceedings;
    (b) sent by fax to the number specified for the proceedings; or
    (c) sent or delivered by such other method as the Upper Tribunal may permit or direct.

(2) Subject to paragraph (3), if a party provides a fax number, email address or other details for the electronic transmission of documents to them, that party must accept delivery of documents by that method.

(3) If a party informs the Upper Tribunal and all other parties that a particular form of communication, other than pre-paid post or delivery by hand, should not be used to provide documents to that party, that form of communication must not be so used.

(4) If the Upper Tribunal or a party sends a document to a party or the Upper Tribunal by email or any other electronic means of communication, the recipient may request that the sender provide a hard copy of the document to the recipient. The recipient must make such a request as soon as reasonably practicable after receiving the document electronically.

(5) The Upper Tribunal and each party may assume that the address provided by a party or its representative is and remains the address to which documents should be sent or delivered until receiving written notification to the contrary.

Note
1. Words substituted by Tribunal Procedure (Amendment) Rules 2009/274 rule 10 (1 April 2009)

Use of documents and information

14.—(1) The Upper Tribunal may make an order prohibiting the disclosure or publication of—

Appendix 6

       (a)   specified documents or information relating to the proceedings; or
       (b)   any matter likely to lead members of the public to identify any person whom the Upper Tribunal considers should not be identified.

(2) The Upper Tribunal may give a direction prohibiting the disclosure of a document or information to a person if—

       (a)   the Upper Tribunal is satisfied that such disclosure would be likely to cause that person or some other person serious harm; and
       (b)   the Upper Tribunal is satisfied, having regard to the interests of justice, that it is proportionate to give such a direction.

(3) If a party ("the first party") considers that the Upper Tribunal should give a direction under paragraph (2) prohibiting the disclosure of a document or information to another party ("the second party"), the first party must—

       (a)   exclude the relevant document or information from any documents that will be provided to the second party; and
       (b)   provide to the Upper Tribunal the excluded document or information, and the reason for its exclusion, so that the Upper Tribunal may decide whether the document or information should be disclosed to the second party or should be the subject of a direction under paragraph (2).

(4) The Upper Tribunal must conduct proceedings as appropriate in order to give effect to a direction given under paragraph (2).

(5) If the Upper Tribunal gives a direction under paragraph (2) which prevents disclosure to a party who has appointed a representative, the Upper Tribunal may give a direction that the documents or information be disclosed to that representative if the Upper Tribunal is satisfied that—

       (a)   disclosure to the representative would be in the interests of the party; and
       (b)   the representative will act in accordance with paragraph (6).

(6) Documents or information disclosed to a representative in accordance with a direction under paragraph (5) must not be disclosed either directly or indirectly to any other person without the Upper Tribunal's consent.

(7) Unless the Upper Tribunal gives a direction to the contrary, information about mental health cases and the names of any persons concerned in such cases must not be made public.

Evidence and submissions

15.—(1) Without restriction on the general powers in rule 5(1) and (2) (case management powers), the Upper Tribunal may give directions as to—

       (a)   issues on which it requires evidence or submissions;
       (b)   the nature of the evidence or submissions it requires;
       (c)   whether the parties are permitted or required to provide expert evidence, and if so whether the parties must jointly appoint a single expert to provide such evidence;
       (d)   any limit on the number of witnesses whose evidence a party may put forward, whether in relation to a particular issue or generally;
       (e)   the manner in which any evidence or submissions are to be provided, which may include a direction for them to be given—
              (i)   orally at a hearing; or
              (ii)   by written submissions or witness statement; and
       (f)   the time at which any evidence or submissions are to be provided.

Appendix 6

(2) The Upper Tribunal may—

    (a) admit evidence whether or not—
        (i) the evidence would be admissible in a civil trial in the United Kingdom; or
        (ii) the evidence was available to a previous decision maker; or
    (b) exclude evidence that would otherwise be admissible where—
        (i) the evidence was not provided within the time allowed by a direction or a practice direction;
        (ii) the evidence was otherwise provided in a manner that did not comply with a direction or a practice direction; or
        (iii) it would otherwise be unfair to admit the evidence.

(3) The Upper Tribunal may consent to a witness giving, or require any witness to give, evidence on oath, and may administer an oath for that purpose.

Summoning or citation of witnesses and orders to answer questions or produce documents

16.— (1) On the application of a party or on its own initiative, the Upper Tribunal may—

    (a) by summons (or, in Scotland, citation) require any person to attend as a witness at a hearing at the time and place specified in the summons or citation; or
    (b) order any person to answer any questions or produce any documents in that person's possession or control which relate to any issue in the proceedings.

(2) A summons or citation under paragraph (1)(a) must—

    (a) give the person required to attend 14 days' notice of the hearing or such shorter period as the Upper Tribunal may direct; and
    (b) where the person is not a party, make provision for the person's necessary expenses of attendance to be paid, and state who is to pay them.

(3) No person may be compelled to give any evidence or produce any document that the person could not be compelled to give or produce on a trial of an action in a court of law in the part of the United Kingdom where the proceedings are due to be determined.

[(4) A person who receives a summons, citation or order may apply to the Upper Tribunal for it to be varied or set aside if they did not have an opportunity to object to it before it was made or issued.

(5) A person making an application under paragraph (4) must do so as soon as reasonably practicable after receiving notice of the summons, citation or order.

(6) A summons, citation or order under this rule must—

    (a) state that the person on whom the requirement is imposed may apply to the Upper Tribunal to vary or set aside the summons, citation or order, if they did not have an opportunity to object to it before it was made or issued; and
    (b) state the consequences of failure to comply with the summons, citation or order.][1]

Note
1. Rule 16(4)-(6) substituted for rule 16(4) by Tribunal Procedure (Amendment) Rules 2009/274 rule 11 (1 April 2009)

Withdrawal

17.—(1) Subject to paragraph (2), a party may give notice of the withdrawal of its case, or any part of it—

Appendix 6

    (a)   at any time before a hearing to consider the disposal of the proceedings (or, if the Upper Tribunal disposes of the proceedings without a hearing, before that disposal), by sending or delivering to the Upper Tribunal a written notice of withdrawal; or

    (b)   orally at a hearing.

(2) Notice of withdrawal will not take effect unless the Upper Tribunal consents to the withdrawal except in relation to an application for permission to appeal.

(3) A party which has withdrawn its case may apply to the Upper Tribunal for the case to be reinstated.

(4) An application under paragraph (3) must be made in writing and be received by the Upper Tribunal within 1 month after—

    (a)   the date on which the Upper Tribunal received the notice under paragraph (1)(a); or

    (b)   the date of the hearing at which the case was withdrawn orally under paragraph (1)(b).

(5) The Upper Tribunal must notify each party in writing of a withdrawal under this rule.

Notice of funding of legal services

18. If a party is granted funding of legal services at any time, that party must as soon as practicable—

    (a)   (i)   if funding is granted by the Legal Services Commission or the Northern Ireland Legal Services Commission, send a copy of the funding notice to the Upper Tribunal; or

            (ii)   if funding is granted by the Scottish Legal Aid Board, send a copy of the legal aid certificate to the Upper Tribunal; and

    (b)   notify every other party in writing that funding has been granted.

Confidentiality in child support or child trust fund cases

19.—(1) Paragraph (3) applies to an appeal against a decision of the First-tier Tribunal in proceedings under the Child Support Act 1991 in the circumstances described in paragraph (2), other than an appeal against a reduced benefit decision (as defined in section 46(10)(b) of the Child Support Act 1991, as that section had effect prior to the commencement of section 15(b) of the Child Maintenance and Other Payments Act 2008).

(2) The circumstances referred to in paragraph (1) are that—

    (a)   in the proceedings in the First-tier Tribunal in respect of which the appeal has been brought, there was an obligation to keep a person's address confidential; or

    (b)   a person whose circumstances are relevant to the proceedings would like their address (or, in the case of the person with care of the child, the child's address) to be kept confidential and has given notice to that effect—

            (i)   to the Upper Tribunal in an application for permission to appeal or notice of appeal;

            (ii)   to the Upper Tribunal within 1 month after an enquiry by the Upper Tribunal; or

            (iii)   to the Secretary of State, the Child Maintenance and Enforcement Commission or the Upper Tribunal when notifying a change of address after proceedings have been started.

Appendix 6

(3) Where this paragraph applies, the Secretary of State, the Child Maintenance and Enforcement Commission and the Upper Tribunal must take appropriate steps to secure the confidentiality of the address, and of any information which could reasonably be expected to enable a person to identify the address, to the extent that the address or that information is not already known to each other party.

(4) Paragraph (6) applies to an appeal against a decision of the First-tier Tribunal in proceedings under the Child Trust Funds Act 2004 in the circumstances described in paragraph (5).

(5) The circumstances referred to in paragraph (4) are that—

 (a) in the proceedings in the First-tier Tribunal in respect of which the appeal has been brought, there was an obligation to keep a person's address confidential; or

 (b) a person whose circumstances are relevant to the proceedings would like their address (or, in the case of the person with care of the eligible child, the child's address) to be kept confidential and has given notice to that effect—
  (i) to the Upper Tribunal in an application for permission to appeal or notice of appeal;
  (ii) to the Upper Tribunal within 1 month after an enquiry by the Upper Tribunal; or
  (iii) to HMRC or the Upper Tribunal when notifying a change of address after proceedings have been started.

(6) Where this paragraph applies, HMRC and the Upper Tribunal must take appropriate steps to secure the confidentiality of the address, and of any information which could reasonably be expected to enable a person to identify the address, to the extent that the address or that information is not already known to each other party.

(7) In this rule—

 "eligible child" has the meaning set out in section 2 of the Child Trust Funds Act 2004; and
 "HMRC" means Her Majesty's Revenue and Customs.

Power to pay expenses and allowances

20.—(1) In proceedings brought under section 4 of the Safeguarding Vulnerable Groups Act 2006 [...]¹ the Secretary of State may pay such allowances for the purpose of or in connection with the attendance of persons at hearings as the Secretary of State may, with the consent of the Treasury, determine.

(2) Paragraph (3) applies to proceedings on appeal from a decision of—

 (a) the First-tier Tribunal in proceedings under the Child Support Act 1991, section 12 of the Social Security Act 1998 or paragraph 6 of Schedule 7 to the Child Support, Pensions and Social Security Act 2000;
 (b) the First-tier Tribunal in a war pensions and armed forces case (as defined in the Tribunal Procedure (First-tier Tribunal) (War Pensions and Armed Forces Compensation Chamber) Rules 2008); or
 (c) a Pensions Appeal Tribunal for Scotland or Northern Ireland.

(3) The Lord Chancellor (or, in Scotland, the Secretary of State) may pay to any person who attends any hearing such travelling and other allowances, including compensation for loss of remunerative time, as the Lord Chancellor (or, in Scotland, the Secretary of State) may determine.

Appendix 6

Note
1. Words repealed by Tribunal Procedure (Amendment) Rules 2009/274 rule 12 (1 April 2009)

PART 3

Appeals and references to the Upper Tribunal

Application to the Upper Tribunal for permission to appeal

21.—(1) This rule applies to an application for permission to appeal to the Upper Tribunal against any decision.

(2) A person may apply to the Upper Tribunal for permission to appeal to the Upper Tribunal against a decision of another tribunal only if—

    (a) they have made an application for permission to appeal to the tribunal which made the decision challenged; and

    (b) that application has been refused or has not been admitted.

(3) An application for permission to appeal must be made in writing and received by the Upper Tribunal no later than—

    (a) in the case of an application under section 4 of the Safeguarding Vulnerable Groups Act 2006, 3 months after the date on which written notice of the decision being challenged was sent to the appellant; or

    (b) otherwise, a month after the date on which the tribunal that made the decision under challenge sent notice of its refusal of permission to appeal, or refusal to admit the application for permission to appeal, to the appellant.

(4) The application must state—

    (a) the name and address of the appellant;

    (b) the name and address of the representative (if any) of the appellant;

    (c) an address where documents for the appellant may be sent or delivered;

    (d) details (including the full reference) of the decision challenged;

    (e) the grounds on which the appellant relies; and

    (f) whether the appellant wants the application to be dealt with at a hearing.

(5) The appellant must provide with the application a copy of—

    (a) any written record of the decision being challenged;

    (b) any separate written statement of reasons for that decision; and

    (c) if the application is for permission to appeal against a decision of another tribunal, the notice of refusal of permission to appeal, or notice of refusal to admit the application for permission to appeal, from that other tribunal.

(6) If the appellant provides the application to the Upper Tribunal later than the time required by paragraph (3) or by an extension of time allowed under rule 5(3)(a) (power to extend time)—

    (a) the application must include a request for an extension of time and the reason why the application was not provided in time; and

    (b) unless the Upper Tribunal extends time for the application under rule 5(3)(a) (power to extend time) the Upper Tribunal must not admit the application.

(7) If the appellant makes an application to the Upper Tribunal for permission to appeal against the decision of another tribunal, and that other tribunal refused to admit the appellant's application for permission to appeal because the application for permission or for a written statement of reasons was not made in time—

Appendix 6

    (a)   the application to the Upper Tribunal for permission to appeal must include the reason why the application to the other tribunal for permission to appeal or for a written statement of reasons, as the case may be, was not made in time; and

    (b)   the Upper Tribunal must only admit the application if the Upper Tribunal considers that it is in the interests of justice for it to do so.

Decision in relation to permission to appeal

22.—(1) If the Upper Tribunal refuses permission to appeal, it must send written notice of the refusal and of the reasons for the refusal to the appellant.

(2)   If the Upper Tribunal gives permission to appeal—

    (a)   the Upper Tribunal must send written notice of the permission, and of the reasons for any limitations or conditions on such permission, to each party;

    (b)   subject to any direction by the Upper Tribunal, the application for permission to appeal stands as the notice of appeal and the Upper Tribunal must send to each respondent a copy of the application for permission to appeal and any documents provided with it by the appellant; and

    (c)   the Upper Tribunal may, with the consent of the appellant and each respondent, determine the appeal without obtaining any further response.

[(3)   Paragraph (4) applies where the Upper Tribunal, without a hearing, determines an application for permission to appeal—

    (a)   against a decision of—
        (i)   the Tax Chamber of the First-tier Tribunal;
        (ii)   the Health, Education and Social Care Chamber of the First-tier Tribunal[2];
        (iii)   the Mental Health Review Tribunal for Wales; or
        (iv)   the Special Educational Needs Tribunal for Wales; or

    (b)   under section 4 of the Safeguarding Vulnerable Groups Act 2006.][1]

(4)   In the circumstances set out at paragraph (3) the appellant may apply for the decision to be reconsidered at a hearing if the Upper Tribunal—

    (a)   refuses permission to appeal; or

    (b)   gives permission to appeal on limited grounds or subject to conditions.

(5)   An application under paragraph (4) must be made in writing and received by the Upper Tribunal within 14 days after the date on which the Upper Tribunal sent written notice of its decision regarding the application to the appellant.

Notes
1. Substituted by Tribunal Procedure (Amendment) Rules 2009/274 rule 14 (1 April 2009)
2. S.I. 2008/2684. The Order is amended by the First-tier Tribunal and Upper Tribunal (Chambers) (Amendment) Order 2009 (S.I. 2009/196).

Notice of appeal

23.—(1) This rule applies—

    (a)   if another tribunal has given permission for a party to appeal to the Upper Tribunal; or

    (b)   subject to any other direction by the Upper Tribunal, if the Upper Tribunal has given permission to appeal and has given a direction that the application for permission to appeal does not stand as the notice of appeal.

Appendix 6

(2) The appellant must provide a notice of appeal to the Upper Tribunal so that it is received within 1 month after the tribunal that gave permission to appeal sent notice of such permission to the appellant.

(3) The notice of appeal must include the information listed in rule 21(4)(a) to (e) (content of the application for permission to appeal) and, where the Upper Tribunal has given permission to appeal, the Upper Tribunal's case reference.

(4) If another tribunal has granted permission to appeal, the appellant must provide with the notice of appeal a copy of—

    (a) any written record of the decision being challenged;
    (b) any separate written statement of reasons for that decision; and
    (c) the notice of permission to appeal.

(5) If the appellant provides the notice of appeal to the Upper Tribunal later than the time required by paragraph (2) or by an extension of time allowed under rule 5(3)(a) (power to extend time)—

    (a) the notice of appeal must include a request for an extension of time and the reason why the notice was not provided in time; and
    (b) unless the Upper Tribunal extends time for the notice of appeal under rule 5(3)(a) (power to extend time) the Upper Tribunal must not admit the notice of appeal.

(6) When the Upper Tribunal receives the notice of appeal it must send a copy of the notice and any accompanying documents to each respondent.

Response to the notice of appeal

24.—(1) Subject to any direction given by the Upper Tribunal, a respondent may provide a response to the notice of appeal.

(2) Any response provided under paragraph (1) must be in writing and must be sent or delivered to the Upper Tribunal so that it is received—

    (a) if the application for permission stands as the notice of appeal, no later than 1 month after the date on which the Upper Tribunal sent notice that it had granted permission to appeal to the respondent; or
    (b) in any other case, no later than 1 month after the date on which the Upper Tribunal sent a copy of the notice of appeal to the respondent.

(3) The response must state—

    (a) the name and address of the respondent;
    (b) the name and address of the representative (if any) of the respondent;
    (c) an address where documents for the respondent may be sent or delivered;
    (d) whether the respondent opposes the appeal;
    (e) the grounds on which the respondent relies, including any grounds on which the respondent was unsuccessful in the proceedings which are the subject of the appeal, but intends to rely in the appeal; and
    (f) whether the respondent wants the case to be dealt with at a hearing.

(4) If the respondent provides the response to the Upper Tribunal later than the time required by paragraph (2) or by an extension of time allowed under rule 5(3)(a) (power to extend time), the response must include a request for an extension of time and the reason why the [response]¹ was not provided in time.

(5) When the Upper Tribunal receives the response it must send a copy of the response and any accompanying documents to the appellant and each other party.

Appendix 6

Note
1. Word substituted by Tribunal Procedure (Amendment) Rules 2009/274 rule 15 (1 April 2009)

Appellant's reply

25.—(1) Subject to any direction given by the Upper Tribunal, the appellant may provide a reply to any response provided under rule 24 (response to the notice of appeal).

(2) Any reply provided under paragraph (1) must be in writing and must be sent or delivered to the Upper Tribunal so that it is received within one month after the date on which the Upper Tribunal sent a copy of the response to the appellant.

(3) When the Upper Tribunal receives the reply it must send a copy of the reply and any accompanying documents to each respondent.

References under the Forfeiture Act 1982

26.—(1) If a question arises which is required to be determined by the Upper Tribunal under section 4 of the Forfeiture Act 1982, the person to whom the application for the relevant benefit or advantage has been made must refer the question to the Upper Tribunal.

(2) The reference must be in writing and must include—

   (a) a statement of the question for determination;
   (b) a statement of the relevant facts;
   (c) the grounds upon which the reference is made; and
   (d) an address for sending documents to the person making the reference and each respondent.

(3) When the Upper Tribunal receives the reference it must send a copy of the reference and any accompanying documents to each respondent.

(4) Rules 24 (response to the notice of appeal) and 25 (appellant's reply) apply to a reference made under this rule as if it were a notice of appeal.

[Cases transferred or referred to the Upper Tribunal, applications made directly to the Upper Tribunal and proceedings without notice to a respondent

26A.—(1) Paragraphs (2) and (3) apply to a case which—

   (a) has been transferred or referred to the Upper Tribunal from the First-tier Tribunal; or
   (b) is a case, other than an appeal or a case to which rule 26 (references under the Forfeiture Act 1982) applies, which is started by an application made directly to the Upper Tribunal.

(2) In a case to which this paragraph applies—

   (a) the Upper Tribunal must give directions as to the procedure to be followed in the consideration and disposal of the proceedings; and
   (b) the preceding rules in this Part will only apply to the proceedings to the extent provided for by such directions.

(3) If a case or matter to which this paragraph applies is to be determined without notice to or the involvement of a respondent—

   (a) any provision in these Rules requiring a document to be provided by or to a respondent; and

Appendix 6

    (b)   any other provision in these Rules permitting a respondent to participate in the proceedings does not apply to that case or matter.]¹

Note
1. Added by Tribunal Procedure (Amendment) Rules 2009/274 rule 16 (1 April 2009)

PART 4
Judicial review proceedings in the Upper Tribunal

Application of this Part to judicial review proceedings transferred to the Upper Tribunal

27.—(1) When a court transfers judicial review proceedings to the Upper Tribunal, the Upper Tribunal—

    (a)   must notify each party in writing that the proceedings have been transferred to the Upper Tribunal; and

    (b)   must give directions as to the future conduct of the proceedings.

(2)   The directions given under paragraph (1)(b) may modify or disapply for the purposes of the proceedings any of the provisions of the following rules in this Part.

(3)   In proceedings transferred from the Court of Session under section 20(1) of the 2007 Act, the directions given under paragraph (1)(b) must—

    (a)   if the Court of Session did not make a first order specifying the required intimation, service and advertisement of the petition, state the Upper Tribunal's requirements in relation to those matters;

    (b)   state whether the Upper Tribunal will consider summary dismissal of the proceedings; and

    (c)   where necessary, modify or disapply provisions relating to permission in the following rules in this Part.

Applications for permission to bring judicial review proceedings

28.—(1) A person seeking permission to bring judicial review proceedings before the Upper Tribunal under section 16 of the 2007 Act must make a written application to the Upper Tribunal for such permission.

(2)   Subject to paragraph (3), an application under paragraph (1) must be made promptly and, unless any other enactment specifies a shorter time limit, must be sent or delivered to the Upper Tribunal so that it is received no later than 3 months after the date of the decision [, action or omission]¹ to which the application relates.

(3)   An application for permission to bring judicial review proceedings challenging a decision of the First-tier Tribunal may be made later than the time required by paragraph (2) if it is made within 1 month after the date on which the First-tier Tribunal sent—

    (a)   written reasons for the decision; or

    (b)   notification that an application for the decision to be set aside has been unsuccessful, provided that that application was made in time.

(4)   The application must state—

    (a)   the name and address of the applicant, the respondent and any other person whom the applicant considers to be an interested party;

    (b)   the name and address of the applicant's representative (if any);

Appendix 6

- (c) an address where documents for the applicant may be sent or delivered;
- (d) details of the decision challenged (including the date, the full reference and the identity of the decision maker);
- (e) that the application is for permission to bring judicial review proceedings;
- (f) the outcome that the applicant is seeking; and
- (g) the facts and grounds on which the applicant relies.

(5) If the application relates to proceedings in a court or tribunal, the application must name as an interested party each party to those proceedings who is not the applicant or a respondent.

(6) The applicant must send with the application—

- (a) a copy of any written record of the decision in the applicant's possession or control; and
- (b) copies of any other documents in the applicant's possession or control on which the applicant intends to rely.

(7) If the applicant provides the application to the Upper Tribunal later than the time required by paragraph (2) or (3) or by an extension of time allowed under rule 5(3)(a) (power to extend time)—

- (a) the application must include a request for an extension of time and the reason why the application was not provided in time; and
- (b) unless the Upper Tribunal extends time for the application under rule 5(3)(a) (power to extend time) the Upper Tribunal must not admit the application.

(8) When the Upper Tribunal receives the application it must send a copy of the application and any accompanying documents to each person named in the application as a respondent or interested party.

Note
1. Words inserted by Tribunal Procedure (Amendment) Rules 2009/274 rule 17 (1 April 2009)

Acknowledgment of service

29.—(1) A person who is sent a copy of an application for permission under rule 28(8) (application for permission to bring judicial review proceedings) and wishes to take part in the proceedings must send or deliver to the Upper Tribunal an acknowledgment of service so that it is received no later than 21 days after the date on which the Upper Tribunal sent a copy of the application to that person.

(2) An acknowledgment of service under paragraph (1) must be in writing and state—

- (a) whether the person intends to [support or]¹ oppose the application for permission;
- (b) their grounds for any [support or]² opposition under sub-paragraph (a), or any other submission or information which it considers may assist the Upper Tribunal; and
- (c) the name and address of any other person not named in the application as a respondent or interested party whom the person providing the acknowledgment considers to be an interested party.

(3) A person who is sent a copy of an application for permission under rule 28(8) but does not provide an acknowledgment of service may not take part in the application for permission, but may take part in the subsequent proceedings if the application is successful.

Appendix 6

Notes
1. Words inserted by Tribunal Procedure (Amendment) Rules 2009/274 rule 18(a) (1 April 2009)
2. Words inserted by Tribunal Procedure (Amendment) Rules 2009/274 rule 18(b) (1 April 2009)

Decision on permission or summary dismissal, and reconsideration of permission or summary dismissal at a hearing

30.—(1) The Upper Tribunal must send to the applicant, each respondent and any other person who provided an acknowledgment of service to the Upper Tribunal, and may send to any other person who may have an interest in the proceedings, written notice of—

(a) its decision in relation to the application for permission; and
(b) the reasons for any refusal of the application, or any limitations or conditions on permission.

(2) In proceedings transferred from the Court of Session under section 20(1) of the 2007 Act, where the Upper Tribunal has considered whether summarily to dismiss of the proceedings, the Upper Tribunal must send to the applicant and each respondent, and may send to any other person who may have an interest in the proceedings, written notice of—

(a) its decision in relation to the summary dismissal of proceedings; and
(b) the reasons for any decision summarily to dismiss part or all of the proceedings, or any limitations or conditions on the continuation of such proceedings.

(3) Paragraph (4) applies where the Upper Tribunal, without a hearing—

(a) determines an application for permission to bring judicial review proceedings and either refuses permission, or gives permission on limited grounds or subject to conditions; or
(b) in proceedings transferred from the Court of Session, summarily dismisses part or all of the proceedings, or imposes any limitations or conditions on the continuation of such proceedings.

(4) In the circumstances specified in paragraph (3) the applicant may apply for the decision to be reconsidered at a hearing.

(5) An application under paragraph (4) must be made in writing and must be sent or delivered to the Upper Tribunal so that it is received within 14 days after the date on which the Upper Tribunal sent written notice of its decision regarding the application to the applicant.

Responses

31.—(1) Any person to whom the Upper Tribunal has sent notice of the grant of permission under rule 30(1) (notification of decision on permission), and who wishes to contest the application or support it on additional grounds, must provide detailed grounds for contesting or supporting the application to the Upper Tribunal.

(2) Any detailed grounds must be provided in writing and must be sent or delivered to the Upper Tribunal so that they are received not more than 35 days after the Upper Tribunal sent notice of the grant of permission under rule 30(1).

Applicant seeking to rely on additional grounds

32. The applicant may not rely on any grounds, other than those grounds on which the applicant obtained permission for the judicial review proceedings, without the consent of the Upper Tribunal.

Appendix 6

Right to make representations

33. Each party and, with the permission of the Upper Tribunal, any other person, may—
- (a) submit evidence, except at the hearing of an application for permission;
- (b) make representations at any hearing which they are entitled to attend; and
- (c) make written representations in relation to a decision to be made without a hearing.

PART 5

Hearings

Decision with or without a hearing

34.—(1) Subject to paragraph (2), the Upper Tribunal may make any decision without a hearing.

(2) The Upper Tribunal must have regard to any view expressed by a party when deciding whether to hold a hearing to consider any matter, and the form of any such hearing.

Entitlement to attend a hearing

35. Subject to rule 37(4) (exclusion of a person from a hearing), each party is entitled to attend a hearing.

Notice of hearings

36.—(1) The Upper Tribunal must give each party entitled to attend a hearing reasonable notice of the time and place of the hearing (including any adjourned or postponed hearing) and any change to the time and place of the hearing.

(2) The period of notice under paragraph (1) must be at least 14 days except that—
- (a) in applications for permission to bring judicial review proceedings, the period of notice must be at least 2 working days; and
- (b) the Upper Tribunal may give shorter notice—
  - (i) with the parties' consent; or
  - (ii) in urgent or exceptional cases.

Public and private hearings

37.—(1) Subject to the following paragraphs, all hearings must be held in public.

(2) The Upper Tribunal may give a direction that a hearing, or part of it, is to be held in private.

(3) Where a hearing, or part of it, is to be held in private, the Upper Tribunal may determine who is entitled to attend the hearing or part of it.

(4) The Upper Tribunal may give a direction excluding from any hearing, or part of it—
- (a) any person whose conduct the Upper Tribunal considers is disrupting or is likely to disrupt the hearing;
- (b) any person whose presence the Upper Tribunal considers is likely to prevent another person from giving evidence or making submissions freely;

(c) any person who the Upper Tribunal considers should be excluded in order to give effect to a direction under rule 14(2) (withholding information likely to cause harm); [...]¹
(d) any person where the purpose of the hearing would be defeated by the attendance of that person [; or]²
[(e) a person under the age of eighteen years.]²

(5) The Upper Tribunal may give a direction excluding a witness from a hearing until that witness gives evidence.

Notes
1. Word repealed by Tribunal Procedure (Amendment) Rules 2009/274 rule 19(a) (1 April 2009)
2. Added by Tribunal Procedure (Amendment) Rules 2009/274 rule 19(b) (1 April 2009)

Hearings in a party's absence

38. If a party fails to attend a hearing, the Upper Tribunal may proceed with the hearing if the Upper Tribunal—

(a) is satisfied that the party has been notified of the hearing or that reasonable steps have been taken to notify the party of the hearing; and
(b) considers that it is in the interests of justice to proceed with the hearing.

PART 6

Decisions

Consent orders

39.—(1) The Upper Tribunal may, at the request of the parties but only if it considers it appropriate, make a consent order disposing of the proceedings and making such other appropriate provision as the parties have agreed.

(2) Notwithstanding any other provision of these Rules, the Tribunal need not hold a hearing before making an order under paragraph (1) [...]¹.

Note
1. Words repealed by Tribunal Procedure (Amendment) Rules 2009/274 rule 20 (1 April 2009)

Decisions

40.—(1) The Upper Tribunal may give a decision orally at a hearing.

(2) [The]¹ Upper Tribunal must provide to each party as soon as reasonably practicable after making a decision which finally disposes of all issues in the proceedings (except a decision under Part 7)—

(a) a decision notice stating the Tribunal's decision; and
(b) notification of any rights of review or appeal against the decision and the time and manner in which such rights of review or appeal may be exercised.

(3) [Subject to rule 14(2) (withholding harmful information), the]² Upper Tribunal must provide written reasons for its decision with a decision notice provided under paragraph (2)(a) unless—

(a) the decision was made with the consent of the parties; or
(b) the parties have consented to the Upper Tribunal not giving written reasons.

(4) The Tribunal may provide written reasons for any decision to which paragraph (2) does not apply.

Notes
1. Words repealed by Tribunal Procedure (Amendment) Rules 2009/274 rule 21(a) (1 April 2009)
2. Words inserted by Tribunal Procedure (Amendment) Rules 2009/274 rule 21(b) (1 April 2009)

PART 7
Correcting, setting aside, reviewing and appealing decisions of the Upper Tribunal

Interpretation

41. In this Part—

"appeal" [, except in rule 44(2) (application for permission to appeal),][1] means the exercise of a right of appeal under section 13 of the 2007 Act; and

"review" means the review of a decision by the Upper Tribunal under section 10 of the 2007 Act.

Note
1. Words inserted by Tribunal Procedure (Amendment) Rules 2009/274 rule 22 (1 April 2009)

Clerical mistakes and accidental slips or omissions

42. The Upper Tribunal may at any time correct any clerical mistake or other accidental slip or omission in a decision or record of a decision by—

(a) sending notification of the amended decision, or a copy of the amended record, to all parties; and

(b) making any necessary amendment to any information published in relation to the decision or record.

Setting aside a decision which disposes of proceedings

43.—(1) The Upper Tribunal may set aside a decision which disposes of proceedings, or part of such a decision, and re-make the decision or the relevant part of it, if—

(a) the Upper Tribunal considers that it is in the interests of justice to do so; and
(b) one or more of the conditions in paragraph (2) are satisfied.

(2) The conditions are—

(a) a document relating to the proceedings was not sent to, or was not received at an appropriate time by, a party or a party's representative;
(b) a document relating to the proceedings was not sent to the Upper Tribunal at an appropriate time;
(c) a party, or a party's representative, was not present at a hearing related to the proceedings; or
(d) there has been some other procedural irregularity in the proceedings.

(3) A party applying for a decision, or part of a decision, to be set aside under paragraph (1) must make a written application to the Upper Tribunal so that it is received no later than 1 month after the date on which the Tribunal sent notice of the decision to the party.

Appendix 6

Application for permission to appeal

44.—(1) A person seeking permission to appeal must make a written application to the Upper Tribunal for permission to appeal.

(2) Paragraph (3) applies to an application under paragraph (1) in respect of a decision—

    (a)   on an appeal against a decision in a social security and child support case (as defined in the Tribunal Procedure (First-tier Tribunal) (Social Entitlement Chamber) Rules 2008);

    (b)   on an appeal against a decision in proceedings in the War Pensions and Armed Forces Compensation Chamber of the First-tier Tribunal[1] ; [...][2]

    [(ba)   on an appeal against a decision of a Pensions Appeal Tribunal for Scotland or Northern Ireland; or][3]

    (c)   in proceedings under the Forfeiture Act 1982.

(3) Where this paragraph applies, the application must be sent or delivered to the Upper Tribunal so that it is received within 3 months after the date on which the Upper Tribunal sent to the person making the application—

    (a)   written notice of the decision;

    (b)   notification of amended reasons for, or correction of, the decision following a review; or

    (c)   notification that an application for the decision to be set aside has been unsuccessful.

(4) Where paragraph (3) does not apply, an application under paragraph (1) must be sent or delivered to the Upper Tribunal so that it is received within 1 month after the latest of the dates on which the Upper Tribunal sent to the person making the application—

    (a)   written reasons for the decision;

    (b)   notification of amended reasons for, or correction of, the decision following a review; or

    (c)   notification that an application for the decision to be set aside has been unsuccessful.

(5) The date in paragraph (3)(c) or (4)(c) applies only if the application for the decision to be set aside was made within the time stipulated in rule 43 (setting aside a decision which disposes of proceedings) or any extension of that time granted by the Upper Tribunal.

(6) If the person seeking permission to appeal provides the application to the Upper Tribunal later than the time required by paragraph (3) or (4), or by any extension of time under rule 5(3)(a) (power to extend time)—

    (a)   the application must include a request for an extension of time and the reason why the application notice was not provided in time; and

    (b)   unless the Upper Tribunal extends time for the application under rule 5(3)(a) (power to extend time) the Upper Tribunal must refuse the application.

(7) An application under paragraph (1) must—

    (a)   identify the decision of the Tribunal to which it relates;

    (b)   identify the alleged error or errors of law in the decision; and

    (c)   state the result the party making the application is seeking.

Notes
1. The War Pensions and Armed Forces Compensation Chamber of the First-tier Tribunal is established by the First-tier Tribunal and Upper Tribunal (Chambers) Order 2008 (S.I. 2008/2684).
2. Word repealed by Tribunal Procedure (Amendment) Rules 2009/274 rule 23(a) (1 April 2009)
3. Added by Tribunal Procedure (Amendment) Rules 2009/274 rule 23(b) (1 April 2009)

Appendix 6

Upper Tribunal's consideration of application for permission to appeal

45.—(1) On receiving an application for permission to appeal the Upper Tribunal may review the decision in accordance with rule 46 (review of a decision), but may only do so if—

(a) when making the decision the Upper Tribunal overlooked a legislative provision or binding authority which could have had a material effect on the decision; or

(b) since the Upper Tribunal's decision, a court has made a decision which is binding on the Upper Tribunal and which, had it been made before the Upper Tribunal's decision, could have had a material effect on the decision.

(2) If the Upper Tribunal decides not to review the decision, or reviews the decision and decides to take no action in relation to the decision or part of it, the Upper Tribunal must consider whether to give permission to appeal in relation to the decision or that part of it.

(3) The Upper Tribunal must send a record of its decision to the parties as soon as practicable.

(4) If the Upper Tribunal refuses permission to appeal it must send with the record of its decision—

(a) a statement of its reasons for such refusal; and

(b) notification of the right to make an application to the relevant appellate court for permission to appeal and the time within which, and the method by which, such application must be made.

(5) The Upper Tribunal may give permission to appeal on limited grounds, but must comply with paragraph (4) in relation to any grounds on which it has refused permission.

Review of a decision

46.—(1) The Upper Tribunal may only undertake a review of a decision—

(a) pursuant to rule 45(1) (review on an application for permission to appeal); or

(b) pursuant to rule 47 (reviews of decisions in proceedings under the Forfeiture Act 1982).

(2) The Upper Tribunal must notify the parties in writing of the outcome of any review and of any rights of review or appeal in relation to the outcome.

(3) If the Upper Tribunal decides to take any action in relation to a decision following a review without first giving every party an opportunity to make representations, the notice under paragraph (2) must state that any party that did not have an opportunity to make representations may apply for such action to be set aside and for the decision to be reviewed again.

Review of a decision in proceedings under the Forfeiture Act 1982

47.—(1) A person who referred a question to the Upper Tribunal under rule 26 (references under the Forfeiture Act 1982) must refer the Upper Tribunal's previous decision in relation to the question to the Upper Tribunal if they—

(a) consider that the decision should be reviewed; or

(b) have received a written application for the decision to be reviewed from the person to whom the decision related.

(2) The Upper Tribunal may review the decision if—

Appendix 6

        (a)   the decision was erroneous in point of law;
        (b)   the decision was made in ignorance of, or was based on a mistake as to, some material fact; or
        (c)   there has been a relevant change in circumstances since the decision was made.

(3)   When a person makes the reference to the Upper Tribunal, they must also notify the person to whom the question relates that the reference has been made.

(4)   The Upper Tribunal must notify the person who made the reference and the person who to whom the question relates of the outcome of the reference.

(5)   If the Upper Tribunal decides to take any action in relation to a decision following a review under this rule without first giving the person who made the reference and the person to whom the question relates an opportunity to make representations, the notice under paragraph (4) must state that either of those persons who did not have an opportunity to make representations may apply for such action to be set aside and for the decision to be reviewed again.

Index

[All references are to paragraph number]

Addressing the tribunal members
   presentation of appeal, and, 18.26–18.34
Administrative procedures
   preparation for appeal, and, 17.17–17.25
Advertisement for work
   HMRC inquiries, and, 15.41
Advice to client
   agree and implement written contract, 20.1–20.4
   maintain due diligence records, 20.5–20.9
   taking professional advice in event of HMRC challenge, 20.10
Advocacy
   formalities of appeal, and, 16.18–16.24
Agencies
   identity of client, and, 6.8–6.9
Agency/end user contract
   case study, 8.1
   common sense and equity, 8.32–8.41
   existing case law, 8.42–8.51
   'hypothetical contract', and
      generally, 8.17–8.24
      introduction, 8.6
   introduction, 8.1–8.4
   ITEPA 2003, Pt 2, Ch 8, and
      generally, 8.6–8.16
      'hypothetical contract', and, 8.17–8.24
      use of 'contracts', 8.25–8.28
   privity of contract doctrine, 8.29–8.31
   reasons for lack of relevance, 8.5
   summary, 8.52
Agency rules
   avoidance of trap
      demonstrating services are being supplied, 9.21–9.25
      demonstrating terms of statutory provision not met, 9.12–9.20
      introduction, 9.11
   generally, 9.2–9.10
   introduction, 9.1
   summary, 9.26–9.29
Agreed statement of facts
   preparation for appeal, and, 17.6–17.14

Agreeing contractual terms falling outside IR35
   And see Contractual terms falling outside IR35
   agency/end user contract, 8.1–8.52
   agency rules, and, 9.1–9.29
   case law, 11.1–11.290
   composite companies, 10.1–10.12
   contractual requirements, 7.1–7.62
   employment status, 5.1–5.191
   HMRC contract review, 12.1–12.16
   identity of client, 6.1–6.15
   importance of case law, 4.1–4.2
   introduction, 2.4–2.7
'Another person'
   identity of client, and, 6.11
Appeals to tribunal
   administrative procedures, 17.17–17.25
   advocacy, 16.18–16.24
   agreed statement of facts, 17.6–17.14
   appeals units, 11.288–11.289
   arrangements for hearing, 16.25–16.31
   burden of proof, 16.37–16.41
   'calling the HMRC's bluff', 16.32–16.36
   clarifying determination sought, 17.43
   documentation
      generally, 17.28–17.42
      legal bundle, 17.32–17.33
      non-legal bundle, 17.30–17.31
   first-tier tribunal, 16.10–16.12
   further appeal
      introduction, 18.90
      taxpayer has lost, where, 19.12–19.16
      taxpayer has won, where, 19.1–19.11
   General Commissioners, 16.9
   internal reviews, 16.13–16.15
   introduction, 2.9
   legal bundle, 17.32–17.33
   listing for hearing, 16.16–16.31
   non-legal bundle, 17.30–17.31
   onus of proof, 17.26
   opinion, and, 17.27
   post-hearing procedure
      summary, 19.19–19.20

339

Index

Appeals to tribunal—*contd*
  post-hearing procedure—*contd*
    taxpayer has lost, where, 19.12–19.16
    taxpayer has won, where, 19.1–19.11
  preparation for hearing
    administrative procedures, 17.17–17.25
    agreed statement of facts, 17.6–17.14
    clarifying determination sought, 17.43
    documentation, 17.28–17.42
    generally, 17.5
    introduction, 17.1–17.4
    legal bundle, 17.32–17.33
    non-legal bundle, 17.30–17.31
    onus of proof, 17.26
    opinion, and, 17.27
    question for determination, 17.15–17.16
    summary, 17.59–17.63
    witness summons, 17.53–17.58
    witnesses, 17.44–17.52
  presentation
    addressing the tribunal members, 18.26–18.34
    avoiding mistakes, 18.95–18.96
    blueprint for defence and appeal, 18.100
    brief summary of case, 18.35–18.38
    calling witnesses, 18.39–18.50
    conduct of proceedings, 18.20–18.25
    constitution of first-tier tax tribunal, 18.10–18.15
    cross-examination of inspector's witnesses, 18.70–18.79
    cross-examination of taxpayer and witnesses, 18.51–18.55
    decision, 18.87–18.90
    evidence on oath, 18.41
    examining witnesses, 18.39–18.50
    hearsay evidence, 18.40
    hostile witnesses, 18.75
    inspector-advocate, 18.17
    introducing the client, 18.26–18.34
    introduction, 18.1–18.2
    layout of meeting room, 18.18–18.19
    leading questions, 18.44
    legal submissions by inspector-advocate, 18.84–18.66
    legal submissions by taxpayer, 18.62–18.66
    location, 18.3–18.5
    opening summary of case, 18.35–18.38

Appeals to tribunal—*contd*
  presentation—*contd*
    questions by tribunal to inspector, 18.81–18.82
    questions by tribunal to taxpayer, 18.61
    re-examination of inspector-advocate, 18.80
    re-examination of taxpayer and witnesses, 18.56–18.60
    representation, 18.6–18.9
    response of inspector-advocate, 18.68–18.69
    style of advocates, 18.91–18.94
    summary of case by inspector-advocate, 18.85
    summary of case by taxpayer, 18.67
    summary of case on closing by taxpayer, 18.86
    summary of case on opening, 18.35–18.38
    tax tribunal judge, 18.16
    'without prejudice' evidence, 18.40
    witness summonses, 18.76–18.78
  procedure
    internal reviews, 16.13–16.15
    introduction, 16.1–16.8
    listing for hearing, 16.16–16.31
    tribunal system, 16.9–16.12
  question for determination, 17.15–17.16
  Special Commissioners, 16.9
  Tax Chamber, 16.10
  tax tribunals, 16.9–16.12
  Upper Tribunal, 16.10–16.12
  Upper Tribunal, to
    introduction, 18.90
    taxpayer has lost, where, 19.12–19.16
    taxpayer has won, where, 19.1–19.11
  witness summons, 17.53–17.58
  witnesses, 17.44–17.52

Basis of remuneration
  contractual arrangements, and, 7.55
  employment status, and, 5.185–5.188
Bundles of documents
  generally, 17.28–17.42
  legal bundle, 17.32–17.33
  non-legal bundle, 17.30–17.31
Burden of proof
  formalities of appeal, and, 16.37–16.41
'Business on own account'
  contractual arrangements, and, 7.9–7.11
  employment status, and, 5.143–5.151

Index

Business organisation
 contractual arrangements, and, 7.42–7.44

Calling witnesses
 presentation of appeal, and, 18.39–18.50

Case law
 Alternative Book Company Ltd v HMRC, 11.247–11.262
 Ansell Computer Services Ltd v Richardson, 11.112–11.120
 Battersby v Campbell, 11.2–11.7
 control
  Alternative Book Company Ltd v HMRC, 11.256–11.257
  Dragonfly Consulting Ltd v HMRC, 11.272, 11.279–11.281
  First Word Software Ltd v HMRC, 11.196–11.199
  Larkstar Data Ltd v HMRC, 11.239–11.243
  MKM Computing Ltd v HMRC, 11.226–11.227
  Netherlane Ltd v York, 11.154–11.155
 Datagate Services Ltd v HMRC, 11.202–11.215
 Dragonfly Consulting Ltd v HMRC, 11.263–11.287
 employment status
  And see Employment status
  basis of payment, 5.185–5.188
  control, 5.104–5.139
  delegated control, 5.137
  Dragonfly Consulting Ltd v HMRC, 11.285–11.286
  employee-style benefits, 5.184
  financial risk, 5.165–5.169
  freedom to offer services, 5.170–5.174
  in business on own account, 5.143–5.151
  intention of the parties, 5.155–5.164
  introduction, 5.1–5.8
  mutuality of obligation, 5.65–5.103
  other factors, 5.140–5.142
  previous HMRC determinations, 5.175–5.176
  profit, 5.165–5.169
  provision of equipment, 5.177–5.183
  recognised custom and practice, 5.189
  series of engagements, 5.152–5.154
  substitution, 5.9–5.64
  summary, 5.190–5.191
 First Word Software Ltd v HMRC, 11.188–11.201

Case law—*contd*
 F S Consulting v McCaul, 11.8–11.17
 Future Online v S K Faulds, 11.93–11.111, 11.132–11.143
 hierarchy of tribunals and courts, 4.7–4.13
 importance
  generally, 4.1–4.6
  hierarchy of tribunals and courts, 4.7–4.13
  precedent, 4.14–4.22
  stare decisis, 4.17
  summary, 4.23
  understanding law and fact, 4.14–4.22
 in business on own account
  Synaptek Ltd v Young, 11.25
 introduction, 11.1
 Island Consultants Ltd v HMRC, 11.165–11.187
 Larkstar Data Ltd v HMRC, 11.229–11.246
 Lime-IT Ltd v Justin, 11.41–11.55
 MKM Computing Ltd v HMRC, 11.216–11.228
 mutual intention
  Alternative Book Company Ltd v HMRC, 11.260, 11.282–11.284
 mutuality of obligations
  Alternative Book Company Ltd v HMRC, 11.258–11.259
  Dragonfly Consulting Ltd v HMRC, 11.273–11.274
  First Word Software Ltd v HMRC, 11.200–11.201
  Larkstar Data Ltd v HMRC, 11.244
  MKM Computing Ltd v HMRC, 11.224–11.225
  Netherlane Ltd v York, 11.151–11.153
  Synaptek Ltd v Young, 11.26–11.28
  Usetech Ltd v Young, 11.128–11.131
 Netherlane Ltd v York, 11.144–11.164
 personal service
  Alternative Book Company Ltd v HMRC, 11.254–11.255
  Dragonfly Consulting Ltd v HMRC, 11.271, 11.276–11.278
  First Word Software Ltd v HMRC, 11.194–11.195
  Larkstar Data Ltd v HMRC, 11.238
  MKM Computing Ltd v HMRC, 11.220–11.223
  Netherlane Ltd v York, 11.156–11.157
 precedent, 4.14–4.22
 stare decisis, 4.17

Index

Case law—*contd*
summary, 11.290
substitution right
  Alternative Book Company Ltd v HMRC, 11.254–11.255
  First Word Software Ltd v HMRC, 11.194–11.195
  Larkstar Data Ltd v HMRC, 11.238
  MKM Computing Ltd v HMRC, 11.220–11.223
  Netherlane Ltd v York, 11.156–11.157
  Synaptek Ltd v Young, 11.29–11.32
  Tilbury Consulting Ltd v Gittins, 11.76–11.79
  Usetech Ltd v Young, 11.123–11.127
Synaptek Ltd v Young, 11.18–11.40
Tilbury Consulting Ltd v Gittins, 11.56–11.92
understanding law and fact, 4.14–4.22
Usetech Ltd v Young, 11.121–11.131

Client's identity
agency's role, 6.8–6.9
'another person', 6.11
commercial contracts with multiple parties, 6.10
contractual relationship, 6.4–6.6
financial relationship, 6.7
HMRC's view, 6.14
introduction, 6.1–6.3
ITEPA 2003, s 49(1)(a), 6.11–6.13
summary, 6.15

Compliance process
And see HMRC compliance process
employer compliance inspections, 15.1–15.87
introduction, 2.8

Composite companies
background, 10.1–10.3
managed service company rules, 10.4–10.9
summary, 10.12
'umbrella' companies, 10.10–10.11

Conditions applicable to IR35
generally, 3.4
introduction, 3.1–3.3
s 49(1)(a) ITEPA 2003, 3.5–3.9
s 49(1)(b) ITEPA 2003, 3.10–3.19
s 49(1)(c) ITEPA 2003, 3.20–3.21
summary, 3.30–3.31

Conduct of proceedings
presentation of appeal, and, 18.20–18.25

Constitution of first-tier tax tribunal
presentation of appeal, and, 18.10–18.15

Contract for services
And see Employment status
meaning, 4.1–4.6

Contract of service
And see Employment status
meaning, 4.1–4.6

Contract review
generally, 12.1–12.15
HMRC inquiries, and, 15.81
summary, 12.16
targeting by HMRC, and, 14.15

Contractual arrangements
basis of payment, 7.55
'business on own account' approach, 7.9–7.11
business organisation, 7.42–7.44
control, 7.25–7.27
employee benefits, 7.51–7.52
factors of secondary importance
  basis of payment, 7.55
  employee benefits, 7.51–7.52
  provision of equipment, 7.53–7.54
financial risk, 7.31–7.41
freedom to offer services, 7.45
general considerations, 7.56–7.59
HMRC inquiries, and, 15.23–15.26
important terms and conditions
  business organisation, 7.42–7.44
  control, 7.25–7.27
  financial risk, 7.31–7.41
  freedom to offer services, 7.45
  intention of parties, 7.46
  introduction, 7.12–7.13
  mutuality of obligations, 7.22–7.24
  other terms, 7.30
  personal service, 7.15–7.21
  substitution, 7.15–7.21
  summary, 7.28–7.29
intention of parties, 7.46
introduction, 7.1–7.4
invoicing, 7.7
'looking beyond the terms of the contract', 7.9–7.11
modus operandi of contractor, 7.5–7.7
mutuality of obligations, 7.22–7.24
non-contractual factors, 7.8
personal service, 7.15–7.21
provision of equipment, 7.53–7.54
substitution, 7.15–7.21
summary, 7.60–7.62

Contractual relationships
identity of client, and, 6.4–6.6

Index

Contractual terms falling outside IR35
And see under individual headings
agency/end user contract
  case study, 8.1
  common sense and equity, 8.32–8.41
  existing case law, 8.42–8.51
  introduction, 8.1–8.4
  ITEPA 2003, Pt 2, Ch 8, and, 8.6–8.28
  privity of contract doctrine, 8.29–8.31
  reasons for lack of relevance, 8.5
  summary, 8.52
agency rules, and
  avoidance of trap, 9.11–9.25
  demonstrating services are being supplied, 9.21–9.25
  demonstrating terms of statutory provision not met, 9.12–9.20
  generally, 9.2–9.10
  introduction, 9.1
  summary, 9.26–9.29
case law
  Alternative Book Company Ltd v HMRC, 11.247–11.262
  Ansell Computer Services Ltd v Richardson, 11.112–11.120
  Battersby v Campbell, 11.2–11.7
  Datagate Services Ltd v HMRC, 11.202–11.215
  Dragonfly Consulting Ltd v HMRC, 11.263–11.287
  First Word Software Ltd v HMRC, 11.188–11.201
  F S Consulting v McCaul, 11.8–11.17
  Future Online v S K Faulds, 11.93–11.111, 11.132–11.143
  introduction, 11.1
  Island Consultants Ltd v HMRC, 11.165–11.187
  Larkstar Data Ltd v HMRC, 11.229–11.246
  Lime-IT Ltd v Justin, 11.41–11.55
  MKM Computing Ltd v HMRC, 11.216–11.228
  Netherlane Ltd v York, 11.144–11.164
  summary, 11.290
  Synaptek Ltd v Young, 11.18–11.40
  Tilbury Consulting Ltd v Gittins, 11.56–11.92
  Usetech Ltd v Young, 11.121–11.131
composite companies
  background, 10.1–10.3
  managed service company rules, 10.4–10.9
  summary, 10.12

Contractual terms falling outside IR35
composite companies—*contd*
  'umbrella' companies, 10.10–10.11
contractual arrangements
  basis of payment, 7.55
  'business on own account' approach, 7.9–7.11
  business organisation, 7.42–7.44
  control, 7.25–7.27
  employee benefits, 7.51–7.52
  factors of secondary importance, 7.51–7.55
  financial risk, 7.31–7.41
  freedom to provide services, 7.45
  general considerations, 7.56–7.59
  important terms and conditions, 7.12–7.50
  intention of parties, 7.46
  introduction, 7.1–7.4
  invoicing, 7.7
  'looking beyond the terms of the contract', 7.9–7.11
  modus operandi of contractor, 7.5–7.7
  mutuality of obligations, 7.22–7.24
  non-contractual factors, 7.8
  personal service, 7.15–7.21
  provision of equipment, 7.53–7.54
  summary, 7.60–7.62
employment status
  And see Employment status
  basis of payment, 5.185–5.188
  control, 5.104–5.139
  delegated control, 5.137
  employee-style benefits, 5.184
  financial risk, 5.165–5.169
  freedom to offer services, 5.170–5.174
  in business on own account, 5.143–5.151
  intention of the parties, 5.155–5.164
  introduction, 5.1–5.8
  mutuality of obligation, 5.65–5.103
  other factors, 5.140–5.142
  previous HMRC determinations, 5.175–5.176
  profit, 5.165–5.169
  provision of equipment, 5.177–5.183
  recognised custom and practice, 5.189
  series of engagements, 5.152–5.154
  substitution, 5.9–5.64
  summary, 5.190–5.191
HMRC contract review, 12.1–12.16
identity of client
  agency's role, 6.8–6.9
  'another person', 6.11

Index

Contractual terms falling outside IR35
identity of client—*contd*
  commercial contracts with multiple parties, 6.10
  contractual relationship, 6.4–6.6
  financial relationship, 6.7
  HMRC's view, 6.14
  introduction, 6.1–6.3
  ITEPA 2003, s 49(1)(a), 6.11–6.13
  summary, 6.15
importance of case law
  generally, 4.1–4.6
  hierarchy of tribunals and courts, 4.7–4.13
  precedent, 4.14–4.22
  stare decisis, 4.17
  summary, 4.23
  understanding law and fact, 4.14–4.22
introduction, 2.4–2.7

Control
And see Employment status
case law
  Alternative Book Company Ltd v HMRC, 11.256–11.257
  Dragonfly Consulting Ltd v HMRC, 11.272, 11.279–11.281
  First Word Software Ltd v HMRC, 11.196–11.199
  Larkstar Data Ltd v HMRC, 11.239–11.243
  MKM Computing Ltd v HMRC, 11.226–11.227
  Netherlane Ltd v York, 11.154–11.155
contractual arrangements, and, 7.25–7.27
delegation, and, 5.137
generally, 5.104–5.133
HMRC inquiries, and, 15.43–15.45
implication, by, 5.134–5.136
summary, 5.138–5.139

Cross-examination
inspector's witnesses, of, 18.70–18.79
taxpayer and witnesses, of, 18.51–18.55

Custom and practice
employment status, and, 5.189

Customer service enquiries
HMRC inquiries, and, 15.81

Decision
appeal procedure, and, 18.87–18.90

Defence strategies
agreeing contractual terms falling outside IR35
  agency/end user contract, 8.1–8.52
  agency rules, and, 9.1–9.29

Defence strategies
agreeing contractual terms falling outside IR35—*contd*
  case law, 11.1–11.290
  composite companies, 10.1–10.12
  contractual terms, 7.1–7.62
  employment status, 5.1–5.191
  HMRC contract review, 12.1–12.16
  identity of client, 6.1–6.15
  importance of case law, 4.1–4.23
  introduction, 2.4–2.7
appeals to tribunal
  introduction, 2.9
  post-hearing procedure, 19.1–19.20
  preparation, 17.1–17.63
  presentation, 18.1–18.100
  procedure, 16.1–16.42
application of principles, 2.10–2.13
critical analysis of legislation
  generally, 3.1–3.31
  introduction, 2.2–2.3
implementing contractual terms falling outside IR35
  agency/end user contract, 8.1–8.52
  agency rules, and, 9.1–9.29
  case law, 11.1–11.290
  case law decisions, 5.1–5.191
  composite companies, 10.1–10.12
  contractual terms, 7.1–7.62
  HMRC contract review, 12.1–12.16
  identity of client, 6.1–6.15
  importance of case law, 4.1–4.23
  introduction, 2.4–2.7
introduction, 2.1
principles
  application, 2.10–2.13
  general, 2.2–2.9
  introduction, 2.1
  summary, 2.14
understanding HMRC compliance process
  HMRC interviews, 15.4–15.87
  introduction, 2.8

Delegated control
employment status, and, 5.137

Documentation for appeal
generally, 17.28–17.42
legal bundle, 17.32–17.33
non-legal bundle, 17.30–17.31

Employee benefits
contractual arrangements, and, 7.51–7.52
employment status, and, 5.184

Employer compliance inspections
And see HMRC inquiries
contracts, 15.23–15.26
employment status inspectors, 15.27–15.36
factors to be considered, 15.37–15.68
factsheets, 15.18–15.22
introduction, 15.1–15.3
interview notes, 15.69–15.70
special status inspectors, 15.27–15.36
start of inspection, 15.4–15.17
summary, 15.87
tactical developments, 15.71–15.86
Employment status
basis of payment, 5.185–5.188
control
　delegation, and, 5.137
　generally, 5.104–5.133
　implication, by, 5.134–5.136
　summary, 5.138–5.139
delegated control, 5.137
employee-style benefits, 5.184
engagements, 5.152–5.154
financial risk, 5.165–5.169
formation of contract, 5.69
freedom to offer services, 5.170–5.174
in business on own account, 5.143–5.151
intention of the parties
　generally, 5.155–5.164
　introduction, 5.69
introduction, 5.1–5.8
mutual intention
　generally, 5.155–5.164
　introduction, 5.69
mutuality of obligation
　case law decisions, 5.78–5.93
　HMRC view, 5.94–5.102
　importance, 5.66–5.68
　introduction, 5.65
　meaning, 5.69–5.77
　summary, 5.103
other factors, 5.140–5.142
previous HMRC determinations, 5.175–5.176
profit, 5.165–5.169
provision of equipment, 5.177–5.183
recognised custom and practice, 5.189
series of engagements, 5.152–5.154
sub-contracting, 5.11–5.39
substitution
　case law decisions, 5.17–5.39
　contracts silent on issue, 5.62–5.63
　external rights, 5.11–5.14
　hiring helpers, 5.60–5.61

Employment status
substitution—*contd*
　HMRC view, 5.40–5.59
　internal rights, 5.11–5.14
　introduction, 5.9–5.10
　sub-contracting, 5.15–5.16
　summary, 5.64
summary, 5.190–5.191
Employment status inspectors
HMRC inquiries, and, 15.27–15.36
End-user evidence
HMRC inquiries, and, 15.80
Engagements
employment status, and, 5.152–5.154
Equipment provision
contractual arrangements, and, 7.53–7.54
employment status, and, 5.177–5.183
'Error or mistake' relief claim
generally, 13.20
Evidence on oath
presentation of appeal, and, 18.41
Examining witnesses
presentation of appeal, and, 18.39–18.50
Exclusivity
HMRC inquiries, and, 15.64–15.67

Factsheets
HMRC inquiries, and, 15.18–15.22
Financial relationships
identity of client, and, 6.7
Financial risk
contractual arrangements, and, 7.31–7.41
employment status, and, 5.165–5.169
HMRC inquiries, and, 15.52–15.53
First-tier tribunal
And see Appeals
generally, 16.10–16.12
Foreign companies
intermediary arrangements, and, 3.19
Form P35
answering box 6, 14.2–14.6
Freedom to offer services
contractual arrangements, and, 7.45
employment status, and, 5.170–5.174

General Commissioners
And see Appeals
generally, 16.9

Hearsay evidence
presentation of appeal, and, 18.40
HMRC determinations
employment status, and, 5.175–5.176

Index

HMRC inquiries
  contract review, and, 15.81
  contracts, 15.23–15.26
  customer service enquiries, 15.81
  employer compliance inspections
    contracts, 15.23–15.26
    employment status inspectors, 15.27–15.36
    factors to be considered, 15.37–15.68
    factsheets, 15.18–15.22
    introduction, 15.1–15.3
    interview notes, 15.69–15.70
    special status inspectors, 15.27–15.36
    start of inspection, 15.4–15.17
    summary, 15.87
    tactical developments, 15.71–15.86
  employment status inspectors, 15.27–15.36
  end-user evidence, 15.80
  factors to be considered
    advertisement for work, 15.41
    client's business, 15.38
    control, 15.43–15.45
    exclusivity, 15.64–15.67
    financial risk, 15.52–15.53
    holiday pay entitlement, 15.60
    in business on own account, 15.42
    intention of parties, 15.68
    introduction, 15.37
    mutuality of obligation, 15.57–15.59
    nature of client's business, 15.38
    opportunity to profit, 15.54–15.56
    other workers doing same job, 15.39–15.40
    personal service, 15.46–15.48
    provision of equipment, 15.49–15.51
    sick pay entitlement, 15.60
    substitution, 15.46–15.48
    termination, 15.61–15.63
  factsheets, 15.18–15.22
  information notices, 15.71–15.79
  introduction, 15.1–15.3
  interview notes, 15.69–15.70
  overview, 2.8
  special status inspectors, 15.27–15.36
  start of inspection, 15.4–15.17
  substitution, and, 15.82–15.85
  summary, 15.87
  tactical developments, 15.71–15.86
  targeting by HMRC, and, 14.10–14.14
Holiday pay entitlement
  HMRC inquiries, and, 15.60
Hostile witnesses
  presentation of appeal, and, 18.75

'Hypothetical contract'
  agency/end user contract, and
    generally, 8.17–8.24
    introduction, 8.6
  contractual terms falling outside IR35, 2.4
  identity of client, and, 6.12
  intention of parties, and, 5.164
  mutuality of obligations, and, 5.100
  national insurance legislation, and, 3.27

Identity of client
  agency's role, 6.8–6.9
  'another person', 6.11
  commercial contracts with multiple parties, 6.10
  contractual relationship, 6.4–6.6
  financial relationship, 6.7
  HMRC's view, 6.14
  introduction, 6.1–6.3
  ITEPA 2003, s 49(1)(a), 6.11–6.13
  summary, 6.15
Implementing contractual terms falling outside IR35
  And see Contractual terms falling outside IR35
  agency/end user contract, 8.1–8.52
  agency rules, and, 9.1–9.29
  case law, 11.1–11.290
  case law decisions, 5.1–5.191
  composite companies, 10.1–10.12
  contractual requirements, 7.1–7.62
  HMRC contract review, 12.1–12.16
  identity of client, 6.1–6.15
  importance of case law, 4.1–4.23
  introduction, 2.4–2.7
In business on own account
  contractual arrangements, and, 7.9–7.11
  employment status, and, 5.143–5.151
  HMRC inquiries, and, 15.42
  Synaptek Ltd v Young, 11.25
Informants
  targeting by HMRC, and, 14.20–14.21
Information notices
  HMRC inquiries, and, 15.71–15.79
Inquiries by HMRC
  contract review, and, 15.81
  contracts, 15.23–15.26
  customer service enquiries, 15.81
  employer compliance inspections
    contracts, 15.23–15.26
    employment status inspectors, 15.27–15.36
    factors to be considered, 15.37–15.68

Inquiries by HMRC
employer compliance inspections—*contd*
  factsheets, 15.18–15.22
  introduction, 15.1–15.3
  interview notes, 15.69–15.70
  special status inspectors, 15.27–15.36
  start of inspection, 15.4–15.17
  summary, 15.87
  tactical developments, 15.71–15.86
employment status inspectors, 15.27–15.36
end-user evidence, 15.80
factors to be considered
  advertisement for work, 15.41
  client's business, 15.38
  control, 15.43–15.45
  exclusivity, 15.64–15.67
  financial risk, 15.52–15.53
  holiday pay entitlement, 15.60
  in business on own account, 15.42
  intention of parties, 15.68
  introduction, 15.37
  mutuality of obligation, 15.57–15.59
  nature of client's business, 15.38
  opportunity to profit, 15.54–15.56
  other workers doing same job, 15.39–15.40
  personal service, 15.46–15.48
  provision of equipment, 15.49–15.51
  sick pay entitlement, 15.60
  substitution, 15.46–15.48
  termination, 15.61–15.63
factsheets, 15.18–15.22
information notices, 15.71–15.79
introduction, 15.1–15.3
interview notes, 15.69–15.70
overview, 2.8
special status inspectors, 15.27–15.36
start of inspection, 15.4–15.17
substitution, and, 15.82–15.85
summary, 15.87
tactical developments, 15.71–15.86
targeting by HMRC, and, 14.10–14.14
Inspection powers
targeting by HMRC, and, 14.12–14.14
Inspector-advocate
presentation of appeal, and, 18.17
Intention of the parties
And see Employment status
Alternative Book Company Ltd v HMRC, 11.260, 11.282–11.284
contractual arrangements, and, 7.46
generally, 5.155–5.164
HMRC inquiries, and, 15.68
introduction, 5.69

Interest charges
generally, 13.4
Intermediary arrangements
conditions applicable to IR35, and, 3.10–3.19
Internal reviews
formalities of appeal, and, 16.13–16.15
Interview notes
HMRC inquiries, and, 15.69–15.70
Invoicing
contractual arrangements, and, 7.7
IR35
'agency rules', 1.12–1.13
background, 1.5–1.39
Budget Press Release (March 1999), 1.6
consequences of application, 1.40–1.51
consultation document, 1.29–1.30
criticisms, 1.2–1.4
disadvantages, 1.40–1.51
future developments, 21.26–21.27
introduction, 1.1
legislative basis
  generally, 3.1–3.31
  introduction, 2.2–2.3
misunderstandings
  5% shareholding in intermediary company, 1.61–1.63
  completion of time sheets, 1.67–1.69
  existence of company affects employee status, 1.70–1.71
  HMRC published guidance, 1.59–1.60
  liability of agency/end user, 1.57–1.58
  standard agency contracts, 1.64–1.66
status test, 1.52–1.56
summary, 1.72
overview, 1.2–1.4
recent developments, 21.1–21.25
ITEPA 2003, ss 44–47
avoidance of trap
  demonstrating services are being supplied, 9.21–9.25
  demonstrating terms of statutory provision not met, 9.12–9.20
  introduction, 9.11
generally, 9.2–9.10
introduction, 9.1
summary, 9.26–9.29
ITEPA 2003, s 49(1)(a)
generally, 3.5–3.9
identity of client, and, 6.11–6.13
ITEPA 2003, s 49(1)(b)
generally, 3.10–3.19

347

Index

ITEPA 2003, s 49(1)(c)
generally, 3.20–3.21
'hypothetical contract', and, 8.17–8.24

Layout of meeting room
presentation of appeal, and, 18.18–18.19

Leading questions
presentation of appeal, and, 18.44

Legal bundle
preparation for appeal, and, 17.32–17.33

Legal submissions
inspector-advocate, by, 18.84–18.66
taxpayer, by, 18.62–18.66

Legislative basis of IR35
generally, 3.1–3.3
introduction, 2.2–2.3
ITEPA 2003, Pt 2, Ch 8
  introduction, 3.4
  s 49(1)(a), 3.5–3.9
  s 49(1)(b), 3.10–3.19
  s 49(1)(c), 3.20–3.21
Social Security Contributions and Benefits Act 1992, s 4A, 3.22–3.29
summary, 3.30–3.31

Listing for hearing
preparation for appeal, and, 16.16–16.31

Location of proceedings
presentation of appeal, and, 18.3–18.5

'Looking beyond the terms of the contract'
contractual arrangements, and, 7.9–7.11

Managed service companies
generally, 10.4–10.9

Material interest
intermediary arrangements, and, 3.15

Modus operandi of contractor
appraisal of case, and, 13.2
contractual arrangements, and, 7.5–7.7

Mutual intention
And see Employment status
Alternative Book Company Ltd v HMRC, 11.260, 11.282–11.284
generally, 5.155–5.164
introduction, 5.69

Mutuality of obligations
And see Employment status
case law
  Alternative Book Company Ltd v HMRC, 11.258–11.259
  Dragonfly Consulting Ltd v HMRC, 11.273–11.274
  First Word Software Ltd v HMRC, 11.200–11.201

Mutuality of obligations
case law—*contd*
  generally, 5.78–5.93
  Larkstar Data Ltd v HMRC, 11.244
  MKM Computing Ltd v HMRC, 11.224–11.225
  Netherlane Ltd v York, 11.151–11.153
  Synaptek Ltd v Young, 11.26–11.28
  Usetech Ltd v Young, 11.128–11.131
contractual arrangements, and, 7.22–7.24
HMRC inquiries, and, 15.57–15.59
HMRC view, 5.94–5.102
importance, 5.66–5.68
introduction, 5.65
meaning, 5.69–5.77
summary, 5.103

National insurance legislation
generally, 3.22–3.29

Non-legal bundle
preparation for appeal, and, 17.30–17.31

Notices requiring agencies to provide details of payments to PSBs
targeting by HMRC, and, 14.16–14.18

'Obligation to perform'
conditions applicable to IR35, and, 3.6–3.9

Onus of proof
preparation for appeal, and, 17.26

Opening summary of case
presentation of appeal, and, 18.35–18.38

Opinion
preparation for appeal, and, 17.27

Opportunity to profit
HMRC inquiries, and, 15.54–15.56

Partnerships
generally, 3.12
material interest, 3.16

Payment basis
contractual arrangements, and, 7.55
employment status, and, 5.185–5.188

Penalties
generally, 13.5
'new' regime, 13.6–13.8
'old' regime, 13.9–13.12

'Performs'
conditions applicable to IR35, and, 3.6–3.9

Personal liability
generally, 13.13–13.18

Personal service
case law
Alternative Book Company Ltd v HMRC, 11.254–11.255
Dragonfly Consulting Ltd v HMRC, 11.271, 11.276–11.278
First Word Software Ltd v HMRC, 11.194–11.195
Larkstar Data Ltd v HMRC, 11.238
MKM Computing Ltd v HMRC, 11.220–11.223
Netherlane Ltd v York, 11.156–11.157
contractual arrangements, and, 7.15–7.21
HMRC inquiries, and, 15.46–15.48
Presentation of appeal
addressing the tribunal members, 18.26–18.34
avoiding mistakes, 18.95–18.96
blueprint for defence and appeal, 18.100
brief summary of case, 18.35–18.38
calling witnesses, 18.39–18.50
conduct of proceedings, 18.20–18.25
constitution of first-tier tax tribunal, 18.10–18.15
cross-examination
inspector's witnesses, of, 18.70–18.79
taxpayer and witnesses, of, 18.51–18.55
decision, 18.87–18.90
evidence on oath, 18.41
examining witnesses, 18.39–18.50
hearsay evidence, 18.40
hostile witnesses, 18.75
inspector-advocate, 18.17
introducing the client, 18.26–18.34
introduction, 18.1–18.2
layout of meeting room, 18.18–18.19
leading questions, 18.44
legal submissions
inspector-advocate, by, 18.84–18.66
taxpayer, by, 18.62–18.66
location, 18.3–18.5
opening summary of case, 18.35–18.38
questions by tribunal
inspector, to, 18.81–18.82
taxpayer, to, 18.61
re-examination
inspector-advocate, of, 18.80
taxpayer and witnesses, of, 18.56–18.60
representation, 18.6–18.9
response of inspector-advocate, 18.68–18.69
style of advocates, 18.91–18.94

Presentation of appeal
summary of case
closing by taxpayer, on, 18.86
end of case by inspector-advocate, at, 18.85
end of case by taxpayer, at, 18.67
opening by taxpayer, on, 18.35–18.38
tax tribunal judge, 18.16
'without prejudice' evidence, 18.40
witness summonses, 18.76–18.78
Privity of contract
agency/end user contract, and, 8.29–8.31
Profit
employment status, and, 5.165–5.169
Provision of equipment
contractual arrangements, and, 7.53–7.54
employment status, and, 5.177–5.183
HMRC inquiries, and, 15.49–15.51
Provision of information
HMRC powers, and, 14.12–14.14

Questions by tribunal
inspector, to, 18.81–18.82
taxpayer, to, 18.61

Random enquiries
targeting by HMRC, and, 14.22
Reclaiming tax
generally, 13.19–13.22
Re-examination
inspector-advocate, of, 18.80
taxpayer and witnesses, of, 18.56–18.60
Remuneration basis
contractual arrangements, and, 7.55
employment status, and, 5.185–5.188
Representation
presentation of appeal, and, 18.6–18.9
Research team results
targeting by HMRC, and, 14.23

s 49(1)(a) ITEPA 2003
generally, 3.5–3.9
identity of client, and, 6.11–6.13
s 49(1)(b) ITEPA 2003
generally, 3.10–3.19
s 49(1)(c) ITEPA 2003
generally, 3.20–3.21
Self-assessment returns
targeting by HMRC, and, 14.7–14.9
Series of engagements
employment status, and, 5.152–5.154
'Service company'
meaning, 14.3

Index

Sick pay entitlement
HMRC inquiries, and, 15.60
Special Commissioners
And see Appeals
generally, 16.9
Special status inspectors
HMRC inquiries, and, 15.27–15.36
Status of worker
basis of payment, 5.185–5.188
control
  delegation, and, 5.137
  generally, 5.104–5.133
  implication, by, 5.134–5.136
  summary, 5.138–5.139
delegated control, 5.137
employee-style benefits, 5.184
engagements, 5.152–5.154
financial risk, 5.165–5.169
formation of contract, 5.69
freedom to offer services, 5.170–5.174
in business on own account, 5.143–5.151
intention of the parties
  generally, 5.155–5.164
  introduction, 5.69
introduction, 5.1–5.8
mutual intention
  generally, 5.155–5.164
  introduction, 5.69
mutuality of obligation
  case law decisions, 5.78–5.93
  HMRC view, 5.94–5.102
  importance, 5.66–5.68
  introduction, 5.65
  meaning, 5.69–5.77
  summary, 5.103
other factors, 5.140–5.142
previous HMRC determinations, 5.175–5.176
profit, 5.165–5.169
provision of equipment, 5.177–5.183
recognised custom and practice, 5.189
series of engagements, 5.152–5.154
sub-contracting, 5.11–5.39
substitution
  case law decisions, 5.17–5.39
  contracts silent on issue, 5.62–5.63
  external rights, 5.11–5.14
  hiring helpers, 5.60–5.61
  HMRC view, 5.40–5.59
  internal rights, 5.11–5.14
  introduction, 5.9–5.10
  sub-contracting, 5.15–5.16
  summary, 5.64
summary, 5.190–5.191

Statutory basis of IR35
generally, 3.1–3.3
introduction, 2.2–2.3
ITEPA 2003, Pt 2, Ch 8
  introduction, 3.4
  s 49(1)(a), 3.5–3.9
  s 49(1)(b), 3.10–3.19
  s 49(1)(c), 3.20–3.21
Social Security Contributions and Benefits Act 1992, s 4A, 3.22–3.29
summary, 3.30–3.31
Sub-contracting
employment status, and, 5.11–5.39
Substitution
And see Employment status
case law
  Alternative Book Company Ltd v HMRC, 11.254–11.255
  First Word Software Ltd v HMRC, 11.194–11.195
  generally, 5.17–5.39
  Larkstar Data Ltd v HMRC, 11.238
  MKM Computing Ltd v HMRC, 11.220–11.223
  Netherlane Ltd v York, 11.156–11.157
  Synaptek Ltd v Young, 11.29–11.32
  Tilbury Consulting Ltd v Gittins, 11.76–11.79
  Usetech Ltd v Young, 11.123–11.127
contracts silent on issue, 5.62–5.63
contractual arrangements, and, 7.15–7.21
external rights, 5.11–5.14
hiring helpers, 5.60–5.61
HMRC inquiries, and
  factors to be considered, 15.46–15.48
  generally, 15.82–15.85
HMRC view, 5.40–5.59
internal rights, 5.11–5.14
introduction, 5.9–5.10
sub-contracting, 5.15–5.16
summary, 5.64
Summary of case
closing by taxpayer, on, 18.86
end of case, at
  inspector-advocate, by, 18.85
  taxpayer, by, 18.67
opening by taxpayer, on, 18.35–18.38

Targeting by HMRC
answering box 6 on Form P35, 14.2–14.6
compliance visits, 14.10–14.14
examination of self-assessment return, 14.7–14.9
informants, 14.20–14.21

Targeting by HMRC—*contd*
  inspection powers, 14.12–14.14
  introduction, 14.1
  notices requiring agencies to provide details of payments to PSBs, 14.16–14.18
  provision of information powers, 14.12–14.14
  random enquiries, 14.22
  research team results, 14.23
  schemes advertised as 'avoiding IR35', 14.24
  submission of contract review, 14.15
  summary, 14.25–14.28
Tax Chamber
  And see Appeals
  generally, 16.10
Tax tribunal judge
  presentation of appeal, and, 18.16
Tax tribunals
  And see Appeals
  first-tier tribunals, 16.9
  Upper Tribunal, 16.10–16.12
Termination of contracts
  HMRC inquiries, and, 15.61–15.63

'Umbrella' companies
  generally, 10.10–10.11
Understanding HMRC compliance process
  And see HMRC compliance process
  employer compliance inspections, 15.1–15.87
  introduction, 2.8
Unincorporated associations
  intermediary arrangements, and, 3.12
Upper Tribunal
  And see Appeals
  generally, 16.10–16.12

'Without prejudice' evidence
  presentation of appeal, and, 18.40
Witness examination
  presentation of appeal, and, 18.39–18.50
Witness summons
  preparation of appeal, and, 17.53–17.58
  presentation of appeal, and, 18.76–18.78
Witnesses
  presentation of appeal, and, 17.44–17.52